SELECTING
EFFECTIVE
TREATMENTS

Linda Seligman

SELECTING EFFECTIVE TREATMENTS

A Comprehensive, Systematic Guide to Treating Adult Mental Disorders

 Jossey-Bass Publishers · San Francisco

SELECTING EFFECTIVE TREATMENTS
A Comprehensive, Systematic Guide to Treating Adult Mental Disorders
by Linda Seligman

Copyright © 1990 by: Jossey-Bass Inc., Publishers
350 Sansome Street
San Francisco, California 94104

Library of Congress Cataloging-in-Publication Data

Seligman, Linda.
    Selecting effective treatments : a comprehensive, systematic guide
to treating adult mental disorders / Linda Seligman. — 1st ed.
       p.   cm.—(The Jossey-Bass social and behavioral science
series)
    Includes bibliographical references.
    ISBN 1-55542-232-2 (alk. paper)
    1. Mental illness—Treatment. I. Title. II. Series.
    [DNLM: 1. Mental Disorders—therapy. WM 400 S465s]
RC480.S342   1990
616.89′1—dc20
DNLM/DLC
for Library of Congress   89-26975
                                         CIP

Manufactured in the United States of America on Lyons Falls
Pathfinder Tradebook. This paper is acid-free and 100 percent
totally chlorine-free.

JACKET DESIGN BY WILLI BAUM

FIRST EDITION

HB Printing   10 9 8 7 6

Code 9032

The Jossey-Bass
Social and
Behavioral Science Series

Contents

Part Two: Effective Treatments of Adult Mental Disorders

4. Situationally Precipitated Disorders   61

5. Mood Disorders   77

Preface

Only a relatively few years ago were beliefs that psychotherapy was effective reinforced by the landmark research of Smith, Glass, and Miller (1980), Bergin (1971), and others. For most, this work seemed to answer the question of psychotherapy's value in the affirmative, and researchers have since turned to studying *differential therapeutics.* They seek now to determine which approaches to psychotherapy are effective in treating which mental disorders, under what conditions, with which clients, and to what ends.

Although our understanding of differential diagnosis of mental disorders has advanced greatly in the past decade, culminating in the publication of the latest edition of the *Diagnostic and Statistical Manual of Mental Disorders (DSM-III-R)* in 1987,* our understanding of differential therapeutics has lagged behind. Many books have been published that focus on a particular disorder, espouse a preferred mode of treatment, or offer a compendium of articles by different authors. However, no one volume presents a systematic, research-based approach to the treatment of the major mental disorders. As a result, approaches to treatment are often haphazard, with clinicians relying on familiar or comfortable models rather than on what has demonstrated the greatest effectiveness.

Note: Work has already begun on the next edition. Publication of *DSM-IV* is expected in 1993.

xiii

In *Selecting Effective Treatments*, I present an overview of the major forms of mental disorder accompanied by an approach to treatment selection that is structured, comprehensive, and grounded in research. This information should help clinicians better understand these mental disorders and enable them to provide their clients with more effective treatments. In addition, use of the model provided in this book should increase psychotherapists' accountability and enable them to deal more effectively with the intricacies of third-party payments and peer reviews.

A caution: This book is not intended to be a cookbook or to constrict clinicians' approaches to a narrow range of techniques. Neither does it advocate the universal application of a particular technique or theoretical model. Research does not support such a circumscribed view of therapy, nor would such an approach promote optimal use of the special talents of each therapist. Rather, this book seeks to increase clinicians' understanding of the symptoms and dynamics of the major mental disorders and to provide a range of treatment options for each disorder, allowing practitioners to blend their own therapeutic strengths and preferences with those approaches that have been demonstrated to be effective.

Intended Audiences

The intended audiences for this book are primarily nonmedical mental health practitioners (psychologists, counselors, and social workers) as well as students in those fields who have at least a basic understanding of approaches to psychotherapy. Clinicians, researchers, and educators in all mental health fields should be able to use this book in their work.

Most existing books on treating mental disorders are written from a medical perspective, yet most of the actual treatment is provided by psychologists, counselors, and social workers. *Selecting Effective Treatments*, therefore, fills another gap in the literature by focusing on the needs of nonmedical mental health practitioners and recognizing the increasingly important part they play in serving clients. After reading this book, these clinicians will have greater understanding of the complexities of diagnosis and of the *DSM-III-R*, will be able to develop sound treatment plans, and will have greater confidence and credibility. They will also be better able to assess when their services are not appropriate and when clients should be referred for medical treatment.

Overview of the Contents

This book is organized to facilitate understanding and application of information. The mental disorders (discussed in Chapters Four through Ten) are grouped into seven broad categories on the basis of similarity of disorder and treatment. The material on each of the mental disorders is organized into five categories: (1) a description of the disorder, (2) an overview of characteristics of people with the disorder, (3) qualities of style and personality typifying clinicians likely to be successful in treating the disorder, (4) a review of research on the treatment of the disorder, and (5) information on the prognosis of the disorder. The use of this format should enable readers to understand the differences and similarities in the disorders, their dynamics, and their treatment. (In many instances, clients with a specific disorder will have symptoms of an accompanying disorder. Therefore, a system of cross-referencing has been designed to give readers easy access to the accompanying or similar disorder.)

A systematic approach to treatment planning, termed "DO A CLIENT MAP," is also presented. At the beginning of each of the seven chapters on the mental disorders, a case study of a client with the specific disorder is presented. At the end of each of these chapters, the nature and treatment of the disorders are summarized according to the client map format and a client map for the client described in the case study is provided. (To protect clients' privacy, all the case studies appearing in this book are made up of composite characters.) In addition, a brief list of recommended readings on each category of disorder is provided at the ends of Chapters Four through Ten. A list of books containing further information on diagnosis and treatment of the whole range of mental disorders is included at the end of this preface.

This book consists of eleven chapters. The first three chapters (concerning the nature of effective treatment) introduce the reader to the process of treatment planning and review current knowledge on psychotherapy. Chapter One reviews the importance of systematic and effective treatment planning and presents the client map, a structured approach to treatment planning. Chapter Two summarizes the literature on the effectiveness of the various dimensions of psychotherapy and examines the decisions that must be made as part of treatment planning. Chapter Three looks at the client, the therapist, and their relationship, exploring those personal and interpersonal variables that maximize the chances for effective treatment.

Chapters Four through Ten explore the nature and treatment of the major mental disorders. Chapter Four looks at situationally precipitated disorders, the mildest of the disorders, involving problems of adjusting and coping. Chapter Five considers disorders of mood—specifically, the disorders characterized primarily by depressed or extremely elevated moods. Chapter Six examines disorders manifested through anxiety and fearfulness. Chapter Seven focuses on disorders of behavior and impulse control, including substance use disorders, eating disorders, sexual disorders, other impulse control disorders, and sleep disorders. Chapter Eight examines disorders in which physical and psychological factors combine and delineates the collaborative efforts of medical and nonmedical practitioners in treating these challenging disorders. Personality disorders, their nature and treatment, are the focus of Chapter Nine, designed to help clinicians ameliorate these longstanding and often treatment-resistant disorders. Chapter Ten focuses on those mental disorders that involve a loss of contact with reality, examining their differences and similarities as well as effective interventions. Finally, Chapter Eleven looks at the future of diagnosis and treatment planning. A comprehensive list of references is provided at the back of the book.

Knowledge of differential therapeutics for mental disorders is still in the early stages. However, the comprehensive scope of this book, its grounding in research and in the *DSM-III-R*, its systematic and structured approach, and its use of case studies and examples of treatment plans should help clinicians make better use of the knowledge currently available on treatment of mental disorders and enable clinicians to serve their clients most effectively.

Acknowledgments

I received a great deal of personal and professional support in writing this book. George Mason University gave me a research leave that afforded me the time to write this book. Larry Bowen, Albert Edgemon, and Barry Beyer provided ideas, encouragement, and additional time. Personal support was provided by my "old" family—my father, Irving Goldberg; my mother, Florence Goldberg; and my sisters, Terri Karol and Gerri Cotton—and my "new" family—my mother-in-law, Helen Zeskind; my stepdaughter, Rachel Zeskind; and, most of all, my husband, Robert Zeskind. This book is dedicated to my father, Irving Goldberg, who always encouraged my writing and scholarship. This book was completed on his eighty-fifth birthday.

Alexandria, Virginia   Linda Seligman
February 1990

Recommended Readings

American Psychiatric Association. (1987). *Diagnostic and statistical manual of mental disorders* (3rd ed., rev.) Washington, DC: Author. (Referred to in text as *DSM-III-R*.)

Atwood, J. D., & Chester, R. (1987). *Treatment techniques for common mental disorders*. New York: Jason Aronson.

Barlow, D. H. (Ed.). (1985). *Clinical handbook of psychological disorders*. New York: Guilford Press.

Cooper, A. M., Frances, A. J., & Sacks, M. H. (Eds.). (1986). *The personality disorders and neuroses*. Philadelphia: Lippincott.

Frances, A., Clarkin, J., & Perry, S. (1984). *Differential therapeutics in psychiatry*. New York: Brunner/Mazel.

Garfield, S. L., & Bergin, A. E. (Eds.). (1986). *Handbook of psychotherapy and behavior change*. New York: Wiley.

Greist, J. H., Jefferson, J. W., & Spitzer, R. L. (Eds.). (1982). *Treatment of mental disorders*. New York: Oxford University Press.

Helzer, J. E., & Guze, S. B. (Eds.). (1986). *Psychoses, affective disorders, and dementia*. New York: Basic Books.

Kaplan, H. I., & Sadock, B. J. (1988). *Synopsis of psychiatry*. Baltimore: Williams & Wilkins.

Maxmen, J. S. (1986). *Essential psychopathology*. New York: Norton.

Millman, H. L., Huber, J. T., & Diggins, D. R. (1982). *Therapies for adults: Depressive, anxiety, and personality disorders*. San Francisco: Jossey-Bass.

Nicholi, A. M., Jr. (Ed.). (1988). *The new Harvard guide to psychiatry*. Cambridge, MA: Harvard University Press.

Seligman, L. (1986). *Diagnosis and treatment planning in counseling*. New York: Human Sciences Press.

Turner, S. M., & Hersen, M. (Eds.). (1984). *Adult psychopathology and diagnosis*. New York: Wiley.

The Author

Linda Seligman is professor of counseling and development at George Mason University, Fairfax, Virginia. She is also director of the Center for Counseling and Consultation, a group private practice in Springfield, Virginia. She received her A.B. degree (1966) from Brandeis University in English and American literature; her M.A. degree (1968) from Teachers College, Columbia University, in guidance and counseling; and her Ph.D. degree (1974) from Columbia University in counseling psychology. Seligman is a licensed psychologist in Virginia, Maryland, New York, and New Jersey and a licensed professional counselor in Virginia.

Seligman's main research interests have been in diagnosis and treatment planning and in career counseling. She has written two previous books, *Assessment in Developmental Career Counseling* (1980) and *Diagnosis and Treatment Planning in Counseling* (1986), as well as over thirty-five professional articles. She was editor of the *American Mental Health Counselors Association Journal* from 1984 to 1987 and was president of the Virginia Mental Health Counselors Association. She has served as consultant for many government and human service agencies, is a member of the editorial board of the *Journal of Counseling and Development,* and has given over fifty lectures and workshops on diagnosis and treatment planning.

SELECTING
EFFECTIVE
TREATMENTS

Part One

What Is Effective Treatment Planning?

Chapter One

▌▌

Laying
the Foundation
for Effective
Treatment Planning

All mental health professionals have the same primary goal. Whether they are counselors, social workers, psychologists, psychiatrists, or members of another discipline; whether they are engaged in career counseling, sex therapy, or stress management; whether their clients are abused children, mid-life career changers, or people with phobias, their goal is to help people feel better about themselves and their lives. Similarly, the fundamental goal of treatment planning is to help mental health professionals make sound therapeutic decisions about their clients and services, so that the clients can ameliorate their difficulties and achieve the goals they have established with the therapist.

The study of differential therapeutics is a new one, little more than ten years old. We have only recently passed the point of arguing whether therapy is effective at all and have just begun to ask why, when, how, where, which, and for whom. The purpose of this book is to provide the most up-to-date answers available to those questions and to facilitate the process of treatment planning by linking our knowledge of treatment to our knowledge of diagnosis, usually made by using the latest edition of the *Diagnostic and Statistical Manual of Mental Disorders* (*DSM-III-R*) (1987), the most widely accepted system for describing and diagnosing mental disorders. This book is not designed to present a rigid formula for treatment planning; the state of the art does not allow that, and it probably would not be desirable, even if it were possible. Therapeutic effectiveness depends not only on the application of well-defined methods of intervention but also on such indefinable and intricate ingredients as the purity of the therapist's style, the expertise of the therapist, and the bond between the therapist and the client. In therapy, there are many roads to the same goal. This book seeks to point out which roads are likely to be smooth and rewarding and which are full of ruts and barriers. Plotting the course is up to the therapist and the client.

A need for accountability as well as for effectiveness mandates systematic treatment planning. As health care costs rise, Civilian Health and Medical Programs of the Uniformed Services (CHAMPUS) as well as some insurance companies have instituted a peer review process in an effort to contain costs and to ensure that only effective and necessary treatments are provided. Peer review is a process by which mental health professionals are asked to describe and justify their treatment plans, in writing, after a predetermined number of sessions. A group of mental health practitioners, usually psychologists or psychiatrists, serving as consultants to the insurance companies, review the treatment plans and determine whether they are appropriate. If the plans do not seem sound, third-party payments can be denied or withheld until a more appropriate plan is submitted. Clearly, if mental health professionals are to prepare sound reports for peer review, they must have a knowledge of treatment planning.

Requests for accountability also come from mental health agencies and clinics; from counseling centers at the schools, hospitals, and residential facilities where therapy is done; and from funding agencies. Funding for mental health services is rarely ample, and funding agencies often require statistical documentation of effectiveness. Statistics would typically be maintained on the number of clients seen, their diagnoses, the nature and duration of the treatment provided, and the outcome.

Unfortunately, treatment planning often is viewed as a process that must be done to satisfy bureaucratic requirements. Although that may, in fact, be the motivation behind treatment planning in some cases, the fundamental reason for treatment planning is to facilitate effective treatment. How can professionals know what is working or not working, what needs to be changed or eliminated, if they do not have a clear understanding of what they are doing? Systematic treatment planning is designed to allow clinicians to map the therapeutic journey, to revise the route as needed, and to repeat the trip with others if it turns out to be worthwhile, without compromising the spontaneity of the traveler or the guide.

1.1 Research on Effectiveness of Therapy

In the 1950s and 1960s, Eysenck (1952, 1966) reviewed a group of studies on psychotherapy outcome and concluded that therapy was not effective. This startling finding triggered a series of studies designed to investigate more thoroughly the question of therapy's effectiveness.

Bergin (1971; Bergin & Lambert, 1978) took on the challenge presented by Eysenck and came to a different conclusion. In a review of fifty-two studies of therapeutic outcome, Bergin found that twenty-two had positive outcomes, fifteen had negative outcomes, and fifteen had questionable outcomes. He concluded that, overall, therapy yielded modestly positive results, with 30 percent of all clients showing spontaneous remission of symptoms.

At about the same time, Meltzoll and Kornreich (1970) reviewed a large number of outcome studies. Of the fifty-seven studies they viewed as adequately designed, forty-eight (or 84 percent) yielded evidence of the effectiveness of therapy. Of forty-four questionable studies, however, only one-third yielded positive results. The quality of the design and execution of the study, therefore, not surprisingly seem important in assessing the true impact of therapy.

Luborsky, Singer, and Luborsky's (1975) review of thirty-three outcome studies yielded similar results. They concluded: "Controlled comparative studies indicate that a high percentage of patients who go through any of these psychotherapies gain from them" (p. 1003).

The most definitive study on the subject was published by Smith, Glass, and Miller (1980). They used a sophisticated meta-analysis to summarize numerically the results of all controlled studies they could locate on psychotherapy outcome—a total of 475 studies conducted prior to 1977. They found that "the average person who received therapy is better off at the end of it than 80 percent of those who do not" (p. 87.) Going beyond Bergin, Smith, Glass, and Miller concluded that the effect of therapy is large and clearly substantial. They also examined many aspects of the therapeutic process, including the type of therapy, the relationship between diagnosis and treatment outcome, the relationship between client characteristics and treatment outcome, treatment duration, treatment setting, and medication. These findings will be discussed in Chapter Two (primarily in section 2.4.2).

The findings of Smith, Glass, and Miller have been substantiated by a subsequent analysis of their data. Andrews and Harvey (1981) focused their analysis on people who had sought treatment for neuroses, phobias, and "emotional-somatic complaints." Andrews and Harvey found that the condition of the typical patient was better than that of 77 percent of the untreated members of the control group, measured at the same time. They also found only a small rate of relapse within the first two years after treatment.

As a result of all these studies, the verdict on the outcome of psychotherapy now seems positive: For most people, therapy is more effective at ameliorating emotional disorders than is no treatment. Where do we go from here? Some researchers have suggested that we should place greater emphasis on exploring the therapeutically relevant qualities of the client, the therapist, and their interaction. VandenBos (1986), who believes that research has focused too much on outcome and not enough on process, recommends that current research be comparative, exploring the relative advantages and disadvantages of alternative treatment strategies for clients with different disorders. However, there are many challenges to research on the therapeutic process. Even the best-defined therapy is difficult to reproduce because of its interactive nature. Other problems inherent in the process of research on therapy effectiveness include (1) the large number of client variables, (2) the variation in therapist expertise, (3) the variation in severity of disorders, (4) participant and observer bias, (5) the questionable ethics of establishing true control and placebo groups, and (6) the difficulty in assessing how much progress has been made.

Research on therapy effectiveness is still in its early stages.

According to Stiles, Shapiro, and Elliott (1986), "most reviews of psychotherapy outcome research show little or no differential effectiveness of different psychotherapies" (p. 165). On an even more discouraging note, Uhlenhuth, Balter, Mellinger, Cisin, and Clinthorne (1983) contend that "the majority of persons with serious psychiatric disorders still do not receive treatment or the most appropriate treatment" (p. 1167). Similarly, Perry, Frances, and Clarkin (1985) conclude: "Too often, patients receive the treatment known best to, or practiced primarily by, the first person they consult rather than that from which they might best benefit" (p. xviii).

What follows is a format for treatment planning that is designed to help clinicians conceptualize what works for whom. The large and growing body of literature on that subject will be reviewed in this book. Although some of the conclusions drawn will be tentative, they should provide a basis for future research into treatment planning as well as for the development of the treatment plans themselves.

1.2 An Integrated Model for Treatment Planning

The integrated model for treatment planning, presented here in a skeleton form, will provide the structure for organizing this book. It is a comprehensive outline, encompassing the major elements that therapists should consider when formulating a treatment plan. Although the clinician probably will not have information about all the categories of the outline when assessing a particular client or disorder, complete information is not necessary to make effective use of the model. Gaps in the therapist's knowledge as well as in the information available on the client can be used to guide the development of the treatment plan as well as to indicate areas needing further research or investigation.

I. *Description of Disorder*
    A. *DSM-III-R diagnosis.* The *DSM-III-R* is, as of 1987, the most widely accepted system for classifying mental disorders. Its nomenclature will be used as the standard throughout this book.
    B. *Epidemiology.* Epidemiology includes both the inci-

dence (number of new cases) and prevalence (number of existing cases at a given time) of a disorder. Acute disorders tend to have a higher incidence, whereas chronic disorders tend to have a higher prevalence. Approximately 19 percent of Americans have some type of mental disorder during any six-month period, although less than 20 percent of these people seek treatment during that period (Maxmen, 1986). In general, the more common a disorder and the more established the diagnosis, the more that is known about its treatment because there has been more opportunity for research on the disorder.

C.   *Primary and secondary symptoms.* A mental disorder is typically comprised of a cluster of symptoms, both primary (required to meet the criteria for diagnosis) and secondary or underlying. The *DSM-III-R* will be used as the major source of information on the primary and secondary symptoms associated with the disorders to be discussed. A comparison of the client's presenting symptoms with the standard symptoms associated with a disorder is important in ensuring that the treatment plan meets the needs of a particular client. Treatment should emphasize interventions designed to reduce a client's most prominent and troubling symptoms.

D.   *Typical onset, course, and duration of disorder.* This information can be useful to clients as well as to the clinician engaged in treatment planning. Some disorders often are chronic and need extended follow-up; others tend to run a circumscribed course and frequently remit spontaneously, even without treatment. In general, disorders with a brief duration and a sudden onset following a precipitant have a better prognosis than disorders with a slow, insidious onset and no clear precipitant. Medication and hospitalization are also more likely to be indicated for the latter.

II.   *Relevant Client Characteristics* This section provides typical profiles of clients with particular mental disorders. By comparing these profiles with information gathered on an individual client, the therapist can gain insight into that client's readiness for treatment, the types of treatment that are most likely to be effective, adjunct and referral sources that might be useful, and the prognosis.

A. *Genetic, developmental, or other predisposing factors.* In this section, common etiologies of the disorders will be discussed. For example, many disorders—for example, schizophrenia and bipolar disorder—tend to follow a genetic pattern in that examples of that disorder or related disorders are often noted in the client's family history. By looking for genetic patterns in clients with these disorders, clinicians can plan a treatment that takes account of environmental or family dynamics as possible contributors to the development of a disorder. A family history of a disorder may also imply a biological element to its transmission, suggesting that medication may contribute to treatment. Developmental patterns, such as the age at which a disorder is most likely to emerge, and predisposing factors, such as a precipitating incident or common background, also provide data useful in determining the treatment plan. That information can help the clinician formulate plans to reduce the likelihood of relapse.

B. *Demographics.* Data such as the typical client's age, marital status, and family constellation will be included here.

C. *Source of referral and apparent motivation for treatment.* Clues to a client's probable response to treatment are often provided by the nature of the referral. For example, a client who sought therapy on a recommendation from a career counselor with whom she had worked successfully seems likely to have more intrinsic motivation toward change than a parent who was encouraged to seek counseling because of his child's disruptive behavior at school.

D. *Treatment history.* Information on previous treatment is important in determining what has and what has not been effective in the past. For example, a long treatment history, especially one including numerous treatment failures, suggests a poor prognosis.

E. *Personality profile.* Personality profiles are obtained from psychological assessment, interview, or observation by the clinician. Typical interpersonal and intrapsychic dynamics of clients will be considered, including such aspects as cognitions, affect, behavior, defenses, and lifestyle.

F. *Relevant developmental history.* A review of the client's background—including such areas as family relationships, work history, social and leisure activities, and medical conditions—usually provides valuable information on that client's strengths and areas of difficulty. Information on the client's successes and failures, support systems, and coping mechanisms should help therapists develop a more effective treatment plan.

G. *Mental status examination.* A mental status examination entails an assessment of the client's overall orientation to reality, level of functioning, and impairment.

III. *Relevant Therapist Variables* This section will review the available information on therapist variables that are relevant to treatment of the particular disorder or client. This information might include therapist experience, orientation, and training; relationship of personality and background between client and therapist; and desirable personal and professional qualities in therapists treating clients with the disorder under consideration.

IV. *Intervention Strategies* In this section, what is known about the treatment of the disorder will be reviewed. Recommendations about treatment strategies will be made, and areas where information is lacking will be discussed.

A. *Approach to therapy.* This section will contain a review of the literature on what approaches to therapy seem to work best with the disorder under consideration. The following dimensions of the therapeutic process have been found to be important in treatment planning and may be considered in this section, depending on the information available (Seligman, 1986):

      1.   Level of therapist directiveness
      2.   Level of supportiveness and level of exploration in therapy
      3.   Balance of focus—affective, behavioral, cognitive
      4.   Modality of treatment—individual, family, group
      5.   Techniques of psychotherapy

Details on these dimensions of therapy will be provided in Chapter Two.

    B.   *Medication.* Whether or not medication enhances the treatment of a particular disorder will be considered. The focus of this book is on treatment of mental disorders by nonmedical clinicians who focus on cognitive, affective, and behavioral approaches to treatment rather than on biochemical methods. However, for some disorders, research suggests that a combination of medical treatment and psychological treatment usually is more effective than either treatment alone. Nonmedical therapists need to be aware of these findings, so that they can refer clients with such disorders for a medical evaluation or arrange to provide treatment in collaboration with a psychiatrist or other medical specialist.

    C.   *Duration and pacing of treatment.* This section will focus on the typical length of treatment necessary for amelioration of a disorder and the swiftness of the therapeutic pace.

    D.   *Treatment setting.* Inpatient, partial hospitalization, and outpatient settings will be evaluated as appropriate for treatment of the disorder.

    E.   *Adjunct services.* These services include social and educational programs and peer support groups (for example, Alcoholics Anonymous) as well as therapy-related services (such as assertiveness training or intelligence testing) that might enhance the effectiveness of psychotherapy.

V. *Prognosis* Information will be provided here on how much change or improvement can be expected from people experiencing the disorder, how rapidly progress is likely to occur, and what the overall prognosis is.

1.3 Client Map

The major elements of the treatment plan discussed in this chapter have been organized into a mnemonic device that is intended to facilitate recall of the parts of the plan, to reflect its purpose, and to guide its development. The mnemonic device is the acronym DO A CLIENT MAP. By filling out the format of this acronym as follows, thereby *doing a client map*, clinicians will have developed a treatment plan for working with a particular client.

DO A CLIENT MAP

Diagnosis
Objectives of treatment

Assessments needed (for example, neurological or personality tests)

Clinician characteristics viewed as therapeutic
Location of treatment (for example, hospital or outpatient setting)
Interventions to be used
Emphasis of treatment (level of directiveness; level of supportiveness; cognitive, behavioral, or affective emphasis)
Nature of treatment (individual, couple, family, or group)
Timing (frequency, pacing, duration)

Medications needed
Adjunct services (for example, support groups, legal advice, or education)
Prognosis

The format of the client map will be used throughout this book to illustrate the process of treatment planning for sample cases.

Chapter Two

■ⅡⅡ■ⅢⅢ■■■

Dimensions
and Effectiveness
of Therapy

Smith, Glass, and Miller's (1980) meta-analysis demonstrated that psychotherapy is effective. Few researchers have disputed those findings, and they now seem well established. Research in the 1980s has focused less on whether therapy is effective and more on which approaches to therapy are the most effective and under what circumstances. Although this research is still in the preliminary stages, a great deal has already been learned about differential therapeutics.

The therapeutic process has been divided into a set of parameters delineated and defined by Frances, Clarkin, and Perry (1984), Seligman (1986), and others. Research on these parameters will be discussed in this chapter, in an effort to clarify what is known about the effectiveness of the therapeutic process and to facilitate decisions about treatment planning. Examples of hypothetical clients will be used to illustrate information provided on differential therapeutics.

In general, treatment planning moves from the nature of the disorder, through consideration of the client's characteristics, to the approach to treatment. That will be the sequence followed throughout most of this book. In this chapter, however, the focus will be primarily on the approach to treatment and what is known about its impact on mental disorders. Part IV of the outline provided in

Chapter One (section 1.2) delineates the aspects of treatment planning to be considered here.

2.1 Level of Directiveness

Little research has been conducted on level of directiveness, a continuum that extends from the humanistic, experiential, and person-centered models of therapy to the structured and directive models of the behaviorists and cognitive therapists. However, clinicians have drawn tentative conclusions about when therapists should be directive and when they should lean toward the experiential (Frances, Clarkin, & Perry, 1984; Lambert, 1982; Seligman, 1986). Table 1 describes this continuum and suggests its appropriate use.

Table 1. Levels of Directiveness in Therapy.

Directive	*Experiential*
1. Therapist directed	1. Client directed
2. Structured	2. Amount of structure varies, depending on client
3. Goals: • Changing maladaptive behavior • Reducing symptoms • Making environmental changes • Developing new skills • Solving problems	3. Goals • Developing self-awareness • Reducing identity confusion • Increasing sense of direction • Promoting independence • Building self-confidence
4. Recommended for clients who are: • Willing to take direction from others or unable to establish own direction • Motivated primarily to achieve specific limited goals • Severely disturbed, dysfunctional, fragile • In crisis or experiencing situational problems • Having difficulty setting limits and boundaries, especially in therapy	4. Recommended for clients who are: • Capable of establishing own direction • Guided by broad, far-reaching goals • Functioning acceptably but not up to potential • Not in crisis • Able to establish appropriate interpersonal boundaries, in and out of therapy

According to Perry, Frances, and Clarkin (1985), the directive approach encompasses such techniques as systematic desensitization, flooding, positive reinforcement (for example, token economies, contingency contracting, and extinction), strategic techniques (such as suggestion, paradox, metaphor, humor, and homework assignments), and cognitive techniques. In all these approaches, the therapist assumes an authoritative stance, clearly defines target concerns, and designs a specific program to change overt and covert symptoms. The experiential model, on the other hand, avoids what some view as manipulation of clients by focusing on the therapist-client interaction and allowing the client to guide the therapeutic process. This approach emphasizes catharsis and abreaction, ventilation, empathy and reflection of feeling, support, affection, praise, and unconditional positive regard.

Some approaches fall in the middle of the directive/experiential continuum. In psychoanalysis, for example, the therapist is clearly an authority figure, but some of the techniques used, such as free association, are experiential.

To illustrate appropriate levels of directiveness, let us look at two different clients, Anne and Bettie, with similar presenting problems. Both clients are in their early twenties and sought counseling following a broken engagement. However, their circumstances and their views of therapy are very different and warrant different levels of directiveness.

Anne is in her third month of an unplanned pregnancy. She is receiving little help from her family or her former fiancé. She is unemployed and is living with a single friend who has two children. Anne is not sure what she wants to do about her pregnancy and has been using alcohol as a way to avoid thinking about her difficulties. She has not had previous therapy and is not sure why the nurse with whom she spoke at an abortion clinic referred her to a counselor.

Bettie also feels depressed because her fiancé has ended their engagement, but she views this situation as a time to review her goals. She believes that she has focused too much of her time and energy on her fiancé and has neglected her career and education. She now wants to return to college, to learn more about her aptitudes and preferences, and to establish a better balance between her social life and her career. She had some family therapy when her parents divorced ten years ago and views therapy as a good resource to help her sort out her options, increase her self-confidence, and redirect her life.

Anne does not have the leisure, the sense of direction, or the motivation for an experiential approach; she needs a directive therapist, not to tell her what to do about her pregnancy but to give her a structure in which she can make decisions and gain some control of her life. Bettie, on the other hand, would be more amenable to experiential or person-centered therapy, which would afford her the opportunity to engage in self-examination and goal setting.

2.2 Level of Exploration

Level of exploration also has received little attention in the literature beyond the theoretical. It is, however, often cited in the literature as an important aspect of treatment (Frances, Clarkin, & Perry, 1984; Horowitz, Marmar, Weiss, DeWitt, & Rosenbaum, 1984; Kaplan & Sadock, 1985; Lambert, 1982; Seligman, 1986; Wallerstein, 1986).

Level of exploration is another continuum; it extends from the probing and analytical to the supportive. Its most analytical form is represented by psychoanalysis and psychodynamic psychotherapy, using such techniques as free association, analysis of transference, examination of dreams, and interpretation. In contrast, the behavioral model, with its focus on the present and on circumscribed and measurable changes, is supportive rather than probing. It seeks to reinforce existing coping mechanisms rather than to promote insight into patterns, causes, and dynamics. Of course, models at either end of the continuum as well as those in the middle inevitably include both support and exploration. They are distinguished by the balance of the two, rather than the absence of one. The person-centered model, for example, has both probing and supportive elements; it stresses reinforcement, empathy, summarization, and unconditional positive regard. Table 2 organizes information on this continuum.

One of the few studies of the probing/supportive dimension of therapy is described in *Forty-Two Lives in Treatment* (Waller-

Table 2. Levels of Exploration in Therapy.

Probing	Supportive
1. Seeks to eliminate barriers to growth	1. Builds on existing defenses and strengths
2. Focuses on past as well as present, seeking patterns	2. Focuses on present
3. Provides challenge and stimulus for change, in an accepting context	3. Provides acceptance, protection, reassurance, empathy
4. Helps client find interpretations, information	4. Provides explanations, information
5. Goals: • To promote growth and development • To increase understanding of intrapsychic conflict • To develop new resources	5. Goals: • To promote symptom reduction and improved functioning • To increase self-acceptance • To strengthen existing resources
6. Recommended for clients who are: • Highly motivated, well organized, reasonably healthy, in contact with reality • Insightful, psychologically minded, verbal • Internally controlled, like to see change as a result of own efforts	6. Recommended for clients who are: • Resistant, fragile, highly dysfunctional, in poor contact with reality • Action oriented • Externally controlled, other-directed

stein, 1986). This study followed forty-two patients at the Menninger Foundation for thirty years after treatment. Three modes of treatment were used: psychoanalysis, expressive psychoanalytic psychotherapy, and supportive psychoanalytic psychotherapy. Although this study has limited application because Wallerstein deals only with the psychoanalytic variety of expressive (probing) and supportive therapy, he does draw many worthwhile comparisons between the two approaches.

Wallerstein believes that supportive therapy is most appropriate for people experiencing severe anxiety or a debilitating crisis or for chronic schizophrenic clients, people who are vulnerable and for whom limited goals are in order. Expressive therapy is more suitable for clients with borderline personality disorders, because, according to Wallerstein, their defenses prevent them from accepting support comfortably and require a more probing approach. Wallerstein also found that insight is not always needed for change; in 45 percent of the cases, the changes achieved seemed to go beyond the amount of insight that was achieved, while in only 7 percent of the cases, insight surpassed discerned change. Overall, Wallerstein concluded that supportive therapy is no less effective than exploratory therapy. However, as Lambert, Shapiro, and Bergin (1986) point out, clients need to recognize that their improvement is a result of their own efforts. Even a supportive counseling relationship, then, should emphasize the client's responsibility for growth.

Bettie and Anne, the clients discussed in the previous section, need different levels of exploration. Bettie, a strong client who is interested in personal growth and introspection, seems to be a good candidate for an approach that is at least moderately probing (an approach such as psychodynamic psychotherapy or person-centered therapy). Anne, on the other hand, needs a more supportive approach that will help to reduce the stress she is experiencing and enable her to draw on her existing strengths to cope with her situation.

2.3 Modality of Treatment

Research is scarce when the literature comparing modalities of treatment is reviewed. Smith, Glass, and Miller (1980) found no significant differences in the impacts of individual, group, and family therapy. Pilkonis, Imber, Lewis, and Rubinsky (1984) conducted a study in which they randomly assigned sixty-four outpatients to individual, group, or conjoint therapy with experienced clinicians. Diagnoses included affective (mood), anxiety, adjustment, and personality disorders. Clients were seen for an average of 26.8 sessions. All treatments focused on helping clients develop cognitive or affective insight. The sample as a whole demonstrated significant improvement in symptoms, target complaints, self-awareness, and interpersonal and family functioning. That improvement was maintained at a thirty-one-week follow-up. However, the study yielded no clear evidence of the superiority of any one mode of treatment. Differences seemed to be due more to the therapist, the client, and the nature of the client-therapist match than to the modality of treatment. Nevertheless, there were indications that individual therapy was most successful in increasing self-awareness in lower-class clients, while group and family counseling were better at lessening interpersonal problems in the more chronically ill clients.

Other studies have attempted to determine what makes group therapy effective and to compare the impact of group and individual therapy. Bloch, Crouch, and Reibstein (1981) reviewed the literature on group psychotherapy published between 1955 and 1979 and sought to elicit the therapeutic factors and processes that contributed to improvements. Research on self-disclosure, insight, catharsis, interaction, and acceptance/cohesiveness all yielded ambiguous results. The literature, then, sheds little light on those aspects of group therapy that seem to make it effective. Perhaps client and clinician variables are so powerful in determining outcome, and therapy and counseling groups are so varied, that few conclusions can be drawn about group therapy in general. Nonetheless, group therapy does seem to be effective. Luborsky (1972) reviewed twelve studies comparing individual and group psychotherapy and found that the two yielded similar gains. Few subsequent studies have investigated the question further, and those that have been conducted suggest that the two are equally effective (Frances, Clarkin, & Perry, 1984).

Therapy groups may be either heterogeneous or homogeneous (composed of individuals with differing problems or composed of individuals with similar problems). Homogeneous groups seem particularly effective with impulse control disorders, posttraumatic stress disorders, substance abuse, psychophysiological concerns, developmental issues, and phobias.

Recent research seems to give marital and family therapy an edge over individual therapy for family concerns and suggests that individual therapy may even be harmful in cases where only one member of a troubled family is seen in treatment. Most of the information in the literature on the respective strengths and benefits of the three primary modalities of therapy (individual, group, and family therapy) is inferential, however. Table 3 summarizes the findings on these modalities.

Table 3. Modalities of Treatment.

Individual Therapy Recommended for:

- Highly anxious, withdrawn, isolated, or introverted clients
- Clients who have difficulty with ambiguity
- Clients seeking help with intrapsychic concerns
- Suspicious, guarded, hostile, antisocial, or destructive clients who have difficulty with trust
- Clients seeking independence and individualization
- Very intimate or idiosyncratic concerns
- Concerns of very long duration
- Crises

Group Therapy Recommended for:

- Anxious clients with authority concerns
- Dependent clients (after or in combination with some individual therapy)
- Interpersonal concerns
- Clients who may feel stigmatized or scapegoated as a result of individual therapy (for instance, the identified patient in a family)
- Clients who are likely to give the therapist excessive power
- Clients who need reality testing and group feedback
- Specific behavioral concerns, shared with other group members
- Clients with limited financial resources

Family Therapy Recommended for:

- Problems in the family structure
- Intergenerational or other family conflicts
- Family communication problems
- Families needing consolidation
- Acting-out adolescents
- Families with limited resources when more than one family member needs help
- Families with no severe pathology

2.4 Therapy Techniques

Once clinicians have defined the parameters of the therapeutic model that seems most appropriate for use with a particular client, the next step probably will be to determine the specific approaches and techniques that will guide treatment.

2.4.1 Elements Common to Therapy Techniques

A great many psychotherapeutic approaches are available to the clinician. Kazdin (1986) observes that more than four hundred psychotherapies have been advanced. However, according to Perry, Frances, and Clarkin (1985), the following elements or strategies are common to almost all approaches to psychotherapy:

1. Establishing and maintaining a therapeutic relationship
2. Providing support via reality testing, suggestions, structure, confirmation, acceptance, validation, and communication of a sense of optimism and confidence
3. Providing information and education
4. Reducing painful feelings, especially anxiety and depression
5. Decreasing specific maladaptive behaviors
6. Modifying specific misperceptions
7. Helping clients put their concerns in context and make sense of them
8. Expanding emotional awareness
9. Enhancing interpersonal effectiveness

Smith, Glass, and Miller (1980) found the following three commonalities in therapies: persuading; treating clients as rational, thinking persons; and encouraging honesty and self-examination. Karasu (1986) presents yet another useful framework for assessing differences among treatment models. According to Karasu, all approaches to therapy involve three therapeutic change agents: affective experiencing, cognitive mastery, and behavioral regulation. The various approaches simply give different amounts of attention to these three vehicles for change. Although different terminology is used in each research study, leading to different sets of commonalities, these studies suggest that there are not really more than four hundred discrete approaches to psychotherapy but, rather, many variations on a far smaller number of well-established themes.

2.4.2 Differential Effectiveness of Therapy Techniques

The existence of so many commonalities in therapeutic approaches also raises the question of whether the differences among therapies are genuine and have differential effectiveness or whether they are simply artifacts, with differential effectiveness due more to therapist effectiveness or the particular chemistry of a therapeutic relationship. This question should be borne in mind when the research on the impact of the major approaches to therapy is reviewed.

In Chapter One (section 1.1), the overall effectiveness of psychotherapy was discussed. Findings of Lambert, Shapiro, and Bergin (1986) seem typical; outcome research suggests that 66 percent of clients are improved, 26 percent are unchanged, and 8 percent are worse after therapy. Once it was established that most clients do benefit from psychotherapy, the fundamental question became "What forms of psychotherapy are the most effective, and what are the common ingredients that maximize their effectiveness?" Although there still are no conclusive answers to that question, there is a considerable body of research that addresses the question, beginning with the work of Smith, Glass, and Miller (1980).

Smith, Glass, and Miller Findings on Differential Effectiveness. Smith, Glass, and Miller examined not only the overall effectiveness of psychotherapy but also the differential effectiveness of the major approaches. On the broadest scale, they compared the effectiveness of behavioral therapies, verbal therapies (including dynamic therapy, cognitive therapy, Rational-Emotive Therapy, Transactional Analysis, humanistic models, and Gestalt models), and developmental therapies. All three categories of therapies seemed to be equally effective in the treatment of psychotic clients, but the behavioral group seemed best for the treatment of so-called neurotic and phobic clients and in the treatment of global adjustment problems. The verbal and behavioral approaches seemed to be equally effective in treating fear and anxiety, specific adjustment concerns, dysfunctional personality traits, psychophysiological conditions, addictions, sociopathy, and social, career, and academic concerns. The verbal approach seemed most effective at improving clients' self-esteem.

Andrews and Harvey (1981) reassessed some of the data gathered by Smith, Glass, and Miller. Their results were similar but more conclusive. They found that the behavioral therapies were more effective than the verbal therapies and that the verbal therapies were more effective than the developmental approaches. The differences among the three classes of psychotherapies were significant.

Smith, Glass, and Miller also compared the following six subclasses of therapies, listed in order of effect size:

Therapy	Effect Size
1. Cognitive (Reality Therapy, Rational-Emotive, transactional analysis, other)	1.31
2. Cognitive-behavioral	1.24
3. Behavioral (systematic desensitization, implosion, behavior modification)	0.91
4. Dynamic (psychodynamic, hypnotherapy, Adlerian, other)	0.78
5. Humanistic (client-centered, Gestalt)	0.63
6. Developmental (vocational-personal, other)	0.42

Similarly, Shapiro and Shapiro (1982), in a review of the literature, found that cognitive and behavioral therapies yielded more favorable outcomes (1.00 and 1.06 effect sizes) than other therapies with which they were compared, while dynamic and humanistic therapies tended to yield inferior outcomes (0.40 effect size). However, they observed that this finding was partly a result of the client populations and problems studied (for example, it is easier to produce and measure progress in treating a phobia than a personality disorder).

Taking an even more specific look at the effectiveness of the various types of therapy, Smith, Glass, and Miller reviewed studies on eighteen specific approaches to therapy. Cognitive, cognitive-behavioral, and behavioral therapy, as well as hypnotherapy, achieved the highest effect sizes. These approaches use such techniques as contingency contracting, desensitization, systematic rational restructuring, cognitive rehearsal, and fixed-role therapy as well as active persuasion and confrontation of dysfunctional ideas and beliefs. Reality Therapy, client-centered therapy, Adlerian therapy, and Gestalt therapy had the lowest effect sizes.

However, as Shapiro and Shapiro point out, these results must be interpreted cautiously. Some of the therapies, such as Reality Therapy, had received little attention in the literature prior to the Smith, Glass, and Miller study. Consequently, the low effect size may be due more to a combination of a dearth of literature, a bias in the existing literature, and diversity in client populations than to a significant deficit in the therapeutic approach. At the same time, this exhaustive research does provide important information on the differential effectiveness of the various psychotherapies. However, when client and diagnostic differences were controlled, "comparisons yielded no reliable differences in effectiveness of behavioral and verbal therapies" (Smith, Glass, & Miller, 1980, p. 125).

Smith, Glass, and Miller also looked at the relationship between treatment effectiveness and diagnosis. They found that simple phobias and depression showed a particularly strong positive response to treatment. Focusing on problems rather than diagnoses, Smith, Glass, and Miller found that psychotherapy had the greatest impact on fear/anxiety, followed by (in descending order) addiction, global adjustment, vocational-personal concerns, emotional-somatic complaints, sociopathic disorders, work-school achievement, life adjustment, personality traits, self-esteem, and physiological states.

Finally, Smith, Glass, and Miller looked at the relationship between diagnostic type and therapy type. They found that clients with neuroses and broad-based phobias responded best to Rational-Emotive Therapy, implosive therapy, cognitive-behavioral therapy, and systematic desensitization. Clients with simple phobias were helped most by the cognitive therapies, followed by cognitive-behavioral therapy and systematic desensitization; psychotic clients received the most benefit from psychodynamic therapy and behavior modification.

A synthesis of the very rich data in the Smith, Glass, and Miller study yields the following observations about the major approaches to psychotherapy:

1. The behavioral approaches tend to be highly effective with a broad range of disorders and are particularly powerful in the treatment of fear/anxiety, simple phobias, global adjustment, depression, and vocational-personal development. Systematic desensitization, a form of behavior therapy, achieved a relatively high effect score in treatment of fear/anxiety, emotional-somatic complaints, and global adjustment.

2. The cognitive therapies, too, have a broad range of effectiveness and have a particularly strong impact in the treatment of fear/anxiety, global adjustment, and simple phobias. In general, Smith, Glass, and Miller found the cognitive therapies to be somewhat more powerful than the behavioral approaches, although Shapiro and Shapiro (1982) found little difference in their effectiveness. A combination of the two, cognitive-behavioral therapy, also seems effective with some disorders, notably disorders of social behavior, simple phobias, fear/anxiety, and global adjustment.

3. The dynamic, dynamic-eclectic, and psychodynamic approaches to therapy seem nearly as effective as the behavioral and cognitive approaches and are especially effective with social, career, or academic concerns; fear/anxiety; criminal behavior; addiction; and emotional-somatic complaints.

4. Research on the person-centered or humanistic approach has not shown the positive outcomes of the cognitive or behavioral approaches, partly because there has been less systematic research on the person-centered model than there has on the cognitive and behavioral approaches. However, the person-centered approach does seem to make an important contribution to building self-esteem.

5. Only limited research was available to Smith, Glass, and Miller on the effectiveness of the developmental approaches. These approaches do seem to ameliorate vocational-personal concerns but do not demonstrate a high overall level of effectiveness.

6. Smith, Glass, and Miller found that the effect size of many of the psychotherapies (psychodynamic, person-centered, vocational-personal developmental, cognitive-behavioral, and implosion therapy) was not affected by whether the client was neurotic, psychotic, or phobic. Placebo treatment and systematic desensitization, however, were more effective at treating simple phobias than neurotic disorders. Behavior modification was more effective in treating psychoses and simple phobias than neurotic disorders. Rational-Emotive Therapy, on the other hand, was more effective in the treatment of phobias than neuroses, while dynamic-eclectic therapy was more effective with neurotic than psychotic disorders.

These results, although helpful to the process of treatment

planning, should be interpreted cautiously. The findings were not based on one large well-planned experimental study but, rather, on a meta-analysis of data from over four hundred studies. Consequently, there were many gaps in the available data, and the omission of an approach to therapy from the Smith, Glass, and Miller study may mean only that not enough studies were conducted on the effectiveness of that approach to yield meaningful data. Moreover, several researchers have raised questions about the value of Smith, Glass, and Miller's conclusions. Searles (1985), for example, claims that they emphasize behavioral over psychodynamic approaches. He also calls the measure of effect size used by Smith and his colleagues "a labile and manipulable measure" (p. 453).

Despite the valuable direction provided in their research, Smith, Glass, and Miller are cautious in interpreting their own data: "Different types of psychotherapy (verbal or behavioral; psychodynamic, client-centered, or systematic desensitization) do not produce different types or degrees of benefit" (p. 184). Luborsky, Singer, and Luborsky (1975) agree. In their view, the comparative research yields a dodo bird verdict. (The dodo bird, in *Alice in Wonderland,* concluded that everyone has won and all must have prizes.)

Smith, Glass, and Miller react to their accumulation of data by recommending a pluralistic approach to treatment. By pluralism, they seem to mean an approach to treatment planning that touches many fronts and combines methods in a logical and systematic way to maximize the chance of a positive therapeutic impact. To Smith, Glass, and Miller, this approach seems preferable to a cookbook approach that would dictate a specific type of therapy for a specific disorder. Recent research has reflected this shift toward pluralism (or eclecticism, as it is more commonly and less precisely known). In a recent survey of psychologists, 44.2 percent described their primary theoretical orientation as eclectic (Wogan & Norcross, 1983). Integrated and eclectic models that have been developed include Lazarus's Multimodal Therapy; Beutler's Eclectic Psychotherapy; Brammer and Shostrom's Actualizing Therapy; and Howard, Nance, and Myers's Adaptive Counseling and Therapy (1987). All these models offer promising ideas to the therapist, but their effectiveness has not yet been well substantiated.

Other Research on Effectiveness of Psychotherapy Approaches. A study with intriguing implications was conducted by Luborsky, McLellan, Woody, O'Brien, and Auerbach (1985). They studied nine therapists, treating 110 male veterans who were on methadone maintenance for drug abuse. Three of the therapists provided supportive-expressive counseling (SE) and medication, three provided cognitive-behavioral psychotherapy (CB) and medication, and three provided only drug counseling (DC). Although all groups improved, large differences were found among the outcomes. Overall, the SE treatment was more effective than the CB treatment, which was more effective than the DC treatment. The addition of medication to therapy (see section 2.5) as well as the establishment of a positive therapeutic relationship (see Chapter Three, especially section 3.3) seemed to increase the likelihood of a positive outcome.

One of the most interesting findings of the above study was the observation that purity of technique (that is, close adherence to the prescribed techniques, as presented in a manual) was significantly correlated with outcome. This finding seems to conflict with the recommendation of Smith and his colleagues, who advocate pluralism in therapy, and the tendency for most therapists to identify themselves as eclectic (Howard, Nance, & Myers, 1987). A question not answered by Luborsky and his colleagues is whether the use of a relatively pure model of therapy promotes a positive outcome or whether therapy that is moving in a positive direction facilitates the application of a pure model because the therapist need not innovate or experiment in order to effect progress.

Frances, Clarkin, and Perry (1984) consider but do not make a judgment about the question of combined versus pure approaches to treatment. They see both advantages and disadvantages to combined treatment. The advantages include the synergistic component to some treatment combinations, as well as the ability to focus different interventions on different target symptoms; to dilute the transference (if a team approach is used); and to induce changes in different areas at different rates of speed, with progress in one area optimally paving the way for progress in another. The disadvantages include the possibility of negative interaction of therapies, a conflict or lack of clarity of direction or responsibility (especially if more than one therapist is involved), cost, possibility of increasing client dependency or exaggerating the client's perception of the severity of the disorder, confusion about what is really helping the client, and the possible failure to obtain a holistic picture of the client.

Aside from the studies of Smith and Luborsky and their colleagues, few studies have been made of the effectiveness of therapies across many orientations. However, studies focusing on only one or two approaches also provide useful information on the effectiveness of the various psychotherapies.

2.4.3 Psychoanalysis

Few studies of the effectiveness of psychoanalysis are available, in part because the process is so lengthy and intense that each analyst can treat only a small number of clients. One of the most thorough studies of psychotherapy effectiveness does, however, focus on clients treated with psychoanalysis. The Psychotherapy Research Project (PRP) of the Menninger Foundation collected data for thirty years (1954–1984) on a cohort of forty-two former patients (Wallerstein, 1986). Half had been treated with psychoanalysis, half with "equally long-term expressive and supportive psychoanalytic psychotherapies" (p. vii), approaches that have a more limited focus than psychoanalysis and do not seek to evoke a full transference. In general, those selected for psychoanalysis were functioning initially at a higher level. Length of treatment ranged from seven months to ten years. Those in psychoanalysis had an average of five and two-thirds years and 1,017 hours of treatment (five sessions per week); those in psychotherapy averaged four and one-third years and 316 hours of treatment (one to three sessions per week). Clients were diagnosed as having "severe symptom neuroses, severe character neuroses, impulse neuroses (alcohol, addictive, sexual), narcissistic and borderline personality disorders" (p. 91) as their primary diagnoses. Most also had anxiety and/or depression, uncontrolled aggression, sexual difficulties, somatic symptoms, and marital problems. Twenty-three of the patients had been hospitalized at some time, generally for substance abuse problems.

Outcome was very similar for psychoanalysis and psychotherapy; 63 percent of the former group and 58 percent of the latter group had good or moderate outcomes. Those with hysteric or phobic disorders tended to improve, while those diagnosed as paranoid, borderline, or obese were not likely to improve. Adolescent and female patients also were likely to improve. Patients who were themselves employed in the helping professions were often resistant to treatment and generally did not show good improvement. A high percentage of those with good results had what Wallerstein terms transference cures, in which the clients were strongly motivated by a wish to please their therapists. Education and information provided during treatment, not usually viewed as major components of intensive psychotherapy, seemed to be important positive ingredients in the treatment. Conflict resolution, too, was associated with improvement. There was no clear indication that insight was necessary for positive change. Improvement typically continued at follow-up, and regression was noted in less than 25 percent of the clients, primarily those who had not had a good outcome initially.

Since the treatment of the clients in the Menninger study, there has been a trend in the literature away from prolonged psychoanalysis and other treatments of long duration and toward the briefer psychotherapies. Psychoanalysis is not commonly recommended as a treatment of choice today except for clients with ample time and finances who have a strong interest in personal growth and change. Nevertheless, the Menninger study provides a useful basis of comparison, some support for principles and procedures of psychoanalysis, and some information on the sort of client who responds best to this approach to treatment (for example, young clients with nonpsychotic disorders of moderate severity). It also demonstrates that even the most intensive treatments fail to work in some cases; approximately 40 percent of the clients in this study showed little or no improvement.

2.4.4 Psychodynamic Approach

The psychodynamic approach to treatment borrows heavily from the psychoanalytic model but is a briefer, more directive, and more problem-focused version of that approach. According to Frances, Clarkin, and Perry (1984), the psychodynamic approach is best suited to clients suffering intrapsychic conflicts who are seeking personality change in at least one area. Ideal clients for this approach seem to be motivated, straightforward, willing to commit time and money to therapy, psychologically minded, able to tolerate and discuss painful feelings, intelligent, verbal, and in possession of relatively high ego strength. They have no urgent concerns and are not likely to regress or become psychologically disabled. Kaplan and Sadock (1985) emphasize that candidates for this approach must be motivated toward insight and must be able to form relationships and to benefit from interpretation.

2.4.5 Brief Dynamic Psychotherapy

Brief dynamic psychotherapy is a form of psychodynamic psychotherapy. Typical outcomes of brief dynamic therapy include symptom relief, improved relationships, better self-esteem, greater insight and self-awareness, better problem-solving ability, and a sense of accomplishment (Budman, 1981). The approach seems to provide a corrective emotional experience for clients who are not severely dysfunctional but who may be suffering from depression, anxiety, post-traumatic stress disorder, phobic or obsessional disorders, or adjustment difficulties, possibly with mild to moderate personality disorders underlying the symptoms. Their contact with reality is fairly good, as is their capacity for insight and interpersonal relationships; but they feel some dissatisfaction and are probably interested in changing some aspects of themselves. Appropriate clients would be those who have a significant focal concern. They should be able to tolerate separation and loss and have a history of shared and meaningful relationships. The transference relationship and the client's fantasies are deliberately fostered. This approach is not recommended for treatment of severe depression that seems to have a biochemical basis, schizophrenic disorders, long-term substance abuse, and borderline or other severe personality disorders. A time limit is typically set at the onset of treatment, with eighteen sessions being the median for experienced therapists (Horowitz, Marmar, Krupnick, Wilner, Kaltreider, & Wallerstein, 1984); and the primary goal is to ameliorate the focal concern and to enable the client to handle similar concerns in the future.

Marziali (1984) studied twenty-five clients treated with brief dynamic psychotherapy. Outcome measures included friendships, intimacy, capacity to use support, self-esteem, and assertiveness. Marziali found a positive association between favorable outcome and the frequency with which the therapist interpreted emotions experienced in the transference relationship that were similar to those experienced in the clients' other important relationships. Most of these clients presented problems of anxiety, depression, or adjustment, with underlying compulsive, histrionic, or narcissistic personality disorders. Although relatively few studies have been conducted of this fairly new approach to treatment, the Marziali study is typical in providing encouraging results in treatment of appropriate clients.

2.4.6 Behavior Therapy

Many studies substantiate the value of behavior therapy. According to Wilson (1981), no study published prior to 1981 had shown behavior therapy to be inferior to psychotherapy, and many showed it to be marginally or significantly more effective than an alternative. In addition, no studies have shown that symptom substitution—the shifting of the focus of a problem from one symptom to another after treatment has effected improvement in the first symptom—took place. On the contrary, studies yielded evidence of spontaneous improvement of untreated areas following successful behavior therapy focusing on one symptom.

Wilson believes that behavior therapy can bring about improvement in overall psychological functioning, as well as in target symptoms, and asserts that behavior therapy should not be regarded as simply a way to enhance more traditional approaches to therapy. Matthews, Gelder, and Johnson (1981) found that flooding and systematic desensitization were more successful than placebo treatment in helping agoraphobic clients. Luborsky, Singer, and Luborsky (1975), in a review of studies that compared the effectiveness of behavioral and verbal therapy, found that behavior therapy was superior in six studies while the two were not significantly different in twelve studies. Kazdin and Wilson (1978) found behavior therapy to be more effective overall than verbal therapy, especially in the treatment of neurotic depression, addiction, and inpatient management of psychotic disorders. Home-based behavioral therapy also was effective with a group of female clients when their husbands followed a manual of instruction and acted as cotherapists. Wilson (1981) found that phobic clients showed considerable improvement after about six sessions of participant modeling or graduated *in vivo* exposure to the feared object. *In vivo* behavior therapy seems to be a particularly efficient form of treatment, not only because it is brief but also because it is at least as effective in group treatment as it is in individual therapy (Frances, Clarkin, & Perry, 1984).

Clients are most likely to benefit from behavior therapy if they are motivated to change, follow through on homework assignments or self-help programs, and have friends and family who support their efforts to change. Clients who are "action-oriented" seem to respond particularly well to behavior therapy (Lambert, 1982, p. 33). Clearly, there are many positive reports of the effectiveness of behavior therapy. Nevertheless, Frances, Clarkin, and Perry (1984) conclude: "Despite many myths to the contrary, the documented advantage of behavioral techniques for phobic patients has not been impressive" (p. 140).

Duration of treatment seems to be a critical variable in determining the effectiveness of behavior therapy. A single two-hour session of *in vivo* exposure seems to be more effective than four half-hour sessions, for example. Flooding can actually increase anxiety if it is not maintained long enough for the anxiety reaction to subside. In the treatment of phobias, obsessive compulsive disorders, and sexual disorders, performance-based *in vivo* exposure methods are more effective than methods that employ imaginal symbolic procedures.

Clearly, behavior modification can have a powerful therapeutic impact on a broad range of disorders. However, as Frances and his colleagues remind us, we still do not have a clear picture of its power nor do we know definitively what form of behavior modification works best with a given disorder. More research is still needed in this area.

2.4.7 Cognitive Therapy

Just as psychoanalysis might be viewed as the therapy of the past, cognitive therapy may be seen as the therapy of the present.

Developed by Beck and his colleagues (Beck, Rush, Shaw, & Emery, 1979), it is used primarily for the treatment of anxiety; depression; and related disorders, such as phobias. It assumes that clients' cognitions represent their view of themselves, their world, their past, and their future (in other words, their phenomenal field). Cognitive structures, then, are the primary determinants of clients' affective states and behavioral patterns. Through cognitive therapy, clients are helped to become aware of their cognitive distortions and to correct their dysfunctional constructs, leading to clinical improvement. The focus of the treatment is on the present, and homework assignments are an important part of the treatment.

Current literature reveals a sort of rivalry between behavior therapy and cognitive therapy. Berman, Miller, and Massman (1985) reviewed and summarized twenty-five studies comparing the relative effectiveness of the two therapies. Sixty percent of those studies focused on the treatment of anxiety-related disorders; 28 percent focused on treating phobias; and 12 percent included treatment of other disorders, such as stuttering, obsessive compulsive disorders, and lack of assertiveness. Berman and colleagues found that the two therapies were approximately equal in efficacy and that treatment via a combination of the two was no more effective than treatment by either alone. They therefore disagree with the earlier findings of Shapiro and Shapiro (1982), who concluded that cognitive therapy is generally more effective than treatment via imaginal or *in vivo* desensitization.

Beck, Rush, Shaw, and Emery (1979) reviewed eight studies of the effectiveness of cognitive therapy and found that cognitive and cognitive-behavioral therapy were superior to nontreatment and to other approaches in treating depression at all levels of severity. However, Beck and his colleagues also concluded that cognitive therapy is not indicated if there is a family history of bipolar illness or a coexisting diagnosis of schizophrenia, organicity, mental retardation, or substance abuse.

2.4.8 No Treatment

Bergin and Lambert (1978) summarized seventeen studies and found a median rate for spontaneous improvement of 43 percent; in these instances, ingredients in the client's experience or environment other than psychotherapy served as the catalyst for change. Frances, Clarkin, and Perry (1984) concluded that, in most studies of psychotherapy and psychotropic medication, the rate of positive response is about 60–70 percent. These figures suggest that at least 17–27 percent of clients who improve during psychotherapy do so as a result of the therapeutic process. (This rate of improvement probably does not fully reflect the benefits of therapy, since it does not consider extent of improvement and since some of those who did not improve might have deteriorated further without intervention.)

Despite the demonstrated effectiveness of therapy, 30–40 percent of psychotherapy clients do not show clear benefit from that process. There is little research on the iatrogenic or negative effects of psychotherapy. However, Frances and his colleagues offer some guidelines for determining when no treatment may be the best recommendation. They suggest that the "no treatment" option be considered for the following groups of clients:

1. Clients at risk for a negative response—for example, clients with severe narcissistic, masochistic, or oppositional personality patterns; clients with borderline personality disorders and a history of treatment failures; and clients who want to support a lawsuit or disability claim and so may have an investment in failing to make progress
2. Clients at risk for no response—for example, clients who are poorly motivated and not incapacitated, clients with antisocial or criminal histories, clients with malingering or factitious illnesses, and those who seem likely to become infantilized by the therapeutic process
3. Clients likely to show spontaneous improvement—for example, healthy clients in crisis or with minor chronic concerns
4. Clients likely to benefit from a strategic use of the "no treatment" recommendation—for example, oppositional clients who refuse treatment and clients whose adaptive defenses would be supported by that recommendation

The "no treatment" recommendation would be designed to protect the client from harm, protect client and therapist from wasting their time, delay therapy until the client is more receptive to it, support prior gains, and give clients the message that they can survive without therapy. Although this option may make sense theoretically, it does not seem to be used frequently by clinicians— at least in part because of the great difficulty of predicting who will not benefit from therapy and the risk involved in discouraging a client from beginning therapy when that client might really be able to make good use of it.

2.4.9 Current State of the Art

Perry, Frances, and Clarkin (1985) conclude: "It is sad but true that it will be a long time before treatment selection in psychiatry will have a solid foundation" (p. 361). At the same time, they encourage clinicians to continue efforts to determine the most effective treatment approach for disorders by reviewing the literature and by generalizing from available studies and cases. Stiles, Shapiro, and Elliott (1986) echo these ideas by expressing dismay over the current state of the art of differential therapeutics while, at the same time, calling for greater precision and specificity of theory.

Some of the reasons for the lack of clarity in treatment specificity are obvious. The challenges of conducting research on something as ill defined and variable as psychotherapy without jeopardizing clients' right to the best possible treatment are enormous. In addition, as discussed earlier in this chapter, the various therapies have many underlying similarities. Could it be that the underlying similarities are more important than the overt differences and tend to blur the distinctions among therapies, thereby leading to inconclusive research? Or, as will be considered in Chapter Three, could it be that client and therapist variables are really at least as important as variables characterizing the various approaches to therapy? Regardless of the answers to these questions, research in this area will continue for the foreseeable future, examining the many approaches to psychotherapy as well as client and clinician variables and their interaction, and the field will continue to evolve.

Researchers have predicted the following trends in psycho-

therapy (Millman, Huber, & Diggins, 1982; Perry, Frances, & Clarkin, 1985):

1. More teaching of functional attitudes and coping skills
2. More group counseling
3. More homework assignments and other procedures designed to
   put increased responsibility on the client
4. More overt collaboration with the client and other clinicians
5. More feedback given to the client
6. More use of family members as aids to the counseling process
7. More use of brief therapy approaches
8. More use of multiple therapies and eclectic approaches, and
   expanded views of the dynamics and treatment of mental
   disorders

2.5 Psychotropic Medication

Although this book is directed toward nonmedical clinicians,
who do not prescribe medication as part of the treatment they provide, all clinicians should have an understanding of the role that
medication can play in the treatment of mental disorders. In that
way, nonmedical clinicians will know when collaboration with a
physician may accelerate a client's progress. Many studies suggest
that, for most of the severe mental disorders, a combination of medication and psychotherapy is better than treatment by either alone
(Luborsky, Singer, & Luborsky, 1975). For example, in a study
discussed earlier in this chapter, Luborsky, McLellan, Woody,
O'Brien, and Auerbach (1985) found that medication enhanced the
effectiveness of psychotherapy provided to clients in a methadone
maintenance program. May, Tuma, and Dixon (1976) obtained a
similar outcome in their study of the treatment of hospitalized
schizophrenic clients.

Medication and psychotherapy often have different effects on
a given mental disorder. For example, Klerman, Dimascio, and
Weissman (1974), in a study of the treatment of moderately depressed female outpatients, found that amitriptyline significantly
reduced the relapse rate but had no effect on social adjustment,
while supportive psychotherapy did not prevent relapse or symp-

tom return but did improve social adjustment, work performance, and family communication and reduced feelings of stress, resentment, and dissatisfaction. Karasu (1982), summarizing the differential effects of psychotherapy and medication, indicates that drugs help to relieve symptoms and affective distress while therapy improves interpersonal relations and social adjustment.

Those studies that do show a difference in the degree of effectiveness of medication and psychotherapy suggest that psychotherapy has a greater positive impact, to some extent because of client attitudes toward the two modes of treatment. For example, Rush, Beck, Kovacs, and Hollon (1977) compared the effects of cognitive therapy and imipramine in the treatment of clients with unipolar depression. After three months, the therapy group showed greater improvement; but there were no significant differences between the two groups after six months. However, more clients dropped out of treatment in the medication group than in the therapy group. Beck, Rush, Shaw, and Emery (1979) also found a higher attrition rate (25-30 percent) for clients receiving antidepressant medication than for those receiving cognitive therapy. Although psychotherapy may be more time consuming and appear less magical and powerful than medication, clients generally seem more comfortable with psychotherapy as the chosen mode of treatment than they do with medication.

Medication seems most useful for disorders involving debilitating anxiety, endogenous depression, mania, or psychosis; therapy seems more effective in treating problems of adjustment, behavior, relationships, mild to moderate anxiety, reactive depression, and personality disorders. The effects of therapy may not appear until later than those of medication, but they are likely to last longer. Medication, then, may be used to provide fairly rapid relief and to facilitate a client's engagement in psychotherapy, while therapy seems to be the foundation for treatment of most mental disorders. When medication is used, most clinicians seem to agree with Perry, Frances, and Clarkin (1985), who state, "To increase compliance and to enhance the placebo effect, somatic treatments should always be provided within the context of a therapeutic relationship" (p. 363).

Psychotropic medications can be divided into the following

four groups (Perry, Frances, & Clarkin, 1985; Frances, Clarkin & Perry, 1984):

1. Antipsychotic medication—primarily for treatment of acute schizophrenia and other disorders involving delusions and hallucinations
2. Antidepressants—including tricyclic antidepressants and mono-amine oxidase (MAO) inhibitors. Tricyclic antidepressants seem to facilitate the treatment of moderate to severe major depression with melancholia; panic attacks; bipolar depression; and eating, sleeping, and obsessive compulsive disorders. MAO inhibitors tend to be effective with atypical depressions associated with prominent phobias, anxiety, and reverse vegetative signs (for example, increased eating and early-morning awakening); panic attacks; and related disorders that have not responded to tricyclics
3. Lithium—for treatment of bipolar disorders and some types of cyclothymia
4. Antianxiety agents—for reduction of anxiety

Smith, Glass, and Miller (1980), reviewing 112 studies of the use of medication in the treatment of emotional disorders, concluded: "Psychotherapy enjoys near parity with drug therapy in treating even the very serious disorders" (p. 189) and "When the two therapies are combined, the net benefits are less than the sum of their separate benefits" but more than either alone (p. 188), particularly in treatment of the psychotic disorders.

2.6 Frequency and Duration of Treatment

In addition to determining levels of directiveness and probing, the modality of treatment, the therapeutic approaches and techniques to be used, and whether a referral for a medical evaluation is indicated, clinicians must also decide how frequently to schedule a client's appointments, how long each session should be, and approximately how long a particular client will need to be in therapy. Typical of most approaches to psychotherapy is one session of 45–50 minutes per week. In practice, however, the frequency of therapy sessions varies from every other week (often used in supportive therapy, particularly toward the end of treatment) to five times per week (in psychoanalysis). Duration of therapy, of course, varies widely and is often difficult to predict.

The available research gives some help to clinicians in making these decisions. Pilkonis, Imber, Lewis, and Rubinsky (1984) studied sixty-four outpatients who received an average of 26.8 sessions of therapy. They found some indication that longer treatment was associated with a more negative outcome, especially for those clients who had a clear idea of the sort of treatment they preferred. Orlinsky and Howard (1986) also reviewed studies of the relationship between outcome and total number of therapy sessions; their findings suggest a different conclusion. They found twenty studies that showed a positive relationship between outcome and number of sessions, seven that showed no significant relationship, and six that showed a curvilinear relationship. In addition, twelve studies showed a positive relationship between outcome and total time in treatment, nine showed no significant relationship, and one showed a negative relationship. Orlinsky and Howard therefore concluded that total number of sessions and, to a lesser extent, duration of treatment correlate positively with therapeutic benefit.

In the 475 studies analyzed by Smith, Glass, and Miller (1980), clients were seen for an average of 17.8 sessions, with a range of 1–100 sessions. (Gurman, 1981, found that marriage and family counseling, too, lasts just over seventeen sessions on the average.) Smith, Glass, and Miller found no clear relationship between treatment duration and improvement. A reanalysis of the Smith, Glass, and Miller data by Andrews and Harvey (1981) yielded an average effect size of 0.68 for brief therapy (0–9 hours), 0.73 for short therapy (10–19 sessions), and 0.86 for longer therapy (20–100 hours). However, the differences among these figures were not significant. There was some indication that the greatest progress was made during the first seven sessions and between the nineteenth and twenty-fifth sessions (Smith, Glass, & Miller, 1980). In a review of the literature on brief forms of psychotherapy, Horowitz, Marmar, Weiss, DeWitt, and Rosenbaum (1984) found that treatment of "circumscribed neurotic conflict" required 5–15 one-hour sessions; treatment with multiple foci required 15–25 sessions; and treatment of severe longstanding character pathology required 20-30 sessions. Generally, the more specific the symptom, the shorter the treatment.

Frances, Clarkin, and Perry (1984) suggest that the following variables increase the duration of therapy, while their converse tend to shorten the therapy: a chronic disorder, poor functioning prior to the onset of the presenting concerns, ambitious treatment goals, motivation toward an enduring therapeutic relationship, a client expectation of change as a lengthy process, a therapist expectation of many target symptoms, no acute precipitant, extensive resources, a geographically convenient therapist, client age between twenty-five and fifty, an emphasis on an exploratory and/or psychoanalytic approach to therapy, a maintenance (rather than repairative) setting, and a heterogeneous group as the mode of treatment.

Bloom (1981) found that single-session episodes of care were quite common, especially among clients in lower socioeconomic groups. In general, 30-35 percent of clients seen at family counseling agencies, 25-30 percent of clients seen at community mental health centers, and 15 percent of clients seen at university-based mental health centers received only one counseling session, sometimes because of the therapist's recommendation and sometimes because of what may be perceived as premature termination on the client's part. However, one study found that two-thirds of clients who had only one therapy session felt that they had been helped. Bloom concluded that "a single contact, virtually regardless of the nature of that contact, appears to have salutary consequences" (p. 179). In fact, Howard, Kopta, Krause, and Orlinsky (1986) found that 10-18 percent of clients improve before the first session just by virtue of having made contact with a potential source of help.

Howard and colleagues also found that, overall, approximately 50 percent of clients were measurably improved by eight sessions of therapy; 75 percent, by twenty-six sessions; and 85 percent, by one year. However, they also found that speed of response to therapy is related to diagnosis. Depressive clients responded fairly quickly to treatment, with 53 percent showing improvement by eight sessions. Forty-six percent of clients being treated for anxiety and 33 percent of clients with borderline personality disorders showed improvement by the eighth session. By the fifty-second session, the numbers were much closer, ranging from 74 percent of clients with anxiety disorders to 77 percent of clients with depression showing improvement. Howard and colleagues recommend that, by the twenty-sixth session, therapists should thoroughly review cases that have shown little or no improvement, since the majority of cases will have responded to treatment by that time.

Research on frequency of sessions and length of sessions is rather sparse. Frances, Clarkin, and Perry (1984) reviewed a group of studies on the topic and found that most yielded little significant information. At least one study, however, found that clients who were seen twice a week did less well than clients who were seen once a week, partially because the more severely disturbed clients had difficulty handling the intensity of the twice-weekly relationship. Research does not support the superiority of the fifty-minute hour, and variations on that standard seem to be increasing. Sessions lasting twenty to thirty minutes are sometimes used to monitor progress and provide support, and sessions of several hours' duration are used to weaken defenses and curtail client avoidance of difficult issues. Lambert, Shapiro, and Bergin (1986) recommend monthly sessions, serving as booster shots to maintain progress.

The literature on duration and frequency of treatment is contradictory and often flawed methodologically (for example, failing to control for severity of disturbance). In general, however, most studies do not indicate that longer treatment has a clear advantage over brief therapy. In light of the added cost in money, time, and emotional investment of longer treatment, the research suggests that brief therapy should be the treatment of choice in most cases. At the same time, no harm has been shown to come from longer treatment; and, in some cases, extended treatment and treatment with a frequency of more than once a week have been shown to be advantageous (Orlinsky & Howard, 1986). A related and positive finding is that improvement made during therapy tends to hold up over time after the completion of treatment (Nicholson & Berman, 1983).

2.7 Treatment Setting

Research is even more limited on treatment setting than it is on duration and frequency of therapy. Smith, Glass, and Miller (1980) found a more positive outcome connected with therapy offered in college settings than in public schools, mental health centers, hospitals, prisons, residential facilities, and other settings. However, the superiority of the college setting seems to have more to do with the typically healthy, youthful, motivated, and intelligent nature of the college population than it does with the therapeutic power of the setting.

Schwartz and Schwartzburg (1976) found that schizophrenic clients comprised 27 percent of psychiatric hospitalizations; depressed clients, 22.5 percent; substance-abusing clients, 21 percent; and the balance, a broad range of other disorders. Frances, Clarkin, and Perry (1984) believe that treatment setting is primarily a function of the goal of the therapy rather than the severity of the disorder. There may even be a negative relationship, in some cases, between severity of disorder and duration of hospitalization. For example, narrower goals usually will be set for chronic schizophrenic clients with poor adjustment prior to the onset of their symptoms than would be set for clients with a reactive schizophrenic disorder whose functioning had been fairly good. The more demanding goals may require a longer hospitalization.

Frances, Clarkin, and Perry also recommend that consideration be given to client preference and motivation. They suggest that the goal of acute care can be met through intensive-care hospitalization, partial hospitalization, or an outpatient crisis intervention program. Rehabilitation can be accomplished through longer-term full or partial hospitalization or through outpatient psychotherapy. Maintenance can be achieved in chronic-care hospitalization, partial hospitalization, or outpatient programs.

Treatment setting, like many of the other decisions that must be made as part of treatment planning, requires clinical judgment, since the literature gives only sketchy guidelines. In general, however, hospitalization seems most appropriate for clients with schizophrenic disorders, major depression, severe substance abuse, or bipolar disorders. It is also indicated for clients who need a high level of supervision because of suicidal or homicidal ideation, bizarre behavior, or an inability to care for themselves. Some studies indicate that a brief hospital stay followed by aftercare is more therapeutic than a longer stay. In general, the most efficient, least confining treatment setting should be used to reduce stigma, maintain client independence and connection to the community, and reduce costs.

Conclusion

Application of the information in this chapter to Bettie and Anne provides clarification of their treatment. Although both women were coping with broken engagements, Anne was also dealing with an unplanned pregnancy and used alcohol and avoidance as coping mechanisms. Bettie, on the other hand, had more self-confidence and personal resources and viewed her unexpected change of plans as an opportunity for personal growth.

Both women probably would benefit from short-term therapy. Bettie should be seen weekly, and Anne should be seen more frequently until she has resolved her immediate crisis. Bettie is more self-directed; and, although some cognitive dysfunction and mild depression are evident, she might respond well to a modified form of person-centered therapy that encourages her to develop her self confidence and self-awareness and establish goals and direction as well as interpersonal skills. Anne is less motivated toward self-exploration and is primarily interested in resolving her immediate concerns. Her therapy would be likely to focus more on cognitive-behavioral areas, emphasizing decision making and behavioral change.

Anne seems likely to respond best to individual therapy because she is in crisis, must make a rapid decision about her pregnancy, and is not presently interested in personal growth and development. Bettie would probably benefit from either individual or group psychotherapy or from a combination of the two, perhaps short-term individual therapy followed by participation in a personal growth group for women or a psychotherapy group for young adults. Neither Anne nor Bettie seems in need of medication, although Anne's therapist should make sure that she is receiving necessary medical care. Both Anne and Bettie are capable of self-regulation and are in touch with reality. An outpatient treatment setting, such as a community mental health center or private practice, seems an appropriate location for their treatment. Adjunct services such as Alcoholics Anonymous and even inpatient treatment may need to be considered for Anne, depending on the severity of her alcohol abuse.

After their immediate concerns have been resolved, both Bettie and Anne might decide to continue treatment beyond the short term. However, their goals are likely to differ. Bettie will probably seek to improve her relationship skills, to clarify goals and direction, and to enhance self-esteem, whereas Anne will probably need to develop better coping mechanisms and greater independence.

Although the research on therapy variables does not provide definitive descriptions of exactly what type of therapy would be best for each of these women, it does give guidelines for shaping an approach to therapy that is likely to be effective with each of them. Subsequent chapters of this book will provide a closer look at the relationship between client and therapist dynamics and therapy effect as well as between diagnosis and therapy effect.

Chapter Three

▮▮▮

How Therapist and Client Characteristics Affect Treatment

Chapter Two reviewed the literature on the effectiveness of psychotherapy in general, as well as on the effectiveness of particular approaches to psychotherapy. Although psychotherapy itself was found to be generally effective, the research on the differential effectiveness of the various psychotherapies was inconclusive. That may be because therapy is an inexact science. Even with the recent advent of manuals to direct the therapeutic process—bringing some uniformity and consistency to that process—therapy inevitably varies widely, depending on the nature of the therapist, the client, and their interaction. As Pilkonis, Imber, Lewis, and Rubinsky (1984) concluded, differences in outcome may be due more to the therapist, the client, and their fit than to aspects of the particular therapeutic model being used. Maximizing the effectiveness of psychotherapy, then, requires an understanding not only of the therapeutic models and techniques used but also of the client and the clinician. This chapter will review and discuss the literature on therapeutically relevant aspects of the therapist, the client, and their interaction.

3.1 Therapist Variables

As Luborsky, McLellan, Woody, O'Brien, and Auerbach (1985) point out, "the therapist is not simply the transmitter of a standard therapeutic agent. Rather, the therapist is an important, independent agent of change with the ability to magnify or reduce the effects of a therapy" (p. 609). The literature on therapist effectiveness can be organized into three categories: demographic information; professional background; and personal, relational, and therapeutic style and values.

3.1.1 Demographic Information

Gender of the therapist as well as interaction of therapist and client genders seem likely to have an impact on the development of the therapeutic relationship. Mogul (1982) found that clients were more satisfied with female than with male therapists and suggests that selecting the gender of the therapist in light of the client's history might contribute to therapeutic effectiveness. For example, clients might be assigned a therapist of the same gender as a parent they had lost in childhood or the parent with whom they had moderate (but not disabling) conflict. Mogul also suggests that women who have been victims of rape or incest might work better with female therapists and that adolescents might be more comfortable with same-sex therapists. Beutler, Crago, and Arizmendi (1986), too, found that female therapists as well as gender matching of client and therapist contributed to effectiveness, especially if the therapist did not communicate attitudes that promoted gender stereotyping. They also found that clients tended to respond better when treatment was provided by a therapist of the sex they had preferred or requested. Perry, Frances, and Clarkin (1985) recommend that "treatment aimed at character change should probably be conducted by a therapist whose sex presents the most difficulties for the patient, whereas treatments designed to alleviate symptoms should most often be conducted by a therapist whose sex poses the least problems for the patient" (p. 364).

In general, Mogul concludes, the gender of the therapist might be important to individual clients and is worth considering—especially for short-term counseling, where the rapid establishment of a positive therapeutic allliance is important. However, "No specific conclusions as to optimal patient-therapist matches on the basis of therapist sex appear warranted" (p. 1). This general conclusion seems sound in light of the limited research on this variable.

Berman and Norton (1985), in a comparative study of professional and paraprofessional therapists, addressed the variables of therapist and client age and their relationship. They found that the professional therapists (who tended to be older) seemed to work better with older clients, while the paraprofessionals had a slight edge in their effectiveness with younger clients. These findings suggest that age similarity could contribute to effectiveness and that older clients might respond better to the credentials and sense of professionalism of well-educated therapists than they would to paraprofessionals. These results were confirmed by Beutler, Crago, and Arizmendi (1986), who found a modest positive effect in age similarity of therapist and client.

Beutler and his colleagues reviewed the literature on therapist ethnicity and socioeconomic status and found that, beyond the need for therapists to have flexible and egalitarian attitudes and to be aware of ethnic differences, no clear conclusions could be drawn. Lambert (1982), too, found no clear evidence that the therapist's race or the similarity of therapist's and client's race affects outcome. However, Lambert also noted that black clients leave therapy at higher than usual rates when they are working with white therapists, suggesting that under some circumstances race may indeed be a factor in determining outcome. Smith, Glass, and Miller (1980) did find a small positive correlation between outcome and client-therapist similarity in education and socioeconomic status. This finding may, however, simply indicate that clients of higher education and socioeconomic status benefit from therapy more than those of lower status; or it could reflect a sampling bias, since most therapists probably do not come from lower-class backgrounds.

3.1.2 Professional Background

Research on the impact of therapist training, experience, and professional affiliation is unclear and often contradictory. Parloff (1986) found no clear correlation between the length of the therapist's experience and the therapeutic outcome. Beutler, Crago, and Arizmendi (1986), however, concluded that the therapist's experience is positively correlated with outcome, particularly with clients' likelihood of remaining in treatment. Lambert (1982), too, found that the therapist's experience has a "reliable relationship to outcome"

(p. 60). The literature suggests that experienced therapists are more similar to each other than are inexperienced ones. Perhaps experience balances out some of the unevenness in therapists' knowledge, teaching them what works and what does not work and increasing uniformity in the characteristics of effective therapist style. This hypothesis makes sense in light of the finding that therapist skillfulness is significantly related to outcome (Beutler, Crago, & Arizmendi, 1986), since, presumably, therapist experience is positively correlated with therapist skillfulness.

Beutler, Crago, and Arizmendi found no relationship between the therapist's discipline and outcome. Berman and Norton (1985), in fact, found that, overall, professionals and paraprofessionals were equally effective. Smith, Glass, and Miller (1980), however, found that those trained in psychology seemed to have a greater positive effect than did those trained in psychiatry or education. Greenspan and Kulish (1985), in their study of 273 clients who terminated treatment prematurely after at least six months of treatment, echo those findings. Greenspan and Kulish found that therapists with Ph.D. degrees, as well as those who had gone through personal therapy, had lower rates of client terminations than did those with M.D. or M.S.W. degrees. However, the nature of these data suggests that they be interpreted cautiously. For example, premature termination does not mean that treatment has been unsuccessful. No conclusive relationship has yet been found between length of training, personal therapy, or professional discipline and outcome.

3.1.3 Personal, Relational, and Therapeutic Style and Values

According to Strupp (1981), motivated clients who have good ego strength are less affected by the therapist's "human qualities" than are clients who are resistant and low in ego strength. He further observed that therapists with strong human qualities and low technical skill still obtain moderate outcomes, but therapists with high technical skills and low human qualities tend to obtain poor outcomes. Human qualities, then, are not sufficient to effect optimal gains in therapy but do seem to be an important ingredient of that process.

More research has been conducted in this area than on the

previous two categories. The following therapist attitudes and approaches have been found to correlate with effectiveness:

1. Acceptance of clients' beliefs and values and use of interventions that reflect that acceptance (Beutler, Crago, & Arizmendi, 1986)
2. Engagement of clients at an emotional level, with an emphasis on apprehensions and feelings expressed in therapy that mirror those experienced by clients in other significant relationships (Beutler, Crago, & Arizmendi, 1986; Marziali, 1984; Shapiro & Shapiro, 1982)
3. Emphasis on support rather than interpretation or insight (Buckley, Conte, Plutchik, Wild, & Karasu, 1984)
4. Communication of accurate empathy, reassurance, positive regard, warmth, and genuineness (Lambert, 1982; Shapiro & Shapiro, 1982)
5. Self-disclosure and expressiveness (in appropriate, moderate amounts)
6. Engagement in the therapeutic process (Beutler, Crago, & Arizmendi, 1986)
7. Credibility and confidence
8. Demonstration of attentiveness to and interest in the client (when the attentiveness and interest are perceived by the client)
9. Communication of the expectation that clients will assume responsibility and take steps to make positive change (Shapiro & Shapiro, 1982)
10. Ability to give direction and coherence to the session, identifying focal concerns and keeping clients on task (Sachs, 1983)

These findings suggest that the therapist most likely to achieve a positive outcome is active, optimistic, expressive, straightforward yet supportive, involved, and in charge of the therapeutic process but also able to encourage client responsibility. Not surprisingly, research has also suggested that therapists who are themselves psychologically healthy are more likely to promote health in their clients (Lambert, 1982).

Beutler, Crago, and Arizmendi (1986) found that social influence variables—such as expertness, trustworthiness, attractiveness, credibility, and persuasiveness—also are positively related to outcome, with expertness a particularly potent variable.

Research suggests that therapists have a good sense of their own skills as well as those of their colleagues. Luborsky, McLellan, Woody, O'Brien, and Auerbach (1985) found that therapists are able to identify other potentially effective therapists and to discriminate them from those therapists who are less effective. In addition, Morgan, Luborsky, Crits-Christoph, Curtis, and Solomon (1982) observed that therapists seem to have a good sense of those clients they can work with effectively; a better outcome was obtained when therapists chose their clients than when clients were randomly assigned. Included in the list of variables that seem to predict therapist effectiveness, then, should be the therapist's assessment of what and who is likely to work effectively with a given client.

3.2 Client Variables

No matter how wisely therapists select their intervention strategies and no matter how abundantly they demonstrate those qualities that correlate positively with outcome, therapy will not be effective if the client is not ready or able to benefit from those techniques. Stiles, Shapiro, and Elliott (1986), in fact, believe that the key to therapeutic effectiveness is more likely to be found in the clients or in the therapeutic alliance than in the therapist. Attention should be given, then, to those qualities in clients that are correlated with treatment effectiveness.

3.2.1 Client Assessment

Developing a treatment plan for a given client begins with obtaining a thorough understanding of that client. Formats for extensive intake interviews and mental status examinations are readily available elsewhere (Seligman, 1986) and are beyond the scope of this volume. However, a brief and useful overview of relevant aspects of the client is provided by Longabough, Fowler, Stout, and Kriebel (1983). They suggest that information should be obtained on the following ten dimensions of the client: physical characteristics, behavior, affect, thought problems, sexual problems, social behavior problems, life-task problems, patient role, environment, and any other relevant areas. Maxmen (1986) elaborates further on the process by describing the seven steps in diagnosis: collecting data, identifying psychopathology, evaluating reliability of data, determining overall distinctive features, arriving at a diagnosis, checking diagnostic criteria, and resolving diagnostic uncertainty.

Therapists seem to be making increasing use of diagnostic interviews, inventories, and rating scales—both in the preliminary stages of therapy (to gather information on client dynamics) and in the termination stages (to gather information on progress and outcome). Projective testing also is sometimes used to provide an understanding of clients. Many inventories and guidelines developed in recent years can play an important role in client screening. Some of those that seem particularly useful will be described briefly here:

1. NIMH Diagnostic Interview Schedule (NIMH-DIS). This structured interview format allows clinicians to make diagnoses according to several established paradigms (*DSM-III*, Research Diagnostic Criteria) and has been termed "a reasonably satisfactory instrument" (Robins, Helzer, Croughan, & Ratcliff, 1981, p. 389).

2. Schedule for Affective Disorders and Schizophrenia. This semistructured interview format is designed to help the clinician explore clients' past and present disorders. It is available in several versions and is congruent with the NIMH-DIS (Hesselbrock, Stabenau, Hesselbrock, Mirkin, & Meyer, 1982).

3. Brief Psychiatric Rating Scale. This scale provides a format for a twenty-minute structured interview, yielding ratings on sixteen psychiatric symptoms. It has been found to have good interrater reliability (Hurt, Holzman, & David, 1983).

4. Beck Depression Inventory, Hamilton Depression Rating Scale. These brief inventories are useful in assessing the severity of depression, both at the outset of therapy and as therapy progresses (Endicott, Cohen, Nee, Fleiss, & Sarantakos, 1981).

5. Millon Clinical Multiaxial Inventory-II (and its companion, the Millon Adolescent Personality Inventory). These inventories are reminiscent of the Minnesota Multiphasic Personality

Inventory but are linked to the *DSM* and provide up-to-date information on diagnosis and treatment (Millon, 1987).

Marziali (1984) and Lambert, Shapiro, and Bergin (1986) suggest that clinicians supplement the structured interviews and inventories by exploring with the client (and, if appropriate, the client's family members and friends) the following measures of client difficulty and/or improvement:

1. Friendships, support systems, capacity for intimacy
2. Ability to express thoughts, feelings, and impulses constructively and appropriately
3. Self-esteem, self-acceptance, and self-image
4. Ability to realize one's potential
5. Perception of the world (for example, realistic or unrealistic, distorted and delusional or free of distortions and delusions)
6. Reported level of distress and changes in symptoms
7. Observable maladjustment
8. Frequency counts of dysfunctional behaviors

The above information provides only a partial list of approaches to client and outcome assessment. Therapists have available a broad repertoire of approaches, depending on personal preference and client concerns. Whatever vehicle is used, assessment is an important component of treatment planning and should be done with care. Effective treatment planning is probably impossible unless the clinician has made an accurate diagnosis and has a good understanding of the client's development, concerns, strengths, and difficulties.

3.2.2 Demographic and Personality Variables

Approximately 18.7 percent of Americans have some type of mental disorder during any six-month period (Maxmen, 1986). Somewhere between 20 percent and 50 percent of people who are advised to seek therapy refuse it, and less than 10 percent of people who are disturbed seek treatment (Garfield, 1986). What distinguishes those people who seek therapy for their concerns and benefit from that process from those who do not? Those who do seek treatment are more likely to be female, college educated, from the middle to upper classes, and with reasonable expectations of how therapy can help them. Clients who continue in therapy tend to be more dependable, more intelligent, better educated, less likely to have a history of antisocial behavior, and more anxious and dissatisfied with themselves than those who leave therapy prematurely (Garfield, 1986).

Black clients as well as those under forty are especially likely to fail to keep therapy appointments; and black clients and clients with lower socioeconomic status are especially likely to drop out of therapy. In addition, those who refuse treatment are typically younger people who did not seek therapy on their own initiative; who are receiving third-party payments for their treatment; whose problem is acute, nonpsychotic, and situational (for example, a family or an interpersonal problem or a reactive depression); and who have few prior episodes of emotional disorder and no prior therapy (Greenspan & Kulish, 1985; Hoffman, 1985; Rabin, Kaslow, & Rehm, 1985).

Lambert (1982), in a review of the literature, found no clear relationship between outcome and client age, race, or gender. Other research has yielded different findings. Smith, Glass, and Miller (1980) concluded that females benefit more from therapy than males do, and they also found a curvilinear relationship between age and effect size; that is, clients in the nineteen- to twenty-two-year-old age group benefited from therapy more than older and younger clients did. Pilkonis, Imber, Lewis, and Rubinsky (1984) found, in their study of sixty-four outpatients, that lower socioeconomic status and chronicity of the emotional disorder were predictive of a poorer outcome.

Beutler, Crago, and Arizmendi (1986) found that clients who were open, in touch with their emotions, and able to express their thoughts and feelings in therapy had a positive prognosis. Moras and Strupp (1982) concluded, "Pretherapy level of interpersonal relations predicted patients' level of collaborative, positively toned participation in a therapeutic relationship" (p. 405) and had a modest correlation with outcome. Garfield (1986) found a correlation between anxiety and positive outcome as well as between likability of the client and outcome. A high tolerance for frustration and anxiety and low levels of guilt or self-destructive behavior also have been associated with a good prognosis (Wallerstein, 1986). Clients who could express their feelings readily and easily were more likely to have a positive outcome in therapy than clients without that ability. Likelihood of a positive outcome was also increased if clients demon-strated good ego strength and could take responsibility for their problems rather than viewing them as external sources of difficulty.

Buckley, Conte, Plutchik, Wild, and Karasu (1984) conducted a study of twenty-one medical students seeking therapy and found that the following variables were all significantly correlated with outcome: high-level ego-defenses (reaction formation, undoing, rationalization), independent personality (negative correlation), withdrawal, stress, projection, blame, and isolation. These results are interesting but may be limited in generalizability because of the initially healthy nature of the population.

Schramski, Beutler, Lauver, Arizmendi, and Shanfield (1984) studied thirty outpatients at termination of treatment and at a six-month follow-up. They found that 77 percent had maintained or improved their progress. Socioeconomic status and extroversion were positively correlated with outcome, while negative life events, marital change, age, and total number of therapy sessions were negatively correlated with outcome. This finding suggests that increased life stress during and shortly after therapy can offset some of the gains from that process.

Research on the relationship between client personality characteristics and outcome is suggestive but is not yet conclusive (Garfield, 1986). Overall, indications are that therapy is particularly effective with young white females who are intelligent, motivated, expressive, and not severely dysfunctional. Although therapy can, of course, be very helpful to people who do not fit this description, these findings point out some of the limitations of psychotherapy as well as the difficulty in adapting that process to the needs of a particular client.

3.2.3 Diagnosis

Research suggests that the most prevalent disorders in men are (in order) alcohol abuse or dependence, phobias, dysthymia, and antisocial personality disorder; in women, they are phobias, major depression, dysthymia, substance abuse, and obsessive compulsive disorder (Myers & others, 1984). Lambert, Shapiro, and Bergin (1986) observed that clients with severe diagnoses (for example, schizophrenia, depression, alcoholism, or antisocial patterns) showed less improvement than those with circumscribed problems (such as phobias or specific anxieties). This conclusion is consistent with the findings of Horowitz, Marmar, Weiss, DeWitt, and Rosenbaum (1984), who noted that pretreatment levels of client functioning and developmental levels of their self-concepts were significantly related to outcome. However, according to Smith, Glass, and Miller's (1980) findings, "Therapy with psychotics was no less successful than therapy with neurotics, both showing around a two-third standard deviation effect" (p. 113). All these findings can be correct; clients who start at lower levels before therapy are still at lower levels after therapy than those who started at higher levels, even though both may have improved equally.

3.2.4 Perceptions

Horowitz, Marmar, Weiss, DeWitt, and Rosenbaum (1984), in their extensive review of the literature, concluded: "What has emerged as the most consistent process predictor of improvement is the patient's subjective perception of the therapist-offered relationship" (p. 439). Research by Morgan and colleagues (1982) supports this conclusion. In this study, clients who believed that their therapists were helping them and that they were working as a team with their therapists were likely to show more benefit from therapy than clients who did not share those perceptions. Similarly, Beutler, Crago, and Arizmendi (1986) noted a moderately positive correlation between outcome and clients' positive perceptions of their therapists' facilitative attitudes (empathy, genuineness, congruence, nonpossessive warmth, and unconditional positive regard).

Sloane, Staples, Cristol, Yorkston, and Whipple (1975) also investigated the relationship between clients' perceptions and therapy outcome. More than 70 percent of the clients they studied who had had successful therapy reported the following to be extremely or very important in contributing to their improvement: the therapist's personality; the therapist's skill in providing help and encouragement, enabling clients to face their problems and to understand their problems and themselves; and the therapist's presence as an understanding person to talk to. Clients' perceptions of the therapeutic process, therefore, seem to be an important ingredient in determining outcome.

3.2.5 Readiness

Clients enter therapy with a broad range of expectations and attitudes. The well-known self-fulfilling prophecy seems to hold true; those clients who expect positive and realistic outcomes from therapy and whose expectations are congruent with those of their therapists are more likely to achieve some outcomes, while those who are resistant to change are less likely to benefit from therapy (Beutler, Crago, & Arizmendi, 1986; Lambert, 1982). Perry, Frances, and Clarkin (1985) suggest that attending to preferences clients express for their treatment (for example, specific form of treatment; conditions of treatment—place, cost, time, frequency; and desired type of therapist) should increase the likelihood of a positive outcome.

Howard, Nance, and Myers (1987) believe that client readiness consists of three components: motivation, ability, and self-confidence. Clients with a high degree of readiness are active; relatively independent; have a broad repertoire of behaviors; have mature and enduring interests; can take a broad perspective that includes past, present, and future; relate to others as equals or superiors; and have adequate self-control and a good sense of themselves. Howard, Nance, and Myers developed a model for matching therapist style to client readiness. According to this model, clients with a very low level of readiness need a therapist with a strong power base who emphasizes "telling" and who is high in directiveness and low in support (for example, a Rational-Emotive or a behavior therapist). Clients with a moderately low level of readiness seem most likely to benefit from a therapist with a "teaching" approach, who provides a high degree of directiveness and support (for example, a Reality therapist or an Adlerian therapist). Those with a moderately high level of readiness tend to respond best to a therapist who emphasizes "understanding" and is low in directiveness but high in support (for example, a client-centered therapist), while clients with high readiness are capable of benefiting from a therapist who observes and delegates responsibility to the client, providing only limited directiveness and support (for example, a psychoanalyst). This seems to be a useful model in helping therapists individualize their treatment plans.

Horowitz, Marmar, Krupnick, Wilner, Kaltreider, and Wallerstein (1984) attempted to match levels of client motivation with levels of exploration in therapy. They concluded that clients who are motivated and stable seem to benefit most from an exploratory approach, while those at lower levels of motivation and stability respond better to a supportive approach.

A process called role induction seems helpful in developing attitudes in clients that are conducive to a positive outcome. In role induction, clients are oriented to the therapeutic process and are given clear information on what is expected of them, what the therapist can offer, and what therapy will probably be like. Role induction seems likely to increase client engagement in the therapeutic process, another variable correlated with positive outcome. Garfield (1986) found that clients who complete a questionnaire before beginning therapy are more likely to continue in that process—perhaps because, in completing the questionnaire, they are making an investment in the process. Role induction and use of pretreatment questionnaires, then, seem to be ways to maximize client readiness for therapy.

3.3 Therapeutic Alliance

In addition to research on the impact of therapist and client variables on outcome, some research has also been conducted on the interactive and synergistic effect of the therapist-client relationship on outcome. A feeling of mutual warmth, affirmation, and respect and a positive therapeutic climate seem to contribute to outcome (Waterhouse & Strupp, 1984). Luborsky, McLellan, Woody, O'Brien, and Auerbach (1985) support these findings. In their study, the client-therapist relationship—as rated by both client and therapist during the third therapy session via the Helping Alliance Questionnaire—was significantly correlated with outcome.

Several researchers have explored the question of therapist-client similarity and have found some indication that it is positively related to outcome (Garfield, 1986). Lambert (1982), however, arrived at a discrepant conclusion, suggesting that complementary matching of therapist and client (for example, a dominant therapist with a submissive client) is positively correlated with outcome. Both conclusions have a logical appeal. Similarity between therapist and client seems likely to promote the rapid establishment of a comfortable working alliance, in which goals and values are compatible. At the same time, complementary matching can offer the client an important learning experience through the therapist's modeling of ways of behaving and coping that are unfamiliar to the client. This is an intriguing and potentially fruitful area of research that warrants further study.

The client's identification with the therapist is another ingredient in determining outcome. Beutler, Crago, and Arizmendi (1986) concluded, "There is apparently a decided tendency for successful therapy dyads to be associated with the patients' acquiring therapists' belief systems, both about religious and moral attitudes and about more general concepts as well" (p. 275). This conclusion is consistent with the finding that similarity seems to improve outcome. However, it does raise a philosophical question: Is a major element of therapy the process of promoting middle-class values in clients?

Conclusion

This chapter has reviewed the literature on the contributions made to outcome by qualities of the therapist, the client, and their interaction. Demographic, personal, and professional qualities discussed certainly seem to have an impact on the effectiveness of therapy. The next chapters will present another perspective on the process of effective treatment planning. Focus will be on those disorders frequently presented by adult clients seeking treatment and the research on effective treatment models for those disorders.

Part Two

Effective
Treatments
of Adult
Mental Disorders

▪▪▪

Chapter Four

Situationally
Precipitated
Disorders

Case Study: Susan B.

Susan B., a forty-nine-year-old white female, sought counseling about three months after her third and youngest child left for college. She had been married for twenty-five years, and for most of that time her focus had been on her family. She had not been a salaried employee since she was twenty-four years old, although she had done a great deal of volunteer work, in organizations such as the Girl Scouts and Sunday school, which her children attended, and in organizations for abused women and displaced homemakers, to which she had a strong commitment. Susan had enjoyed her years of child rearing and—although she expressed some regret that she had not used her college degree professionally or pursued occupational goals—felt comfortable with the lifestyle she had chosen.

In recent months, however, she had been aware of a lack of direction in her life. Her children were at college, and her husband was involved with his own successful career. Her volunteer activities and tennis games with friends did not seem to be enough for her. In addition, the family had some financial concerns because of the expense of college tuition and would benefit from another income. However, Susan felt that she might not be able to locate employment because she had been out of the job market for so long.

Susan had been an English major in college and had intended to become a teacher. However, she had never taught but, instead, had had a series of sales and secretarial positions before her children were born. At present, she expressed little interest in teaching or in working with young people. Interest inventories suggested that Susan was still interested in occupations that involved helping people and using language skills, but the inventories also reflected her strong commitment to social justice. Susan was willing to further her education but, at the same time, did not want to become the fourth family member in college. She was eager to obtain a position that would pay relatively well as quickly as possible.

Overview of Situationally Precipitated Disorders

Susan is an emotionally healthy woman who has functioned well throughout her life. She has good relationships with family and friends, rewarding interests, and an optimistic view of her life and herself. However, normal developmental changes in her life, such as the departure of her children from home, have left her feeling without direction and in need of a career path. Susan is experiencing what is referred to in the *DSM-III-R* as "conditions not attributable to a mental disorder that are a focus of attention or treatment," also known as V code conditions. This chapter will focus on V code conditions and on adjustment disorders, the two mildest conditions described in the *DSM-III-R*.

Description of Disorder. Both of these categories of disorder, V code conditions and adjustment disorders, typically have an identifiable precipitant or cause and are relatively mild and usually transient disorders. Causes are most likely to be common life events or developmental processes, such as marriage, divorce, relocation, or retirement. Any emotional symptoms that result are clearly connected to the precipitant, although the client may react with some generalized dysfunction.

Several other disorders in the *DSM-III-R*—for example, major depression without melancholia (discussed in this book in section 5.1) or brief reactive psychosis (section 10.2)—also tend to be precipitated by an external stressor. However, the severity of their symptoms typically obscures the role of the precipitant, and it is the symptoms rather than the stressful life circumstances that, at least initially, become the focus of the treatment. In contrast, for adjustment disorders and V code conditions, the precipitant and its impact on the client's lifestyle and adjustment are the primary focus of treatment, while the emotional upset and dysfunctional behavior resulting from the precipitant receive secondary attention. These dysfunctional symptoms, it usually is assumed, will spontaneously be alleviated or eliminated if clients can gain a realistic view of the precipitant, adapt to and manage the changes it has produced, and increase their sense of control over their lives and their responses. For example, Myra sought counseling because she felt discouraged and full of self-doubts following an unanticipated marital separation. However, once she obtained more information on her husband's decision to divorce her, the help he was willing to provide, and the options open to her, her symptoms subsided. Although she was still saddened at the end of her marriage, she became involved in the process of moving into the city and completing her college education, which she had wanted to do for many years.

It is sometimes difficult to determine whether a client is experiencing a V code condition or an adjustment disorder. Adjustment disorders, by definition, will result in noticeable impairment or dysfunction, accompanied by symptoms that are beyond the expectable. V code conditions, the milder of the two, describe normal or expectable reactions to life events. For example, Myra had symptoms of low self-esteem, tearfulness, and hopelessness, typifying an adjustment disorder with depressed mood. Had she been saddened by the end of her marriage but in control of her grief and ready to plan for her future, she would be described as experiencing a V code condition or life circumstance problem.

Relevant Client Characteristics. Nearly everyone has experienced either an adjustment disorder or a V code condition or both. These disorders may be triggered by positive or negative transitions and changes (such as graduation from college, birth of a child, bereavement, or a career shift). They may also reflect and be related to common problems of living, such as occupational dissatisfaction, marital conflict, and the care of an ill and elderly parent. Although it seems impossible to go through life without experiencing a V code condition or adjustment disorder, some people—that is, people with effective coping mechanisms and ways of handling stress, with support systems and confidants, with a track record of successfully coping with previous stressors, and with good overall functioning—are less likely to be troubled by these disorders. In addition, people are typically more successful at handling stressful life circumstances if those events are not severely disruptive and if the stressors are not multiple. Stressors seem to have an additive impact, so that a major stressor accompanied by several minor stressors (for example, divorce accompanied by relocation and a new job) probably will have a much greater impact than an isolated major stressor.

Relevant Therapist Variables. Because treatment of these disorders is typically short term, focused on helping clients cope more effectively with stressful changes or circumstances, therapists should be comfortable with brief, structured interventions that may involve some teaching and referral but are unlikely to involve extended exploration. They should also be comfortable dealing with clients in crisis who may be feeling overwhelmed, discouraged, and even suicidal. Clients with these disorders typically work best with therapists who are supportive and empathic but, at the same time, able to provide the structure and stimulus needed for clients to mobilize themselves and use their resources more effectively.

Intervention Strategies. Treatment for these disorders varies, depending on the associated crisis or life circumstance. In general, however, treatment will be designed to help clients understand the crisis, their reactions to it, and their options. Therapy will seek to elicit or develop the skills and insights that will enable clients to cope more effectively with the stressors. For example, clients with marital problems typically would be helped to improve their communication, to clarify their expectations of their spouses, and to seek a mutually agreed-upon and rewarding marital relationships; clients who have experienced a bereavement usually will need help in expressing and managing their grief, in dealing with the impact the loss has had on their lives, and in establishing new and rewarding goals, directions, friends, and activities for themselves. Clients' current resources and coping mechanisms provide the foundation for treatment, and efforts will be made to increase clients' awareness of existing strengths and to build on those strengths.

Prognosis. The prognosis for returning clients with these disorders to their previous levels of functioning is excellent. In fact, some clients seem to function even better after experiencing one of these conditions than they did earlier, because of the self-confidence they gained from handling the situation effectively and because of the skills they developed or improved during the course of therapy. Treatment of these disorders, then, is often a growth-promoting experience for clients.

4.1 Adjustment Disorders

Description of Disorder. Adjustment disorders are more severe and less prevalent than V code conditions. According to the *DSM-III-R* (1987), "The essential feature of this disorder is a mal-adaptive reaction to an identifiable psychosocial stressor, or stressors, that occurs within three months after onset of the stressor, and has persisted for no longer than six months" (p. 329). Stressors may be single events (such as a divorce or the birth of a child) or continuous circumstances (such as marital stress or chronic illness), but they are within the realm of normal experience (unlike the precipitants for post-traumatic stress disorder, discussed in section 6.5). The most common stressors for adults are marital difficulties, divorce or separation, and moving; for adolescents, school-related problems, conflict with parents, and substance abuse (Maxmen, 1986). Adjustment disorders seem to develop when a stressor impinges on an area of client vulnerability and leads to an adverse reaction.

The *DSM-III-R* specifies nine types of adjustment disorders. When the diagnosis is made, the clinician should specify whether the type is adjustment disorder with anxious mood, depressed mood, disturbance of conduct, mixed disturbance of emotions and conduct, mixed emotional features, physical complaints (fatigue, aches, and pains that are not diagnosed as specific medical condition), withdrawal, work (or academic) inhibition, or not otherwise specified. Depression seems to be the most common accompaniment of adjustment disorders in adults, while disturbances of conduct are particularly common among adolescents with adjustment disorders (Maxmen, 1986). Anxiety and psychophysiological symptoms are found in approximately one-third of clients with adjustment disorders (Marshall & Barbaree, 1984).

Kaplan and Sadock (1985) report that adjustment disorders are experienced by 10–15 percent of the population. Maxmen (1986) indicates that these disorders are even more prevalent and typically more severe in adolescents, with as many as one-third experiencing adjustment disorders. However, because many with adjustment disorders do not seek treatment and experience a spontaneous remission of symptoms, the incidence of these disorders is difficult to assess and may be considerably higher than the above estimates.

Relevant Client Characteristics. Adjustment disorders occur in all types of people. However, as mentioned, they are more prevalent in those with limited resources and support systems, poor or underdeveloped coping mechanisms, little experience in dealing effectively with previous stressful events, and multiple stressors.

Relevant Therapist Variables. Most clients with adjustment disorders have a relatively high level of previous functioning. They probably are capable of handling the stressor themselves but have been daunted by its suddenness or by their own lack of self-esteem. Therefore, the therapist must express confidence that, with some support and direction, the clients will be able to resolve these problems themselves. This optimistic attitude should serve to strengthen their coping mechanisms and encourage them to face the stressors.

Intervention Strategies. Although most adjustment disorders improve spontaneously without treatment, therapy can facilitate recovery. It can hasten improvement, provide coping skills and adaptive mechanisms to avert future crises, and minimize poor choices and self-destructive behaviors that may have adverse consequences (Maxmen, 1986).

A flexible crisis intervention model probably best describes the therapy that is usually recommended to treat this disorder. This therapy will focus both on relieving the acute symptoms the clients are experiencing and on helping clients adapt to and cope with the stressors. Therapy will support the clients' strengths and pay little attention to past problems unless they suggest patterns that must be addressed in order to promote effective coping with the present stressors. Education and information usually are provided as part of the treatment, to help clients take a realistic look at their situations and become aware of options and resources that might be useful to them. The overriding goal of this brief, problem-focused orientation to treatment is to return the clients to their previous or higher levels of functioning and to change some self-destructive behaviors and reactions, so that chances of a recurrence with the next life change are reduced.

The specific interventions to be employed will depend on the symptoms associated with the adjustment disorder as well as on the nature of the stressors. Approximately one-third of those with adjustment disorders are suicidal, particularly adolescents with adjustment disorders (Maxmen, 1986). Of course, preventing suicide must be a priority of treatment. Clients with depressive symptoms (see Chapter Five) probably will respond to techniques borrowed from cognitive and interpersonal therapy; anxious clients (see Chapter Six) probably will benefit from learning relaxation techniques; and clients with work or academic inhibition are likely to respond to behavioral therapy, to cite a few of the diverse approaches that might be used.

The specific nature of the crisis also indicates appropriate interventions. Environmental manipulation—such as a change of residence, a job change, employment of help to assist with a new baby, or reorganization of shared duties at home or at work—can be useful. Bibliotherapy, the assignment of books written by others who may have experienced similar concerns, can provide useful information and a clearer perspective. Excellent books are available, for example, on such topics as improving marital relationships (Scarf, 1987), dealing with divorce or bereavement (Caine, 1974; Viorst, 1986), making a career change (Bolles, 1988), and handling various personal crises (Stearns, 1984). Tools to promote self-awareness and clarify options—for example, interest inventories; inventories of marital satisfaction; and personality inventories, such as the Myers-Briggs Type Indicator (Myers & McCauley, 1985)—also can help clients understand why they are having difficulty with a particular situation, what resources they might draw on, and what options they have.

Gutsch (1988) views adjustment disorders as stress disorders and recommends a stress inoculation approach to treatment. His model includes the following four phases: (1) understanding stress in general and the specific stressor in question, (2) developing coping strategies (for example, relaxation or decision making), (3) application of coping strategies to the current problems, and (4) assessing and revising strategies as necessary and reinforcing the self for successes. Gutsch also suggests a multifaceted approach, in which techniques such as modeling, role playing, and cognitive rehearsal are used to teach clients how to cope.

Brief psychodynamically oriented psychotherapy also seems to be a useful approach in treating these disorders (Koss & Butcher, 1986). Although this approach does involve interpretation and the use of positive transference, techniques usually associated with long-term psychoanalytic treatment, brief psychotherapy tends to focus on a single concern presented by the client. Treatment, therefore, may be crisis oriented, involving environmental manipulation and crisis resolution as well as promoting an understanding of the relationship between the impact of the crisis and the client's personality dynamics.

Therapists using brief psychodynamic psychotherapy typically are supportive, active, flexible, and goal directed, working in a time-limited context (usually a maximum of twenty-five sessions) to restore clients' previous level of equilibrium. This model seems particularly well suited to treating problems of acute onset, experienced by clients who have had a good prior adjustment, who can relate to others and engage in a therapeutic relationship, and who are highly motivated toward treatment. The approach is generally not indicated for those who have underlying personality disorders (described in Chapter Nine).

According to Koss and Butcher (1986), studies using this model report improvement rates of over 70 percent but also indicate that more than half of the clients later return for additional treatment. Research on the effectiveness of brief psychotherapy is in the preliminary stages but seems to suggest that it is effective primarily in accelerating change, rather than in producing change that would not otherwise have occurred. However, because most adjustment disorders tend to remit spontaneously, brief psychodynamically oriented psychotherapy may be helpful in quickening the pace of clients' ability to deal with disconcerting life changes.

It is unfortunate that many people with this relatively mild disorder do not seek treatment for their symptoms, because early awareness and detection of the dysfunctional reaction seem to enhance the prognosis for improvement (Meyer, 1983). Clients should be encouraged to resume their former lifestyles, to expect to be back to normal in a relatively short time, and to deal with the stressor as expeditiously as possible. Typically, the longer the clients avoid dealing with the stressful situation, the more difficult it will be for them to handle it effectively. Therefore, timing is an important variable in treatment of this disorder.

Group therapy may be a useful addition to treatment. It can provide a support system, teach and reinforce coping mechanisms, improve self-esteem, and promote reality testing through the group members' shared perceptions of the client's situation. Groups comprised of clients going through similar life circumstances (such as marital separation, divorce, or bereavement) can be particularly helpful. However, group therapy typically does not provide crisis intervention and so may not be sufficient to respond to the urgency of the client's situation. A combination of group and individual therapy may be particularly useful to some clients with adjustment disorders; the individual therapy can focus on the immediate crisis, while the group therapy can provide support and an arena for testing new ideas and behaviors. If the stressor involves the client's family, directly or indirectly, at least a few sessions of family therapy might be useful to solidify the support the client is receiving, to ensure that the client's efforts to cope with the stressor are not being undermined by the family, and to deal with any family circumstances that might be related to the stressful situation.

Medication is almost never necessary to treat adjustment disorders. In rare cases, it may help clients manage anxiety or depression, but its use should be time limited and it should be perceived as secondary to the therapy.

Prognosis. The prognosis for treatment of adjustment disorders seems to be one of the most positive of all the disorders and is particularly good for adults with these disorders. Three- to five-year follow-up studies of adults treated for this disorder indicated that 59–71 percent of them were functioning well, although only 44 percent of the adolescents with this disorder were functioning well (Maxmen, 1986). Andreasen and Hoenk (1983) conducted a five-year follow-up of one hundred adults and adolescents with adjustment disorders and found that 79 percent seemed to be well at follow-up, although 8 percent had developed intervening problems, most commonly alcohol abuse (see section 7.1.1) or major depression (section 5.1). Although Andreasen and Hoenk concluded that the overall prognosis for treatment of adjustment disorders was excellent, it was relatively less good for males and for those with behavioral symptoms.

There seems to be a tendency for clients with adjustment disorders to require subsequent treatment (Donovan, Bennett, & McElroy, 1981). Whether this pattern reflects an incomplete recovery from the adjustment disorder, a subsequent adjustment disorder, or the onset of another disorder is not clear in the literature. It does, however, emphasize the importance of including a preventive component in the treatment of adjustment disorders.

4.2 V Codes for Conditions Not Attributable to a Mental Disorder That Are a Focus of Attention or Treatment

Description of Disorder. These conditions—referred to here as V code conditions, as they are designated in the *DSM-III-R*—encompass concerns that may well benefit from treatment but are not, in themselves, mental disorders (unlike adjustment disorders) and have not resulted from mental disorders. Clients may or may not have coexisting and unrelated mental disorders, but the diagnosis of a V code condition implies that the focus of treatment will be on that condition rather than on any mental disorder that may be present. For example, a client whose wife is threatening to leave him because of his excessive consumption of alcohol would not be diagnosed as having a V code condition of marital problem, because his marital difficulties are related to another disorder, alcohol abuse. On the other hand, a client with a simple phobia (fear of snakes) who is having marital difficulties unrelated to the phobia would receive two diagnoses, marital problem and simple phobia. (Simple phobia is discussed in section 6.3.2.)

The *DSM-III-R* lists the following thirteen V code conditions: academic problem, adult antisocial problem, borderline intellectual functioning, childhood or adolescent antisocial problem, malingering, marital problem, noncompliance with treatment, occupational problem, parent-child problem, other interpersonal problem, other specified family circumstances, phase of life problem or other life circumstance problem, and uncomplicated bereavement. These are problems in living that are experienced by most people. In general, these disorders go untreated, and people manage to deal with them with varying degrees of success. These conditions do not cause people to become severely dysfunctional for long periods of time, nor do they cause extreme and persistent emotional reactions. Typically, clients with these conditions are in good contact with reality, and their reactions seem consistent with the stressors or life circumstances they are experiencing. However, they may be experiencing considerable unhappiness and dissatisfaction with their lives and may benefit from therapy.

Relevant Client Characteristics. V code conditions are most likely to be diagnosed in fairly healthy clients with relatively good ego strength and self-esteem. Although they may have coexisting severe mental disorders, that is not likely, because clients with severe disorders typically react to life stressors in more dysfunctional ways.

Relevant Therapist Variables. Therapist variables indicated for treatment of V code conditions are similar to those indicated for treatment of adjustment disorders. Clients probably will respond best to therapists who are supportive and flexible but, at the same time, challenge the clients to grow and develop. These therapists should be able to encourage clients to take responsibility for their own treatment when possible but also should provide direction, resources, and information when needed (Gutsch, 1988; Maxmen, 1986). Therapists should maintain an attitude that is optimistic and that anticipates fairly rapid progress.

Intervention Strategies. No controlled studies were located on the overall treatment of V code conditions. However, suggestions for treatment can be inferred from studies of treatment of specific types of V code conditions and from information on the treatment of related disorders. Treatment of these conditions will typically be fairly similar to treatment for adjustment disorders. The major difference is that less attention probably will be paid to the clients' emotional, social, and occupational dysfunction, and more attention will be paid to the presenting concern. Clients can benefit from support and from the reassurance of being told that their reactions are not abnormal. Clients experiencing V code conditions typically need education and information about their situations and about options that are available to them. Environmental changes can be useful, and others involved in the problem (for instance, family, friends, or business colleagues) might profitably be included in the therapy.

Specific approaches to therapy have been developed to ameliorate some of the V code conditions. For example, the large body of literature available on theories and techniques of career counseling can guide therapy for clients coping with occupational problems (Seligman, 1980). Typically, current approaches to career counseling have a strong behavioral flavor, promote information seeking and appropriate decision making, and teach such skills as interviewing and résumé writing (Myers, 1986). Similarly, many books are available to familiarize therapists and clients with patterns of family change and ways to deal with them effectively (see, for example, Carter & McGoldrick, 1988; Nichols, 1984).

Support groups can be particularly useful to clients with V code conditions and sometimes provide all the treatment that is needed. Therapy or self-help groups comprised of clients with similar life circumstances (such as bereavement, retirement, or recent marriage) may be particularly helpful in offering information and modeling coping mechanisms as well as providing support. Nonprofessional, socially oriented groups such as Parents Without Partners can be a valuable adjunct to treatment.

Prognosis. The prognosis for treatment of V code conditions seems quite good, although the diversity of conditions and clients involved in this disorder suggests caution in generalizing. Figures are available to support a positive prognosis in some areas. For example, studies of the effectiveness of career counseling indicate a success rate ranging from 73 percent to 93 percent, depending on the length of the follow-up (Myers, 1986). Horowitz, Marmar, Weiss, DeWitt, and Rosenbaum (1984) surveyed the impact of time-limited dynamic psychotherapy on fifty-two clients coping with bereavements. They found that outcomes were generally favorable; that is, clients experienced symptom relief and improved social and occupational functioning. The clients who benefited most from treatment were those who had the highest pretreatment levels of functioning and self-concepts and who were motivated for treatment.

Summary of Treatment Recommendations

The following table organizes the recommendations made in this chapter for the treatment of situationally precipitated disorders (adjustment disorders and V code conditions) according to the DO A CLIENT MAP model presented earlier in this book. A summary organized according to that model will be presented at the end of each of the chapters focusing on the treatment of specific disorders so that readers can quickly obtain an overview of the information presented and compare treatment recommendations for different categories of disorders.

> *Diagnoses.* Adjustment disorders and V codes for conditions not attributable to a mental disorder
>
> *Objectives.* Relieve symptoms, improve coping, restore at least prior level of functioning
>
> *Assessments.* Generally none, although measures of transient anxiety, depression, and stress might be useful
>
> *Clinician.* Flexible yet structured, present oriented, optimistic
>
> *Location.* Outpatient
>
> *Interventions.* Crisis intervention, brief psychodynamically oriented psychotherapy, stress management, other short-term/active approaches

Emphasis. Encourage client responsibility, moderately supportive, probing only when relevant to current concerns, with focus determined by specific precipitant and response

Nature. Individual therapy and/or peer support group; possibly some family sessions

Timing. Brief duration, rapid pace

Medication. Rarely needed

Adjunct services. Inventories to clarify goals and direction; education and information very important; possibly environmental manipulation

Prognosis. Excellent, especially when no underlying mental disorder is present

Client Map of Susan B.

The case of Susan B., a forty-nine-year-old woman experiencing many changes in her life, was presented at the beginning of this chapter. This chapter will conclude with a client map of Susan.

Diagnosis. Axis I: V62.89—Phase of life problem; V62.20—Occupational problem

Axis II: V71.09—No diagnosis or condition

Axis III: No physical disorders

Axis IV: Psychosocial stressors: Departure of youngest child for college. Severity: 2—mild, acute

Axis V: Current Global Assessment of Functioning: 80; highest GAF past year: 85

Objectives. (1) Develop rewarding and realistic career goals and plans

(2) Increase comfort and ability to deal with new phase of life

Assessments. Strong-Campbell Interest Inventory, Myers-Briggs Type Indicator

Clinician. Supportive and accepting yet action oriented, knowledgeable about career counseling

Location. Outpatient, college counseling center with community services

Interventions. Emphasis is on career counseling in the context of a supportive therapeutic relationship designed to build self-esteem and clarify goals and direction

Emphasis. High in supportiveness, low in directiveness, emphasis on cognitions (self-doubts) with a secondary focus on behavior and affect

Nature. Primarily individual therapy with a few couples sessions

Timing. Short-term, weekly sessions, moderate pace

Medication. None needed

Adjunct services. Support group for reentry women

Prognosis. Excellent

Exploration of relatively short-term programs that might build on Susan's interests and college courses revealed a local training program in paralegal education. This curriculum seemed to combine Susan's strongest interest areas: helping people, writing, and advancing social justice. It also would enable her to begin earning money fairly soon. Susan decided to enroll in this program while simultaneously joining a support group for reentry women, to help with some of her apprehension about returning to school and beginning a new career. One therapy session was held with Susan and her husband, to help her explain her plans to him and elicit his support. Follow-up sessions as Susan neared the completion of her education were used to help her prepare a résumé and refine her interviewing skills. Bimonthly sessions provided support while Susan sought employment and made an adjustment to a new job. Therapy was terminated when Susan felt she had achieved her goals and found a rewarding career direction for herself.

Like most clients with V code conditions, Susan needed only some short-term counseling to help her mobilize her resources and establish a rewarding direction for herself. The self-awareness, support systems, and coping strategies she gained from the counseling process should enable her to cope more effectively with future life transitions. The next chapter will focus on another prevalent group of disorders but one that typically causes more dysfunction than those in this chapter: disorders characterized primarily by depression.

Recommended Readings

Gutsch, K. U. (1988). *Psychotherapeutic approaches to specific DSM-III-R categories*. Springfield, IL: Thomas.

Maxmen, J. S. (1986). *Essential psychopathology*. New York: Norton.

Stearns, A. K. (1984). *Living through personal crisis*. New York: Ballantine Books.

Viorst, J. (1986). *Necessary losses*. New York: Fawcett.

Chapter Five

■■

Mood Disorders

Case Study: Karen C.

Karen C., a thirty-year-old married black female, was brought to a therapist in private practice by her mother. Karen reported feelings of severe depression and hopelessness. She was barely able to care for her child and her home and had not been to work for over two weeks. Accompanying symptoms included loss of appetite, difficulty falling asleep, feelings of fatigue, and severe guilt.

Karen and her husband had been married for eight years and had a five-year-old child. Her husband was in the military, necessitating frequent absences from home. Karen had always found these absences difficult and had encouraged her husband to leave the service. He complained that she was too dependent on him and urged her to develop her own interests. She did work part-time as an aide in her child's school but otherwise had few outside activities and few supports outside of her mother, who had been widowed when Karen was a child. Conflict had been increasing in the marriage and reached a peak about three weeks ago, when Karen's husband went on a tour of duty away from home. Karen was convinced that he would become involved with another woman and would never return home. She berated herself for not being a good wife for her husband and stated that life was not worth living without him.

Karen was an only child and had been raised by her mother after the death of her father. Her mother had not remarried and told Karen that she had been so devastated by the death of Karen's father that she would never get involved with another man. Episodes of severe depression seem to have been present in the mother, although she had never received treatment. Karen had an unremarkable developmental history except that she had been ill quite a bit. She graduated from high school and worked as a secretary, living with her mother until her marriage. She had dated little before her marriage.

Overview of Mood Disorders

Description of Disorder. Karen is suffering from a severe depression that has considerably impaired her level of functioning. Although there is an identifiable precipitant for Karen's current episode of depression, Karen's symptoms do not reflect either an adjustment disorder (section 4.1) or a V code condition (section 4.2); her reaction reflects too much dysfunction to be described as either of those conditions; and the precipitant, her husband's tour of duty, is less disruptive than those that usually would spark a situationally precipitated disorder. Karen is experiencing another prevalent condition, a mood disorder, characterized by depression. This chapter will review the nature of mood disorders and their treatment and then will provide information on the diagnosis and treatment of the major types of mood disorders. The *DSM-III-R* (1987) lists the following mood disorders: major depression, dysthymia, depressive disorder not otherwise specified, bipolar disorder, bipolar disorder not otherwise specified, and cyclothymia. All these disorders typically have depression as a prominent feature but vary in intensity, duration, and pattern of onset. Bipolar disorders and cyclothymia are also characterized by unpredictable shifts in mood as well as extremely elevated moods. However, the focus here will be on depression, the common ingredient in these disorders.

As many as 30 percent of the population will experience some form of mood disorder during their lives. Depression is the most common and probably the most lethal mental disorder (via suicide). However, only 20–25 percent of those who experience clinical depression will receive treatment. Depression has a broad range of severity. Most people with depression are able to struggle on with their lives, perhaps even succeeding in concealing their symptoms from others. In some, depression may be present at a subclinical level for many years, becoming a deeply ingrained part of the personality. Those with severe depression, however, typically manifest significantly impaired functioning.

Approximately one in fifty depressed clients is hospitalized, and depression accounts for 75 percent of psychiatric hospitalizations. One in a hundred people suffering from depression commits suicide (Gotlib & Colby, 1987), while 15 percent of those with chronic, recurrent depression commit suicide (Klerman, Weissman, Rounsaville, & Chevron, 1984). The prevalence of clinical depression seems to be increasing, and its onset seems to be occurring at an earlier age (Klerman & others, 1985). Women are twice as likely to be depressed as men (Atwood & Chester, 1987); whether a hormonal or an environmental and social factor is responsible for this disparity is unclear. Currently and formerly married women are more likely to be depressed than those who have never married; the opposite is true for men (Gotlib & Colby, 1987). Depression seems particularly common among married women of lower socioeconomic levels who are full-time homemakers with young children. Whites, urbanites, and Jews also seem to have a disproportionate incidence of depression (Maxmen, 1986).

Many theories have been advanced to explain the origin of depression. To Freud, depression represents the symbolic loss of a love object, accompanied by the turning inward of anger toward the parents. Under those circumstances, according to Freud, self-esteem becomes contingent on constant affirmation from others. The social learning theorists believe that depression may become a learned response when it is rewarded and reinforced. The secondary gains it brings outweigh the negative experience of being depressed. To Beck (Beck, Rush, Shaw, & Emery, 1979) and other cognitive theorists, depression results from faulty logic and misinterpretation, involving a negative cognitive set. Behavioral theorists hypothesize that depressed clients have poor social and other skills and, therefore, receive little positive social reinforcement. The interpersonal model explains depression as stemming from undue dependency on others as well as friction and poor communication in relationships.

Biological approaches view depression as resulting from a dysfunctional level of serotonin, a neurotransmitter (Atwood & Chester, 1987), while developmental models suggest that depressed clients are likely to have had aversive childhoods with parental discord, an inappropriate level of maternal care, low cohesion or adaptability in the family, and controlling and/or rejecting parents (Gotlib & Colby, 1987).

The onset of depression often follows one or more negative and stressful life events, frequently involving a real or threatened loss of a relationship. The anticipation of loss may trigger a return of unresolved feelings about an earlier loss. This pattern is particularly likely to occur in people with few social supports, no intimate confidants, and generally negative social relationships. The proverbial vicious cycle unfortunately is likely here: the clients' depression is exacerbated by a lack of friends, but they cannot readily make friends because they are depressed.

Depression often has a genetic component, particularly in men whose mothers were depressed (Gutsch, 1988). In addition, people with depression often have a history of early developmental difficulties. History taking, then, should include questions about a familial background of depression and about childhood development. Information revealing a family history of depression and of early developmental problems in the client may help both therapist and client understand the nature and dynamics of the disorder.

Primary symptoms of depression are feelings of discouragement and hopelessness, a dysphoric mood, a loss of energy, and a sense of worthlessness. Physiological changes and complaints are common and typically include changes in appetite and sleep, with insomnia and loss of appetite the most common. A medical examination sometimes is indicated to ascertain whether medical treatment is needed for the physical complaints.

Some sources (for example, Atwood & Chester, 1987) have distinguished between exogenous or reactive depression (precipitated by some external event or situation) and endogenous or biochemical depression (having a physiological cause). Endogenous depressions are less common than reactive ones. Severe and reverse physiological symptoms (such as increased appetite or early-morning awakening rather than insomnia) seem more common in endogenous depression. Melancholia or an absence of pleasure or interest typicallly accompanies this form of depression. Endogenous depressions also are far more likely than reactive ones to involve delusions or hallucinations, psychomotor retardation or agitation, and extreme guilt (Gotlib & Colby, 1987). Endogenous depressions typically are most severe in the morning, while the severity of reactive depressions depends more on what is happening than on the time of day. Depressions beginning during the postpartum or involutional period (late in life) are more likely to be endogenous (Atwood & Chester, 1987).

Suicidal ideation is a pervasive secondary or underlying symptom in depression, one that obviously requires attention. People suffering from depression may be in such severe emotional pain that they feel as though their symptoms will never end. Suicide may seem to be the only escape. There are approximately 200,000 suicide attempts and 25,000 suicides annually in the United States; 80 percent of these seem linked to depression (Gotlib & Colby, 1987). Suicidal ideation, like depression, seems to have a genetic component. Roy (1983) studied 243 people with a family history of suicide and found that 48.6 percent of them had attempted suicide and that 84.4 percent had experienced a depressive episode. Depressed clients with a concurrent diagnosis of borderline personality disorder (see section 9.7) or with accompanying delusions are particularly likely to commit suicide (Roose, Glassman, Walsh, Woodring, & Vital-Herne, 1983).

Depressed clients, then, should be asked about suicidal thinking ("Have you thought about hurting or killing yourself?"). If suicidal ideation is present, information should be gathered about any plans that have been formulated and the availability of means. Preventing suicide must take priority. If there is a threat of suicide, the therapist should consider hospitalizing the client, notifying friends and relatives (ideally with the client's consent), and developing a written agreement with the client, designed to ensure safety and specify alternatives to self-injury.

Most people with mood disorders are not psychotic. They do not have hallucinations or delusions, although their reality testing is likely to be impaired. They generally will not manifest severe paranoia but are likely to feel bereft of supports and to feel that even those who care about them are undermining them.

Gotlib and Colby (1987) provide the following comprehensive list of symptoms that typically accompany a mood disorder:

Emotional—anxiety, guilt, anger/hostility, irritability, social and marital distress

Behavioral—crying, neglect of appearance, withdrawal, dependency, lethargy, reduced activity, poor social skills, psychomotor retardation or agitation

Attitudinal—pessimism, helplessness, thoughts of death/suicide, low self-esteem

Cognitive—reduced concentration, indecisiveness, cognitive distortion

Physiological—sleep disturbances, loss of appetite, decreased sexual interest, gastrointestinal and menstrual difficulties, muscle pains, headaches

A first episode of depression generally occurs during young or middle adulthood but may occur at any age, as can recurrences. The initial episode of depression tends to occur earlier in women than in men, who are more likely to have an initial episode in midlife. Depression may be primary; or it may be secondary to a preexisting, chronic mental or physical disorder—such as alcohol abuse (section 7.1.1). It is fairly common for depression to coexist with a personality disorder—for example, borderline (section 9.7), histrionic (section 9.5), or dependent (section 9.9).

Relevant Client Characteristics. Seligman (1975) has written about the importance of "learned helplessness" in the dynamics of depression. According to Seligman, many depressed clients have longstanding motivational, interpersonal, cognitive, and affective deficits as well as low self-esteem—all resulting from a series of uncontrollable and painful events that have made these clients depression prone. They tend to set unrealistic goals, have little sense of competence, and view others as more powerful and capable than themselves.

People suffering from depression frequently experience marital discord. Clients hospitalized for depression were found to have a postdischarge rate of divorce that was nine times the average (Maxmen, 1986). Gotlib and Colby (1987) believe that the course of the depression may be related to the course of the marriage. They therefore suggest that mild to moderate depression will often respond to a structural approach to family therapy.

Hirschfeld, Klerman, Clayton, and Keller (1983), in their study of a group of women who had recovered from depression, found that these women tended to be introverted, submissive, passive, and interpersonally dependent but had normal emotional strength. Whether these traits reflect a predisposition to depression, a subclinical manifestation of the disorder, or part of the aftermath of depression remains unclear. In addition, Gutsch (1988) reports that depressed clients turn anger inward, experience conflicts between their dependency and autonomy needs, and believe that they have failed to live up to their goals and ideals.

Relevant Therapist Variables. Perry, Frances, and Clarkin (1985) emphasize the importance of quickly establishing and maintaining a positive and encouraging therapeutic relationship with depressed clients. Ideally, the therapist should communicate strongly the core conditions required for effective therapy (for example, genuineness, caring, acceptance, and empathy) and should be capable of providing support, structure, reality testing, optimism, reinforcement, and a strong role model. The therapist also must be prepared to intervene actively if suicide is threatened.

Schmitt (1983) urges the therapist to assume a directive role and warns that a person-centered approach, in which all client behaviors receive approval, can lead to a sense of helplessness in depressed clients, although it may increase their sense of responsibility. The therapist should not be threatened, gratified, or frustrated by the client's dependency and neediness but should gradually promote client independence. Depressed clients sometimes direct their anger and disappointment at their therapists and may invite rejection; it is important that therapists maintain objectivity despite the challenge presented by these clients.

Intervention Strategies. Depression takes many forms, and diagnosis of the particular form is crucial in determining the best treatment. In general—especially for reactive or exogenous depressions—individual psychotherapy without medication is appropriate for treatment of mild to moderate depression, uncomplicated by a bipolar pattern (see section 5.4), coexisting schizophrenia (section 10.1), organicity (section 10.6), mental retardation, or substance abuse (section 7.1) (Beck, Rush, Shaw, & Emery, 1979). For severe or complex forms of depression, medication, typically combined with psychotherapy, is often recommended; and a referral for a medical evaluation usually would be indicated. Marital and family therapy also seem to enhance treatment, since such therapy provides support to the families and ameliorates family conflict that may be contributing to the depression. Group therapy generally does not seem appropriate as the primary mode of treatment for depressed clients; their hopelessness and lack of energy make it difficult for them to engage actively in group therapy.

Recent findings by the Treatment of Depression Collaborative Research Program (TDCRP), established by the National Institute of Mental Health, provide helpful information. Mildly depressed clients treated with either the drug imipramine, behavioral therapy, or interpersonal therapy for sixteen weeks all showed relief of depressive symptoms and improvement of general functioning and had better outcomes than clients treated with placebos (National Institutes of Health, n.d.). In another study, comparing the impact of imipramine, cognitive therapy, and interpersonal therapy on severely depressed clients, both imipramine and interpersonal therapy seemed effective, but the impact of cognitive therapy was less well established (National Institutes of Health, n.d.).

Other research, however, has supported the use of *cognitive and cognitive-behavioral* approaches in treating depression. Emmelkamp (1986), for example, found that an approach initially focusing on behavioral and social skills and progressing to cognitive restructuring seemed to bring about an improvement in depressed subjects. Smith, Glass, and Miller (1980) found that a behavioral approach had a sizable impact (1.18 effect size) on depression. In another study, behavior therapy proved superior to insight-oriented psychotherapy and to medication and relaxation therapy in ten-week treatment of moderately depressed clients (McLean & Hakstian, 1979). Rush, Beck, Kovacs, and Holon (1977) compared cognitive-behavior therapy to imipramine over eleven weeks of treatment and found that 79 percent were at least markedly improved with psychotherapy, while only 23 percent were markedly improved with pharmacotherapy. In addition, the medication group had a higher dropout rate. Hollon and Beck (1986) also concluded that cognitive therapy works at least as well as medication in treating acute episodes of depression. Jarrett and Rush (1986) found that cognitive-behavioral therapy was associated with lower relapse rates than was short-term dynamic therapy (9 percent versus 56 percent relapsed at one-year follow-up).

Cognitive therapy or cognitive-behavioral therapy may work better with some types of clients than with others. Hollon and Beck (1986) suggest that clients who are high in self-control will respond well to cognitive therapy, whereas those who are low in self-control seem to do better with pharmacotherapy. Jarrett and Rush (1986) believe that cognitive-behavioral therapy is particularly effective with young clients who have a sense of mastery, view their families as supportive, and have a good reading level.

Perry, Frances, and Clarkin (1985) question whether cognitive therapy should be used with depressions that are not cognitively based. These investigators also suggest that not all clients can handle either the active role required of them by the cognitive model or the relatively confrontational stance of the cognitive therapist. Layne (1984) also raises questions about the emphasis on cognitive distortion, since depressed clients do not seem to have more distortion than others. Simons, Garfield, and Murphy (1984) speculate that cognitive distortions might be symptoms rather than causes of depression.

Kornblith, Rehm, O'Hara, and Lamparski (1983) and Lewinsohn and Hoberman (1982), in their review of the cognitive-behavioral approaches to the treatment of depression, found that the following ingredients in these approaches are instrumental in producing positive change:

1. Present a concrete rationale for depression and treatment as well as a vocabulary for defining and describing the problem
2. Are highly structured and offer clear plans for change, giving clients a sense of control

3. Provide feedback and support, so that clients can see change, receive reinforcement, and attribute improvement to their own efforts
4. Teach skills that will increase personal effectiveness and independence

These qualities may contribute at least as much to the clients' improvement as does the modification of cognitions. Consequently, although the reviews of cognitive-behavior therapy as a treatment for depression are not wholly positive, this mode of treatment for depression does seem quite promising.

Interpersonal psychotherapy (IPT), based on the work of Harry Stack Sullivan and the psychodynamic therapists, and developed by Klerman, Weissman, Rounsaville, and Chevron (1984), has received growing attention as an approach to treating depression. Klerman and his colleagues describe IPT as "a focused, short-term, time-limited therapy that emphasizes the current interpersonal relations of the depressed patient while recognizing the role of genetic, biochemical, developmental, and personality factors in causation and vulnerability to depression" (p. 5). They view depression as having three components: symptom function, social and interpersonal relations, and personality and character problems. IPT focuses on the first two of these, while taking account of the third in formulating interventions.

IPT holds that depression is caused by the early loss of a parent and a lack of adequate replacements. According to this model, four problem areas play key roles in depression: abnormal grief, interpersonal role disputes (nonreciprocal role expectations in significant relationships), role transitions (for example, marriage or divorce), and interpersonal deficits. The IPT model has developed strategies for dealing with each of these problem areas and matches treatment focus to client concerns. In general, IPT concentrates on clients' history of significant relationships, the quality and patterns of their interactions, their cognitions about themselves and their relationships, and associated emotions. Attention also is paid to strengthening clients' assets, increasing optimism and acceptance, developing coping mechanisms, providing information, and building competence. IPT differs from the cognitive-behavioral approaches in that it uses little homework and places less emphasis on planning action and assessing progress. The IPT model was originally developed for treating ambulatory clients with nonpsychotic major depression but is being used more broadly.

Another model that has been advanced to treat depression is *self-control therapy*, developed by Rehm (1984), Kanfer (1972), and others. Proponents of this approach believe that depressed clients feel responsible for their failures but not for their successes. This model—which emphasizes goal setting, self-administered rewards, and self-monitoring of levels of depression and progress—seems likely to be effective in the treatment of mild to moderate depression and can be conducted in both group and individual therapy settings. It seems more effective than no treatment or social skills training and just as effective as cognitive and learned helplessness models of treatment (Jarrett & Rush, 1986).

Brief psychoanalytic psychotherapy has also received some attention in the literature as a treatment of depression (Millman, Huber, & Diggins, 1982). However, only limited research is available to substantiate the efficacy of that model. Comparative studies tend to favor behavioral (Liberman & Eckman, 1981) and other more active, present-oriented models.

Lewinsohn, Sullivan, and Grosscup (1980) present a clear and straightforward model for treating depression. This model incorporates many of the features of the cognitive-behavioral, self-control, and interpersonal models of treatment and includes the following steps:

1. Examine feelings, actions, and thoughts that need to be changed.
2. Understand when depression emerges and learn to anticipate and recognize antecedent events.
3. Discover and explore reactions to antecedent events and consequences of those reactions and events.
4. Develop ways to change feelings and reactions.
5. Chart progress and reward self for positive change.
6. Learn when to seek help.

In addition to the above steps, the model incorporates relaxation techniques; techniques for counterpoising negative ideas with pleasant experiences, developing interpersonal skills, and controlling negative ideation; and homework assignments (for example, schedule, relaxation log, activity schedule).

Brown and Lewinsohn (1984) and Steinmetz, Lewinsohn, and Antonuccio (1983) have had some success in treating unipolar depression via a psychoeducational model of therapy. Three eight-week treatment conditions (a two-hour twelve-session class, individual tutoring, and minimal contact involving one session to establish assignments and subsequent telephone contact) were all more effective than no treatment. All the treatment conditions had low dropout rates (4.6 percent) and yielded marked improvement in nearly all clients, though treatment was less helpful to those reporting significant life stress who had become depressed relatively early in life.

Whichever of these models the therapist chooses to follow, it seems important to promote a realistic appraisal of alternatives and goal setting, a sense of mastery amd improved self-esteem, better reality testing, clearer boundaries between self and others, and a repertoire of problem-solving skills and coping mechanisms. Therapy will typically be action rather than interpretation oriented, with more focus on the present than on the past. It also will probably be moderately high in directiveness, at least in the early stages of treatment. Decreasing directiveness gradually over the course of treatment should prevent clients from becoming too dependent on their therapists and should help to increase clients' self-esteem. Supportiveness, too, will need to be fairly high initially; depressed clients are in considerable pain, and a probing approach runs the risk of opening new painful areas. Clients also will need considerable acceptance and positive regard at the start of therapy because of the fragility of their self-concepts.

Focus usually will be more on cognitive and behavioral areas of concern than on affective ones. The affective component should certainly receive some attention; however, extensive discussion of depression tends to entrench the symptoms and contributes to the clients' sense of discouragement and hopelessness. A focus on cognitive or behavioral areas is more likely to mobilize clients.

Treatment will probably be multifaceted, involving individual and family treatment; regular assessment of level of depression;

and home-based tasks, such as planned activities and charts to rate mastery and describe dysfunctional cognitions. The genetic nature of some forms of depression provides an important rationale for family therapy. If any other family members manifest overt or underlying depression or are at risk for developing such disorders, these family members also would benefit from therapy.

Treatment will typically be provided one to two times a week in an outpatient setting and will be paced fairly rapidly, but not so rapidly as to threaten or discourage clients. Inventories such as the Beck Depression Inventory and concrete, mutually agreed-upon assignments can give clients optimism and a sense of progress and direction. Therapy for depression tends to be short term (three months seems typical) and would rarely take as long as a year. Adjunct services to help clients establish a sense of direction and become involved in rewarding activities that are likely to increase their sense of competence and confidence (for example, social groups, sports, or weight control clinics) can enhance the treatment of depression.

New approaches for the treatment of depression are currently being studied. For example, some researchers have found that deprivation of one night's sleep seems to reduce depression (Roy-Byrne, Unde, & Post, 1986). Such techniques as guided imagery, social skills training (Bellack, Hersen, & Himmelhoch, 1983), simulated rites of passage (for example, a staged funeral), and flooding have been used effectively to help clients cope with grief and move ahead with their lives (Millman, Huber, & Diggins, 1982). Running and other forms of exercise have also been found to contribute to relief of depression (Millman, Huber, & Diggins, 1982).

Prognosis. The prognosis for a positive response to treatment for depression is excellent; a high percentage of clients improve, regardless of which of the treatments discussed in this chapter is used. In general, prognosis is correlated with severity of depression (Stewart & others, 1983), with previous level of adjustment, and with initial response to treatment (Baker & Wilson, 1985). Making new friends during treatment is also positively related to outcome (Monroe, Bellack, Hersen, & Himmelhoch, 1983).

Depression tends to be a self-limiting disorder and rarely lasts longer than six to twelve months (Wolman, 1976). However, there is a high risk of relapse for depressed clients, especially during the first few months after treatment. Baker and Wilson (1985), for example, found that 46–60 percent of clients reported depressive symptoms during a follow-up phase. Clients with a poor previous adjustment are particularly likely to experience a relapse (Lambert, 1982). In light of these findings, treatment might involve follow-up sessions, perhaps at monthly intervals, to maintain progress and facilitate rapid treatment for relapses. However, research has yet to clearly substantiate the value of such follow-up treatment.

5.1 Major Depression

Description of Disorder. According to the *DSM-III-R*, a major depression is manifested by the presence of at least five of the following symptoms (including one or both of the first two) nearly every day for at least two weeks: (1) depressed mood, (2) markedly reduced interest or pleasure in almost everything, (3) significant weight or appetite change (found in over 70 percent of cases), (4) insomnia or hypersomnia (in nearly 90 percent), (5) psychomotor retardation or agitation, (6) fatigue or loss of energy (in 78 percent) (Craighead, Kennedy, Raczynski, & Dow, 1984), (7) feelings of guilt or worthlessness, (8) reduced ability to think or concentrate, and (9) recurrent thoughts of death or suicide. These symptoms are not caused by an organic condition, and they do not represent a normal reaction to a bereavement.

In making a diagnosis of major depression, the clinician must assess the following features:

1. Severity—mild, moderate, severe, in partial remission, or in full remission (no symptoms for six months or more).
2. Presence of psychotic features—mood-congruent (consistent with the depressive attitudes), mood-incongruent, or none. Psychotic features are found in 10–35 percent of clients with major depression.
3. Chronic—episode continuing for at least two years (with symptom-free intervals, if any, lasting less than two months).

Approximately 20–35 percent of clients with major depression have chronic symptoms (Millman, Huber, & Diggins, 1982).

4. Melancholic—presence of at least five of the following symptoms suggesting a depression of endogenous or biochemical origins: (1) loss of interest or pleasure, (2) lack of reactivity to pleasurable events, (3) symptoms worse in morning, (4) early-morning awakening, (5) psychomotor retardation or agitation, (6) significant weight loss, (7) no significant antecedent personality disturbance, (8) one or more previous episodes with recovery, (9) positive response to somatic treatment for depression (for example, antidepressant medication). The dexamethasone suppression test, a biochemical measure, and EEG sleep patterns are both useful in discriminating endogenous from reactive depressions (Feinberg & Carroll, 1984).

5. Seasonal pattern—at least three depressive episodes linked to a particular sixty-day period of the year, with at least two in consecutive years. This pattern suggests a depression that is related to the amount of available natural light and is most common during the late fall. The key to treatment for this type of mood disorder is exposure to bright, white lights.

The average age at onset of major depression is the late twenties, but it may occur at any age (*DSM-III-R*, 1987). Symptoms usually develop fairly rapidly (within several days or weeks), beginning with dysphoria and biological symptoms; but onset may be sudden, following a loss or other stressor. Without treatment, this disorder typically runs its course in about six months to one year, but residual symptoms may be present for two years or more. Some overall impairment during episodes is typical, and the impairment may be so severe as to prevent even minimal functioning. Constant feelings of lethargy and hopelessness may be present, and clients may have to struggle to perform daily routines or even to get dressed in the morning.

Relevant Client Characteristics. Approximately 18–23 percent of women and 8–11 percent of men experience a major depression during their lifetime; and approximately 3 percent of men and 6 percent of women have a major depressive episode of sufficient severity to require hospitalization (Millman, Huber, & Diggins, 1982). Women not only are more prone to depression but also tend to have an earlier onset (Hirschfeld & Cross, 1982). Incidence peaks in women between thirty-five and forty-five and in men over fifty-five (Kaplan & Sadock, 1985).

There is a tendency for major depression to be associated with a family history of depression and/or alcohol abuse, particularly if the family environment was a negative one (Boyd & Weissman, 1982). This relationship seems to hold true for women more than for men (Kaplan & Sadock, 1985).

Major depression is often precipitated by a stressor, particularly one involving the loss of a relationship (such as the death of a spouse or the end of a marriage), and is frequently associated with childbirth, substance abuse, and chronic physical illness. The clinician should bear in mind that drugs, alcohol, and medication can precipitate depressive symptoms.

Several studies have found an association between personality type and incidence of major depression and suggest that the combination of a stressor and a depression-prone personality has a high correlation with the onset of a major depression. Cofer and Wittenborn (1980) found that women who experienced major depressions tended to have a sense of hopelessness, pessimism, and failure; to be self-critical and vulnerable; and to be from lower socio-economic groups. Cofer and Wittenborn also found that clients with this disorder often had a critical mother and a dependency-fostering father. Hirschfeld and Cross (1982) describe two depression-prone personality types: (1) low self-esteem and high obsessionality; (2) low frustration tolerance, dependent, emotionally labile, and vulnerable to the impact of stressors. Boyd and Weissman (1982) found that clients who experienced major depressions typically had difficulty in handling stress and were low in energy, insecure, introverted, anxious, low in assertiveness, dependent, and obsessional. Other personal qualities associated with susceptibility to a major depression include a strong superego and narcissism (Kaplan & Sadock, 1985). Many studies, then, affirm a connection between major depression and a preexisting personality pattern, including low self-esteem, dependency, anxiety, and fragility.

Relevant Therapist Variables. As discussed in the "overview" section of this chapter, therapists who are likely to be effective in treating depressed clients are those who are structured, focus on the present, attend to interpersonal issues and deficits, establish clear and realistic goals with clients, and encourage optimism and an increased activity level.

Intervention Strategies. The "overview" section of this chapter reviewed approaches to psychotherapy (for example, cognitive therapy and interpersonal therapy) that were most likely to be effective in treatment of depression. That information would apply to treatment of major depression.

A variety of medications also have been used in the treatment of major depression—mainly tricyclic antidepressants (TCAs) and MAO inhibitors. Beck, Rush, Shaw, and Emery (1979) estimate that 60–65 percent of depressed clients show definite improvement in response to TCAs. The particular nature of the depression and its accompanying symptoms suggest which medication is most likely to be helpful. For example, desipramine hydrochloride seems particularly effective with depressed clients who also have panic attacks (see section 6.2) (Stewart & others, 1985). Tricyclic antidepressants seem to be particularly helpful to depressed clients who are extremely orderly, in contact with reality, conscientious, and dependent; MAO inhibitors seem effective for atypical, fluctuating depressions (Millman, Huber, & Diggins, 1982). On the other hand, clients whose depression is accompanied by somatization (see Chapter Eight) and antisocial and other personality disorders (see Chapter Nine) tend not to respond well to medication (VanValkenburg & Akiskal, 1985). Medication seems particularly indicated for clients with endogenous (rather than reactive) depressions, including such symptoms as significant biological disturbance, a family history of depression, and the lack of a clear precipitant.

Electroconvulsive therapy (ECT) is also used to treat depression, particularly severe medication-resistant endogenous varieties. According to Maxmen (1986), after two to six weeks of treatment ECT leads to improvement in 78 percent of clients; TCAs, in 70 percent. However, both ECT and antidepressant medication have side effects. L-tryptophan, available without a prescription, has also demonstrated some effectiveness in relieving depression (Mindham, 1982); so have lithium and Trazodone, a nontricyclic antidepressant (Rickels & Case, 1982), although their impact on depression is not yet fully clarified.

Considerable controversy exists about the role of medication in the treatment of major depression. Until recently, medication was almost automatically prescribed for cases of severe depression. Current research, however, suggests that psychotherapy has a more enduring and equally powerful impact on depression.

The primary approaches to psychotherapy for clients with major depression include cognitive, cognitive-behavioral, and interpersonal therapy, discussed earlier in this chapter. Steinbrueck, Maxwell, and Howard (1983) conducted a meta-analysis of fifty-six outcome studies on the impact of psychotherapy and medication on depression. They concluded that psychotherapy, with a mean effect size of 1.22, was superior to pharmacotherapy, with a mean effect size of .61. Murphy, Simons, Wetzel, and Lustman (1984) found that twelve weeks of treatment via cognitive therapy, pharmacotherapy (tricyclic antidepressant), a combination of the two, and therapy with an active placebo all effected improvement, although 19 percent of the clients were still at least moderately depressed at a one-month follow-up. Clients were more receptive to treatment by psychotherapy than by medication, and therapy was particularly beneficial to clients who were high in resourcefulness. In a similar study, Kovacs, Rush, Beck, and Hollon (1981) found that those receiving cognitive therapy had a greater reduction in symptoms and a higher treatment completion rate than did those on medication. Weissman, Klerman, Prusoff, Sholomskas, and Padian (1981) compared interpersonal therapy and medication in four-month treatment of nonpsychotic acutely depressed clients and found that both had an approximately equal impact on symptoms but that clients who had received therapy made greater improvement in social and leisure areas. These investigators also found that the combination of medication and psychotherapy was even more powerful than either alone. Lambert (1982) also advocates a combination of medication and psychotherapy, suggesting that the medication acts on the biological complaints and that the therapy acts on the depression, low self-esteem, and skill deficits.

Conte, Plutchik, Wild, and Karasu (1986) reviewed all controlled studies of treatment of depressed outpatients conducted between 1974 and 1984. They concluded that, especially for endogenous depressions, the combination of drugs and psychotherapy was "appreciably more effective than the placebo conditions but only slightly superior to psychotherapy alone, pharmacotherapy alone, or either combined with a placebo" (p. 471). The research, then, supports Arieti's (1982) conclusion: "Individual psychotherapy should play a major role in most cases of depression, from the mildest to the most severe" (p. 297). However, medication may enhance the impact of therapy of severe depression. Clinicians should consider referring severely depressed clients for medical evaluations to determine their need for medication.

Prognosis. The prognosis for fairly rapid symptom relief via medication and/or psychotherapy is very good, and seems better for endogenous than for reactive major depressions (Coryell & Winokur, 1982). However, 15-20 percent do not recover fully from a given episode of major depression and have persistent symptoms for at least two years (National Institutes of Health, n.d.). In addition, recurrences ranging from mild, transient symptoms to full-blown major depressions are reported in approximately half of all clients during the first year after treatment (Kovacs, Rush, Beck, & Hollon, 1981). Approximately half of those will have yet another recurrence (Maxmen, 1986). Recurrence rates are highest during the first four to six months after recovery and have a negative correlation with response to treatment.

Keller, Lavori, Endicott, Coryell, and Klerman (1983) found that 25 percent of clients with a major depression had a preexisting chronic mild depression and that the chances for relapse for this group were greater than for those who did not have a prior underlying depression; 62 percent of the group with double depression (a major depression combined with an underlying mild to moderate depression) had a relapse within two years of recovery, while only 33 percent of those with single depression (major depression alone) relapsed. Duration of mild depression was correlated with likelihood of recurrence. Lambert (1982) found that, in general, the prognosis was worse for clients with accompanying pervasive maladjustment. On the other hand, a positive prognosis was associated with number and supportiveness of social resources and with positive life changes during treatment (Billings & Moos, 1985). Overall, then, the prognosis for recovery from a given episode of major depression is good, but there is a likelihood of relapse, particularly for those with preexisting mild depression and a history of dysfunction.

5.2 Dysthymia

Description of Disorder. Dysthymia—or depressive neurosis, as it was formerly called—is characterized by the presence of mild to moderate depression manifested almost every day for at least two years. (In children, a minimum duration of one year is required for diagnosis, and the primary manifestation of the disorder may be irritability rather than depression.) According to the *DSM-III-R* (1987), at least two of the following symptoms would also be present: (1) poor appetite or overeating, (2) insomnia or hypersomnia, (3) low energy or fatigue, (4) low self-esteem, (5) difficulty in concentrating or making decisions, and (6) a sense of hopelessness. The disorder would not encompass a manic or hypomanic episode (section 5.4), would not have an organic cause (section 10.6), and would not be superimposed on a chronic psychotic disorder (Chapter Ten). In establishing the diagnosis, the clinician would also make the following determinations about the disorder: (1) primary or secondary to a preexisting chronic nonmood mental or physical disorder (such as anorexia nervosa or multiple sclerosis); (2) early or late (age twenty-one or older) onset. Common periods of onset include late adolescence/early adulthood and middle age (Kaplan & Sadock, 1985).

Dysthymia generally has no clear point of onset or obvious precipitant. Clients with this disorder tend to maintain an acceptable level of social and occupational functioning and often conceal their symptoms from others but may experience mild to moderate impairment or limitations because of their depression.

Dysthymia is a common disorder, particularly among females. In any given year, approximately 4 percent of adults will experience this disorder (Klerman, 1986). At some time during their lives, 45 out of 1,000 people will experience dysthymia (Kaplan &

Sadock, 1985). Some have raised the possibility that dysthymia is really a personality disorder—a longstanding, potentially lifelong way of dealing with the world (Flach, 1987)—rather than a mood disorder.

Relevant Client Characteristics. Clients with dysthymia often have longstanding environmental stressors, most commonly a rejecting, confusing, affectionless, and controlling family background (Sacks, 1986). Men with dysthymia are particularly likely to present accompanying situational problems (such as work or family problems). A history of a childhood mental disorder (for example, conduct disorder, attention deficit hyperactivity disorder, or a specific developmental disorder) often is reported, as is a family history of major depression (*DSM-III-R*, 1987). Dysthymia frequently is accompanied by a personality disorder (see Chapter Nine) or by another mental or physical disorder; anxiety (Chapter Six), eating disorders (section 7.2), and substance abuse (section 7.1) are particularly common.

Personality patterns of dysthymic clients tend to be similar to those of clients with major depression (section 5.1). These clients are often low in self-esteem, introverted, helpless, vulnerable, and narcissistic. They overreact to stressful events or social disappointments (Sacks, 1986). Underlying hostility may be present. Often, people with dysthymia are divorced or separated and come from lower socioeconomic groups. Somatic and physiological complaints, such as eating or sleeping problems, are common and may be the presenting problems when treatment is sought. These clients may have a longstanding pattern of avoiding their difficulties by fleeing into overwork or excessive activity.

In some ways, clients with dysthymia may present more of a challenge to the therapist than do clients with major depression. Dysthymic clients have been depressed for so long that they may not know how to be anything but depressed and may be resistant to and apprehensive about change. Secondary gains, such as attention and reduced demands, may reinforce their depressed and helpless stance; and they may hesitate to relinquish these gains without assurances of continuing rewards and attention. Dysthymic clients also present a suicide risk; although their depression is not as severe as a major depression, they have the resourcefulness and energy to make a suicide attempt, whereas severely depressed clients may be too depressed to even attempt suicide.

Relevant Therapist Variables. Therapists working with dysthymic clients generally should follow recommendations made in earlier sections of this chapter on how to work with depressed clients. With dysthymic clients, however, the therapist can be somewhat less supportive and more confrontational, expecting completion of more extratherapy tasks, because these clients are more functional and resilient than those with major depression or bipolar disorders.

Intervention Strategies. Research on treatment modalities specific to dysthymia is sparse. It seems clear that medication is usually unnecessary and ineffective in the treatment of this disorder (Reid, 1983). Some of the psychotherapeutic approaches discussed earlier in this chapter also would be recommended in treatment of dysthymia—namely, cognitive, cognitive-behavioral, and interpersonal therapy, particularly when combined with development of social and related skills (such as assertiveness and decision making). Wierzbicki and Bartlett (1987), in their study of individual and group cognitive therapy for mild depression, suggest that individual treatment is superior to group treatment and that group treatment, in turn, is superior to no treatment. Harmon, Nelson, and Hayes (1980) found that dysthymic clients showed improvement (reduced depression and increased participation in activities) when they monitored their own mood and activity levels and when they received help in modulating their reactions to temporary discouragement and in overcoming learned helplessness. Meyer (1983) advises therapists to avoid reinforcing the depressive and negative verbalizations of dysthymic clients; negative thoughts, Meyer suggests, should be counteracted with images of pleasurable and successful activities. In the treatment approach recommended by Jacobson and McKinney (1982), the therapist helps clients identify and resolve sources of stress, mobilize energy, and improve self-esteem. The ideal treatment for dysthymia, Jacobson and McKinney believe, combines interpersonal and psychodynamic ingredients. A broad range of cognitive and behavioral interventions and techniques clearly contributes to the treatment of dysthymia.

Supportive therapy and group therapy seem to play a greater role in treatment of dysthymia than in major depression. Because dysthymic clients have more energy and a better level of functioning, they are able to participate in group therapy and make use of purely supportive interventions. Although there is only limited evidence that a modified psychoanalytic approach is useful in the treatment of these disorders, some clinicians have recommended such an approach for long-term dysthymia (Sacks, 1986).

Merikangas (1984) found that depressed clients often have spouses with emotional disorders, raising questions of whether difficult marriages contribute to the incidence of depression or whether depressed clients select mates with similar traits. Regardless of the answers to those questions, family counseling in combination with individual counseling seems indicated for many dysthymic clients as well as for clients with other forms of depression.

Therapists working with dysthymic clients seem to have a broader range of therapeutic options from which to choose than do therapists working with more severely depressed clients. In general, psychotherapy aimed at treating dysthymia seems most likely to be effective if it is moderately supportive, structured, and directive; focuses on cognitions and behavior more than on affect; and includes an array of educational and psychotherapeutic interventions designed to modify cognitions, increase activity, and improve self-esteem and interpersonal skills. Therapists also should probably pay some attention to the past, in an effort to elucidate repetitive and self-destructive patterns and clarify the dynamics that are perpetuating the depression.

Prognosis. Viable goals in the treatment of dysthymia include relief of depression and anxiety, amelioration of somatic and physiological symptoms, increased optimism and sense of control, and improved social and occupational functioning. The literature provides little information on the prognosis for treatment of dysthymia. If the disorder is closely related to major depression, the prognosis is likely to be good although there probably is a high risk for relapse; if the dysthymia is related to a personality disorder, the prognosis for significant and rapid change is not good. Probably the answer is somewhere in between; clients who can recall a healthier way of functioning, who have some good interpersonal skills and support systems, and whose depression is not deeply entrenched can be expected to respond well to treatment, whereas treatment may be long and difficult for clients who do not meet those criteria.

5.3 Depressive Disorder Not Otherwise Specified

As with most of the categories of mental disorder listed in the *DSM-III-R* (1987), there is not a "not otherwise specified" (NOS) category at the end of the section on depression. However, this particular NOS category, unlike most, seems to describe an important and distinct diagnostic entity. This category—which the *DSM* defines as "disorders with depressive features that do not meet the criteria for any specific Mood Disorder or Adjustment Disorder with Depressed Mood" (p. 233)—is usually used to describe a recurrent depression that is accompanied by prominent anxiety, panic, phobias, and/or irritability; histrionic or borderline features; and few or reverse biological symptoms (overeating, oversleeping, increased libido) (Flach, 1987).

Clients with this disorder are particularly prone to substance abuse, suicide attempts, and seductive and manipulative behavior. Their social judgment is poor, and they react strongly to rejection and disappointment. This disorder seems reminiscent of histrionic and borderline personality disorders (see sections 9.5 and 9.7). Nies and Robinson (1982) and others have found that this variety of depression often is responsive to a combination of psychotherapy and MAO inhibitors that act on both the anxiety and depression.

5.4 Bipolar Disorder

Description of Disorder. A bipolar disorder, in its most common form, involves alternating major depressive episodes and manic episodes, usually separated by periods of relatively normal mood. The disorder has no apparent organic cause and is not superimposed on a psychotic or delusional disorder.

The nature of a major depressive episode has been discussed

earlier in this chapter (section 5.1). However, the depressive phase of the bipolar disorder seems somewhat different from the depression associated with a major depression. According to Smith and Winokur (1984), the depression associated with a bipolar disorder entails less anger and somaticizing and more often includes oversleeping and psychomotor retardation.

A manic episode is a period of "elevated, expansive, or irritable mood" (*DSM-III-R*, 1987, p. 214). At least three of the following symptoms accompany the elevated mood: (1) grandiosity, (2) reduced need for sleep, (3) increased talkativeness, (4) racing thoughts, (5) distractibility, (6) increased activity level, and (7) excessive pleasure seeking to a potentially self-destructive extent (for example, excessive spending). A manic episode is sometimes preceded by a hypomanic phase, a less severe variety of the manic episode. The manic episode itself, like an episode of major depression, is typically quite severe and causes impairment in social and occupational functioning. Clients experiencing this phase of the disorder tend to view themselves as powerful and destined for great success. They disregard potential risks of their behavior, as well as the feelings of others, and may become hostile and contentious when challenged. Their judgment and impulse control are poor.

One client who experienced the manic phase of a bipolar disorder was Evelyn R., a twenty-seven-year-old woman with a stable marriage and work history. During the manic phase, she slept little and stayed up most of the night to make plans for her future; she planned, among other things, to purchase several houses and to embark on affairs with many of her co-workers and acquaintances. When her startled husband objected, she informed him that she was in the prime of her life and he should not get in her way. A brief period of hospitalization was required to prevent Evelyn from destroying her marriage and spending all their resources.

In diagnosing a manic episode, the clinician has the same decisions to make as with a major depressive episode: severity, whether or not psychotic features are present, and whether the disorder follows a seasonal pattern. About 20–50 percent of these clients have delusions or hallucinations (usually mood-congruent), which may lead to a misdiagnosis of schizophrenia (Pope, 1987).

There are three types of bipolar disorder: mixed, manic, and depressed. The mixed type involves a rapid alternation and mixture of manic and depressed moods. The manic type would be diagnosed if the client were experiencing a manic episode when the diagnosis was made, and the depressed type would be diagnosed if the client were in a depressed episode and had a history of one or more manic episodes. It is possible for clients with the manic type to report no depressive episodes, but that would be unusual.

A bipolar disorder usually begins with a manic episode (Coryell & Winokur, 1982). However, sometimes a bipolar disorder begins as a series of depressive episodes and is erroneously diagnosed as a recurrent major depression. If the disorder is treated with antidepressant medication, the mania or hypomania typically emerges, thereby clarifying the diagnosis (VanValkenburg & Akiskal, 1985). The nature of a client's first episode tends to reflect the nature of that person's dominant episode for the illness.

The average duration of an episode is two and a half to four months, with an average of thirty-three months between symptoms. Episodes may be as short as a few days and tend to end abruptly. The depressive episodes (average duration of six to nine months) tend to be longer than the manic episodes (two to six weeks) but shorter than episodes of major depression (Maxmen, 1986). Clients with a bipolar disorder have an average of seven episodes, with frequency varying from three a year to one every ten years.

Unipolar depression, or major depression without a history of manic episodes, is much more common than the bipolar disorders, which are found in only 0.5–1 percent of the population (Smith & Winokur, 1984). The onset of this disorder is usually early; in over half of the cases, the disorder begins before the person is twenty-nine years old (Smith & Winokur, 1984). Glassner and Haldipur (1983) suggest that bipolar disorders with an early onset are more likely to be genetic and responsive to medication, whereas those with later onset are more likely to be connected to stressful life events. An approximately equal number of men and women have bipolar disorders (Millon & Klerman, 1986).

Relevant Client Characteristics. Clients with a history of bipolar disorders often also suffer from dysthymia (section 5.2), substance abuse (section 7.1), or anxiety (Chapter Six), sometimes in reaction to their troubling unstable moods. Tyrer and Shopsin (1982) found that many clients with a bipolar disorder have a premorbid cyclothymic (section 5.5) personality style involving unstable but less severe mood changes. Perris (1982) suggests that clients with bipolar disorders are more independent and dominant, less guilty and anxious, and more prone toward instability and risk taking than are clients with major depressions (section 5.1). However, in general, clients with bipolar disorders have underlying personality patterns that are healthier than those of clients with major depressive disorders (Silverman, Silverman, & Eardley, 1984). Biological elements seem to be a more important ingredient than intrapsychic and interpersonal factors in the development and treatment of bipolar disorders; in contrast, major depression seems more closely linked to environmental than to physiological disturbances.

Compared to the general population, clients with bipolar disorders have a higher proportion of first-degree relatives with bipolar disorders (7 percent) or major depression (8 percent), suggesting a genetic component to this disorder (Boyd & Weissman, 1982). Similarly, 15–25 percent of those who have first-degree relatives with bipolar disorders will develop bipolar or unipolar disorders (Kaplan & Sadock, 1985). Clients with bipolar disorders tend to come from higher socioeconomic groups than do clients with major depression and tend to describe their families as socially inferior but upwardly striving, with pressure placed on the client to increase the prestige of the family (Gotlib & Colby, 1987). Obsessionality (section 9.10) is often high in the personalities of bipolar clients. Unlike major depression, bipolar disorders do not seem associated with marital status, although clients with these disorders not surprisingly often report marital conflict (Hirschfeld & Cross, 1982).

Relevant Therapist Variables. Perry, Frances, and Clarkin (1985) recommend that the therapist treating clients during the manic phase should be empathic but should not support the inappropriate behavior; the therapist should be directive, set limits, and promote reality testing. Flexibility on the part of the therapist also seems important, since the client is likely to be unstable and possibly hostile and resistant during the manic phase. Guidelines for the

therapist's role during the depressed phase would be similar to those
for major depression (section 5.1).

   Intervention Strategies. Medication is clearly the primary
mode of treatment for bipolar disorders. Lithium carbonate is the
standard, supplemented by antipsychotic, antidepressant, or other
medications, depending on whether psychotic features or severe mania is present (Klerman, 1986). About 75–80 percent of clients improve on lithium, typically in about ten days (Maxmen, 1986). Millman, Huber, and Diggins (1982) suggest that ECT can also reduce
the severity of this disorder. Bipolar symptoms, particularly those
present during the manic phase, are sometimes so severe and self-
destructive that hospitalization is needed. The period of hospitalization will typically be brief, lasting only until medication has modified the client's mood.

   Individual psychotherapy is used to help clients recover from
the symptoms of their disorder, restore a normal mood, repair damage they have done to relationships and careers as a result of their
disorder, and establish a milieu that offers structure and support.
Providing therapy during the manic phase is likely to be very difficult; clients typically enjoy the manic phase and tend not to believe
that they are ill. Their flight of ideas and high activity level make
analysis and clarification of concerns all but impossible. If therapy
is attempted during the manic phase, it will probably have to be
very structured and concrete, involving short, frequent sessions focusing more on behavior and milieu than on introspection and
exploration of affect.

   On the other hand, treatment during the normal or depressive phases can be very helpful and generally would follow the
guidelines discussed earlier for the psychotherapeutic treatment of
depression. However, treatment will probably tend to be more supportive and less confrontational than therapy for major depression,
since medication is really the primary mode of treatment for this
disorder. The higher level of functioning of most clients with bipolar disorders suggests that less emphasis is needed on social skills,
although educating the clients on the nature of their disorder is an
important element of the treatment. As with any depression, attention should be paid to the possibility of suicide by clients in the

depressed phase. Suicide seems even more likely for clients with bipolar disorders than for other disorders involving depression (Perris, 1982).

Family therapy and education also are important for clients with bipolar disorders, to help the families understand the nature and treatment of this potentially chronic disorder. Group therapy is usually not indicated for clients with bipolar disorders, since the severity of their symptoms makes it difficult for them to engage in the group process. However, Klerman (1986) found that group therapy did enhance treatment compliance and might be useful during the recovery phase. Family group therapy has also been used successfully to promote compliance, stabilization, and socialization.

Prognosis. Bipolar disorders present an even greater risk of recurrence than major depression; and, without treatment, that risk does not decline over time (National Institutes of Health, n.d.). Although the duration of the episodes tends to be fairly constant for a given person, the intervals between episodes tend to decrease. Recurrences are particularly likely for clients with late-onset bipolar disorder (Perris, 1982).

However, the prognosis for controlling the disorder with medication is quite good. Although six to nine months of lithium treatment may suffice after a first episode, extended maintenance on lithium or other medication is strongly recommended for clients who have had recurrent episodes, to reduce the likelihood of future recurrences. Therapy has also been recommended as a preventive procedure, but its efficacy in preventing the disorder has not been well documented (Jacobson & McKinney, 1982). However, perhaps on a reduced schedule, psychotherapy can play an important role in follow-up treatment of bipolar disorder. Even though medication, the central ingredient of treatment for this disorder, is not being provided by the therapists, they can monitor progress, promote appropriate use of the medication, and facilitate the adjustment of clients with a history of bipolar disorders.

5.5 Cyclothymia

Description of Disorder. Cyclothymia is, in a sense, a longer and milder version of bipolar disorder—just as dysthymia is a longer and milder version of major depression (although any biological relationship between the pairs is unclear). Cyclothymia entails a period of at least two years (one year for children and adolescents), during which clients experience numerous periods of hypomania and depression (often with several months of normal mood between episodes) that do not meet the criteria for major depressive episode (*DSM-III-R*, 1987; Kaplan & Sadock, 1985). The mood changes tend to be abrupt and unpredictable and to have no apparent cause.

People with cyclothymia usually are not significantly impaired by their disorder, and their mood cycles are usually briefer and less severe than those typical of bipolar disorder. However, their instability and moodiness tend to make them difficult co-workers and companions, and some social and occupational dysfunction is likely to result.

Lifetime prevalence of this disorder ranges from 0.4 percent to 3.5 percent (*DSM-III-R*,1987). The disorder most commonly begins in late adolescence or early adulthood and tends to have a chronic course without treatment. It is equally common in males and females.

Relevant Client Characteristics. Cyclothymia is associated with an increased incidence of major depression and bipolar disorder in clients' first-degree relatives. Some clinicians have noted a common history of early-childhood trauma and oral fixation in cyclothymic clients (Kaplan & Sadock, 1985). Cyclothymia is often accompanied by substance abuse (section 7.1) and may be a precursor to a bipolar disorder (section 5.4). A concurrent diagnosis of a personality disorder (sections 9.1–9.12) or a somatoform disorder (section 8.1) is also common (VanValkenburg & Akiskal, 1985). Cyclothymic clients often have trouble coping with stress effectively (Goplerud & Depue, 1985). Beyond this, little research is available on family background, personality patterns, and other antecedent variables associated with cyclothymia. To speak of a premorbid personality does not make sense in many cases, because the affective lability characteristic of these clients may have been present throughout most of their lives.

Relevant Therapist Variables. Little information is available on the therapist's role in the treatment of cyclothymia. Logic suggests the need for stability, patience, structure, and flexibility. Role modeling might also be a useful tool for therapists, since cyclothymic clients have no stable sense of themselves and probably will need to clarify values and direction as symptoms are reduced.

Intervention Strategies. Because of the deeply ingrained nature of this disorder, people with cyclothymia are rarely motivated to seek treatment for their symptoms (Kaplan & Sadock, 1985). Consequently, the literature on this disorder is limited. Treatment seems to be most effective when it includes a combination of medication and psychotherapy. Peselow, Dunner, Fieve, and Lautin (1982), in a review of many studies, found that 26–36 percent of cyclothymic clients benefited from treatment with lithium (a much lower rate of effectiveness than in the treatment of bipolar disorders).

Psychotherapy usually will be the primary mode of treatment. Individual therapy should probably follow the cognitive, behavioral, and other models that have demonstrated effectiveness in treating dysthymia (section 5.2), because depression is a central element in cyclothymia and because behavioral and cognitive deficits are likely to accompany the mood shifts. Also, the depressive cycles of this disorder tend to produce more dysfunction than do the manic phases. In addition, since clients with cyclothymia are unlikely to be introspective, affective and analytical approaches do not seem appropriate, at least in the early stages of treatment.

Family therapy is indicated, as it is for most of the disorders in this chapter. The unpredictable mood shifts experienced by these clients may well have damaged their family relationships, and rebuilding as well as education of the family often are needed. Career counseling and interpersonal skill development also will be useful supplements to treating these clients, since their mood changes have probably made it difficult for them to negotiate a smooth career path and to develop a repertoire of positive social skills and coping mechanisms. Group therapy may well be useful also; these clients are generally healthy enough to interact with other group members and might benefit from the opportunity to try out new ways of relating, to receive feedback from group members, and to make use of the role models provided by others. In general, then, psychotherapy for clients with cyclothymia will be multifaceted—including individual psychotherapy and, if indicated, medication (usually lithium), group therapy, family therapy, career counseling, and education. Therapy will be structured and relatively directive, to keep the client focused; it will combine supportive and exploratory elements, to help clients understand their patterns of interaction; and it will focus on cognitive and behavioral areas.

Prognosis. Goals for treatment of cyclothymia should probably be broad based, including not only reduction of symptoms and stabilization of mood but also establishment of a more consistent and rewarding lifestyle and improved relationships and occupational functioning. The literature provides little information on the prognosis for treatment of cyclothymia. Its close relationship to bipolar and other mood disorders, as well as its functional similarity to some of the personality disorders, suggests that therapy, possibly combined with medication, has a good likelihood of reducing symptoms and effecting improvement. However, because of the longstanding nature of this disorder and the chronicity of related disorders, effecting a complete recovery from the disorder may be difficult and may require relatively long-term therapy.

Summary of Treatment Recommendations

Five types of mood disorder have been discussed in this chapter: major depression, dysthymia, depressive disorder not otherwise specified, bipolar disorder, and cyclothymia. Information on the treatment of these disorders is summarized here.

Diagnoses. Mood disorders (major depression, dysthymia, atypical depression, bipolar disorder, cyclothymia)

Objectives. Stabilize mood; alleviate depression and mania; prevent relapse; improve coping mechanisms, relationships, and overall adjustment

Assessments. Measures of depression and suicidal ideation; medical examination for physical symptoms

Clinician. High in core conditions (such as empathy, acceptance, and genuineness), comfortable with client's dependency and discouragement, able to promote independence and optimism, structured, present oriented

Location. Usually outpatient but inpatient if symptoms are severe, risk of suicide is high, or loss of contact with reality is pronounced

Interventions. Cognitive-behavioral, interpersonal, and related models of treatment

Emphasis. On cognitions and behavior; directive and supportive initially but shifting to a less directive, more exploratory style

Nature. Usually individual therapy, accompanied by family therapy and possibly support groups once symptoms have abated

Timing. Medium duration (three to six months), possibly with extended follow-up; moderate pace, one to two sessions per week

Medication. Medication combined with psychotherapy often indicated for severe forms of these disorders

Adjunct services. Increased activities, homework assignments, career counseling, social skills development

Prognosis. Very good for recovery from each episode, although relapses are common

Client Map of Karen C.

This chapter began with a description of Karen C., a thirty-year-old woman experiencing severe depression following her husband's departure for a tour of duty. Karen shows many of the characteristics of clients suffering from depression. Her mother had episodes of depression, a disorder that often has a genetic component. Karen herself had suffered an early loss with the death of her father, was dependent and low in self-esteem, had few resources and interests, and looked to others for structure and support. Her depression seemed to be a reactive one, triggered by her perception that she was about to lose her husband to another woman. Her symptoms, typical of major depression, included both emotional (hopelessness, guilt) and somatic (sleep and appetite disturbances, fatigue) features. The following client map outlines the treatment for Karen.

Diagnosis. Axis I: 296.23—Major depression, single episode, severe, without psychotic features

Axis II: Dependent personality traits

Axis III: No known physical disorders or conditions, but weight loss and insomnia are reported

Axis IV: Psychosocial stressors: separation from husband, marital conflict. Severity: 2— mild (predominantly enduring circumstances)

Axis V: Current Global Assessment of Functioning: 45; highest GAF past year: 63

Objectives. (1) Reduce level of depression

(2) Eliminate physiological complaints

(3) Improve social and occupational functioning

(4) Increase self-esteem, sense of independence, and activity level

(5) Improve communication and differentiation in marital relationship, reduce marital stress and conflict

(6) Reduce cognitive distortions and unwarranted assumptions

Assessments. The Beck Depression Inventory will be used at the start of each session. In addition, to avert a suicide attempt, a contract in which Karen agrees not to harm herself will be used after discussion of her suicidal ideation. (It is assumed that this client is not acutely suicidal.) A physical examination is recommended.

Clinician. Karen seems likely to benefit most from working with a therapist who is supportive and patient yet structured, who can model and teach effective interpersonal functioning, and who can rapidly build a working alliance with a discouraged and potentially suicidal client.

Location. Efforts will be made to see Karen in an outpatient setting. However, if she does not respond to treatment quickly and remains relatively immobilized by her depression, a brief period of hospitalization will be considered.

Interventions. In accordance with the guidelines for interpersonal psychotherapy (Klerman, Weissman, Rounsaville, & Chevron, 1984), attention will be paid to Karen's history of significant relationships (for example, her early loss of her father, her dependent and enmeshed relationship with her mother, and her extended conflict with her husband), the nature and patterns of her social interactions, her thoughts about herself and her roles and relationships, and associated emotions. However, focus will be on her present relationship with her husband and her lack of self-direction (interpersonal role disputes and interpersonal deficits). Karen will be helped to clarify and communicate her expectations and wishes to her husband and to renegotiate their relationship. She will also be encouraged to review strengths and weaknesses of past and present relationships and to try out improved ways of relating both at home and in therapy sessions. Techniques such as role playing, examination of logic and belief systems, communication analysis, and modeling will be used.

Emphasis. Because Karen is nearly immobilized by her depression, she requires a high level of directiveness. She has no sense of how to help herself and needs the therapist to provide direction and structure. Over time, it is anticipated that this directiveness will be reduced somewhat, to increase Karen's own sense of mastery and competence and help her take responsibility for her life.

Karen has few friends and confidants and will require a high degree of support at the outset. As symptoms abate and as Karen begins to develop some additional outside support systems, focus will shift to include more exploration and education; but support will remain relatively high.

Although Karen presents with primarily affective difficulties, to focus on her feelings of depression would probably only entrench her sense of hopelessness. Both cognitive dysfunction (inappropriate generalization, self-blame) and behavioral deficits (few activities, poor social and interpersonal skills, dependence on others to take care of her) are present. Because the precipitant of her present depression seems primarily interpersonal, the primary emphasis of treatment will be on her relationships.

Nature. Individual therapy will be the focus of treatment. However, marital counseling is also indicated once her husband returns home.

Timing. Karen initially will be seen twice a week, to facilitate reduction of depression and improve her functioning. Once she is able to return to work, this schedule may be reduced to once a week. Counseling will move as quickly as Karen's fragile condition allows, but pacing will need to be relatively gradual and supportive at first. Treatment of three to nine months' duration is anticipated. Although major depression generally responds to treatment fairly rapidly, Karen's dependent personality traits may retard progress and may merit attention even after the depressive symptoms have been alleviated. Extending treatment beyond symptom abatement would probably also have a preventive impact and might avert the recurrences that often follow an episode of major depression.

Medication. Although medication is often helpful in treating major depression, Karen seems to be experiencing a reactive rather than an endogenous depression. If Karen can engage rapidly in a productive therapeutic relationship, medication is probably not necessary. However, if her symptoms of depression and hopelessness are so prominent that therapy is hampered, she will be referred to a psychiatrist to determine whether medication is indicated, since medication and psychotherapy seem to have a synergistic effect in the treatment of major depressions.

Adjunct services. Some nondemanding tasks will be suggested to Karen to do outside of the session, such as reading about assertiveness and increasing and listing her pleasurable activities, particularly those involving socialization. A women's support group might also be useful once depression has been relieved.

Prognosis. The prognosis for symptom reduction in major depression, single episode, is excellent. However, the prognosis for greatly modifying Karen's underlying dependent personality traits is less optimistic. Improvement will probably be observed as a result of psychotherapy, but a total personality change is unlikely to result from relatively short-term psychotherapy. In addition, there is approximately a 50 percent chance of a recurrence, and this possibility should be discussed with Karen and her family and addressed via extended treatment and/or follow-up.

Although depression is the symptom most often presented in psychotherapy, anxiety is a close second. The next chapter will review the diagnosis and treatment of those disorders characterized primarily by anxiety.

Recommended Readings

Beck, A. T., Rush, A. J., Shaw, B. F., & Emery, G. (1979). *Cognitive therapy of depression.* New York: Guilford Press.

Gotlib, I. H., & Colby, C. A. (1987). *Treatment of depression.* Elmsford, NY: Pergamon Press.

Klerman, G. L., Weissman, M. M., Rounsaville, B. J., & Chevron, E. S. (1984). *Interpersonal psychotherapy of depression.* New York: Basic Books.

Seligman, M. (1975). *Helplessness: On depression, development, and death.* New York: Freeman.

Turner, S. M., & Hersen, M. (Eds.). (1984). *Adult psychopathology and diagnosis.* New York: Wiley.

Chapter Six

▐▌▌▐▌▌▌▐▌▌▐▌▌▌▐▌▌▐▌▌▌▐▌▌▌▐▌▌▐▌▌▐▌▌▌▐▌▌▌▐▌▌▐▌▌▐▌▌▌▐▌

Anxiety
Disorders

Case Study: Sharon A.

Sharon A., a twenty-five-year-old single white female, requested psychotherapy at a community mental health center for help with what she described as overwhelming fear and anxiety. She had been experiencing these feelings almost constantly for the past nine months. Accompanying symptoms included feelings of exhaustion, even upon awakening, difficulty concentrating on her work, muscle tension, apprehensiveness, irritability, dizziness, and feelings of being on edge and of being smothered. When asked about the impact of these symptoms on her work and social life, Sharon reported that her work was certainly affected.

Symptoms began shortly after Sharon, who was a sales representative for a computer software firm, was transferred from the company's main office on the West Coast to Boston, where she was to develop a new market for the firm's products. She had only one colleague in the Boston area, and most of her work was done out of her apartment or on the road. Sharon said that she felt anxious at home and when calling on prospective clients and found herself putting off both paperwork and client visits. She felt uncomfortable with the clients and was convinced that she was not presenting herself or the company adequately. She said that her social life had not been affected because she had not yet developed any social life in Boston.

Sharon was an only child whose parents divorced when she was in elementary school. Sharon had had little contact with her father since then and had lived with her mother in the same house in the same town until the transfer to Boston. A popular and above-average student, she had worked hard to make friends and earn good grades. After graduating from college, with a major in business, she was immediately employed by the software company where she still worked. Her life on the West Coast had been very rewarding to her; she maintained close contact with friends from high school and college and did well at her job. She did not date much but spent time at parties and outings with both male and female friends. She had become a good tennis player, and much of her social life revolved around tennis. Although she did not feel a great deal of anxiety prior to the move to Boston, Sharon said that she often felt uneasy when meeting new people and worried that she was not as attractive or sophisticated as her friends.

Overview of Anxiety Disorders

Description of Disorder. Sharon is experiencing an anxiety disorder, typified by emotional and physiological sensations of tension and apprehension. Although there is an apparent precipitant for her symptoms, her move to Boston, her disorder is too long-standing and probably too severe to be classified as either a V code condition (section 4.2) or an adjustment disorder (section 4.1). Although underlying depression is present, Sharon's overriding emotion is anxiety. This chapter will review the diagnosis and treatment of five categories of anxiety disorder: generalized anxiety disorder, panic disorders, phobias (including agoraphobia, simple phobia, and social phobia), obsessive compulsive disorder, and post-traumatic stress disorder. Although these disorders differ in duration, precipitant, secondary symptoms, and impact, they are all characterized primarily by anxiety.

Anxiety disorders are among the most prevalent forms of mental illness in the United States (Thyer, 1987). Approximately 2-5 percent of the people have, at one time, suffered from anxiety disorders (Millman, Huber, & Diggins, 1982). More women than men suffer from these disorders, especially in the sixteen- to forty-year-old age group (Beck & Emery, 1985). Anxiety is the primary symptom in 20–25 percent of all psychiatric disorders (Turner & Hersen, 1984). In addition, stress, related to anxiety, is a significant factor in 30–70 percent of patients who are seeing physicians for physical ailments.

Anxiety may be free-floating and apparently without cause, or it may occur in response to a fear-inducing stimulus (such as a snake or the recollection of an accident). Like depression, anxiety takes many forms but is usually not debilitating or accompanied by loss of contact with reality. Most people with anxiety try to manage or conceal their symptoms and go about their lives. However, the symptoms of the disorder—such as heart palpitations and shortness of breath—are in themselves frightening and may lead clients to believe they are having a heart attack or other serious physical ailment. Anxiety, then, often breeds further anxiety.

Not a great deal is known about the origins of anxiety. Speilberger, Pollans, and Worden (1984) believe that it is caused by a combination of constitutional or biological predispositions and environmental factors. Others, taking a more psychoanalytic view, suggest that anxiety may be the product of experiences in which internal impulses, previously punished and repressed, evoke anxiety, which signals danger of further punishment if the impulses are expressed. Or, in cognitive terms, a stressor produces a perception of threat, which, in turn, produces a dysfunctional emotional reaction (anxiety). According to that interpretation, it is the cognitive processes that lead us to define something as threatening.

Relevant Client Characteristics. The onset of severe anxiety is often preceded by financial or marital problems, a bereavement, or another event that places stress in an area where people are vulnerable, increases their responsibilities, and weakens their support systems. People who are prone to excessive anxiety often come from a background including poverty, a breakup of the family, separation from the mother in childhood, and critical and demanding parents (Turner & Hersen, 1984). Like depression, anxiety tends to run in families (Kaplan & Sadock, 1985), though this is less clearly true of generalized anxiety disorder than it is of panic disorder. More females than males seek treatment for anxiety disorders—perhaps because anxious men often turn to alcohol rather than to therapy (Gorman & Liebowitz, 1986).

Anxiety is often accompanied by secondary symptoms. When depression is present, the result may be what has been termed an agitated depression. Substance abuse and dependency on others are also common and may represent efforts to control the symptoms through self-medication and a reliance on support symptoms. Unfortunately, the substance abuse and dependency seem more likely to worsen than to alleviate the anxiety.

Relevant Therapist Variables. The ideal therapist for treating anxiety seems to be one who is flexible and can draw from a variety of therapeutic approaches to find an optimal balance of techniques. Therapists need to be sufficiently comfortable with clients' pain and tension that they refrain from controlling the therapeutic process, yet they also need to have sufficient concern and compassion that they keep trying to find an approach that has an impact on the client.

Although there is little research on the optimal therapist for the anxious client, it would seem to be a therapist who is calm, not troubled by anxiety, and able to exert a tranquilizing and reassuring effect on the client. Beck and Emery (1985) suggest that the therapist should be a model of patience and persistence and should encourage rather than force change. Horowitz, Marmar, Krupnick, Wilner, Kaltreider, and Wallerstein (1984) suggest that "Frequently, stress-related symptoms subside rapidly once a firm therapeutic alliance is established." In their view, the best therapist for anxiety disorders is an "expert and healer" (p. 42) who is compassionate, understanding, nonjudgmental, and genuine. It seems to be the consensus, then, that the therapeutic relationship can have a powerful impact on symptoms of anxiety.

Intervention Strategies. Optimal treatment of anxiety disorders seems to involve a combination of behavioral and cognitive therapy. Smith, Glass, and Miller (1980) found that cognitive-behavioral and cognitive approaches yielded the largest effect sizes

(1.78 and 1.67, respectively) in the treatment of fear and anxiety, followed by the behavioral approach (1.12). Dynamic, humanistic, and developmental approaches were not nearly as effective in the treatment of these disorders. According to Barrow (1979), relaxation should be the focus of treatment if emotions are the source of the anxiety, while cognitive methods should be the focus if thoughts are the source. In general, he recommends cognitive methods because they promote client self-control more than does behavior therapy.

Another approach to treating anxiety disorders is anxiety management training (AMT), developed by Suinn and Deffenbacher (1988). AMT is a relaxation-based self-control therapy, in which clients are taught to identify cognitive and physical signs of the onset of anxiety and to develop responses, such as imagery and relaxation, that they can use to reduce or eliminate those symptoms. AMT is especially useful for treating forms of anxiety in which there is no obvious precipitant, because AMT can be integrated with cognitive restructuring and skills training.

A similar approach is described by Meichenbaum and Deffenbacher (1988). Their model, stress inoculation training (SIT), includes three phases: (1) conceptualization of problem and rapport building, (2) skill acquisition and rehearsal, and (3) application and follow-through. The teaching of relaxation and cognitive coping skills (problem-oriented self-instruction, restructuring negative cognitions, and self-reward/self-efficacy statements) is an important component of this useful model. Imaginal and *in vivo* desensitization, hypnotherapy, and other techniques designed to reduce fear and anxiety may also be useful in treatment of these disorders, depending on the nature of the particular disorder.

Psychoanalysis, psychodynamic therapy, and related approaches have not been found effective in treating anxiety. Their use cannot be recommended for anxiety disorders (Klerman, 1986).

Therapists treating anxiety, like those treating depression, will probably use a moderate level of directiveness and a high level of supportiveness at the beginning of treatment. Clients typically feel fragile and apprehensive and need support and encouragement to help them engage in therapy, although they usually will be eager to work collaboratively with the therapist to relieve their anxiety. Once the debilitating anxiety has been reduced, therapists can assume a more probing stance; most clients with anxiety will have had a period of relatively healthy functioning prior to the onset of symptoms and should be able to respond to and grow from some exploration.

Group therapy often is used along with or in lieu of individual therapy in the treatment of anxiety. Clients with similar anxiety-related symptoms and experiences—such as a post-traumatic stress disorder following a rape (see section 6.5) or the fear of social situations—can provide one another with a powerful source of encouragement, role models, and reinforcement.

Family counseling can be a useful adjunct to treatment. A highly anxious and constricted person in a family may have a strong impact on the life of the family, and family members may benefit from help in understanding the disorder and in learning how to respond supportively and helpfully without providing secondary gains that would reinforce the symptoms.

Collaboration with a physician is important when one is treating anxiety disorders, because physical disorders (for example, cardiopulmonary disorders, such as mitral valve prolapse, angina pectoris, and cardiac arrhythmia; endocrine disorders, such as hyperthyroidism and hypoglycemia; neurological disorders; metabolic disorders; and abuse of such substances as diet or cold pills, caffeine, nicotine, or cocaine) can cause anxiety symptoms. It is important to determine whether the physical is causing the psychological or vice versa (Deitch, 1981). Medication can accelerate the treatment of some anxiety disorders (such as a panic disorder or an obsessive compulsive disorder), but hospitalization is rarely necessary. Outpatient psychotherapy of medium duration (months rather than weeks or years), combining cognitive and behavioral interventions with between-session practice, usually will be the major ingredient in treating anxiety disorders.

Prognosis. Prognosis for treatment of the anxiety disorders varies widely, depending on the specific disorder in question. Some disorders, such as phobias, respond very well to treatment; others, such as obsessive compulsive disorder, are often resistant to treatment. Recurrences of anxiety disorders, like the mood disorders, are common. Goal setting, focusing on measurable behavioral and affective changes, is integral to treatment; and procedures for assessing progress—such as observation, checklists, diaries, questionnaires, inventories, and even videotapes—often are used to monitor change. Subsequent sections of this chapter, focusing on the specific disorders, provide more information on prognosis.

6.1 Generalized Anxiety Disorder

Description of Disorder. Generalized anxiety is a pervasive disorder that affects almost every system of the body: physiological, cognitive, motivational, affective, and behavioral (Beck & Emery, 1985). According to the *DSM-III-R* (1987), clients with a generalized anxiety disorder have had "unrealistic and excessive worry" about at least two life circumstances for most days during a period of at least six months. The worry is also accompanied by at least six of the following physiological symptoms:

Motor tension—trembling or twitching, muscle tension or soreness, restlessness, tiring easily

Autonomic hyperactivity—shortness of breath or smothering sensations, sweating or cold and clammy hands, dry mouth, dizziness or lightheadedness, nausea or diarrhea or other abdominal discomfort, flushes or chills, frequent urination, discomfort swallowing

Vigilance and scanning—feeling on edge, extreme startle response, anxiety-related trouble concentrating, sleep disturbance, irritability

The most common affective and somatic symptoms of generalized anxiety disorder include inability to relax (96.6 percent), tension (86.2 percent), fright (79.3 percent), jumpiness (72.4 percent), and unsteadiness (62.1 percent) (Beck & Emery, 1985). The most common cognitive and behavioral symptoms include difficulty in concentrating (86.2 percent), fear of losing control (75.9 percent), fear of being rejected (72.4 percent), inability to control thinking (72.4 percent), and confusion (69 percent). For the diagnosis to be made, the symptoms should not be caused by an organic factor or by another Axis I mental disorder.

Common secondary symptoms include emotional outbursts and hypersensitivity, reduced sexual and interpersonal activity, and perfectionism (Rosenthal & Rosenthal, 1985). Clients with generalized anxiety disorder typically have low self-esteem; feel insecure, indecisive, and socially inadequate; and have strong needs for affection and approval (Speilberger, Pollans, & Worden, 1984). Depression often underlies anxiety; Anderson, Noyes, and Crowe (1984) found that 37 percent of their clients with generalized anxiety disorder also had a secondary diagnosis of depression (Chapter Five). Clients may seem confused and have a sense of unreality as well as a loss of objectivity and a fear of losing control (Beck & Emery, 1985). They are also prone to insomnia and anxiety-laden dreams (Atwood & Chester, 1987). Anticipatory anxiety is a prominent manifestation of the disorder. Clients have motivation and energy and are not disabled by the disorder but are inhibited by their fears. Beck and Emery (1985) found that over 80 percent of those with generalized anxiety had also experienced phobias (section 6.3) or panic attacks (section 6.2) at some time in their lives. Generalized anxiety disorder is clearly not a misnomer; the anxiety expresses itself through a multitude of pervasive symptoms that typically are without an obvious immediate precipitant and that leave clients feeling frightened and overwhelmed by what is happening to them.

Because of the often misleading physiological nature of many of the symptoms of generalized anxiety disorder, it is important to gather data on variables that may have precipitated or may be perpetuating the disorder, so that some understanding of its origins and dynamics is gained. The disorder tends to have a fairly gradual onset, although it is often triggered by an experience of loss or separation.

Relevant Client Characteristics. Generalized anxiety disorder tends to develop early, with 40 percent reporting onset before age twenty and onset rare beyond the mid-thirties (Thyer, 1987). Gender distribution is approximately equal. The disorder seems to be most prevalent among young adults, particularly those with a history of physical disease or substance abuse (Beck & Emery, 1985). The little research available on these clients suggests that they come from disrupted families and had patterns of adjustment that involved dependency and low self-esteem.

Both men and women with generalized anxiety were likely to have had one or more negative, important, and unexpected life events associated with the onset of the disorder. For men, the number of these events was also correlated with incidence of the disorder (Blazer, Hughes, & George, 1987).

Barbaree and Marshall (1985) suggest that an intake interview with clients suffering from generalized anxiety disorder should cover the following: relevant cognitions (self-statements, expectations, fears, attributions, evaluations), somatic/physiological complaints, relevant behaviors, severity and generalizability of disorder, antecedents and precipitants, consequences and responses of others, family and individual history of emotional disorders, previous attempts to manage anxiety, and information on overall lifestyle. A comprehensive interview of this kind can provide important information on the dynamics of the disorder, which can, in turn, dispel some of the client's fears about their symptoms.

Relevant Therapist Variables. Information provided in the "overview" section is relevant here. In addition, the therapist should have a wide repertoire of anxiety management techniques. Since not all of these techniques are effective with all clients, the therapist needs to select approaches most likely to work with a given client.

Intervention Strategies. Several studies have sought to determine the relative effectiveness of various cognitive and behavioral therapies in the treatment of generalized anxiety disorder. Their conclusions provide a framework for intervention.

Hutchings, Denney, Basgall, and Houston (1980) divided sixty-three clients with chronic generalized anxiety into three groups and assessed the effect of the following treatments: (1) applied relaxation training with practice; (2) anxiety management training, including relaxation training and structured rehearsal (visualization with relaxation); and (3) relaxation without application. The second procedure was the most effective; the third, the least. The authors concluded that people need to know not only how to relax but also how to channel that technique so that it enables them to cope with their anxiety.

Woodward and Jones (1980) treated twenty-seven clients with generalized anxiety who had had their symptoms for an average of thirty months. They found that cognitive restructuring—focusing on self-defeating statements, irrational beliefs, and coping skills—was more effective when combined with systematic desensitization than was either alone. The greater the frequency and severity of the symptoms, the more positive was the effect of the treatment.

Kanter and Goldfried (1979) found that systematic rational restructuring more effectively reduced anxiety and irrational beliefs than did self-control desensitization. Treatment had an equal effect on behavioral and physiological manifestations of anxiety.

Durham and Turvey (1987) compared clients with chronic anxiety who had received a maximum of sixteen sessions of behavioral or cognitive therapy. They found that both groups had made equal progress at the end of treatment; but at a six-month follow-up, the clients who had received cognitive therapy had maintained or improved upon their gains, while the other group showed some decline.

These studies give cognitive interventions an edge over behavioral ones in the treatment of generalized anxiety disorder. However, a combination of behavioral and cognitive techniques seems particularly powerful in ameliorating generalized anxiety.

The primary goal of behavior therapy for generalized anxiety disorders is stress management. Rosenthal and Rosenthal (1985) suggest many approaches to helping anxious clients manage stress: progressive muscle relaxation, autogenic training, guided imagery, yoga, mental discipline, meditation, the Lamaze method, and Meichenbaum's self-instruction (see Meichenbaum & Deffenbacher, 1988) are among them.

Beiman, Israel, and Johnson (1978) studied forty adults with high general anxiety and compared live presentation by the therapist of progressive relaxation techniques, taped presentation of the same techniques, self-relaxation, and biofeedback. After six thirty-minute sessions, physiological and self-reports indicated that live presentation of progressive relaxation was the most effective technique.

Morgan (1979) found that vigorous exercise, especially combined with pleasant fantasy and systematic desensitization, lowered anxiety, as did rest, meditation, and biofeedback. Fishbein (1985) reviewed the literature on behavioral approaches to anxiety reduction and concluded that biofeedback, transcendental meditation, and progressive relaxation are all equally effective in contributing to the improvement of clients with anxiety disorders.

Clearly, there are many effective approaches to reducing anxiety through stress management. When planning a specific approach to stress management, therapists should consider their own and their clients' preferences, clients' lifestyles, and the dynamics of the stress. However, single-focus interventions such as progressive relaxation, biofeedback, and meditation do not seem sufficient to relieve the disorder. They can enhance a multifaceted treatment plan designed to relieve anxiety but should not constitute the primary approach to treatment (Thyer, 1987). As mentioned, behavior therapy is sometimes combined with cognitive therapy to form a more powerful and all-encompassing treatment.

Among those who propose cognitive therapy as a treatment for generalized anxiety, Beck and Emery (1985) describe a brief and time-limited approach (five to twenty sessions is typical), emphasizing a sound collaborative therapeutic relationship. Therapy is present oriented, structured, directive, and problem oriented, based on the inductive/Socratic method of teaching (questions are the primary form of intervention), with homework an important component of treatment. Four stages of treatment are described: relieving symptoms, clarifying distorted automatic thoughts, teaching logic and reason, and modifying long-held dysfunctional assumptions underlying major concerns. Techniques suggested by Beck and Emery include the use of logic, educational stories, visual images, and the active voice; data gathering and experimental testing of beliefs; examination of automatic thoughts via free association and behavioral tasks; an emphasis on "how" rather than "why" inquiry; reattribution; and decatastrophizing. This approach is active, logical, and organized.

Barrow (1979) describes a four-stage model of cognitive therapy, which also seems well suited to treatment of generalized anxiety disorders:

1. Early-detection training. Clients learn to become alert to the onset of anxiety and to determine thoughts and situations that seem to promote anxiety.

2. Analyzing self-talk. Clients look at self-statements or interpretations that mediate between their experience of a situation and the development of anxiety. Particular focus is on cognitions related to worrying about performing adequately or winning the approval of others.

3. Redirecting self-talk. Clients are taught to challenge the accuracy of their self-statements, to shift their focus off themselves and onto situations and tasks, and to stop negative thoughts and take positive action.

4. Transfer of training. Learning is expanded and generalized. Additional coping skills are taught as needed.

Cognitive and behavioral components probably will be emphasized over the affective in the treatment of generalized anxiety. However, to facilitate the decrease of anxiety, some direct attention should be paid to the affective component. Beck and Emery (1985) propose a five-step process (AWARE) for dealing with the affective component of an anxiety disorder:

A Accept feelings; normalize, identify, and express them. Clients are encouraged to go on with life despite anxiety and to learn strategies, such as self-talk, to develop some mastery of their anxiety.

W Watch the anxiety, seeking objectivity and distance. Use diaries and ratings to demonstrate that the anxiety is situational, time limited, and able to be controlled.

A Act with the anxiety, rather than fighting it in dysfunctional ways. Confront fears rather than trying to avoid them; act against inclination. Deliberately seek out anxiety-provoking situations to inoculate against anxiety.

R Repeat the steps, to establish the learning and facilitate the process.

E Expect the best; maintain an optimistic outlook.

Although research on treatment of this disorder is fairly limited, the Beck and Emery model is consistent with what is known about the treatment of generalized anxiety. Their multifaceted treat-ment approach—beginning with feelings and behaviors, and moving on to automatic thoughts, underlying assumptions, and major concerns—seems to be one of the clearest and most useful approaches in the treatment of anxiety.

Medication is not often necessary for the treatment of generalized anxiety. In an early study, Greenblatt and Shader (1974) found that benzodiazepines (such as Valium, Librium, and Serax) were effective in reducing anxiety. Since that study, much has been learned about the addictive potential of benzodiazepines. At present, they are used with considerable caution, especially with clients who express suicidal ideation. Antidepressants, Chlordiazepoxide (a benzodiazepine), and Xanax (a drug that acts on both anxiety and depression) have been found useful in cases where medication is indicated (Breier, Charney, & Heninger, 1985; Kahn & others, 1986; Kaplan & Sadock, 1985); but medication should be used with considerable caution and monitored carefully with anxious clients. The risks inherent in the medication may not be worth the anxiety relief provided; other approaches to anxiety reduction may be safer and at least as effective, though somewhat slower.

Prognosis. There is little clear information on the prognosis for treating clients with generalized anxiety disorder (Kaplan & Sadock, 1985) except the finding that spontaneous remission is uncommon (Gorman & Liebowitz, 1986). Although most clients demonstrate a fairly rapid response to treatment and 50–60 percent of those with generalized anxiety disorder do manifest significant improvement after treatment, some follow-up studies suggest that less than 25 percent of those with anxiety disorders recover completely (Breier, Charney, & Heninger, 1985). Therapists should recognize that this disorder sometimes does not remit fully and should include preventive and coping mechanisms to help clients continue to manage anxiety and stress effectively on their own.

6.2 Panic Disorder

Description of Disorder. Maxmen (1986) reports that 1–2 percent of the people in the United States suffer from panic disorders and that the disorder is two to three times more common in women than in men, particularly in the sixteen- to forty-year-old age group. Beck and Emery (1985) believe that panic attacks occur in 2–5 percent of the population.

A panic attack is a circumscribed period of intense fear or discomfort that has no obvious precipitant or reason for occurring. Maxmen (1986) found that the attacks typically last three to ten minutes and are never longer than thirty minutes, although other reports suggest that they may be of longer duration. Beck and Emery (1985) hypothesize that one of the following three fears is at the core of acute attacks of panic: fear of internal physical disaster (such as cancer), fear of a mental disorder, or fear of a social catastrophe or public disgrace.

According to the *DSM-III-R* (1987), the following criteria must be met for a diagnosis of panic disorder:

1. There are at least three panic attacks within a three-week period or there is a period of at least a month of persistent fear of another attack following a panic attack.
2. At least four of the following symptoms are present during at least one attack: shortness of breath or smothering, choking, accelerated heart rate or palpitations, chest pain or discomfort, sweating, faintness, dizziness or lightheadedness, nausea or abdominal discomfort, depersonalization or derealization, numbness or tingling sensations, flushes or chills, trembling or shaking, fear of dying, fear of loss of control or going crazy. These symptoms are similar to the somatic symptoms that accompany generalized anxiety disorder but tend to be even more pronounced in panic disorders (Anderson, Noyes, & Crowe, 1984).
3. During some of the attacks, at least four of the symptoms occur within ten minutes of the start of the first one.
4. There is no organic cause for the symptoms.

Panic disorder is often accompanied by phobic avoidance or agoraphobia (section 6.3.1). People with panic attacks associate the attack with the place where it occurred and avoid that place in an effort to avert future attacks. As the panic attacks occur in more and more places, people with this disorder tend to restrict their activities until, in severe cases, they refuse to leave home. The *DSM-III-R* recognizes the connection between panic disorder and phobic avoidance by establishing three subtypes of panic disorder: panic disorder with extensive phobic avoidance (agoraphobia), panic disorder without phobic avoidance, and limited symptom attacks with phobic avoidance (agoraphobia without panic attacks).

Alcohol abuse (section 7.1.1) and depression (Chapter Five) are other frequent concomitants of panic disorder. The alcohol seems to be used as a sort of self-medication, an effort to control the attacks.

Panic disorder is more likely to have a sudden onset (beginning with a severe panic attack) than is generalized anxiety disorder. Panic disorder tends to begin at a slightly later age than generalized anxiety disorder—most often in late adolescence or early adulthood. In about 50 percent of the cases, there is a clear precipitant, usually a stressful life event (Anderson, Noyes, & Crowe, 1984). However, the panic attacks tend to recur, even after the stressor is resolved (Gorman & Liebowitz, 1986). The attacks may vary in frequency from one or two a day to less than one a month and may occur when clients are asleep as well as while they are awake (Atwood & Chester, 1987). Anticipatory anxiety and phobic avoidance of potentially anxiety-provoking situations are common secondary symptoms following an initial panic attack.

Relevant Client Characteristics. Both panic disorder and its close relative, agoraphobia (section 6.3.1), seem to be familial disorders (Harris, Noyes, Crowe, & Chaudhry, 1983). The risk for the first-degree relatives of those with these disorders to develop an anxiety disorder themselves is twice as high as it is for the general population. The risk is particularly high for the female relatives; the male relatives of people with panic disorders seem to be at particular risk for alcohol abuse, often a mechanism for coping with anxiety. Breier, Charney, and Heninger (1985) suggest that panic disorder and depression may have a genetic relationship. People with a combination of major depression (section 5.1) and panic attacks seem particularly likely to have relatives with a variety of emotional disorders (Leckman, Weissman, Merikangas, Pauls, & Prusoff, 1983).

Raskin, Peeke, Dickman, and Pinsker (1982) compared the family backgrounds of people with panic disorder to those of people with a generalized anxiety disorder. They found that both groups had a similar high incidence of early separations and that separation was a common precipitant of both disorders. However, those with panic disorder had a higher incidence of grossly disturbed childhood environments (70 percent versus 30 percent) and were more likely to have experienced major depressive episodes and separation anxiety disorder as children (20–50 percent) (Gorman & Liebowitz, 1986).

Many of those with panic disorder seem to have been depressed, dependent, and passive, even before the panic attacks began. Relationship difficulties are often prominent (Barbaree & Marshall, 1985). Psychoanalytic theory attributes panic attacks to a failure of the ego-defenses to control unacceptable impulses or to threatened or experienced loss of support (Atwood & Chester, 1987). This disorder has also been attributed to cognitive and anxiety-provoking interpretations of environmental events and to avoidance or escape learning that has been conditioned. However, at present there is no conclusive explanation for the dynamics of panic disorder.

Relevant Therapist Variables. No information was located that describes specific qualities needed in therapists who treat panic disorders. Information provided in the "overview" section, as well as in the section on therapist variables recommended in the treatment of phobias (section 6.3), seems pertinent here.

Intervention Strategies. Treatment of panic attacks is, to a large extent, similar to treatment of generalized anxiety disorder (section 6.1). Both behavioral and cognitive interventions are paramount in amelioration of the disorder, and some combination of the two approaches seems to be the most powerful in treating panic disorder (Barlow & Waddell, 1985). Very limited research is available on the treatment of panic disorder; most of the literature considers it along with generalized anxiety disorder and agoraphobia.

The sections on those two disorders (sections 6.1 and 6.3.1) should be reviewed for more detailed information on treatment.

Barlow and colleagues (1984) demonstrated that eighteen sessions of electromyogram (EMG) biofeedback and relaxation effected significant improvement in the anxiety and panic of clients diagnosed as having panic disorder as well as clients with generalized anxiety disorder. Both groups responded equally well and continued to improve during the follow-up period, while a control group showed no improvement. Meyer (1983) recommends systematic relaxation training and yoga for treatment of panic disorder and suggests a group format to promote relaxation and support. Atwood and Chester (1987) provide general suggestions for treatment: neutralize anxiety, teach relaxation, promote accurate reality testing and a sense of control, and develop support systems.

Medication seems to be a more significant part of the treatment plan for panic disorder than it is for generalized anxiety. From a review of the literature, Breier, Charney, and Heninger (1985) concluded that tricyclic antidepressants, MAO inhibitors, and Alprazolam (Xanax) all seemed to have a positive effect in the treatment of panic attacks. Garakani, Zitrin, and Klein (1984) found that all their clients showed a cessation of panic attacks as well as overall improvement after two to three weeks of treatment with imipramine, a tricyclic antidepressant. Although those who stopped treatment in less than two months tended to relapse, those who continued on medication for five or more months generally showed marked and sustained improvement. Barbaree and Marshall (1985) found that antidepressant medication suppressed the panic attacks but did not diminish the anticipatory anxiety, while anxiolytics, as well as behavior therapy, reduced the overall anxiety but did not affect the panic attacks.

It is not surprising that medication would play a significant role in the treatment of this disorder, since indications are that panic disorder has a genetic/familial and biochemical component. However, some researchers believe that it is countertherapeutic to suppress the panic attacks pharamacologically. The research on that question is not yet clear (Barbaree & Marshall, 1985).

Despite the demonstrated effectiveness of medication in treating this disorder, medication should almost never be the sole modality of treatment. Clients with this disorder tend to have concerns, such as low self-esteem and interpersonal difficulties, that precede and underlie the panic attacks. Eliminating the panic attacks is not necessarily equivalent to treating the qualities that predisposed the client to a panic disorder. Chronicity and incomplete remission are significant concerns in the treatment of this disorder; psychotherapy, with or without medication, seems necessary to help effect those personal changes that are likely to prevent future episodes of anxiety disorders. Lifestyle changes, too, can contribute to relief of panic disorder. For example, caffeine is likely to increase the frequency and severity of panic attacks. Its use should be discouraged in clients with this disorder (Maxmen, 1986).

As with generalized anxiety disorder, a referral for a physical examination is recommended for clients with the somatic symptoms of panic disorder, to determine whether a physical ailment is present. Mitral valve prolapse, a cardiovascular disorder in which a heart valve does not close properly, for example, is found in 40-50 percent of clients with panic disorder (Maxmen, 1986). Clients often believe that their panic disorder is physiological in origin and so are likely to be receptive to the suggestion of a physical examination.

Prognosis. The prognosis for panic disorder seems less optimistic than it is for generalized anxiety disorder, although some cases remit spontaneously or with relatively brief treatment. In a study conducted by Breier, Charney, and Heninger (1985), only 15 percent of clients with panic disorder showed significant improvement, as opposed to 50-60 percent of those with generalized anxiety disorder. Maxmen (1986) arrived at a more positive conclusion; he found that only 20 percent of clients with panic attacks remained moderately impaired after treatment. As with generalized anxiety disorder, the prognosis seems fairly good for a relatively rapid response to treatment. However, a complete elimination of panic and anxiety symptoms will not be achieved in many cases.

6.3 Phobias

Description of Disorder. Phobias are characterized by two circumstances: (1) a persistent unwarranted or disproportionate fear of an actual or anticipated environmental stimulus (such as snakes or solitude or public speaking) and (2) a dysfunctional way of coping with that fear, resulting in impairment in social or occupational functioning (for example, refusing to leave the house). People with phobias typically are aware that their reactions are unreasonable, but they feel powerless to change them. Beck and Emery (1985) suggest that people react to these exaggerated and disabling fears with self-protective primal reactions (fight, flight, freeze, or faint). They believe that a core concern about acceptance, competence, or control generally underlies extreme, unwarranted fears. Thirty percent of those with phobias, particularly those with agoraphobia, also have panic attacks (Beck & Emery, 1985).

The *DSM-III-R* (1987) describes three categories of phobia, which will be discussed here: agoraphobia (section 6.3.1), simple phobia (section 6.3.2), and social phobia (section 6.3.3). The one-year prevalence of agoraphobia is 1.2 percent; of other phobias, 2.3 percent (Uhlenhuth, Balter, Mellinger, Cisin, & Clinthorne, 1983). Atwood and Chester (1987) report a prevalence figure of 7.7 percent but state that less than 1 percent of these phobias are severe. Phobias are more common in women (Fyer & Klein, 1986). The incidence of new phobias is highest in childhood and then decreases with maturity, although many have a chronic course. Most phobias develop suddenly; agoraphobia, however, tends to have a gradual onset. Phobias, particularly agoraphobia and social and animal phobias, seem to run in families, but whether that is the result of learning or of genetics is unclear (Kaplan & Sadock, 1985). People with phobias reduce their anxiety by avoiding the feared stimulus but simultaneously reinforce the fear through phobic avoidance. Consequently, phobias that have been present for longer than one year are unlikely to remit spontaneously (Maxmen, 1986).

Several explanations have been advanced to explain phobias. The psychoanalytic model suggests that they develop in situations that cause great internal conflict; to avoid the internal conflict, the phobic individual displaces or projects that conflict onto an external situation. Social learning theorists believe that phobias result from conditioning, stimulus generalization, and secondary gains (such as attention or the avoidance of challenging situations). Cognitive-behavioral theory views phobias as the result of illogical thinking and such cognitive distortions as overgeneralization, selective perception, and a negative view of the self and the world. Finally, biological theorists suggest that some people have a biological predisposition to avoid certain situations (Atwood & Chester, 1987). Clearly, there are many different explanations for phobias; and, as with panic attacks, a conclusive explanation has not yet been found.

Relevant Client Characteristics. Clients with phobias tend not to have the pessimism of most depressed clients and some of those with generalized anxiety disorder. They see hope for the future and do not condemn themselves for their shortcomings. Their worries and self-doubts are likely to have a specific rather than a general focus, and they do not pervade all aspects of these clients' lives. However, people with phobias tend to be apprehensive and tentative, fearing failure and exposure, particularly when approaching new experiences (Beck & Emery, 1985). They often feel vulnerable and have deficits in social skills and coping mechanisms.

Relevant Therapist Variables. The therapist treating phobias needs to be flexible; treatment may have to begin at the client's home or be scheduled at places that evoke the fear (such as elevators or doctors' offices). Contextual therapy is often used to accommodate to the client's limitations and provide *in vivo* exposure. The therapist needs to be comfortable taking charge of the therapy and providing structure, direction, and suggested assignments while developing a positive working relationship. Kaplan and Sadock (1985) report that encouragement, instruction, suggestion, exhortation, support, and modeling on the part of the therapist can all contribute to client improvement.

Intervention Strategies. Most of the approaches suggested for treating phobias seem to be derived from behavioral models of psychotherapy, employing a range of techniques designed to reduce anxiety while increasing clients' comfort with the feared stimulus. Most also are structured and directive, including procedures to quantify and measure the presenting problem and to monitor progress. For example, progress with clients with agoraphobia would be measured by their range of movement: how far from home they will travel and how anxious they become when away from home. An anxiety hierarchy might be established, beginning with "standing at the opened front door," and progressing through "walking down the driveway," "walking one block," "getting into the car," "driving around the block," "going into someone else's house," and so on, until the client can drive, shop, visit, and even go to a place of employment comfortably and independently.

Research suggests that the behavioral approaches are particularly effective in treating agoraphobia; other phobias seem to respond equally well to both cognitive and behavioral approaches (Hollon & Beck, 1986). However, Marks (1982) believes that *in vivo* desensitization—giving clients direct exposure to their feared objects or situations—is the most effective treatment ingredient for all phobias. In Marks's view, neither cognitive therapy nor relaxation is needed to enhance the effectiveness of *in vivo* desensitization in treating phobias. *In vivo* desensitization seems to work faster than imaginal desensitization (developing comfort with images of the feared object or situation) and seems to help an equal number of clients (Zitrin, Klein, Woerner, & Ross, 1983).

Others agree that exposure is the key element in relieving phobias (Lambert, 1982). Frances, Clarkin, and Perry (1984) suggest that *in vivo* desensitization can be conducted as effectively in group as in individual therapy, and the group setting offers the advantages of support and modeling. Although the number of participants for *in vivo* treatment does not seem critical, the duration of treatment does seem important; Wilson (1981) found, for example, that one two-hour exposure session was more effective than four half-hour sessions. Linden (1981) recommends sixty-minute exposure sessions.

A typical approach to treating phobias is Joseph Wolpe's Reciprocal Inhibition. In this approach, as described by Gutsch (1988), "a response inhibitory of anxiety is counterpoised with anxiety-evoking stimuli to weaken the bond between the stimuli and the anxiety" (p. 7). The treatment has two phases. During the assessment phase, clients learn a measure of anxiety, Subjective Units of Disturbance (SUDS), a rating of the anxiety and distress they are feeling, ranging from 0 (calm) to 100 (extreme anxiety).

Once they have mastered the use of relaxation to reduce their level of anxiety below 10, they are ready for the treatment phase. With therapist assistance, clients construct rank-ordered lists of anxiety-provoking situations and stimuli (anxiety hierarchies). Beginning with the least threatening, clients imagine the anxiety-evoking stimuli for five to seven seconds and then experience a ten- to twenty-second interval of relaxation. As clients acclimate to the lower-level anxieties, they deal with increasing levels of anxiety-provoking situations.

A related approach, Self-Directed Systematic Desensitization, is a client-directed model developed by Weinrach, Dawley, and General (1976). This three-stage model (building anxiety hierarchies, learning to relax, and rehearsing feared scenes while relaxed) also has proved helpful to clients with phobias. Common ingredients of approaches that are successful in treating phobias include (1) development of anxiety hierarchies; (2) relaxation; (3) imaginal or *in vivo* systematic desensitization, possibly via modeling; (4) encouragement of expression of feeling, sense of responsibility, and self-confidence; and (5) consideration of any family issues that might impinge on or be affected by the phobia.

Flooding or implosion (prolonged exposure to the feared object, until satiation and reduction of fears result) is another behavioral approach to the treatment of phobias. For example, a client with a fear of elevators might spend hours riding up and down a variety of elevators, under supervision of a therapist, until the fear is reduced to a manageable level. Marshall (1985) found that teaching clients to use coping self-statements enhanced the impact of the implosion. This approach seems less appealing than desensitization to clients and has a higher risk; exposure of insufficient duration can actually increase fears (Wilson, 1981). In addition, related emotional disorders or physical disorders (such as heart disease) may be worsened by the discomfort induced by implosion. Consequently, implosion seems to be used less than desensitization, and clients should be selected carefully for implosion.

Cognitive therapy is another frequently used approach to treatment of phobias, either alone or in combination with behavioral therapy. Cognitive therapy, behavioral therapy, and a combination of the two have all received support in the literature, although treatment combining behavioral and cognitive therapy does not seem to be more effective than either alone (Berman, Miller, & Massman, 1985).

According to the cognitive approach, inordinate fears are maintained by a mistaken or dysfunctional appraisal of a situation. The goal of therapy is to help clients understand, normalize, and manage their fears (Beck & Emery, 1985). Therapy is typically brief and time limited (five to twenty sessions, one to two hours each), structured, directive, and problem oriented. Socratic questions, designed to elucidate cognitive distortions and encourage testing of their validity, are the primary mode of intervention. Manageable homework assignments are a central feature of the treatment and are designed to help clients face their fears and test their cognitions. These assignments include such experiences as gradually increasing exposure to the feared stimulus, telling others about the fears in order to reduce shame, and assessing the veracity of beliefs. The principle of overcoming fears by confronting them is stressed.

Another approach to treating phobias was suggested by Bibring (1954), who took a psychoanalytic perspective. Viewing problems as the result of repression and displacement, Bibring emphasized the importance of uncovering the repressed material. An updated version of Bibring's model is Nexus Psychotherapy, developed by Gutsch and Ritenour (Gutsch, 1988). This is a cognitive approach that "drops the patient back into earlier periods of his or her life until there is reasonable assurance that the original onset of the anxiety condition has been located" (p. 15). Techniques such as biofeedback, imaginal and *in vivo* desensitization, extinction, and fading are used to eliminate the phobia. This type of approach has not received much support because the elimination of a phobia does not seem to promote symptom substitution (the development of another symptom). Regardless of the cause of a phobia, then, it is generally sufficient to focus treatment on symptom removal.

Klein, Zitrin, Woerner, and Ross (1983) compared supportive and behavior therapy in a twenty-six-week course of treatment of phobic clients. They concluded that supportive therapy that is dynamically oriented, nondirective, and empathic and that encourages ventilation is as successful as behavior therapy, largely because both function as motivational devices to increase exposure to feared stimuli.

Medication seems to contribute to the treatment of some phobias but not of others. For example, MAO inhibitors have been found useful in the treatment of severely depressed clients with phobias (Klerman, 1986). Xanax, with both antianxiety and antidepressant qualities, can be helpful on an as-needed basis (Kaplan & Sadock, 1985). However, phobias not accompanied by severe depression or panic attacks generally do not require a referral for medication (Maxmen, 1986).

Prognosis. In general, the prognosis for treatment of phobias is excellent. Linden (1981) reviewed a series of studies of treatment via *in vivo* exposure and found improvement rates ranging from 58 percent to 100 percent. Complete remission of symptoms seems unusual, however, and clients tend to remain mildly phobic but with much improved functioning following treatment.

The type of phobia seems unrelated to prognosis. Because the treatment relies heavily on homework assignments, client motivation seems to be a major determinant of outcome (Wilson, 1981). Family and social support is also an important ingredient of outcome; treatment may be undermined by family members who are invested in maintaining the client's illness. Improvement seems to be well maintained (Lambert, 1982), and symptom substitution is uncommon. Some clients, however, do report an increase in depression (Lambert, 1982) as well as marital difficulties following treatment—possibly because the reduction of specific fears has given them the freedom to take a broader view of their lives and acknowledge other troubling concerns.

6.3.1 Agoraphobia

Description of Disorder. Agoraphobia is the most common phobia presented by clients seeking help, representing 60 percent of all phobic disorders seen in therapy (Kaplan & Sadock, 1985); and it seems to be on the increase (Meyer, 1983). (Other phobias may actually be more common but are less disabling and are seen less frequently for treatment.) Agoraphobia is found in 1–5 percent of the population and may be found with or without panic attacks (*DSM-III-R*, 1987). If there are panic attacks, they developed an average of nine years before the agoraphobia (Thyer, 1987). Since panic attacks have been discussed earlier (in section 6.2), this section will focus specifically on agoraphobia.

Agoraphobia is defined as "the fear of being in places or situations from which escape might be difficult (or embarrassing) or in which help might not be available in the event of suddenly developing symptom(s) that could be incapacitating or extremely embarrassing" (*DSM-III-R*, 1987, p. 240). Clients express a fear of losing control and of having what is called a limited symptom attack, developing one or a few specific symptoms (such as the loss of bladder control or the onset of chest pains), although they may or may not have had these symptoms before. As a result of this fear, clients restrict their travel and may refuse to enter certain places without a companion. Places from which escape is difficult (such as cars, beauty shops, or supermarket check-out lines) are particularly frightening. In severe cases, the client may be housebound for many years. This disorder typically begins in the twenties or thirties, later than other phobias. Approximately 75 percent of agoraphobic clients are women (Barlow & Waddell, 1985).

Relevant Client Characteristics. Clients with agoraphobia often develop substance use problems (see section 7.1) in an effort to reduce their anxiety (Barlow & Waddell, 1985). Accompanying personality disorders—such as avoidant personality disorder (section 9.8) or dependent personality disorder (section 9.9)—may be reported. A history of generalized anxiety disorder (section 6.1) and of separation anxiety disorder and social isolation in childhood also is often reported, as is a family history of agoraphobia.

People with agoraphobia tend to be anxious, apprehensive, low in self-esteem, socially uncomfortable, vigilant, concerned about their health, and occasionally obsessive. Depression, anticipatory anxiety, and passivity also are common; these characteristics both exacerbate and are reactions to clients' circumscribed lives. Medical problems often are presented and may be viewed by clients as the reason for their restrictions.

People with agoraphobia may feel simultaneously dominated by and dependent on a significant person in their lives. For many clients, this is their "safe person," the one they feel most comfortable with; yet this person often contributes to the dynamics of their disorder. A wife may be her husband's safe person, for example, but may covertly reinforce his fears to prevent him from becoming involved with other women.

Agoraphobia is sometimes triggered by an increase in responsibility or a threatened interpersonal loss (Beck & Emery, 1985). Clients have sometimes been experiencing marital difficulties, and the agoraphobia may offer the secondary gain of cementing the marital relationship out of need. For some clients, symptoms are particularly severe just before and after menstruation (Barlow & Waddell, 1985) and may be worsened by caffeine consumption. Inventories such as the Beck Depression Inventory and the Mobility Inventory for Agoraphobia can be useful in assessing symptoms (Thyer, 1987).

Relevant Therapist Variables. In treating clients with agoraphobia, therapists must provide support, suggestions, and empathy. Praise and reinforcement can also help clients take risks. Comfort with contextual therapy is particularly important in the treatment of agoraphobia.

Intervention Strategies. Medication, particularly drugs designed to reduce anxiety, is a frequent component of the treatment of agoraphobia; and therapists working with agoraphobic clients probably will want to work collaboratively with a physician or a psychiatrist. According to one survey, 59 percent of clients with agoraphobia had received medication, while only 21 percent of those with other phobias were treated with drugs (Uhlenhuth, Balter, Mellinger, Cisin, & Clinthorne, 1983). There seems to be particular indication for medication when agoraphobia is accompanied by panic attacks (section 6.2).

Telch, Agras, Taylor, Roth, and Gallen (1985) found that treatment of agoraphobia combining imipramine and exposure to feared situations was more effective than either alone. Other studies have supported the effectiveness of this combined treatment, but the effect of behavior therapy seems to be more enduring than that of the medication (Klerman, 1986). Thyer (1987) recommends that medication not be used at the beginning of treatment; it can be included at a later stage—but only if the behavior therapy is not working.

Treatment effectiveness is generally high even without medication. Not surprisingly, exposure, in sessions and through homework assignments, is the key element in most treatment approaches to agoraphobia, although many variations have been developed. Clients should remain in the situation of exposure and repeat it frequently enough that anxiety is diminished (habituation). Fear of this procedure may precipitate noncompliance and premature termination of treatment; a carefully paced and supportive approach is indicated to counteract those behaviors.

Ost, Jerremalm, and Jansson (1984) found that both *in vivo* exposure (behavioral focus) and applied relaxation (physiological focus) yielded significant improvement after twelve individual sessions. Mavissakalian, Michelson, Greenwald, Kornblith, and Greenwald (1983) found that paradoxical intention (encouraging clients to welcome and exaggerate their fears) and self-statement training (encouraging clients to make positive statements about their coping abilities), both combined with *in vivo* practice, had a significant positive impact on clients after twelve ninety-minute small-group sessions. Ascher (1981) recommends paradoxical intention as an alternative to flooding, which has not received much support in the treatment of agoraphobia. Techniques such as hypnosis, progressive relaxation, and assertiveness training seem to enhance treatment. Logs of panic attacks and of exposure activities are also useful adjuncts to treatment. Treatment in a group setting can be helpful by reducing dependence on the safe person and by offering models and support.

Clearly, many models have been advanced that seem helpful in treating agoraphobia. In general, behavioral treatment seems superior to cognitive treatment (Millman, Huber, & Diggins, 1982), and analytic and psychodynamic techniques do not seem at all effective in treatment of this disorder (Kaplan & Sadock, 1985).

Several studies suggest that family dynamics should receive attention in the treatment of clients with agoraphobia. For example, Hafner (1984) found that husbands who had adapted to their wives' agoraphobia, as well as husbands who tended to be critical and unsupportive, had negative reactions to their wives' improvement; in contrast, husbands who were supportive and involved reported concurrent marital improvement. This finding suggests that some husbands may undermine treatment and may view their wives' improvement as a threat to the marriage.

Millman, Huber, and Diggins (1982) noted that relapse was associated with marriages in which the client was dependent and fearful of divorce or in which improvement in symptoms focused greater attention on the spouse's inadequacies. Barlow and Waddell (1985) found that home visits and conjoint or group therapy enhanced prognosis. Involving the spouses in treatment, then, as coaches or clients, seems to improve treatment effectiveness. The clients' other social and environmental patterns and relationships should also be considered when treatment is developed, and *in vivo* treatment will often be indicated.

Prognosis. Kaplan and Sadock (1985) concluded that nearly half of the clients with this disorder respond to behavior therapy well enough to resume leading relatively normal lives, although some relapse or do not reach optimal functioning (Barlow & Waddell, 1985). Relapses, however, seem easier to treat than the original disorder.

6.3.2 Simple Phobia

Description of Disorder. The *DSM-III-R* (1987) defines a simple phobia as "a persistent fear of a circumscribed stimulus (object or situation) other than fear of having a panic attack . . . or of humiliation or embarrassment in certain social situations" (p. 243). Common phobias involve fear of dogs, snakes, heights, thunderstorms, and flying. People with a simple phobia recognize the excessive or unreasonable nature of their reaction; nevertheless, the phobia interferes with their activities and relationships and may cause considerable distress.

Phobias in children are relatively common, and most remit spontaneously; if they persist into adulthood, however, they are unlikely to remit without treatment. Phobias may stem from a childhood fear that has not been outgrown and that has been entrenched by avoidance. Sixty percent of phobias result from a trauma; 20 percent, from vicarious experiences; and 10–20 percent, from frightening information (Thyer, 1987). Some clients present multiple phobias; but these phobias often have a common underlying fear, which can provide the focus of treatment.

Women seem more prone to develop phobias, particularly animal phobias. The average age of onset for phobias varies, depending on the particular phobia. Phobias of animals and blood tend to begin during childhood; claustrophobia, about age twenty; and phobias of heights, driving, and air travel usually begin in midlife (DSM-III-R, 1987; Lars-Göran, 1987). Little information is available on the prevalence of phobias, since most people with phobias do not seek treatment for them. Phobias do, however, seem to be quite common. As Meyer (1983) has stated, "most individuals have at least one mild, nondisabling phobia of one sort or another" (p. 115).

Relevant Client Characteristics. Very little information is available about common personality patterns in clients with simple phobias, probably because the disorder is so pervasive and tends to be linked more to experiences than to personality traits. However, clients with phobias tend to have parents with phobias, who perhaps communicated them to their children (Thyer, 1987).

When anticipating or confronting the feared object, clients are likely to become agitated and tearful and may experience physical symptoms of anxiety (such as shortness of breath or heart palpitations). A medical examination may be used as a safeguard in fragile or highly anxious clients, to be sure they can handle the temporarily increased stress caused by treatment.

Relevant Therapist Variables. Treatment of phobias is often anxiety provoking to clients. The therapist who treats such clients should be supportive and optimistic about the outcome of treatment and able to communicate acceptance and empathy while still encouraging clients to experience frightening situations.

Intervention Strategies. In vivo desensitization seems to be the treatment of choice for simple phobias. Combining that approach with relaxation and encouragement of a sense of mastery usually contributes to the effectiveness of the treatment (Emmelkamp, 1986). Other techniques that can enhance treatment include imaginal flooding, positive coping statements, paradoxical intention (focusing on the anticipatory anxiety), thought stopping, thought switching, success rehearsal, assertiveness training, reciprocal inhibition, hypnosis, progressive relaxation, cognitive restructuring, modeling by the therapist or another person, and reinforced practice.

Wilson (1981) found that most specific phobias respond to about six sessions of treatment using participant modeling or graduated *in vivo* exposure. Thyer (1987) emphasizes the importance of practice outside of the sessions and recommends eight hours of outside homework and practice for every two hours of therapy. Clients should be encouraged to keep a diary of their efforts, rating distress experienced and gradually attempting more anxiety-provoking situations while controlling anxiety. Inventories such as the Fear Survey Schedule, the Behavioral Avoidance Test, and the Fear Thermometer (Millman, Huber, & Diggins, 1982) can facilitate assessment of fears and of progress.

These behavioral and cognitive approaches seem effective with all simple phobias; specific approaches do not need to be developed for each phobia. If the phobia is such that *in vivo* exposure is impossible, imaginal desensitization is an effective substitute, possibly enhanced by photographs and films of the feared object. Bourque and Ladouceur (1980), treating clients with fear of heights, also found that they did not need to provide contextual therapy but that homework assignments involving heights were sufficient for effective treatment.

Cognitive therapy has not received much support as the primary mode of treatment for simple phobias (Biran & Wilson, 1981) although Smith, Glass, and Miller (1980) found that both cognitive and cognitive-behavioral therapy had a substantial impact (1.82 and 1.71 effect size) on the treatment of simple phobias—greater than that of behavioral (1.01), dynamic (0.88), and developmental (0.33) therapies. Certainly, cognitive interventions can enhance the impact of behavioral treatment of simple phobias, but most research emphasizes the importance of the behavioral interventions for symptom relief.

Medication is almost never indicated for treatment of this disorder, although some very anxious clients may benefit from medication (such as Xanax or benzodiazepine) taken prior to an exposure session, to increase their relaxation during the session. Education and an emphasis on willpower do not seem to have much effectiveness as treatments for phobias (Beck & Emery, 1985).

Prognosis. The prognosis is generally excellent for the treatment of simple phobias, with most clients (75–100 percent) showing significant improvement (Kocsis & Mann, 1986). In a number of cases, however, some residual apprehension associated with the feared object will remain (Linden, 1981). For most clients, the more anxiety they are willing to tolerate, the faster the progress (Thyer, 1987). Noncompliance may impede treatment effectiveness; if so, the presence of secondary gains should be investigated.

6.3.3 Social Phobia

Description of Disorder. Social phobia is the most recently defined phobia and the least studied (Fyer & Klein, 1986). It is defined by the *DSM-III-R* (1987) as a "persistent fear of one or more situations in which the person is exposed to possible scrutiny by others and fears that he or she may do something or act in a way that will be humiliating or embarrassing" (p. 241). Situations involving evaluation are likely to be particularly threatening. Actual or threatened exposure to such situations produces an immediate anxiety response, leading clients with social phobia to avoid social or occupational situations that are anxiety provoking. The phobia often focuses on one or more specific types of situations, such as speaking to groups, eating in public, using public rest rooms, writing while observed, and being interviewed. Clients with this relatively rare phobia are typically more incapacitated than clients with simple phobias but less incapacitated than those with agoraphobia.

George R. was typical of clients with social phobia. Although he had married (the daughter of a family friend) and secured stable employment, his life had been shaped by his phobia. At age thirty-five, he sought treatment because he realized that he was hurting his family. He had turned down several promotions because he would have to preside at meetings; he refused to attend events at his child's school because of his fear of meeting new people; and he and his wife had little social life outside of their immediate families.

Several explanations have been offered for social phobia, including social skills deficits, conditioned responses to painful experiences, emotional blocks, and deficits in perceptual or cognitive processing. The onset of this phobia tends to be in late adolescence or early adulthood (Speilberger, Pollans, & Worden, 1984). The phobia may quickly follow a humiliating incident, or it may have an insidious onset (Fyer & Klein, 1986). It is not clear whether social phobia is equally prevalent in both sexes or is more prevalent in men. For both men and women, social phobia tends to have a chronic course without treatment.

Relevant Client Characteristics. Social phobia or social inadequacy is associated with a broad range of accompanying disorders, particularly panic disorder (section 6.2), simple phobia (section 6.3.2), substance abuse (section 7.1), and depression (Chapter Five) (*DSM-III-R*, 1987), as well as with marital, occupational, and interpersonal difficulties. It sometimes leads to social isolation. However, it is usually not associated with severe pathology or incapacitation.

Clients with social phobia typically have deficits in social skills, but these deficits may take many forms. For example, some of these clients mask their anxiety with aggression, while others seem shy and insecure. They tend to have difficulty maintaining conversation and eye contact, may be awkward and stiff, and may talk too much about themselves.

Relevant Therapist Variables. Clients with social phobia may bring their interpersonal discomfort with them into the therapy room and feel threatened by what they perceive as the need to perform for the therapist. An important role for the therapist, then, is helping clients manage their initial anxiety enough so that they do not flee therapy before that process can begin.

Intervention Strategies. Treatment of social phobia is more complex than is treatment of a specific simple phobia. Although the repertoire of useful behavioral interventions remains the same for all phobic disorders, the treatment plan for social phobia will typically be a multifaceted one that both reduces fear and improves socialization (Millman, Huber, & Diggins, 1982). Linehan, Goldfried, and Goldfried (1979) found that a combination of skill acquisition, via behavior rehearsal, and cognitive restructuring was more effective than either technique alone. Modeling and assertiveness training also enhanced treatment, but behavioral rehearsal to improve social skills and reduce anxiety seemed to be the most important ingredient of treatment.

Social skills training may focus on communication skills, tone of voice, posture, eye contact, or other aspects of socialization, depending on the needs of the individual client. Some form of self-monitoring is also a valuable aspect of the treatment and may involve soliciting feedback from others, role playing, and rehearsal with video and audiotaping along with rating by self or others. Inventories such as the Rathus Assertiveness Schedule, the Miskimins Self-Goal-Other Discrepancy Scale, the Self-Consciousness Scale, and the Fear of Negative Evaluation Scale can facilitate the process of self-evaluation (Horvath, 1984). Homework assignments are almost always part of the treatment, to facilitate application of in-session learning.

Desensitization, stress management, Rational-Emotive Therapy, flooding, and cognitive restructuring may be included in the treatment but are generally not sufficient to relieve this disorder (Emmelkamp, 1986). Some researchers have been successful, however, in treating social phobia via a cognitive approach (Beck & Emery, 1985). Liebowitz, Gorman, Fyer, and Klein (1985) reviewed a group of studies on treatment of social phobia and concluded that the three principal forms of treatment—desensitization/exposure, social skills training, and cognitive restructuring—all seemed equally effective. Whatever approach to treatment is used, however, probably should be multifaceted and should be designed both to improve social skills and to reduce fears.

Although there is little research on the use of a group format for the treatment of social phobia, it seems to be a valuable approach for those clients who are not so incapacitated by their phobia as to prevent their participation in group therapy. The group interaction gives clients the opportunity to learn new skills from others, to experiment with new ways of relating in a safe setting, and to receive peer feedback.

Minor tranquilizers may help reduce severe anxiety enough so that clients can benefit from treatment. However, medication does not cure the social phobia and is rarely needed in treatment of this disorder.

Prognosis. Although the prognosis for effecting improvement in social phobia in a relatively small number of treatment sessions (five to twenty) is excellent, it is not as good as the prognosis for simple phobia (Maxmen, 1986). Most clients seem to remain somewhat awkward and uncomfortable in social situations. On a positive note, however, Butler, Cullington, Munby, Amies, and Gelder (1984) found that improvement was well maintained for at least six months.

6.4 Obsessive Compulsive Disorder

Description of Disorder. Obsessive compulsive disorder is a relatively rare disorder; its prevalence in the general population is probably approximately 0.05 percent (Shear & Frosch, 1986), although Thyer (1987) reports an incidence of 2 percent. This disorder seems equally common in both sexes (Kaplan & Sadock, 1985). It usually begins with an insidious onset in adolescence or early adulthood (Speilberger, Pollans, & Worden, 1984), although clients sometimes report a stressful event in the year prior to onset (Thyer, 1987). People diagnosed as having obsessive compulsive disorder have either obsessions (thoughts, images, or impulses) or compulsions (repetitive, purposeful behaviors performed in response to obsessions) or a combination of the two. These obsessions and/or compulsions are recurrent and distressing and interfere with daily activities and social and occupational functioning. People with this disorder realize that their thoughts or behaviors are excessive and unreasonable yet are unable to get rid of them. Typically, this chronic disorder will remain static or will worsen without treatment (Rapoport, 1989; Shear & Frosch, 1986).

Obsessions typically have some content that is unacceptable (immoral, illegal, disgusting, or embarrassing) to the client. The most common obsessions are repetitive thoughts of contamination, violence, doubts about religion and sexuality, and self-doubts (Meyer, 1983). The obsessions may have the quality of magical thinking (thinking = doing).

The compulsions or behavioral rituals are designed to prevent some discomfort or unwanted thought or event. According to Stern and Cobb (1978), most people with compulsions (65 percent) regard their rituals as absurd, but only 30 percent make great efforts to resist them. Common compulsions include handwashing, checking (for example, lights, appliances, or locks), counting, repeating, and touching in some ritualistic fashion. About half of those with compulsions have a mixture of three or more rituals, while about one-third confine their rituals to one place, usually the home (Mavissakalian & Barlow, 1981). According to Gutsch (1988), obsessions are thoughts that elicit anxiety, whereas compulsions are acts that reduce anxiety.

Many explanations have been advanced for this disorder. According to psychoanalytic theory, obsessive compulsive disorder represents an underlying conflict between repressed sexual and aggressive impulses and efforts to inhibit them. For example, compulsive cleanliness might be a way of warding off unacceptable sexual impulses. Social learning theory hypothesizes that the obsession or compulsion is a learned response, often acquired from parental models and reinforced because it reduced anxiety. Interpersonal theory suggests that the obsessions or compulsions reflect an underlying fear of humiliation or loss of control in a client with strong feelings of inadequacy. The ritual serves to maintain self-esteem (Atwood & Chester, 1987). Recent research suggests that the disorder has a biological and genetic basis (Rapoport, 1989).

Relevant Client Characteristics. Clients with obsessive compulsive disorder often have social anxiety and other related difficulties that warrant attention in treatment. In Stern and Cobb's (1978) survey, 71 percent of these clients stated that their compulsion was causing moderate to severe family distress. The rate of celibacy of people with obsessive compulsive disorder is unusually high (40 percent), particularly among the males (Shear & Frosch, 1986). Their families tend to have a high incidence of emotional disturbance.

Concurrent disorders with a high incidence in these clients include other anxiety disorders, depression (Chapter Five), substance abuse (section 7.1), obsessive compulsive personality disorder (section 9.10), and Tourette's disorder (a tic disorder). Schizophrenia and suicide are rare (Shear & Frosch, 1986), although thoughts of suicide are common. These clients tend to have rigid consciences and strong feelings of guilt and remorse. They feel driven and pressured, tend to ruminate and doubt themselves, are concerned with control, have a high need for reassurance, and tend to be indecisive and perfectionistic. They often are aggressive and avoid intimacy and affectionate feelings. This disorder seems more common among the affluent and intelligent, possibly because of a connection to capacity for abstract thinking (Atwood & Chester, 1987; Shear & Frosch, 1986).

These clients generally cooperate well with treatment and are motivated to complete homework assignments. However, hospitalization is occasionally necessary to initiate treatment in severe cases.

Relevant Therapist Variables. Atwood & Chester (1987) suggest that the ideal therapist for these clients should be supportive but firm and should be able to promote self-control, problem solving, expression of feelings, and anxiety reduction. Many people with obsessive compulsive disorder are highly embarrassed by their symptoms and have become skilled at concealing them from others. Establishing a therapeutic relationship may, therefore, involve overcoming the clients' resistance to disclosure of the symptoms.

Intervention Strategies. The treatment picture for obsessive compulsive disorder is at a transition point. Until recently, research on available medication and therapy has been ambiguous. Some techniques had a higher probability of being effective than others, but no approaches had demonstrated consistent effectiveness in treating this disorder. However, preliminary studies have shown that clomipramine (Anafranil), a tricyclic antidepressant, has a high probability of effectiveness in treating this disorder via an antiobsessiveness effect (Mavissakalian, Turner, Michelson, & Jacob, 1985; Rapoport, 1989). Use of this drug and related medications in the future, then, will probably improve the prospects for treating this disorder successfully. If severe depression or anxiety is present, other medications also may be used to pave the way for treatment.

The literature on the use of psychotherapy to treat obsessive compulsive disorder suggests that the behavioral model has the most support, while the cognitive model has received little support (Hollon & Beck, 1986; Rapoport, 1989). ECT, psychoanalytically oriented psychotherapy, aversion therapy, and paradoxical intention have all been used to treat this disorder, but their effectiveness has not been clearly demonstrated (Lambert, 1982).

Foa and Steketee (1979) suggest that, as a general principle of treatment, compulsions should be blocked and obsessions should be treated by prolonged exposure. The combination of exposure to anxiety and response prevention seems to be particularly useful in treating compulsions (Kocsis & Mann, 1986). This technique involves exposing clients to anxiety-provoking stimuli, typically for one to two hours, while preventing the ritualistic behaviors they would usually employ to reduce anxiety. Prolonged exposure to this situation often reduces both the anxiety and the compulsive behavior (Lambert, 1982). As with treatment of most anxiety disorders, *in vivo* exposure seems more effective than imaginal desensitization (Wilson, 1981), although Steketee, Foa, and Grayson (1982) found imaginal exposure an effective ingredient in addition to *in vivo* exposure and response prevention for clients who feared future catastrophes.

Therapy is typically of relatively brief duration (ten to twenty-five sessions). However, developing an effective treatment plan for this disorder can be challenging and requires a careful gathering of information on obsessions and rituals, their eliciting stimuli, their frequency and duration, and moderating environmental cues (Beech & Vaughn, 1978). Symptom substitution can occur if the symptom is not appropriately addressed (Queiraz, Motta, Madi, Sossai, & Boren, 1981). The Maudsley Obsessive-Compulsive Inventory, the Leyton Obsessional Inventory, or the Lynnfield Obsessional-Compulsive Questionnaire can be useful in assessment (Steketee & Foa, 1985). Thyer (1987) has recommended long, frequent sessions and frequent assessment of anxiety to guide treatment.

Some clients respond well to various alternate methods of reducing anxiety (for example, assertiveness, attention focusing or distracting, progressive relaxation, planned worrying, coping skills, cognitive rehearsal, imagery of the best or worst that can happen). The focus of treatment, then, should be on the source as well as the symptoms of the anxiety. Homework assignments, possibly aided by a close friend or family member, can also accelerate progress (Emmelkamp, 1986). Other techniques that have been used with some success include shaping, pacing, exaggerating, and scheduling the rituals; paradoxical intention, to intensify the obsession; modeling; covert sensitization (imagining both the compulsion and a consequent punishment); and rewarding a reduction in rituals. Multiple modes of treatment seem more effective than single-focus treatments (Foa, Steketee, Grayson, & Doppelt, 1982; Paquin, 1979).

Treatment of obsessions without accompanying compulsions seems more difficult (Lambert, 1982). Thought stopping, aversive conditioning, and thought satiation via fantasy or via repeated writing, hearing, or verbalizing the obsessions are techniques that have sometimes been effective in treating obsessions. The tedium of repetition can supplant the anxiety.

The prevalent negative impact of this disorder on social adjustment and family life suggests that family therapy might be a useful part of the treatment plan. Group therapy also might be helpful; it can improve socialization and provide needed feedback.

Prognosis. Shear and Frosch (1986) call obsessive compulsive disorders "notoriously difficult to treat" (p. 360). Flare-ups and incomplete remissions are common (Thyer, 1987). Postsession rituals often undo the impact of treatment and must be prevented. Wilson (1981) reports a treatment failure rate of 10–30 percent. At the same time, Christensen, Hadzi-Pavlovic, Andrews, and Mattick (1987), who conducted a meta-analysis of outcome studies on this disorder, concluded that antidepressant medication and psychotherapy have "produced appreciable changes in obsessive-compulsive . . . symptoms" (p. 701).

Foa and colleagues (1983) found that low anxiety and early age of onset and treatment were related to positive outcome, while prominent depression was related to a negative outcome. Mavissakalian and Barlow (1981), however, found that outcome was better for clients with depression and for those who did not regard their fears as realistic. According to Kaplan and Sadock's (1985) findings, outcome was better with shorter duration of symptoms, the presence of an identifiable precipitant, and a positive current environment and adjustment. Maxmen (1986) observed that treatment was more likely to be effective for clients with mild symptoms. Emmelkamp (1986) found that treatment results were generally well maintained, although Steketee and Foa (1985) report a 20 percent relapse rate.

At present, it seems that a substantial number of clients with obsessive compulsive disorder do respond positively to treatment, particularly if symptoms are not deeply entrenched or very pervasive. However, prognosis for treatment of this disorder should become even better as new information becomes available on the impact of combined treatment, behavior therapy and medication, for this disorder.

6.5 Post-Traumatic Stress Disorder

Description of Disorder. Post-traumatic stress disorder (PTSD) is characterized by an extreme and recurring reaction to a traumatic stressor (for example, rape, combat experience, or involvement in the experience or aftermath of a serious accident). Reactions include recurrent recollections of the event, upsetting dreams, severe distress at reminders of the event, and/or a sense of reliving the experience. These symptoms persist for more than a month and are accompanied by efforts to avoid and suppress all reminders of the event and a general withdrawal and decrease in responsiveness. Persistent symptoms of increased arousal (for example, sleeping difficulties, irritability, trouble concentrating, hypervigilance) also are present. This disorder produces anxiety symptoms in all systems—physical, affective, cognitive, and behavioral (Atwood & Chester, 1987). Clients often feel that their previous ways of coping and making sense of the world no longer work, and they are left confused and without direction.

Although people with PTSD may seem to recover from the immediate impact of the trauma, they are often left with residual and underlying symptoms (such as mistrust and avoidance of close relationships) that may appear long after the trauma. For example, children who are sexually abused sometimes repress the experience for many years; active symptoms (such as nightmares or recurrent recollections of the trauma) only surface in adulthood when they encounter upsetting sexual or interpersonal situations, although their self-images and socialization probably have been adversely affected by the abuse for many years. If the onset of the disorder occurs at least six months after the trauma, the disorder is viewed as having a delayed onset (*DSM-III-R*, 1987).

The impact of a trauma seems to be particularly severe and longlasting when it has a human cause; in other words, a rape is likely to be more disturbing than a tornado. The impact also seems worse if there was no warning of the event, if the clients had no prior experience with such events (Atwood & Chester, 1987), and if the clients are perceived by some as deserving their fate (for example, AIDS victims). If the trauma involved others who did not survive, as in war or an accident, the survivor often experiences guilt along with the symptoms of PTSD. Suicidal ideation, somatization, and substance abuse often develop along with PTSD as ways to cope with the distress. Depression, anxiety, and rage may also accompany the disorder. Future stressors become inordinately troubling, and clients feel as though they have little control over their lives. Some clients even seem to undergo a major personality change following a trauma (Horowitz, Marmar, Krupnick, Wilner, Kaltreider, & Wallerstein, 1984). Information is not available on the prevalence of PTSD or its sex ratio. Onset may occur at any age.

Relevant Client Characteristics. Young white Protestant females living alone in lower socioeconomic circumstances with few support systems seem to be particularly prone to PTSD (Atwood & Chester, 1987). The aged, who often have few support systems and a limited sense of control, are also more prone to this disorder (Kaplan & Sadock, 1985). Clients with prior emotional disorders are more likely to develop PTSD following traumatic events. A four-year follow-up of children involved in a school bus kidnapping (in Chowchilla, California) found that all had some post-traumatic symptoms but that the severity of the symptom was related to "prior vulnerabilities, family pathology, and community bonding" (p. 1543). An external locus of control may also increase the likelihood of PTSD (Frye & Stockton, 1982). Clients' functioning prior to a trauma, then, seems to be related to their likelihood of developing PTSD after a trauma.

Relevant Therapist Variables. Therapists treating clients with PTSD must be extremely supportive. At the same time, they must not reinforce the clients' sense of being victims. If the trauma occurred many years prior to treatment, therapy may be a slow process of gradually building trust and helping clients to access troubling memories.

Intervention Strategies. PTSD should be treated as soon as possible—even preventively, before symptoms emerge, for clients who have undergone obvious traumas. Most clients with this disorder respond well to relatively brief treatment. Maxmen (1986) found that five to sixteen weeks of treatment is usually sufficient.

Treatment should not exacerbate anxiety and, if possible, should take place in a setting that is familiar and comfortable. Treatment usually should follow a crisis intervention model, particularly if the trauma was relatively recent, avoiding reinforcement of the sick role and helping clients resume their prior lifestyle as quickly as possible (Meyer, 1983). Some therapists have found that abreaction or reexperiencing the feelings associated with the trauma has been helpful, particularly for chronic or severe cases, but this technique should be used with great care (Kaplan & Sadock, 1985). Although no clear preferred model of treatment for this disorder emerges from the literature, an eclectic mix of psychodynamic, cognitive, and behavioral approaches with a heavy dose of support seems most useful. Mild or acute cases may respond well to support alone (Kaplan & Sadock, 1985).

Atwood and Chester (1987) recommend a two-part model of treatment: (1) promote expression of feelings and control over memories (to dilute pain) and (2) provide acceptance and reassurance (to restore self-concept and previous level of functioning). Other important ingredients of treatment include education on the nature of PTSD, encouragement of assertiveness and mastery experiences, testing and modification of dysfunctional cognitions, and stress management (for example, through relaxation or imagery). A similar model with ten steps has been recommended by Maxmen (1986): (1) history taking, (2) therapist provides realistic appraisal of the event and the client's reactions, (3) themes identified, (4) defenses interpreted (and adaptive defenses reinforced), (5) confrontation of fears and memories encouraged, (6) termination is begun, (7) remaining conflicts and issues clarified, (8) gains summarized, (9) possible future concerns considered, (10) termination.

Developing support systems is an important ingredient in the treatment of PTSD. For this reason, support groups composed of people who have had similar experiences can be very helpful. That seems to have become the primary mode of treatment for Vietnam veterans, for example. If the symptoms of PTSD have been present for an extended period of time, the disorder has probably had a negative impact on clients' social and occupational pursuits and family relationships, and therapy may need to take a broad focus. Vietnam veterans with PTSD, for example, were found to have more difficulty with self-disclosure and expressiveness to their partners, physical aggressiveness toward their partners, and overall adjustment than veterans without PTSD (Carroll, Rueger, Foy, & Donahoe, 1985). Therapy with the troubled veterans, then, would need to go beyond an exploration of their traumatic war experiences and promote improvement in their communication and social skills and their trust of others.

Medication is generally not indicated for PTSD. However, MAO inhibitors may enhance the impact of therapy if therapy alone does not seem to be working (Kocsis & Mann, 1986).

Prognosis. The prognosis for treatment of PTSD is excellent, especially for clients with good functioning prior to the trauma who have strong belief systems and who receive treatment fairly soon after the trauma. However, the prognosis for treatment of delayed-onset PTSD does not seem to be as good as the prognosis for rapid onset, because the delayed-onset type is more often accompanied by another psychological disorder (such as depression or substance abuse) (Maxmen, 1986). Although it seems almost impossible to erase clients' vivid memories of their traumatic experiences, most can readily be helped to resume or even improve upon their former levels of functioning. Relapses are not uncommon but may be averted through an extended follow-up.

Summary of Treatment Recommendations

This chapter has focused on five anxiety disorders: generalized anxiety disorder, panic disorder, phobias (agoraphobia, simple phobia, and social phobia), obsessive compulsive disorder, and post-traumatic stress disorder. The following summary lists the treatment recommendations for these disorders according to the framework of the client map.

Diagnoses. Anxiety disorders (generalized anxiety disorder; panic disorder; phobias—namely agoraphobia, simple phobia, or social phobia; obsessive compulsive disorder; post-traumatic stress disorder)

Objectives. Reduce anxiety and related behavioral and somatic symptoms of disorder; improve stress management, socialization skills, sense of mastery

Assessments. Physical examination often indicated to rule out physical disorder; measures of anxiety or fear

Clinician. Patient, encouraging, supportive but firm, flexible, concerned but not controlling, calming and reassuring, comfortable with a broad range of behavioral and cognitive interventions

Location. Generally outpatient, sometimes contextual

Interventions. Cognitive-behavioral and behavior therapy (especially *in vivo* desensitization), anxiety management training, stress inoculation, problem solving

Emphasis. Usually present oriented, moderately directive, highly supportive, primarily behavioral with a secondary cognitive emphasis

Nature. Individual or group therapy, depending on nature of disorder, with ancillary family therapy as needed

Timing. Typically, weekly treatment of moderate duration, moderate pacing; contextual treatment may necessitate flexible scheduling

Medication. May supplement treatment in some forms of anxiety disorder, especially panic and obsessive compulsive disorders, but otherwise not usually needed unless anxiety is disabling

Adjunct services. Relaxation, hypnotherapy, biofeedback, meditation, and other approaches to stress management; social skills and assertiveness training

Prognosis. Varies, depending on specific disorder, but generally good for amelioration of symptoms

Client Map of Sharon A.

This chapter began with a description of Sharon A., a twenty-five-year-old woman who developed symptoms of strong anxiety after relocating to a new city, where she had few support systems and considerable professional responsibility. The diagnosis and treatment plan for Sharon is presented below according to the client map.

Diagnosis. Axis I: 300.02—Generalized anxiety disorder, moderate severity

Axis II: V71.09—No diagnosis or condition on Axis II

Axis III: Fatigue, dizziness, other physical complaints

Axis IV: Psychosocial stressors: relocation away from friends and family, increased job responsibility. Severity: 3—moderate

Axis V: Current Global Assessment of Functioning: 60; highest GAF past year: 75

Objectives. (1) Reduce level of anxiety and accompanying somatic symptoms

(2) Increase level of self-confidence

(3) Increase productivity at work

(4) Increase social and leisure activities

(5) Decide whether to request a transfer back to the West Coast

(6) Clarify career and personal goals

Assessment. Sharon was referred to a physician for a checkup; findings were negative. The use of a diary and checklist as well as inventories (for example, the State-Trait Anxiety Inventory) were used to provide a baseline measure of Sharon's current feelings and activities.

Clinician. Sharon requested and was given a female therapist. Therapist selected was supportive and encouraging yet skilled at empowering and encouraging clients.

Location. Sharon seemed sufficiently motivated and in control for outpatient therapy.

Interventions. Behavioral interventions were the focus of treatment. Sharon was advised to keep daily records of her anxiety levels; her sense of self-confidence; and business and social activities she had undertaken, as well as cognitions that accompanied those activities. She was helped to identify pleasurable and comfortable leisure activities (such as tennis practice and a walk in the park) and to gradually include more of those activities in her schedule. To facilitate realistic goal setting, she also was helped to develop a plan and schedule for her work. Relaxation strategies that appealed to her were identified and taught for use during times of stress. After some reduction of anxiety, instruction in the development of decision-making and social skills was included in the treatment plan.

Cognitive approaches were combined with the behavioral. In the cognitive area, Sharon expressed quite a few dysfunctional thoughts, for example: "I can't possibly succeed without the support of my friends and family on the West Coast. People in Boston are cold and sophisticated. . . . I'll never be able to make friends here. To succeed at this job, I will have to give up my hopes of marriage and children, since no man would be interested in a hard-working businesswoman. My mother was right; I'm not smart enough to handle this job." At the beginning of treatment, therefore, Sharon was helped to identify thoughts and situations that promoted anxiety and then to examine and dispute those thoughts. Imagery, thought stopping, and other techniques were used to facilitate the development of more positive thoughts.

Emphasis. Sharon felt confused, overwhelmed, and hopeless at the start of treatment. A moderately directive approach was necessary to mobilize her energy and give structure and direction to the treatment. However, she had many strengths and was encouraged to collaborate increasingly with the therapist as her symptoms abated.

A moderately supportive approach was indicated to bolster self-esteem and avoid adding more threat to what the client was already experiencing. However, the dynamics of Sharon's disorder suggested that it would eventually be beneficial for her to look at her patterns, especially in interpersonal relationships, and attempt to effect some long-range changes.

Consistent with the research on the treatment of anxiety disorders, the primary focus of treatment was on cognitive and behavioral areas where there was evident dysfunction. Attention would also be paid to the affective area as needed.

Nature. Individual therapy was the initial mode of treatment. Sharon's anxiety and social discomfort would probably have prevented her from deriving much benefit from group therapy and might have even caused her to terminate treatment. Once symptoms had lessened, however, she might benefit from the opportunity to examine and practice her interpersonal skills in a supportive therapy group.

Timing. Sharon initially was seen twice a week, to facilitate rapid reduction of anxiety. After that, weekly sessions for three to six months were anticipated. Because Sharon's prior level of functioning had been fairly good, and because she was in considerable pain, therapy moved at a moderately rapid pace.

Medication. Medication did not seem indicated, since Sharon was functioning relatively well despite her symptoms.

Adjunct services. Adjunct services such as supportive social groups and informal classes were suggested to enhance the treatment and promote behavioral change. Career counseling was also anticipated.

Prognosis. The prognosis for significant symptom reduction seemed good. There was a clear environmental precipitant. Client had relatively good coping skills and previous adjustment. However, longstanding mild anxiety accompanied by low self-esteem would also need attention. Although the prognosis for effecting change in those longstanding qualities was optimistic, it was not as good as the prognosis for changing the more recent and severe symptoms.

The next chapter will focus on disorders of behavior and impulse control. With those disorders, as with anxiety disorders, behavioral interventions usually are the key to effective treatment.

Recommended Readings

Barlow, D. H., Cohen, A. S., Waddell, M. T., Vermilyea, B. B., Klosko, J. S., Blanchard, E. B., & DiNardo, P. A. (1984). Panic and generalized anxiety disorders: Nature and treatment. *Behavior Therapy, 15,* 431–449.

Beck, A. T., & Emery, G. (1985). *Anxiety disorders and phobias.* New York: Basic Books.

Cooper, A. M., Frances, A. J., & Sacks, M. H. (Eds.). (1986). *The personality disorders and neuroses.* Philadelphia: Lippincott.

Gutsch, K. U. (1988). *Psychotherapeutic approaches to specific DSM-III-R categories.* Springfield, IL: Thomas.

Meichenbaum, D. H., & Deffenbacher, J. L. (1988). Stress inoculation training. *The Counseling Psychologist, 16,* 69–90.

Rapoport, J. L. (1989). *The boy who couldn't stop washing.* New York: Dutton.

Thyer, B. A. (1987). *Treating anxiety disorders.* Newbury Park, CA: Sage.

Chapter Seven

Disorders
of Behavior
and Impulse
Control

Case Study: George W.

George W., a thirty-six-year-old white male, was referred for therapy by the courts. Following his third conviction for driving while intoxicated, George had been sentenced to a six-month stay in a work-release program. Therapy was required as part of his participation in that program.

George began using alcohol when he was fourteen years old and had been drinking excessively since that time. His father, his maternal grandfather, and two of his three brothers all abused alcohol. George had been married to his second wife for two years and had a one-year-old child. His first marriage had ended in divorce four years earlier, partly because his wife would no longer tolerate George's drinking. He had maintained contact with his two children from that marriage.

George was employed as a supervisor for a construction firm. He had been with the same company for over ten years and had a good work record. He consumed little alcohol during the day, but on most evenings he would begin drinking beer as soon as he returned home from work, and he also drank on most weekends. He had tried to stop drinking on his own repeatedly and had been alcohol free for six months when he married his present wife. However, he stated that financial difficulties associated with the birth of their child led him to resume drinking. George reported frequent weekend episodes of binge drinking and occasional blackouts. He said that his wife was unhappy about his drinking and expressed disappointment that they never went out; but since she was always absorbed in caring for the baby, he did not believe that going out mattered any more to her than it did to him.

George reported some mild depression and stated that he was very shy and never felt comfortable around people. Alcohol had helped him feel more self-confident, so that he was able to establish relationships with a group of male peers who also drank to excess. The possibility of an underlying avoidant personality disorder was considered. Otherwise, George's difficulties all seemed related to his alcohol use.

Overview of Disorders of Behavior and Impulse Control

Description of Disorder. George is suffering from a disorder of behavior and impulse control, alcohol dependence. He has had this disorder for over twenty years and, as is common for people with this disorder, reports a family history of alcohol abuse. George also presents other concerns, including marital and social difficulties. However, these are so closely connected to his substance abuse that they cannot be understood or treated except in the context of the alcohol abuse. For many people with disorders of behavior and impulse control, the disorder affects most if not all areas of their lives, and they present with impairment in interpersonal, occupational, and other areas. Their behavioral disorder is, however, at the heart of their difficulties and is the focus of treatment.

This chapter will focus on various behavioral disorders—disorders characterized by excessive behavior (as in drug and alcohol abuse), insufficient behavior (anorexia nervosa), inappropriate behavior (paraphilias), and unrewarding behavior (sexual dysfunctions). These disorders can cause impairment in social and occupational functioning and can even be life threatening. The following categories of disorder will be discussed in this chapter: substance use disorders (alcohol and drug abuse), eating disorders (anorexia nervosa and bulimia nervosa), sexual disorders (paraphilias—such as pedophilia or exhibitionism—and sexual dysfunctions), other impulse control disorders (such as pathological gambling, intermittent explosive disorder, or pyromania), and sleep disorders.

The prevalence of the behavioral disorders varies considerably. Some of these disorders, such as pyromania and fetishism, are not often encountered by the therapist; others, such as drug and alcohol abuse, are among the most frequently presented concerns. Eating disorders and sexual dysfunctions are often encountered by therapists in certain settings (such as college counseling centers or family therapy settings).

The primary symptom of all these disorders is, of course, the undesirable behavior. However, because many of these disorders typically begin in adolescence and persist and often worsen without treatment, people with these concerns often have serious developmental deficits. Instead of going through the normal developmental experiences of adolescence and early adulthood, people with behavioral disorders often focus their lives around the dysfunctional behavior. When they finally are helped to stop abusing substances or to resume healthy eating, it often becomes clear that they have failed to develop age-appropriate maturity and self-confidence, and that becomes an important secondary focus of treatment.

In addition, although anxious or depressed people often can conceal their disorders from their families, friends, and colleagues, the behavioral disorders are difficult to hide because of their external manifestations (such as intoxication or weight loss). Some of these disorders are illegal (for example, pyromania or pedophilia), while others (such as the sexual dysfunctions) involve a partner. For many reasons, then, the reputations, relationships, career development, and self-images of people with these disorders can be damaged. The clients' lifestyles and their behavioral disorders are interconnected, with each having an impact on the other.

The time of onset of these disorders varies, depending on the specific disorder. The most common ones, substance use disorders and eating disorders, usually begin during the adolescent years. Course and duration also vary. Some people may respond to encouragement or exhortation in their environment to control their behavioral difficulties and may curtail or even eliminate their dysfunctional behaviors without therapy. However, such a response is unusual, and it is even less common for these disorders to remit spontaneously. Without treatment, these disorders tend to become deeply entrenched and often worsen.

Relevant Client Characteristics. People who present with disorders of behavior and impulse control typically come from dysfunctional families, where they were not afforded models of positive relationships. Some of these disorders, such as alcohol abuse, have a strong genetic component; others, such as anorexia nervosa, often stem from a characteristic pattern of family interactions and expectations that predisposes the client to develop a particular set of symptoms.

Specific information on personality patterns characterizing people with the disorders in this chapter will be considered in subsequent sections. Contrary to common belief, people with behavioral disorders do not necessarily have other underlying personality or emotional disorders. In some instances, preexisting conditions may have contributed to the development of the behavioral disorder, and some people may develop emotional disorders secondary to their behavioral concerns; but many people—particularly those with sexual dysfunctions and sleep disorders—do not have any other diagnoses accompanying the behavioral disorder.

Relevant Therapist Variables. Therapists treating behavioral disorders have diverse educational and experiential backgrounds. Some have doctoral or master's degrees, while others have associate degrees and certificates in counseling chemically dependent clients. These paraprofessionals usually have had personal experience with the behavioral difficulties that are presented by their clients. Paraprofessional counselors are especially prevalent and helpful in the treatment of clients with drug and alcohol problems. The establishment of a sound collaborative relationship between professional and paraprofessional therapists is an important element in treating these clients.

Therapists working with these clients should be comfortable conducting group and individual sessions and incorporating self-help groups into their treatment plans. Typically, therapists who treat behavioral disorders are called on to coordinate a multifaceted treatment plan. These therapists need to have not only the usual expertise in relationship building and strategies of psychotherapy; they also need to have a good grasp of personal and career development and family dynamics, in order to assess and treat the overall developmental problems related to the behavioral disorder. Therapists also should have a good understanding of the nature of the particular disorder they are treating, since education is typically an important component of the treatment of behavioral disorders. In addition, the therapists should be comfortable with a style of therapy that is directive and structured, that involves goal setting and follow-up, but that is, at the same time, supportive and empathic.

Intervention Strategies. Treatment of disorders of behavior and impulse control not surprisingly emphasizes behavioral interventions such as behavioral counts and checklists; goal setting; learning and mastery of new behaviors; reduction or elimination of dysfunctional behaviors; reinforcement, reward, and punishment; and homework assignments. Information and education are almost always a part of treatment. Clients are taught about the negative impact of their behaviors on their physical and emotional adjustment and learn new and more effective behaviors to replace the old ones.

Group therapy is at least as important a mode of treatment for these disorders as is individual therapy; clients with behavioral disorders seem to benefit from receiving therapy along with others who have experienced similar difficulties, learning from their successes and failures and receiving feedback and encouragement from the group. Group therapy also enables them to increase their social interest and involvement and work on their social skills. It facilitates reality testing and challenging of defenses, provides a point of comparison, promotes self-understanding and acceptance, and is often less threatening than individual therapy. Group therapy is particularly useful in the early stages of treatment, when motivation may be uncertain, but it does not seem indicated for very fragile or disturbed clients.

Self-help peer groups, such as Narcotics Anonymous or Alcoholics Anonymous, often are included in a multifaceted treatment plan for disorders of behavior and impulse control.

Family therapy, too, is a salient component of the treatment of these disorders. The clients' behavioral problems have typically had an adverse impact on their family relationships, and help may be needed there. Family members often need to be given information about the behavioral disorder and shown how to help the clients maintain desired behavioral changes. In addition, the family members are often, themselves, part of a pathological pattern that perpetuates the behavior (for example, the enabling spouse of an alcoholic client or the overwhelmed wife who does not know how to cope with her husband's physical abuse). When family members are helped to change patterns that reinforce and provide secondary gains for the negative behavior, the likelihood of the clients' improvement is increased and the family members also benefit. Multiple family therapy groups (groups composed of a number of families exposed to the same behavioral problem) can provide a useful forum in which families can interact, receive support, and learn from one another.

Medication is almost never the primary mode of treatment for behavioral disorders. However, it can occasionally contribute to the treatment process. For example, Antabuse may help an alcohol-abusing client remain alcohol free; and antidepressant medication may reduce the depression in a bulimic client, so that she is more able to benefit from treatment for her eating disorder.

Many behavioral disorders (for example, substance use disorders or eating disorders) are physically harmful and even life threatening. Other disorders that seem to be behavioral in origin (for example, sexual dysfunction or intermittent explosive disorder) may have a physiological cause. For both of these reasons, it is usually advisable to refer clients with most of the disorders considered in this chapter for a physical examination. Information from that examination can be useful in determining the most appropriate treatment plan for the disorder.

Therapy for behavioral disorders, then, will most likely:

Be high in directiveness
Be moderate in supportiveness, with some attention paid to
    past patterns and difficulties
Emphasize behavioral interventions

Focus on homogeneous group therapy and include individual, family, and self-help groups as appropriate

Make minimal use of medication but probably include a physical examination

Have a fairly rapid pace and brief to medium duration of treatment

Be provided in an outpatient setting, although a period of initial hospitalization may be needed for some of the life-threatening and physically damaging disorders (substance use and eating disorders)

Prognosis. The prognosis for treatment of the behavioral disorders varies, depending on the nature of the disorder and the motivation and lifestyle of the client. Perhaps the greatest barrier to treatment is the inherently gratifying nature of most of these disorders. Although the eating and substance use disorders, for example, often cause physical, social, and possibly occupational difficulties for clients with those disorders, the rewards of being thin or being intoxicated are very powerful and difficult to counteract in therapy. Relapses and decrements in gains made through therapy are common. Therefore, even though the basic treatment program may be relatively brief, extended aftercare via self-help groups, drug testing, medical examinations, homework assignments, and family or individual therapy usually is indicated to consolidate gains, prevent relapse, and help clients cope effectively if relapses do occur. With appropriate treatment, follow-up, and client motivation, the prognosis is good for significant improvement if not complete remission of behavioral symptoms.

7.1 Psychoactive Substance Use Disorders

Description of Disorder. Psychoactive substance use disorders, according to the *DSM-III-R* (1987), deal with "symptoms and maladaptive behavioral changes associated with more or less regular use of psychoactive substances that affect the central nervous system" (p. 165). The *DSM* specifies ten classes of psychoactive substances that often are used in maladaptive ways: alcohol; amphetamines or similarly acting sympathomimetics; cannabis; cocaine;

hallucinogens; inhalants; nicotine; opioids; phencyclidine (PCP) or similarly acting arylcyclohexylamines; and sedatives, hypnotics, or anxiolytics.

Substance use disorders come in two varieties: abuse (the milder of the two) and dependence. Substance abuse is diagnosed in clients who do not meet the criteria for dependence (on that same substance) and who have demonstrated a pattern of "continued use despite knowledge of having a persistent or recurrent social, occupational, psychological, or physical problem that is caused or exacerbated by use of the psychoactive substance *or* recurrent use in situations in which use is physically hazardous (e.g., driving while intoxicated)" (*DSM-III-R*, 1987, p. 169) for at least one month (or repeatedly for a longer period of time). Dependence is diagnosed if the client has met at least three of the following criteria for at least one month (or repeatedly for a longer period of time): (1) using the substance more than intended; (2) persistently wanting the substance or making unsuccessful efforts to control substance use; (3) spending a great deal of time related to the substance (for example, recovering from intoxication); (4) manifesting intoxication or withdrawal that interferes with normal activities, or intoxication that involves physically hazardous use; (5) limiting activities as a result of the substance use; (6) continuing to use the substance despite awareness that it is causing difficulties; (7) showing clear signs of tolerance; (8) having withdrawal symptoms; (9) using the substance to relieve or avoid withdrawal. In diagnosing a psychoactive substance use disorder, the clinician would specify the substance involved and indicate whether there is abuse or dependence and, if there is dependence, the severity of the condition (for example, "alcohol dependence, moderate"). Substance use disorders, then, do not necessarily entail longstanding and pervasive impairment; in fact, most people who abuse drugs or alcohol are employed and have families. Nevertheless, the substance use has a powerful negative impact on the users as well as on the people who are close to them.

Eighteen percent of people in the United States will have a substance use disorder at some point in their lives, and 6.3 percent will manifest the disorder during any six-month time period (Frances & Allen, 1986). The problem is particularly prevalent among young adults (Maxmen, 1986). Many causes have been suggested to explain substance use disorders: biological, cultural, environmental, interpersonal (social, familial), and intrapersonal (developmental, cognitive, affective) (Leigh, 1985), but no conclusive explanation has been found yet for these disorders.

Relevant Client Characteristics. The search for an addictive personality has not been a particularly fruitful one, although some researchers believe there are personality patterns that predispose people toward substance abuse. Forrest (1985), for example, suggests that people with problems of substance abuse have been hurt by significant others and that those who are orally addicted had particular problems with their mothers. In Forrest's view, people who abuse substances experience lifelong anxiety, seek a sense of identity, and are depressed and dependent. He believes that they engage in avoidant behavior and are often suspicious and guilt ridden. To some extent, these behaviors may stem from their efforts to conceal their substance abuse from others and to defend their use of drugs and alcohol. People who use drugs or alcohol to excess may have learned to cope by lying to others or by placating or abusing others; and these patterns may be carried into their therapy.

Approximately two-thirds of those with substance use disorders have another coexisting disorder, most commonly depression (see Chapter Five) (Frances & Allen, 1986). Some of the coexisting disorders are preexisting conditions; others were initiated or worsened by the substance use. People with a family history of alcohol abuse are particularly likely to have coexisting disorders. This pattern is difficult to treat because it becomes a vicious cycle: the substance abuse worsens the coexisting disorder, which, in turn, increases the client's tendency to use drugs or alcohol as a form of self-medication for the coexisting disorder. Also, the substance use often masks the symptoms of the underlying disorder, further complicating the treatment picture.

Suicide and suicidal ideation are frequent in people who abuse substances and seem to increase as the abuse increases (Fowler, Rich, & Young, 1986). The possibility of suicide is of particular concern because substance abusers have an available lethal weapon, drugs or alcohol, and the combination of intoxication and depression may lead them to turn a binge into a suicide attempt. With multiple substance abuse becoming increasingly the norm, suicide becomes even easier via a mixture of drugs (such as alcohol and tranquilizers).

Substance abuse, particularly alcohol abuse, tends to run in families. Leigh (1985) found that family members tend to use the same drugs and in similar amounts.

Relevant Therapist Variables. Forrest (1985) urges the therapist who treats these disorders to take an active role in the therapy and to avoid the more traditional analytical models, which do not seem effective in treating substance abuse. Reid (1983) recommends that therapists be caring yet firm and realistic with substance-abusing clients. The therapists also must be comfortable with limit setting and confrontation. Bratter (1985) suggests that the life-or-death situation presented by many substance abusers requires the therapist to exert external control and even coercion, breaking confidentiality if necessary when the client's life is in danger.

Therapists who work with substance-abusing clients must be prepared to deal with resistance, hostility, manipulativeness, and deception. They also need to handle appropriately their own reactions to the clients' reluctance to change, continuing to communicate empathy and acceptance to even the most hostile and resistant clients. While these behaviors are certainly not descriptive of all clients seeking help for substance use, they are common among these clients. One of the challenges facing the therapist is the reversal of these patterns and the development of an honest relationship.

Because many of the treatment providers in this area are themselves recovering substance abusers, the history of substance use of the therapist often is of interest to clients. Bratter suggests that some judicious sharing of the therapists' own experiences, whether or not they have had problems with substances themselves, can promote rapport and straightforwardness in the therapeutic relationship. However, the focus always should remain on the clients' concerns, and therapists should not assume that what has been helpful to them will necessarily be helpful to others.

Intervention Strategies. Therapy with substance-abusing clients usually will be structured and behaviorally oriented, with abstinence being the goal. Contracts can be useful in affirming that goal and in specifying steps clients can take when they feel the desire for drugs or alcohol. For many clients, substance use is reinforced by the peer group; group counseling as well as self-help groups can counteract the influence of these peer groups.

Forrest (1985) suggests an eclectic approach to treatment. This approach emphasizes behavioral therapy, abstinence, and self-help groups. It also includes "genetic reconstruction," to help clients come to terms with the past, accept reality, and modify defenses. Finally, the approach makes use of interpretation and insight, to help clients understand and manage their feelings. Forrest reports that with six to eight months of treatment following this model, 50 percent of clients are abstinent five years later. Other approaches that have been suggested to supplement treatment include aversive conditioning, assertiveness training to develop social skills, cognitive therapy, and, in the later stages, existential therapy to promote a decision to establish a different lifestyle.

One common approach to treating substance abuse—an approach that Rachman and Raubolt (1985) refer to as "attack therapy"—is most commonly conducted in therapeutic communities, staffed largely by paraprofessionals who are themselves recovering substance abusers. Rachman and Raubolt believe that this approach can promote insularity (a sort of closed community) and can increase clients' hostility, leading them to change in order to placate others rather than out of internal motivation.

Self-help groups such as Alcoholics Anonymous and Narcotics Anonymous are almost always part of the treatment plan for substance abuse and become the central ingredient of most aftercare programs. Auxiliary groups, such as Al-Anon and Adult Children of Alcoholics, help family members deal with the impact of the substance use on them and also show them how to encourage the recovery of the substance abuser.

Education is another important component of most drug and alcohol treatment programs. Clients gain motivation and can deal better with the challenge of abstinence when they understand the negative effects of drug and alcohol and recognize in themselves the patterns of abuse.

Substance abuse, as well as relapse, is associated with stressful life events (Leigh, 1985). To prevent a setback when things do not go well in clients' lives, therapy should help them look realistically at their lives; make needed changes; and develop coping mechanisms, so that they are better prepared to deal with future stress. In addition, therapy should focus on any developmental or lifestyle deficits that may have resulted from prolonged substance abuse. Many clients need assistance with career development and job seeking, socialization and communication, parenting, developing drug-free leisure activities, and improving family relationships. Gurman, Kniskern, and Pinsof (1986) recommend a structural-strategic model of family counseling with substance-abusing clients and their families and suggest that multiple family therapy (including other families with similar difficulties) can be particularly helpful. If there is a coexisting disorder, in addition to the substance use disorder, treatment seems to be most effective if both problem areas are addressed through the treatment (Frances & Allen, 1986).

Some clients have such severe substance use problems that they cannot be treated initially via outpatient therapy. Either their physical addiction makes detoxification dangerous or they are so emotionally addicted that they cannot maintain abstinence independently for any length of time. For such clients, residential treatment is indicated. The standard approach to medical detoxification is a twenty-eight- or thirty-day inpatient program that detoxifies the client under medical supervision and initiates the individual, group, and family therapy that will continue after discharge.

Some clients seem to deteriorate after detoxification. Mild cognitive deficits (such as memory problems) emerge, and a sense of anxiety and feelings of being out of control may develop. If these symptoms are not dealt with through education and therapy, they can frighten clients into a relapse. The early stages of recovery, then, are tenuous ones, and close monitoring and support are needed.

Therapeutic communities or partial hospitalization programs are available for clients who are not ready to live independently immediately after detoxification or who have failed to respond to outpatient programs in the past. Such transitional programs can help clients locate employment and develop skills and resources necessary to become self-sufficient. Token economies, which are sometimes available in such programs, can offer clients additional motivation to change and can solidify their resolve to stop abusing drugs or alcohol. These communities can be particularly helpful to clients with few resources and support systems as well as to those whose peer groups and place of residence have promoted substance abuse, so that they need a comprehensive life change if they are to maintain abstinence.

As Reid (1983) has observed, there is no single approach to treatment that seems best for substance abuse. Rather, a combination of interventions (for example, detoxification, education, individual behavior therapy, multiple family therapy, assertiveness training, and Narcotics Anonymous), individualized to meet the needs of a particular client, seems ideal. Therapy with substance-abusing clients typically follows a series of stages: identify the problem, take a detailed history, provide detoxification if needed, help motivate clients toward change, set goals, provide education and interventions designed to develop coping mechanisms, involve clients in family therapy and self-help groups, help clients maintain change.

Prognosis. Forrest (1985) reports 50–80 percent overall improvement rates for clients with psychoactive substance use disorders, although attrition rates in outpatient programs may be as high as 50–75 percent. Treatment of substance use disorders has a positive prognosis for clients who have a stable work and family life, who manifest little or no accompanying antisocial behavior, and who do not have a family history of alcoholism (Frances & Allen, 1986). The prognosis also seems good for clients who comply with treatment, who can see the positive consequences of not using drugs and alcohol, and who do not have strong guilt and low self-esteem. The prognosis is less optimistic for clients with a coexisting emotional disorder; the more severe the accompanying diagnosis, the worse the prognosis (O'Brien, Woody, & McLellan, 1984). The overall emotional health of the client, then, seems to be a better predictor of outcome than does the severity of the substance use disorder (McLellan, Luborsky, Woody, O'Brien, & Druley, 1983).

7.1.1 Alcohol Abuse

Description of Disorder. There are eight to nine million alcoholics in the United States; about three million of them are women (Atwood & Chester, 1987). Five percent of women and 21 percent of men have an alcohol problem. Less than 5 percent of these people are stereotypical skid row alcoholics. Alcohol abuse tends to begin in adolescence or early adulthood; it rarely begins after age forty-five and tends to remit spontaneously in mid-life (Maxmen, 1986).

Men and women seem to have different patterns of alcohol abuse. Female alcoholics are more likely to drink alone, to feel guilty and attempt to conceal their drinking, to combine alcohol with other drugs, and to suffer from depression, anxiety, and insomnia. Alcohol problems seem to start later and progress faster in women, and are more closely linked to stressful life circumstances.

Some ethnic groups have a higher prevalence of alcohol problems than others. The Irish, for example, are overrepresented among those with alcohol problems, while Jews and Italians are underrepresented (Atwood & Chester, 1987). Alcoholism seems less prevalent in groups where alcohol is an accepted part of dining or religion rather than being used primarily for recreation.

Numerous models have been advanced to explain the development of alcohol abuse (Atwood & Chester, 1987):

1. Disease model. Developed by Jellinek (1971), this model suggests that some people have an inborn vulnerability to the physiological effects of alcohol.
2. Family systems model. Alcoholism is passed on from one generation to the next, whether through modeling or genetic transmission. The genetic theory has received some support from studies of twins.
3. Behavioral/social learning model. Alcohol use is reinforced by its immediate social and physiological rewards.
4. Psychodynamic/psychoanalytic model. Alcohol reflects infantile oral dependency needs and unresolved conflict with parents. The alcohol reduces fear and hostility and gives a sense of power.
5. Humanistic/existential model. Alcohol is a way to receive attention, sympathy, and care and avoid responsibility.

Of these models, the psychodynamic/psychoanalytic model probably has received the least support, while the disease model is widely accepted; the family systems model also is important in present understanding of alcohol abuse.

Relevant Client Characteristics. Meyer (1983) found that, on the Minnesota Multiphasic Personality Inventory, people who abuse alcohol tend to receive high scores in introversion, depression, and somatization; on the California Psychological Inventory, these people score high in imagination, intellectual ability, extroversion, passivity, instability, anxiety, and interpersonal undependability. Also, they tend to have little information on the physiological and interpersonal effects of their substance abuse. Leigh (1985) found that those who abuse alcohol tend to be immature, impulsive, and antisocial, and have poor coping skills and low self-esteem. Maxmen (1986) found that males with alcohol problems often manifest antisocial behaviors and attitudes while women are often depressed and phobic. For women, the pathology seems to precede the alcoholism; the reverse is more common in men, except for those with antisocial personality disorder (section 9.4) and panic disorder (section 6.2) (Hesselbrock, Meyer, & Keener, 1985). Frances and Allen (1986) found that about half of those who abuse alcohol are significantly depressed (Chapter Five). They tend to be anxious, self-centered, and sensitive to stress; have interpersonal difficulties and poor ego strength; perceive themselves as having little control and few options; and overreact to failure (Yost & Mines, 1985). Forrest (1985) suggests that the alcohol abuser's personality is similar to that of the client with a borderline personality disorder (see section 9.7). As children, alcoholic clients often had attention deficit and conduct disorders (Frances & Allen, 1986). Many studies, then, suggest that people who abuse alcohol have a range of associated difficulties—especially depression, low self-esteem, poor coping mechanisms, and interpersonal concerns. Whether these traits preceded or were a consequence of the alcohol abuse is unclear, but what is clear is that therapy should go beyond establishing abstinence in clients who abuse alcohol.

It is not surprising that alcohol abuse seems to play a role in other serious problems. Maxmen (1986) reports that it is a major factor in 20 percent of all divorces and is involved in 25 percent of suicides. Frances and Allen (1986) found that alcoholics have thirty times the suicide risk of the general population. Alcohol is also linked to a large number of homicides. Severe alcoholism reduces life expectancy by ten to twelve years (Atwood & Chester, 1987) and can cause a broad range of physical problems.

Alcohol abuse has a strong tendency to run in families; 30 percent of those with alcohol problems have an alcoholic parent (Leigh, 1985), while 20-25 percent of those from families where alcohol was abused will become alcoholic (Goodwin, 1984). Sons are particularly prone to familial alcoholism, while daughters often marry men with alcohol problems. Familial alcoholism tends to begin earlier and to be more severe than alcoholism in those without a family history of the disorder. Familial alcoholism also tends to be associated with poor coping and social deficits, because those from alcoholic families typically lacked positive role models.

Alcohol abuse is commonly reinforced by peer and social systems. Leigh (1985) found that adolescents often begin drinking beer and wine with their peers, progress to cigarettes and hard liquor, then to marijuana, and finally to other illicit drugs. If this pattern is widespread, it emphasizes the importance of early intervention and attention to environmental factors, especially in the treatment of adolescent alcohol abuse.

Relevant Therapist Variables. As in treatment of other substance use disorders, the therapist working with clients who abuse alcohol should promote optimism, commitment, and a sense of responsibility; facilitate reality testing; and provide structured treatment and limit setting. Confrontation and therapist self-disclosure should be used judiciously but may facilitate progress and reduce resistance to treatment. Therapists should be prepared for clients to engage in some alcohol use while in treatment and should not be too discouraged by that. At the same time, therapy sessions should not be held if clients arrive intoxicated. Some therapists use breath testing immediately before sessions to monitor alcohol use.

Intervention Strategies. The first consideration in treating alcohol use disorders is assessing the extent of the addiction. Withdrawal can be dangerous if alcohol consumption is high; in such instances, hospitalization should be the first step in treatment. At the same time, Miller and Hester (1986) concluded, after reviewing twenty-six controlled studies, that there is "no overall advantage for residential over nonresidential settings, for longer over shorter inpatient programs, or for more intensive over less intensive interventions in treating alcohol abuse" (p. 794) and suggest that less than 10 percent of clients require inpatient detoxification. Even if hospitalization is not indicated, a medical examination probably is, because of the damaging effects of alcohol.

McCrady (1985) reviewed the literature on the treatment of alcoholism and concluded that treatment clearly has a positive impact and that the best outcomes seem to come from therapy that focuses on clients' social systems, facilitating construction of new social systems if necessary. Although the *DSM-III-R* distinguishes between alcohol abuse and alcohol dependence, treatment is basically the same for the two, with the specific ingredients of the treatment plan being individualized (Kaplan & Sadock, 1985). Use of two or more treatment modalities (such as individual and family therapy) increases the percentage of clients who have a positive outcome from treatment.

Most approaches to treating alcohol abuse take a behavioral focus. From a behavioral point of view, maladaptive drinking is triggered by a stimulus and mediated by cognitive, affective, and physiological responses; and the immediate consequences of alcohol provide reinforcement despite subsequent negative consequences (McCrady, 1985). Treatment seeks to modify the stimuli as well as the cognitive, affective, and behavioral responses that are promoting the drinking. A treatment contract, specifying goals as well as duration and ingredients of treatment, can be useful in promoting commitment and abstinence. Common techniques used in treatment include cognitive restructuring, education, keeping daily records of activities and drinking, behavioral rehearsal (for example, rehearsing appropriate ways of refusing a drink that is offered), *in vivo* cue exposure (accompanying clients to a bar and helping them resist the impulse to drink), modeling, overt sensitization (conditioning nausea in response to an imagined drinking scene), social skills training, control of stimulus and consequence, and contingency contracting (returning a prepaid fee if a treatment program is completed successfully).

Sobell and Sobell (1978) compared two groups of clients who had received treatment for alcoholism. For both groups, treatment included hospitalization, group therapy, AA, and chemotherapy; but the experimental group also had seventeen sessions of behavior therapy. Follow-up six months, two years, and three years later indicated that the members of the experimental group were coping with their drinking and related problems better than the members of the control group. Behavior therapy, then, does seem to be an important ingredient in the treatment of alcohol abuse.

Alcohol is often used as a way to manage stress, and alcohol abuse is particularly common among people in stressful occupations (Yost & Mines, 1985). Unfortunately, stress management and relaxation have not been shown to contribute much to the treatment of alcoholism (Miller, 1981). Consequently, to reduce stress and promote abstinence and relapse, therapy should foster coping techniques and environmental change rather than emphasizing specific relaxation techniques.

Research has not supported the use of an analytic or insight-oriented approach to treating alcohol abuse or the use of electric shocks as a form of aversive conditioning (Emmelkamp, 1986). Supportive therapy, as the primary intervention, also has not proven effective.

One of the controversies in the field of alcohol treatment is whether controlled drinking can provide a viable alternative to abstinence. Those who accept the disease concept of alcohol abuse believe that controlled drinking does not work, and most research suggests that therapy with abstinence as a goal seems more effective than therapy with controlled drinking as a goal (Wilson, 1981). Atwood and Chester (1987), for example, report a success rate of only 5 percent in controlled-drinking programs. On the other hand, Sanchez-Craig, Annis, Bornet, and MacDonald (1984) found that brief treatment of early-stage problem drinkers was equally effective whether the goal was abstinence or controlled drinking, that most in both groups became controlled drinkers anyhow, and that clients found the idea of controlled drinking more acceptable than abstinence. Emmelkamp (1986) suggests that controlled drinking is most likely to be effective with younger clients who have brief and mild drinking histories and little coexisting pathology. However, this issue has not yet been resolved.

Participation in Alcoholics Anonymous (AA) seems to have a strong correlation with treatment success; 70 percent of those who are in AA for at least a year "have good sobriety" (McCrady, 1985, p. 247). AA has been in existence since 1935 and currently has over 10,000 groups in the United States. Its primary tenets are that alcoholism is a progressive disease and that a person who has become an alcoholic will remain an alcoholic and cannot stop drinking without help. Some clients are uncomfortable with AA because of its strong spiritual component. Familiarizing clients with this aspect of AA in advance in therapy, and helping them identify their own spirituality, may facilitate clients' involvement with AA.

AA is a very important ingredient in treatment, especially in relapse prevention; but it has not received much support as the primary form of treatment, partly because it tends to have a high dropout rate (Brandsma, Maultsby, & Welsh, 1980). Also, not all people seem to benefit from AA. Clear information is not available on the difference between those who do benefit and those who do not. For maximum effectiveness, then, AA should be part of a multifaceted treatment plan, including psychotherapy.

Antabuse (disulfiram) is sometimes part of the treatment of alcohol abuse, particularly for those who have a long history of abuse and who have failed at efforts to maintain sobriety in the past. An alcohol antagonist that acts as an emetic when taken regularly and when combined with alcohol, Antabuse is most commonly prescribed only for the first 90-120 days of treatment. Combined with other approaches to treatment, it has yielded recovery rates of 60-80 percent (Forrest, 1985). McCrady (1985) agrees that Antabuse seems to enhance treatment outcome but can worsen depression. It should be used cautiously, then, with depressed clients.

Although other medication is not usually needed in treatment of alcohol abuse, severely depressed or anxious clients might benefit from a short course of medication. Research suggests that clients do not substitute one drug for another; so there is not a high risk of their abusing medication, although such a risk must be considered (Kaplan & Sadock, 1985).

As with most forms of substance abuse, treatment of alcohol

abuse should go beyond abstinence and focus on career development, family relationships, leisure activities, and social relationships, and should encourage the development of skills that are
needed to establish a rewarding and alcohol-free lifestyle. Some clinicians have noted that, during the early months of abstinence,
clients go through a dry-drunk phase as they are struggling to ad-
just to sobriety. Halfway houses can facilitate the transition from
severe alcoholism to self-sufficiency for some clients.

Lambert (1982) found that involving their wives in treatment
improved the prognosis for male alcoholics. In alcoholic families,
there is typically more than one client. The children may be suffering from the parents' inconsistent and negative behavior and may
manifest emotional disorders and early alcoholism themselves, as
well as low self-esteem and a poor sense of direction. The spouses
are sometimes enablers who indirectly encourage the alcohol abuse
out of their own dependency needs. Involving the family in the
therapy can also increase the accuracy of available information on
the client's drinking, although most clients are fairly straightforward about their alcohol consumption (Miller, 1981). Therapy,
then, should address the needs of family members, both to treat their
immediate problems and to help them avoid the continuation of
patterns that promote alcoholism. Al-Anon, Al-A-Teen, and Adult
Children of Alcoholics (ACOA) groups can enhance treatment of
family members.

Prognosis. Prognosis for the treatment of alcoholism is better
if the alcoholism started late and developed slowly, and if the client
has strong relationships, is active in work and other pursuits, and
has a history of accomplishments (Atwood & Chester, 1987). Vaillant and Milofsky (1982) found that abstinence was more successful
among clients who found substitutes for the alcohol (for example,
activities, jobs, new relationships, behavior modification programs,
or involvement in religious or AA groups). Rounsaville, Dolinsky,
Babor, and Meyer (1987) found a poorer prognosis for men who had
an emotional disorder in addition to the alcohol abuse, an antisocial personality disorder (section 9.4), or a problem with drug abuse
(section 7.1.2). In contrast, men who had a treatment-responsive
major depression (section 5.1) had a better prognosis. In general,

older clients seem to respond better to treatment than younger clients do, and women seem to respond better than men (Lambert, 1982).

Alcoholics Anonymous reports a recovery rate of 30–35 percent, which seems comparable to statistics reported by many treatment programs for alcohol abuse (Atwood & Chester, 1987). Some studies provide even less encouraging statistics. Polich, Armor, and Braiker (1980) conducted a four-year follow-up study of 922 male alcoholics, 90 percent of whom had serious alcohol-related problems prior to treatment. They found that only 7 percent had been totally abstinent and that 54 percent continued to have alcohol-related problems. Lambert (1982) found that the results of a one-year follow-up to treatment generally predicted long-term progress. This finding suggests that a relapse—if it occurs—will probably occur relatively soon after treatment. Although the prognosis seems good for improvement of alcohol abuse, then, it is only fair for recovery or total abstinence.

7.1.2 Drug Abuse

Description of Disorder. Twenty percent of drug abusers begin taking an addictive drug for medical reasons; medical use subsequently becomes abuse, but that is only one of the ways that drug abuse starts. Leigh (1985) hypothesizes that there are two groups of drug users: one consisting of troubled individuals in emotional or physical pain who are using drugs as a form of self-medication; the other consisting of recreational users who enjoy the sensations afforded by the drugs.

There is an increasing tendency for people to abuse more than one drug (for instance, alcohol, marijuana, and cocaine), although most have a drug of choice. This multiple drug use complicates the treatment picture and makes accidental overdoses more likely.

An important difference between drug abuse and alcohol abuse is that most abused drugs are illegal. Consequently, although alcoholic clients also may have legal difficulties if they are arrested for driving while intoxicated, drug abusers often are involved in serious crimes and devote extensive time and energy to obtaining the funds needed to purchase drugs. Many clients with drug abuse problems (and some of those with alcohol problems) come to therapy involuntarily on a court referral and may be suspicious, guarded, and resentful. Therapists, then, will need to deal with such clients' criminality and anger as well as their substance abuse.

Relevant Client Characteristics. Many of those who abuse drugs have problems with impulse control in other areas and resemble clients with impulse control disorders such as those discussed in section 7.4. Adolescent drug users, in particular, seem to have a high susceptibility to boredom along with a high need to take risks and seek excitement (Leigh, 1985). Men are more likely to abuse illicit drugs; women are more likely to abuse prescription drugs. Those who abuse prescription drugs tend to be dependent, shy, anxious, and socially isolated (Meyer, 1983). Often, conditions such as insomnia or obesity precipitated the drug use.

Research indicates that there may be an association between personality traits and preferred drug. These findings should be viewed as tentative rather than conclusive at present, and overgeneralization should be avoided. However, research on the association between personality and drug of choice may help clinicians understand the personality patterns and choices of their clients. For example, Leigh (1985) suggests that heroin addicts tend to be childlike yet distant and to have one parent who is punitive or distant and one who is overinvolved. Meyer (1983) has observed that opioid users tend to be apathetic, egocentric, narcissistic, easily bored and frustrated, and have difficulty with authority. Rounsaville, Weissman, Kleber, and Wilber (1982) found that most opiate addicts have at least one coexisting emotional disorder, most often major depression (section 5.1), alcoholism (section 7.1.1), antisocial personality disorder (section 9.4), dysthymia (section 5.2), or an anxiety disorder (sections 6.1 to 6.5). They are also likely to come from lower socioeconomic groups. Female heroin addicts often have a history of incest.

Those who abuse amphetamines are also often coping with underlying depression. Amphetamine users may be depressed and suicidal when they are not on drugs; when they are on drugs, they may have symptoms resembling a paranoid psychosis (section 10.1).

In addition, people who abuse amphetamines tend to be agitated and suspicious, and frequently have little sense of direction.

Those who abuse tobacco tend to have some guilt and anxiety and may be angry and defensive as well as impulsive and extroverted (Kaplan & Sadock, 1985). They are also prone to alcohol abuse.

Some studies have found a correlation between cocaine abuse and a high incidence of depressive and bipolar disorders (Chapter Five) (Kleber & Gawin, 1984). Cocaine use, itself, can cause anxiety and suspiciousness as well as temporary energy and self-confidence; and some people may use cocaine to relieve depression.

Barbiturates tend to be abused by people who feel tense, anxious, and inadequate. Barbiturates are highly addictive and are probably the most frequent cause of drug-related deaths.

Chronic marijuana users tend to be passive, lacking in ambition, and prone to depression, suspiciousness, and panic or anxiety attacks (Kaplan & Sadock, 1985).

Meyer (1983) has noted that polydrug abusers tend to be young, venturesome, apathetic, and depressed; to have social problems; and to engage in antisocial behavior. They are often dependent and have confused values and poor problem-solving skills. They seem to be particularly troubled.

Although there is not the clear pattern of genetic transmission that is seen in alcoholism, families of drug abusers have a high incidence of impulse control problems, are conflict ridden and enmeshed, have particularly strong mother-child connections, and are troubled by issues of death and loss (Meyer, 1983). Antisocial behavior and alcoholism are often found in these families, as are high levels of marital disruption, inconsistency, and emotional disorder (Cadoret, Troughton, O'Gorman, & Heywood, 1986). The drug abuser was often the favorite child and had an important role in maintaining the family (Stanton, 1985). Drug abuse is particularly prevalent in immigrant families, possibly as a way to become accepted by a peer group.

Relevant Therapist Variables. Guidelines for therapists working with clients who abuse drugs are similar to those provided in the sections on alcohol abuse (section 7.1.1) and psychoactive substance use disorders (section 7.1).

Intervention Strategies. Treatment for drug abuse is also similar to that for alcohol abuse and usually includes the following: medical and psychological assessment, detoxification and treatment of withdrawal if needed, drug education, behavior therapy for drug use, and psychotherapy for other concerns (such as poor social skills, lack of career direction, or family difficulties). Although behavior therapy has been the most common approach to treating drug abuse, supportive therapy (promoting impulse control and environmental change) and psychodynamic therapy (focusing on insight) have also been used with some success. Kleber and Gawin (1984) found that a combination of all three approaches works better than any one of them alone in treating cocaine abusers.

These clients may not know how to relate to other people without being high. Therefore, they may need help in improving interpersonal skills, so that they can become part of a non-drug-abusing peer group. Developing leisure activities to fill the time that had previously been spent in drug-related activities can also be helpful. Clients with the typical personality patterns of prescription drug abusers (shy, anxious) may benefit from relaxation and assertiveness training.

Group and individual counseling often are part of the treatment plan, as is involvement in self-help groups, notably Narcotics Anonymous (NA). Paraprofessionals who have had drug problems themselves may provide helpful treatment to some drug abusers. O'Brien, Woody, and McLellan (1984) found that, for clients with mild drug abuse problems, drug counseling provided by paraprofessionals could be as effective as cognitive-behavioral therapy and psychodynamic (supportive-expressive) therapy provided by professionals. However, the therapy provided by the professionals was more effective for those with moderate to severe drug abuse.

Family therapy, too, is an important part of the treatment plan. After a review of the literature, Stanton (1985) concluded, "family treatment—especially outpatient-conjoint, multiple family therapy, and group treatment for parents—shows considerable

promise for effectively dealing with problems of drug abuse"
(p. 417).

Methadone, a heroin antagonist, and other drug antagonists
(such as Naloxone or Cyclazocine) sometimes become part of the
treatment program for opoid users. Methadone programs have had
good success rates; Maxmen (1986) reports that, after four years of
methadone maintenance, the majority of former heroin addicts live
productively and 94 percent no longer commit crimes to obtain
drugs. O'Brien, Woody, and McLellan (1984) found that drug abusers with severe pathology benefited more from methadone maintenance than from therapeutic communities, because their social
difficulties led them to feel uncomfortable in close interpersonal
situations. However, methadone maintenance is controversial because it involves substituting one drug for another and because
information is still limited on the long-term physiological effects of
methadone. At present, the Food and Drug Administration recommends no more than two years of methadone treatment.

Other medication (such as tricyclic antidepressants or lithium) may be helpful in controlling underlying symptoms and
thereby facilitating treatment of the drug problem. Gawin and
Kleber (1984), for example, found that medication seems to motivate
cocaine users to continue in treatment. However, medication should
be used cautiously with those who tend to abuse drugs.

Therapeutic communities are another avenue to treatment,
particularly for those with a long history of opioid use. Many of
these communities follow the highly confrontive model popular-
ized by the Synanon program. They encourage responsibility, insist
on honesty and self-examination, and exert peer pressure to effect
change. Recovering drug abusers serve as valuable role models. The
focus of these communities is on the present, on the unlearning and
new learning based on education and feedback, and on rewarding
responsibility and competence (Bratter, Collabolletta, Fossbender,
Pennacchia, & Rubel, 1985). This approach has yielded mixed results (Berger & Dunn, 1982). Bale and associates (1984) found that
therapeutic communities seem most effective when there are program clarity, order, staff control, and a focus on residents' personal
problems.

One of the most common drugs to be abused is nicotine.

Although clients usually do not seek therapy primarily for smoking, many clients present smoking as a secondary concern or seek help from one of the widely available programs for smokers. Most of these programs employ a multifaceted behavior therapy program, using such techniques as rapid smoking, with satiation as an aversive procedure, as well as charting and goal setting with reinforcement. Nicotine antagonists and substitutes have generally not proven helpful (Kaplan & Sadock, 1985).

Drug abusers seem to respond strongly to life crises, especially those involving arguments and losses (Kosten, Rounsaville, & Kleber, 1986). Such events often precipitate a relapse; therefore, therapy should help these clients find effective ways of coping with negative events. Extended aftercare, monitoring and building upon clients' coping mechanisms, is useful in preventing relapse. Periodic blood or urine testing also can be useful in motivating clients to remain drug free and keeping the therapist informed of relapses. Maddux and Desmond (1982) found that relocation prevents relapses. Environmental change is yet another approach to consider as part of aftercare, especially for clients whose families and peer groups encourage their drug abuse. Simpson, Joe, and Bracy (1982) suggest that it takes about three years of abstinence for recovery to be well established. Therefore, an equivalent period of aftercare, follow-up, and NA meetings probably will be required.

Prognosis. High relapse rates, often over 50 percent, are reported for drug abusers (Berger & Dunn, 1982). The prognosis for recovery is better if the drug abuser is not living with relatives and if the abuser's mother is not living alone (and is, therefore, probably less dependent on the abuser) (Stanton, 1985). Simpson (1981) found a correlation between outcome one year after treatment and the length of time clients remained in treatment (methadone maintenance, therapeutic community, or drug-free treatment). Treatments of less than three months' duration seemed to have little impact.

Treatment for smokers yields only 20–30 percent success rates at six-month follow-up, although treatment clearly seems to work better than no treatment (Meyer, 1983). For smokers, a positive prognosis is associated with attributing the change to the self rather than to the program, involvement in maintenance treatment, and having social support for the effort to stop smoking. Duration of smoking and amount smoked are negatively related to outcome (Meyer, 1983). These findings can probably be generalized to the treatment of abuse of other drugs.

7.2 Eating Disorders

Description of Disorder. This section will focus on two eating disorders: anorexia nervosa and bulimia nervosa. Like drug and alcohol abuse, they are disorders of behavior and impulse control that can be physically dangerous and even life threatening. Both anorexia and bulimia are most common in adolescent and young adult women; 3–13 percent of college females have one or both of these disorders. However, they are being reported with increasing frequency in both males and older women. Approximately 10 percent of people with these disorders are men (Andersen, 1987a). People in professions where low weight is desirable (for example, ballet, modeling, or sports) are particularly prone to these disorders.

Anorexia nervosa, according to the *DSM-III-R* (1987), involves a refusal to maintain a normal body weight, a body weight that is 15 percent or more below that expected for age and height, great fear of becoming overweight, a disturbed body image (viewing oneself as fat when one is underweight), and, in females, absence of at least three expected consecutive menstrual cycles (amenorrhea). Other physiological symptoms of anorexia include cold intolerance, dry skin, an increase in fine body hair, low blood pressure, and edema (Agras, 1987). According to Maxmen (1986), the two cardinal features of anorexia are a distorted body perception and a dread of being out of control. In some women, anorexia is associated with apprehension about puberty and seems to represent an effort to delay development. Anorexia is found in approximately 0.5 percent of the general population and is less common than bulimia (Maxmen, 1986).

Although occasional binge eating is common, approximately 2–6 percent of young women are actually bulimic (Agras, 1987). The mean age at onset is 18.4 years. Bulimia nervosa, again according to the *DSM-III-R*, involves an average of at least two episodes of binge eating per week for at least three months; a sense of being out of control during the episodes; excessive and persistent concern with body size; and regular use of self-induced vomiting, laxatives (often 50–100 per day), severely restricted eating, or exercise to prevent weight gain. The purging is often learned from friends and seems to have some support among adolescent girls as an acceptable way to control body weight. Most clients with bulimia do maintain a normal weight. However, some are anorexic while others are obese. The term *bulimarexia,* although not a recognized diagnosis, has been used to characterize people who are both bulimic and anorexic.

Physical signs of bulimia include a swelling of the parotid glands, producing a chipmunk-like appearance; scars on the back of the hand from self-induced vomiting; chronic hoarseness; and dryness of the mouth. Physiological reactions to the disorder include dental cavities and enamel loss, electrolyte imbalance, cardiac and renal problems, and esophageal tears (Agras, 1987).

Relevant Client Characteristics. Clients with anorexia generally are from affluent homes where food has an important role. They tend to have been very well-behaved children and have a major role in holding the family together. Many have been parental children in enmeshed families and have been overprotected and overregulated. They often had eating problems as children and tend to be strongly attached to their mothers (Atwood & Chester, 1987). Gutsch (1988) reports that clients with anorexia typically are dependent, introverted, compulsive, stubborn, perfectionistic, asexual, and shy. They have low self-esteem and feel ineffectual. Their disorder is generally ego-syntonic; and they typically feel little hunger or discomfort with their symptoms, although they may become absorbed with food and its preparation, often cooking for their families but refusing to eat what they have prepared. Their eating disorder is sometimes a form of rebellion, a way to get attention from their families, and a way to avoid having to be mature and responsible. It is unusual for people with anorexia to have other behavioral problems. However, Andersen (1987a) found that approximately 50 percent have or develop another emotional disorder.

Bulimic clients tend to be anxious and depressed, self-critical, socially inhibited, secretive, and ashamed of their bulimia.

They have conflicted feelings about relationships and sex; feel angry and powerless; have difficulty handling pain, loss, and conflict (Gutsch, 1988); are preoccupied with their bodies; and tend to have many physical complaints. They seem to be slightly older, more likely to act out, more extroverted, more emotional, less rigid, more anxious, more guilty, and more depressed than anorexic clients (Andersen, 1987b). People with bulimia feel out of control and demoralized. They tend to have a high incidence of other impulse control problems, such as alcohol abuse and self-mutilation. Hudson, Pope, Yurgelun-Todd, and Jonas (1987) concluded that there is a relationship between bulimia and both substance use disorders (section 7.1) and major affective disorders (Chapter Five). Most bulimic clients report problems with interpersonal relationships (70 percent), family (61 percent), finances (53 percent), and work (50 percent). People with bulimia, then, seem to present more emotional and behavioral disorders, in addition to their eating disorders, than do people with anorexia.

People with bulimia tend to see their families as low in cohesiveness, deemphasizing intellectual and recreational activities, independence, assertiveness, and open expression of feelings. The families tend to have high levels of conflict and often are enmeshed yet disengaged (Johnson & Flach, 1985). Herzog, Norman, Gordon, and Pepose (1984) found that men with eating disorders manifest more severe pathology than women with these disorders.

Bulimia, unlike anorexia, tends to be ego-dystonic, and those with bulimia experience considerable hunger and disappointment with their need to binge and purge. Their episodes of bingeing tend to be late in the day and coincide with dysphoric moods and stressful or unstructured times.

Mitchell, Hatsukami, Eckert, and Pyle (1985) studied 275 bulimic clients and found that 88.1 percent engaged in self-induced vomiting; 60.6 percent, in laxative abuse; 33.1 percent, in diuretic abuse; and 64.5 percent, in chewing and spitting out food. Combinations of methods of purging are common. The self-induced vomiting seems to increase feelings of self-control and reduce anxiety; its secondary gains often make it a difficult behavior to extinguish.

Both those with bulimia and those with anorexia tend to have suicidal ideation. Both tend to have some friends and have fairly successful lifestyles, but they also tend to isolate themselves and have social difficulties.

People with bulimia and people with anorexia are particularly likely to have troubled and chaotic families (Foreyt & Kondo, 1985). They tend to have mothers who doubt themselves and are unresponsive to their daughters and fathers who are distant and have high expectations for their daughters (Atwood & Chester, 1987). Their siblings and parents have an unusually high incidence of eating disorders and of major depression (Agras, 1987). They also are more likely than the general population to have experienced sexual abuse as children.

Relevant Therapist Variables. Clients with eating disorders need considerable support and approval to make the potentially frightening behavioral changes that will be asked of them. Developing strong therapist-client rapport seems integral to treatment. As Bruch (1982) notes, the individuality of these clients has often been denied in their families, and that should not happen in therapy. It is important that they be heard and encouraged to develop separateness and autonomy. Therapists will need to handle clients' strong dependency needs by gently encouraging self-control and independence. At the same time, therapists will also need to be structured and to set limits to protect the clients, hospitalizing them if necessary. Women with eating disorders are often uncomfortable with men and might do better with a female therapist or a male/female cotherapy team.

Intervention Strategies. Both anorexia and bulimia are physically damaging, potentially lethal disorders. Approximately 10–15 percent of those with anorexia die from complications of that disorder (Agras, 1987). The first step in treatment, then, is to assess the client's physiological damage via a careful history taking and a referral for a medical examination. If the weight loss is severe (25 percent or more) or if the client's medical condition is precarious, hospitalization may be needed to supervise eating, prevent vomiting and laxative abuse, and promote weight gain. While hospitalization restores about two-thirds of these clients to normal weight, about half continue to have eating problems after discharge, indicating the need for continued treatment (Agras, 1987). If the client does not seem to be in immediate danger, outpatient treatment may be adequate as long as steps are taken to restore a normal weight and curtail other self-damaging behaviors.

Most treatment programs for clients with eating disorders tend to be relatively brief (eight to twenty sessions) but sometimes include extended follow-up treatment. Therapy for clients with eating disorders, as for most clients with behavioral disorders, typically has several components. Behavior therapy, to promote healthy eating and to eliminate purging, is the core of the treatment. Procedures usually include the gathering of baseline data on clients' weight and related dysfunctional behaviors (such as laxative use), establishment of goals, contingency contracting, monitoring of progress (via a diary or a scale in the office if necessary), reinforcement and rewards for positive change, and relaxation strategies to reduce anxiety and improve self-image and sense of control. Other behavioral techniques—such as assertiveness, communication, and social skills training—can enhance treatment, as can the development of leisure activities and improved relationships to provide alternatives to the dysfunctional eating.

Cognitive and insight-oriented therapy, combined with behavioral treatment, can help clients gain insight into the dynamics of their disorder, improve their self-esteem and sense of control, and contribute to the development of better eating. Psychoanalytic and psychodynamic approaches, however, do not seem promising in the treatment of eating disorders (Kaplan & Sadock, 1985).

Agras (1987) describes a cognitive-behavioral approach to treating bulimic clients. The treatment, fifteen sessions of group therapy, includes shaping diet, providing education, exploring antecedents of the disorder, preventing vomiting, examining cognitions, teaching problem solving and coping mechanisms, providing group support, and preventing relapse. Response prevention is a key element in the treatment. Clients are asked to binge during a therapy session and then are taught effective ways to manage the urge to vomit. Agras concludes, "Cognitive-behavioral treatment, with or without response prevention, results in impressive reductions in binge eating and vomiting, and concomitant improvement in psychological functioning" (p. 66).

Boskind-White and White (1983) suggest that group therapy with a male/female leadership team can be particularly helpful for bulimic women. Their approach to treating bulimia has the following elements: (1) exploration of affect (for example, shame, hostility, isolation, self-esteem), designed to clarify connection between emotions and eating; (2) understanding relationships and the connection between intimacy and responsibility, improvement of social skills; (3) awareness of eating patterns and cues to dysfunctional eating and purging; (4) role playing to develop assertiveness, communication, and other skills; and (5) development of coping strategies. Techniques such as the writing of autobiographies, feedback, values clarification, and self-disclosure also are used to help clients establish and work toward goals.

The treatment programs developed by Agras and by Boskind-White and White are typical of those used to treat eating disorders. Both programs combine cognitive and behavioral interventions with some attention to affect into a structured format that could be used with either individuals or groups.

O'Connor (1984) suggests a paradoxical intervention for bulimic clients. Clients are instructed to think obsessively about food for thirty minutes daily; to develop a mutually exclusive behavior, such as shopping, that they can engage in whenever they feel the urge to purge; and to binge on a schedule. This approach might be effective with clients who are highly resistant to straightforward treatment of their symptoms.

Research suggests that family therapy may be another effective approach in the treatment of eating disorders. Minuchin, Rosman, and Baker (1978) report an 86 percent success rate when family therapy was used to treat anorexia.

Although medication is not usually necessary for the treatment of eating disorders, many people with these disorders suffer from depression (55.6 percent of those with anorexia and 23.6 percent of those with bulimia, in a 1984 study by Herzog). The depression may be primary, with the eating disorder used to relieve symptoms; secondary to the eating disorder; or tertiary, emerging only after the dysfunctional eating patterns have been modified. If the depression is severe, and particularly if it seems to be endogenous or biochemical in nature (see Chapter Five, especially section

5.1), medication (such as MAO inhibitors or tricyclic antidepressants) may contribute to treatment effectiveness, especially for the more troubled bulimic clients. Hughes, Wells, Cunningham, and Ilstrup (1986), for example, found that desipramine reduced binge eating 91 percent over six weeks in bulimic clients. However, Agras (1987) concluded that cognitive-behavioral therapy is a more effective treatment for bulimia than medication is. Usually, then, normal eating, combined with some therapy designed to relieve the depression, will be sufficient to alleviate symptoms; and medication will not be necessary to treat an eating disorder.

Prognosis. In general, the prognosis for treating anorexia is better than for bulimia (Andersen, 1987a), perhaps because anorexic clients tend to have better overall emotional health than bulimic clients. Maxmen (1986) reports that 40 percent of clients with anorexia recover completely through treatment, 30 percent are significantly improved, 20 percent are unimproved, and 5–10 percent die as a result of the disorder. Connors, Johnson, and Stuckey (1984) found that 80 percent of their bulimic clients stopped their dysfunctional behavior in ten weeks of treatment, 93 percent in fourteen weeks. These findings suggest a positive prognosis for treatment of bulimia, although no follow-up data were provided. A positive prognosis is associated with good premorbid functioning, high educational level, early age at onset, feelings of hunger, low weight loss, short duration of disorder, acceptance of illness, overactivity, and psychosexual maturity.

As with most behavioral disorders, relapses are common and are often related to stressful life events. Treatment should be extended via follow-up or support groups to prevent severe setbacks. Follow-up treatment should also be helpful in reducing the family, social, and occupational difficulties that often persist after the eating disorder has been eliminated.

7.3 Sexual Disorders

Sexual disorders, like substance use and eating disorders, involve behavioral patterns that are dysfunctional or self-destructive. Unlike eating or substance use disorders, sexual disorders are not usually physically injurious and usually do not cause pervasive dysfunction; but they may both reflect and cause impairment in relationships.

The *DSM-III-R* divides sexual disorders into two categories: paraphilias and sexual dysfunctions. Although both are, in a sense, disorders of behavior and of dysfunctional and inappropriate responses to stimuli, people with these disorders tend to be very different in their lifestyles and personality patterns, their motivation toward treatment, and their interactions with the therapist; and their disorders tend to differ in duration and impact. Although treatment for the two categories has some common ingredients, the two disorders will be discussed separately because of the important differences between them.

7.3.1 Paraphilias

Description of Disorder. The *DSM-III-R* (1987) describes paraphilias as "characterized by arousal in response to sexual objects or situations that are not part of normative arousal-activity patterns and that in varying degrees may interfere with the capacity for reciprocal, affectionate sexual activity" (p. 279). People with paraphilias are subject to recurrent distressing sexual urges and fantasies or sexual acts "involving either (1) nonhuman objects, (2) suffering or humiliation . . . or (3) children or other nonconsenting persons" (p. 279). The *DSM* provides an extensive list of paraphilias, including exhibitionism, fetishism (sexual activity focusing on objects), frotteurism (touching and rubbing against others without their consent), pedophilia (sexual activity with children), sexual masochism, sexual sadism, transvestic fetishism (cross-dressing), voyeurism, telephone scatologia (lewd telephone calls), necrophilia (sexual interest in corpses), partialism (focus on part of the body), zoophilia (animals), coprophilia (feces), klismaphilia (enemas), and urophilia (urine). Specific criteria are provided in the *DSM* for each of these disorders, but that is beyond the scope of this book. Here, the paraphilias will be considered as a class of disorders.

Paraphilias are far more prevalent in males than in females, although both sexual masochism and sexual sadism are diagnosed with some frequency in females (Person, 1986). Otherwise, little is known about the prevalence and distribution of these disorders, largely because only a small percentage of people with these disorders seek help. Many of those with this disorder have more than one paraphilia. In general, people with this disorder do not see themselves as having an emotional disorder; they tend not to be self-referred for treatment but, rather, come into treatment at the urging of a friend or family member (usually the spouse) or because actions associated with their paraphilia have led to their arrest.

Paraphilic disorders vary widely in severity. Roger had a mild paraphilia. At age thirty-two, he was a successful lawyer and had rewarding intimate relationships with women. However, he fantasized a great deal about causing women to suffer. He bought pornographic magazines with sadistic themes and enjoyed films in which women were injured, raped, or killed. Roger had never hurt a woman, but he sought therapy because he was afraid he would lose control of his fantasies and would injure someone. Steven, on the other hand, had a severe paraphilia, pedophilia. His only sexual experiences had been with young boys. He had been arrested three times and was seen for therapy while in prison. Although he, like Roger, had a professional career, he had lost his job because of his imprisonment and feared that his prison record would prevent him from locating future employment in his field, accounting.

Expression of paraphilic impulses often follows a cycle common to disorders of impulse control. Tension builds in the person until it is relieved by a paraphilic act; then guilt and regret ensue, and the person often promises to change the behavior. However, in time, tension builds and once again is released via the undesirable behavior.

Paraphilias rarely seem to have a biological cause. They are often related to an early-childhood sexual experience (such as being tied up or forced to cross-dress).

Relevant Client Characteristics. Although about half of the clients with this disorder are married, most have some impairment in their capacity for intimate relationships (*DSM-III-R*, 1987). Their sexual activities tend to be ritualized and unspontaneous. Most experience distress and anxiety connected to their disorder, even though they may deny that their paraphilic impulses are a problem (Person, 1986). People with paraphilias are prone to de-pression (Chapter Five) and to substance abuse (section 7.1). They often have unclear and unstable body images (Kaplan & Sadock, 1985). However, with the exception of sexual masochists, people with paraphilias rarely have a severe emotional disturbance.

Pedophilia, often taking the form of incest, is one of the most common paraphilias seen in therapy. Men who engage in pedophil-ia with young girls typically have marital difficulties, are anxious and immature, and have problems with impulse control. Men who molest young boys tend to avoid any adult sexual experiences and are only attracted to children.

Relevant Therapist Variables. Some therapists have strong countertransference reactions to clients with paraphilias, particu-larly those that involve children. One of the challenges for thera-pists treating paraphilias is managing their own feelings so that they do not undermine the therapeutic relationship and increase the clients' guilt and distress.

Both therapists and clients will also have to deal with the low prognosis for success in treating these disorders. Clients with para-philias, like those with drug and alcohol problems, enjoy the behav-iors involved in their disorder. It is the negative consequences rather than the behaviors themselves that typically lead these people to seek treatment. As a result, they may be ambivalent or resistant toward treatment and—especially if they have been ordered by a court to seek treatment—may be guarded and suspicious. Establish-ing a positive therapeutic relationship may, therefore, be difficult with these clients.

Intervention Strategies. Little conclusive information is available on effective approaches to treating paraphilias, although behavioral approaches predominate. Wilson (1981) found that co-vert sensitization—linking, in fantasy, the undesirable behavior with a negative contingency—is effective in treating exhibitionism and transvestic fetishism. Aversion therapy has also been used, pair-ing images of the paraphilic behavior with electric shocks or other negative experiences. A related technique is covert extinction, in which the paraphilic behavior is imagined but without the anticipated reinforcement or positive feeling (Meyer, 1983). Orgasmic reconditioning is another behavioral approach that has been used, particularly in treatment of pedophilia (Emmelkamp, 1986). Thought stopping, too, can be helpful, particularly for disorders that have compulsive qualities.

Behavioral techniques may be effectively supplemented with cognitive therapy, focusing on guilt, responsibility, and expectations in relationships (Meyer, 1983). Some people with paraphilias engage in sexual activities with children, animals, or objects because they are afraid of rejection if they seek sexual relationships with adults. Improvement of social and assertiveness skills as well as education on sexuality can encourage those clients to engage in sexual activities involving peers.

Some theorists have recommended psychoanalysis or psychodynamic therapy to treat paraphilias, focusing treatment on seeking the origins of the disorder (Kaplan & Sadock, 1985). However, research has not substantiated the effectiveness of these approaches.

Antiandrogenic medication has also been used, particularly in the treatment of pedophilic clients. However, this medication produces a general reduction in sexuality and so is resisted by many clients.

Prognosis. Paraphilias tend to be resistant to treatment, although concurrent adjustment and relationship difficulties may improve through therapy. In addition, relapses are common, especially with exhibitionism, which accounts for one-third of all sexual offenses (McConaghy, 1984); short-term improvement, therefore, does not provide assurance of continuing change (Person, 1986). Prognosis seems better for clients with good ego strength and flexibility (Kaplan & Sadock, 1985) and worse for clients with borderline personality traits (see section 9.7) (Person, 1986).

7.3.2 Sexual Dysfunctions

Description of Disorder. This category of disorders involves inhibition in sexual desire or functioning that is not caused by an organic factor or by another Axis I emotional disorder. The *DSM-III-R* (1987) includes the following disorders in this category:

Sexual desire disorders: (1) hypoactive (deficient) sexual desire disorder and (2) sexual aversion disorder

Sexual arousal disorders: (1) female sexual arousal disorder and (2) male erectile disorder, both reflecting a lack of physiological arousal and sexual excitement

Orgasm disorder: (1) inhibited female orgasm, (2) inhibited male orgasm, and (3) premature ejaculation

Sexual pain disorders: (1) dyspareunia (genital pain in males or females) and (2) vaginismus (involuntary vaginal spasms)

To warrant a diagnosis, symptoms must be recurrent and persistent. In making the diagnosis, the clinician would specify the disorder and indicate whether it is psychogenic only or psychogenic and biogenic; lifelong or acquired; and generalized or situational.

Most sexual dysfunctions begin in early adulthood, although some, particularly male erectile disorder, tend to begin later. Treatment for sexual dysfunction typically is not sought until people are in their late twenties or early thirties (Skinner & Becker, 1985). The course of these disorders is extremely variable. Some are situationally related, precipitated by stress or relationship difficulties, and remit spontaneously once the situation has improved. Others are chronic or progressive, worsening as anxiety about the disorder increases. Sexual dysfunctions seem to be very common; for example, 30 percent of females have inhibited female orgasm, and 30 percent of males have premature ejaculation. Kaplan (1986) suggests that 50 percent of the population suffers from a sexual problem at some time.

Marital or relationship difficulties are common secondary symptoms. History taking may indicate that relationship and sexual difficulties developed concurrently or that one seemed to precipitate the onset of the other. In addition to an interpersonal cause, sexual dysfunctions may be caused by intrapsychic factors; a traumatic sexual experience; cultural and family attitudes; illness; medication; and some emotional disorders, such as depression (Chapter Five) and obsessive compulsive disorder (section 6.4) (Maxmen, 1986). Approximately 75 percent of sexual disorders have a psychological, rather than a biogenic, origin (Atwood & Chester, 1987).

Relevant Client Characteristics. There does not seem to be a clear association between particular personality traits or background and sexual dysfunction, although anxiety is almost always a component of the dysfunction. Negative or rigid attitudes toward sexuality, low self-esteem, fear of failure, and sensitivity to rejection, as well as an overall low level of mental health, do seem to bear some relationship to incidence of sexual dysfunction.

Relevant Therapist Variables. In Masters and Johnson's model for conducting sex therapy, a male and a female therapist work as a team with a couple experiencing sexual dysfunction. Although this model allows considerable flexibility and does seem ideal, one therapist seems nearly as effective as a dual-sex treatment team (Kaplan & Sadock, 1985).

Treating sexual dysfunctions can be very challenging to therapists, because they must have expertise in the specific techniques of sex therapy and must also be skilled at providing support, communicating empathy, and establishing a relationship with clients who are likely to feel uncomfortable, embarrassed, and exposed. Many people have never talked openly about their sexual attitudes and behaviors before seeking therapy and will have difficulty doing so with the therapist, possibly avoiding specific details, minimizing the problem, and being unfamiliar with terminology. Therapists must be sure to conduct a detailed inquiry in terms that are comprehensible to clients and that reduce threat and anxiety as much as possible. Maintaining a nonjudgmental stance is particularly important. Orienting clients quickly to the nature of the treatment may also be useful, since they may be apprehensive about what will be required of them.

Intervention Strategies. The first step in treating a sexual dysfunction is determining the cause of the difficulty via a history taking and a referral for a medical examination. Although most sexual disorders are not biogenic in origin, many do have a physiological basis. Prescription medicines as well as other drugs and alcohol, for example, are common physiological causes of sexual dysfunction. Psychotherapy may be indicated, whatever the cause, but medical treatment may also need to be part of the treatment plan.

Great strides have been made in the past fifteen to twenty years in developing treatment strategies for sexual dysfunction. At this point, many highly successful techniques—developed by Masters and Johnson (1970), Helen Singer Kaplan (1979), and others— are available for treating these disorders. A discussion of techniques designed for specific disorders is beyond the scope of this book, and readers are referred to the above authors for that information. However, the common ingredients present in the treatment of most types of sexual dysfunction will be reviewed here.

If the person with a sexual dysfunction has a spouse or another consistent sexual partner, the partner should almost always be involved in the therapy. Sexual dysfunctions grow out of relationships and affect relationships, and so must be considered in context. Information should be gathered on the couple's interpersonal and sexual relationship, to determine whether any difficulties in their interaction might have a bearing on the sexual dysfunction. Data should be gathered from the couple while together and while apart, since they often have discrepant perceptions of their sexual relationship.

In most cases, couples therapy is helpful, focusing on communication, expectations, and sexual desires and behaviors. Satir (1983) provides a useful model for interviewing couples and gathering information on the development of their relationships as well as on their present concerns. Inventories such as the Sexual Interaction Inventory, the Sexual History Form, and the Locke-Wallace Marital Adjustment Inventory can also facilitate history taking (Friedman & Hogan, 1985).

Many people develop or exacerbate sexual dysfunctions because of what has been called spectatoring, the process of watching and monitoring their sexual performance as well as their partners' responses during sexual relations. The tension and anxiety associated with spectatoring typically prevent relaxation and comfortable involvement in sexual activity and worsen the sexual dysfunction—leading to a vicious cycle, in which the sexual dysfunction promotes spectatoring, which increases the dysfunction. Research has shown that behavioral treatment and practice at home between sessions are more effective in treating spectatoring and other symptoms of sexual dysfunction than is traditional, insight-oriented therapy (Lambert, 1982).

Since clients typically delay seeking treatment for sexual dysfunction, often for years, the disorder is likely to be deeply entrenched (Maxmen, 1986). The first step in the behavioral treatment of sexual dysfunction, then, is reduction of spectatoring and its accompanying anxiety. To accomplish this, the couple may be taught nonthreatening relaxation techniques (such as progressive relaxation or nonsexual massage) and typically are asked to refrain from overt sexual activity. Reducing pressure and demands in this way can help the couple gradually resume a more rewarding sexual relationship and apply specific techniques that are designed to modify sexual functioning.

Sensate focusing, a common technique used early in treatment, is designed to help the couple enjoy closeness and intimacy without intercourse. Other specific techniques that might be part of treatment for sexual dysfunction include systematic desensitization, masturbation for women with inhibited orgasm, bridging (making the transition from masturbation or manual stimulation to intercourse), the "squeeze technique" (to teach control for those with premature ejaculation), Kegeling (an exercise to strengthen women's pubococcygeal muscles), and using imagery and fantasy to enhance sexual arousal. To help the couple express their sexual wants and feelings, assertiveness and other communication techniques are also taught.

Education plays an important role in the treatment of sexual dysfunction. Many people are misinformed about the process of sexual arousal and what is considered normal sexual functioning. For example, attitudes about the inappropriateness of sexual activity for older clients or an erroneous belief about the difference between types of female orgasm can inhibit sexual functioning and cause people to feel uncomfortable with healthy feelings and behaviors.

Friedman and Hogan (1985) suggest four components to effective therapy for sexual dysfunction: (1) experiential/sensory awareness exercises; (2) insight, promoting awareness of factors that cause and maintain the disorder; (3) cognitive restructuring, to increase flexibility in attitudes and promote commitment; and (4) behavioral interventions, focusing on both interpersonal and sexual concerns. They emphasize the importance of homework assignments for practicing techniques that have been taught and the need for posttreatment follow-up to deal with any relapses.

Therapy for sexual dysfunctions tends to be about fifteen to twenty-five sessions in duration. Although Masters and Johnson often conducted their therapy sessions on an intensive, daily basis, weekly therapy does not seem to yield inferior results (Emmelkamp, 1986).

In general, therapy for sexual dysfunction is conducted with a couple or, if necessary, with an individual. However, some sexual dysfunctions also seem to benefit from group therapy, designed to provide support as well as education and stress management. Such groups have been used for women with inhibited orgasm and for men with erectile disorders. Couples groups have also been used successfully.

Medication is rarely necessary in treatment of sexual dysfunction. However, there are occasional exceptions. Women with sexual desire disorders, for example, have been treated successfully with androgens (Lambert, 1982). A short course of treatment with medication designed to reduce anxiety can also be useful to highly anxious clients. Since most clients with sexual dysfunction will be referred for a medical examination, the possibility of medication— in those few cases where medication seems likely to enhance treatment—can be raised when the referral is made.

Lief (1981) found that 10 percent of clients with sexual dysfunction needed extensive individual therapy and that 20 percent needed marital therapy before they could benefit from therapy focusing on their sexual dysfunctions. Although therapy for sexual dysfunction will focus primarily on the couple and their relationship and sexual difficulties, sometimes the dysfunction will prove to be intrapsychic in origin and linked to other emotional disorders or underlying pathology. Kaplan (1979) has suggested, for example, that disorders of sexual desire are often associated with underlying anxiety and hostility as well as with marital and relationship difficulties. In such cases, a treatment plan that combines behavioral and couples therapy with some individual cognitive, interpersonal, or psychodynamic therapy for the person experiencing an emotional disorder in addition to the sexual dysfunction may facilitate change. Authorities disagree on this approach, however; Kaplan (1979) advocates a combination of behavioral and psychodynamic approaches in such cases, but Wilson (1981) believes that the combination offers no advantage over behavioral therapy alone. Everaerd and Dekker (1985) suggest that Rational-Emotive Therapy can enhance the impact of sex therapy on couples who also have relationship difficulties; however, their conclusions are not fully substantiated. It is up to the therapist, then, to determine the best way to treat clients who present a combination of sexual dysfunction and other emotional disorders.

Prognosis. In their early research, Masters and Johnson (1970) reported an 80 percent overall success rate for 733 cases receiving two weeks of intensive treatment for sexual dysfunction; only 5 percent had a recurrence within five years. For some disorders, even higher recovery rates have been found (87 percent for vaginismus and nearly 100 percent for premature ejaculation); for others, recovery rates were not quite so high (66 percent for erectile disorder, 63 percent for inhibited orgasm) (Lambert, 1982). However, recent research suggests that these figures may be too optimistic, at least for some disorders. Friedman and Hogan (1985), for example, report a success rate of only 10–15 percent in fifteen sessions of treatment for sexual arousal disorders, one of the most prevalent and treatment-resistant sexual dysfunctions.

Prognosis seems best for orgasm-phase dysfunctions (premature ejaculation, inhibited female orgasm, genital pain disorders), less good for treatment of excitement-phase disorders (erectile disorder), and least positive for treatment of disorders of desire. A positive prognosis is associated with a stable and rewarding marital relationship, brevity and low severity of impairment, specificity of the dysfunction, openness and flexibility, following through on assignments, and interest in sexual activity (Lambert, 1982). However, treatment typically leads to improvement rather than a complete elimination of the problem. In addition, relapses seem fairly common (Friedman & Hogan, 1985). Nevertheless, the prognosis for amelioration of sexual dysfunction is good and often has a ripple effect, improving the relationship as sexual functioning improves (Kaplan, 1986).

7.4 Other Impulse Control Disorders

Description of Disorder. Impulse control disorders typically are characterized by feelings of tension or arousal, which are relieved by yielding to an impulse or temptation to perform an act that is destructive to the self or to others. The act is ego-syntonic (compatible with clients' self-images) and provides gratification and a release of the tension, although it may be followed by feelings of guilt and remorse. The behavioral and impulse control disorders most often presented for treatment (for example, sexual disorders and substance use disorders) have been discussed earlier in this chapter. This section will focus on less prevalent impulse control disorders not discussed elsewhere in this book and included in a category entitled "Impulse Control Disorders Not Otherwise Specified" in the *DSM-III-R* (1987).

1. *Intermittent explosive disorder.* According to the *DSM-III-R*, this disorder involves "discrete episodes of loss of control of aggressive impulses resulting in serious assaultive acts or destruction of property" (p. 321). The symptoms generally are not caused by another disorder or by drug or alcohol use. This rare disorder is most common in males, usually begins in adolescence or early adulthood, and tends to run in families. It is most often found in men who are concerned about their masculine identity (Maxmen, 1986). As children, they typically were hyperactive and had assaultive, hostile parents who evoked feelings of powerlessness (Kaplan & Sadock, 1985). Episodes of this disorder are often triggered by strong feelings of powerlessness.

2. *Kleptomania.* Characterized by recurrent theft of unneeded objects, this rare disorder seems most common in middle-aged females who are mildly depressed and experiencing interpersonal difficulties and who have a sense of injustice and deprivation (Frosch, Frosch, & Frosch, 1986).

3. *Pathological gambling.* The primary feature of this disorder is preoccupation with self-destructive gambling. This disorder is

found in 2–3 percent of the population, is more common in males, usually begins in adolescence, and is often accompanied by substance abuse (section 7.1). Family backgrounds of people with this disorder often include substance abuse, antisocial behavior, gambling, an emphasis on material gain, an early loss, and harsh and inappropriate discipline. The gamblers themselves tend to be intelligent, overconfident, energetic, industrious, and risk taking (Custer, 1984). They also have a high incidence of major depression (see section 5.1) and hypomanic symptoms (McCormick, Russo, Ramirez, & Taber, 1984).

4. *Pyromania.* This disorder involves the repeated setting of fires for pleasure and tension relief rather than for gain, accompanied by an interest in anything associated with fires. This rare disorder tends to be found in males who feel powerless and who come from disrupted homes. Their involvement with fire may provide a sense of power and social prestige. Pyromania is often associated with alcohol abuse, poor social skills, and childhood difficulties (such as enuresis, learning disabilities, or mild mental retardation) (Maxmen, 1986).

5. *Trichotillomania.* Characterized by plucking one's head and body hairs, this disorder is more common in females and tends to be stress related. Little information is available about this newly defined disorder.

Relevant Client Characteristics. Disorders of impulse control are often associated with other disorders, including personality disorders (discussed in Chapter Nine), depression (Chapter Five), anxiety disorders (Chapter Six), and substance abuse (section 7.1). Suicidal ideation is not uncommon, especially among gamblers. Alcohol may be used to reduce self-control and allow the client to act on the impulse. The impulsive behavior itself is typically used to relieve anxiety and depression.

Although clients with these disorders generally are not severely troubled by their symptoms, they recognize that others find them unacceptable; and so they frequently take steps to conceal their behaviors. Consequently, these disorders often have a negative impact on interpersonal relationships, and people with these disorders typically have limited, conflicted, or unrewarding patterns of socialization. Except for the gamblers, these clients tend to be passive and have difficulty expressing their feelings. Some researchers believe that they also have an underlying need for punishment (Kaplan & Sadock, 1985).

The backgrounds of people with these disorders often reveal either too much or too little gratification and a failure to learn to defer gratification (Frosch, Frosch, & Frosch, 1986). They often felt powerless as children and did not do well in school. The impulse control disorder, then, seems to be both a way to express feelings of anger and frustration and a way to feel more powerful.

Relevant Therapist Variables. Clients with these disorders, like those with substance use disorders and paraphilias, typically are resistant to treatment. They may seek therapy only because a court has ordered them to do so or because of pressure from friends and family. Clients with impulse control disorders tend to be defensive, to engage in denial and avoidance, and to resist taking responsibility for the consequences of their behavior. They may insist that others forced them to act as they did and that they themselves are blameless. Their capacity for insight varies greatly; gamblers generally are quite insightful, whereas clients who engage in pyromania usually are low in insight (Kaplan & Sadock, 1985). Engaging these clients in therapy, then, is likely to present quite a challenge to the therapist.

Like clients with paraphilias, these clients may commit acts that are viewed as distasteful and reprehensible, such as a client's physical abuse of a spouse. Another challenge to therapists, then, is managing their own feelings about the clients' behaviors and remaining objective while communicating acceptance and support to the clients.

Intervention Strategies. Little research is available on the treatment of these impulse control disorders. Treatment recommendations are therefore tentative and are based primarily on theory and on what has proved effective in the treatment of related disorders. To develop an appropriate treatment plan, the therapist will need to explore the behavioral, cognitive, and affective components of the disorder as well as the impact of the disorder on the client's lifestyle.

Behavioral techniques usually will form the core of treatment for clients with impulse control disorders. Such techniques as stress management, impulse control, contingency contracting, and aversive conditioning commonly are used to discourage the impulsive behavior. Satiation, under controlled conditions, is another useful behavioral technique for fire setters. Overcorrection, via public confession and restitution, has also been part of the treatment of these clients. Assertiveness training and communication skills development can help alleviate interpersonal difficulties and increase clients' sense of control and power. Exploration of cognitions can help client and therapist understand the thinking that promotes the disorder (for example, "Setting fires will show people I'm not really a weakling"; "If I can only gamble a little longer, I'm sure I'll get that big win"; or "I'll show people they can't take advantage of me, I'll steal from them"). Underlying depression and anxiety also need to be relieved through therapy, since the impulsive behavior is often a way to manage those feelings. Family therapy may be indicated, too, particularly for those with pathological gambling or kleptomania, for those who abuse family members, and for adolescents involved in pyromania.

Because clients with these disorders vary greatly, treatment will need to be individualized to the needs and personality of the particular client. For example, those who are high in insight may benefit from a psychodynamic component to the therapy, while behavioral therapy will probably predominate with those who are low in insight. People who engage in pathological gambling or kleptomania seem particularly responsive to insight-oriented therapy (Kaplan & Sadock, 1985). The gamblers will probably require help in coping with their high need for stimulation, while those diagnosed as having an explosive disorder will need help in managing and expressing anger.

Limit setting is an important component of treatment for these disorders. Clients must deal with the legal or interpersonal consequences of their behaviors. Bailing them out of trouble seems to reinforce and perpetuate the behavior (Custer, 1984). At the same time, therapy needs to attend to the correlates of the disorder, including legal, financial, occupational, and family difficulties. Development of leisure activities and increased involvement in career and family can help replace the impulsive behavior. If the behavior has reached addictive proportions, clients may experience withdrawal-like symptoms in the aftermath of ceasing the behavior, and these symptoms will require attention in therapy in order to prevent relapse.

As with other impulse control disorders, the negative behavior is inherently gratifying and so reinforces itself and makes treatment difficult. Group therapy, with other clients who share the same problems, can often counteract the attraction of the impulse through peer confrontation and support. This approach to treatment is particularly common with pathological gamblers and with spouse abusers diagnosed as having intermittent explosive disorder. Gamblers Anonymous, modeled after Alcoholics Anonymous, offers another avenue to peer support. These groups can help fill the void left when the impulsive behavior is stopped and can offer understanding, concern, role models, and new behaviors.

Medication is occasionally useful in treatment of these disorders, especially for pyromania and explosive disorders. Those disorders may have a neurological component that can be modified by medication (such as lithium or anticonvulsant medication). Referral for a neurological examination should be made if organic impairment is suspected.

Prognosis. As with other impulse control disorders, the prognosis for the disorders reviewed in this section is uncertain, and relapse is common. Few figures are available on success rates for treatment. However, several of the disorders (for example, intermittent explosive disorder or kleptomania) tend to diminish spontaneously over time (Kaplan & Sadock, 1985).

7.5 Sleep Disorders

Description of Disorder. Sleep disorders are a very different type of behavioral disorder than those discussed earlier in this chapter. Unlike most of the other behavioral disorders, these disorders provide few secondary gains and rewards to clients, and they clearly want to be free of their symptoms. Sleep disorders, as described in the *DSM-III-R* (1987), are persistent and chronic disorders of at least one month's duration. They include two major subgroups: dyssomnias and parasomnias. Buchholz (1988) reports that 10–20 percent of the people in the United States have chronic sleep complaints and that insomnia and hypersomnia are the most common of these disorders.

Dyssomnias involve a disturbance in "amount, quality, or timing of sleep" (*DSM-III-R*, 1987, p. 297). They include insomnia (difficulty in falling asleep, maintaining sleep, or feeling rested after sleep), hypersomnia (excessive sleepiness during the day, not caused by lack of sleep), and sleep-wake schedule disorder (diagnosed in people who have difficulty accommodating to frequently changing schedules or whose own body schedule is not synchronized with the schedule they must follow). In making the diagnosis, the clinician would specify whether insomnia and hypersomnia are related to another (nonorganic) mental disorder (such as depression), related to a known organic factor (such as alcohol abuse or sleep apnea), or primary (not related to other factors). Sleep-wake schedule disorder would be described as characterized by a sleeping pattern that is advanced, delayed, disorganized, or frequently changing in relation to required sleeping hours.

The parasomnias, less likely to be seen in treatment, include dream anxiety disorder (nightmare disorder), sleep terror disorder, and sleepwalking disorder. These disorders generally begin in childhood and rarely are presented by adults. Consequently, little attention will be given to them here.

Relevant Client Characteristics. Insomnia, particularly in mild, nonclinical forms, is experienced by approximately 35 percent of adults in a given year. For an extended period of time, these people have required more than about thirty minutes to fall asleep. About half of them—primarily female, older, and experiencing health problems—have a serious sleep disorder (Mellinger, Balter, & Uhlenhuth, 1985).

Hypersomnia is far less common, occurring in only 1–2 percent of the population. When related to narcolepsy, it may have a genetic component (*DSM-III-R*, 1987). People with sleep apnea–related hypersomnia are often obese.

Clients with sleeping disorders often have underlying depression and anxiety (discussed in Chapters Five and Six). They typically have difficulty expressing their feelings directly and tend to somatize (see Chapter Eight). Presentation of their sleep disorder may be a way to seek help for underlying concerns that they are reluctant to acknowledge.

Kales, Soldatos, and Kales (1982) found that adults with parasomnias appear active, outwardly directed, hostile, aggressive, and easily frustrated. Underneath their facades, however, they are often anxious, depressed, or phobic (see section 6.3) and tend to have negative views of themselves.

Relevant Therapist Variables. Therapists treating sleep disorders seem to be most successful if they assume an active, directive, yet supportive stance. Clients with these disorders often have deferred seeking help until the problems became overwhelming, and they need reassurance and active intervention to modify the symptoms quickly. People with sleep disorders will sometimes be resistant to exploration of lifestyle and possible underlying concerns, and this resistance must be addressed and reduced by the therapist.

Intervention Strategies. Insomnia and hypersomnia are often related to or caused by other disorders or situations, such as depression (Chapter Five), stress reactions (section 4.1), and substance use disorders (section 7.1). These other disorders, therefore, also will require attention. Clients with sleep disorders also may have life circumstances that interfere with their obtaining restful sleep (for example, a noisy environment or an uncomfortable living situation). When clients present with symptoms of sleep disorders, then, a careful history taking is indicated to ascertain the dynamics of the disorder. Careful interviewing is particularly indicated with clients who present sleep-wake schedule disorders, since their lifestyle and their work schedules often contribute to this disorder. Another reason for thorough interviewing is that up to 30 percent of those who complain of insomnia actually sleep well (Buchholz, 1988).

If a disorder such as depression or substance abuse seems to be causing the sleep disorder, focusing on the disorder that is exacerbating the sleep problems may take priority, and successful treatment of that disorder may automatically relieve the sleep disorder. However, it is often difficult to shift clients' focus from their sleeping difficulties to their underlying concerns.

Research on the use of psychotherapy to treat sleep disorders is limited. Most of the relevant research has been done by medical researchers working in sleep laboratories. However, some guidelines have been provided for the use of psychotherapy to treat these disorders, once organic causes have been ruled out. If the focus of treatment will be on the sleep disorder, the therapist first should ensure that clients have a sleeping environment that is conducive to restful sleep and should help them to stabilize their sleep schedule, eliminating naps and caffeine and establishing healthy patterns of eating, drinking, and exercising.

A number of behavioral techniques have been used successfully in the treatment of insomnia. Insomnia often has a self-perpetuating course. The sleeping difficulty causes people to worry about not sleeping, and that, in turn, exacerbates the insomnia. Breaking the cycle is important in reducing the symptoms. Clients should be discouraged from lying in bed for long periods of time and worrying about not sleeping; they should get up and engage in another activity, perhaps writing about a source of concern, until they feel tired.

Borkovec (1982) found that relaxation and biofeedback are consistently effective in the treatment of insomnia, yielding an average reduction of 45 percent in latency of sleep onset. Woolfolk and McNulty (1983) also support the use of progressive relaxation, as well as positive imagery. They compared four treatments for insomnia with no treatment. The four treatments included (1) group imagery training, (2) imagery training with muscle relaxation, (3) somatic focusing/focusing on and releasing tension, and (4) progressive relaxation. At six-month follow-up, Woolfolk and McNulty found that all four treatments were better than no treatment and that imagery training seemed to have the greatest positive impact.

Sleep restriction, another technique that has been effective in treating insomnia, is a behavioral-shaping procedure in which clients are instructed not to go to sleep until the time they usually fall asleep. This time is then gradually moved back in increments of fifteen to thirty minutes until the clients are going to sleep at an appropriate time.

Education as part of treatment can provide clients with needed reassurance—for example, the reassurance that no permanent damage will result from missed sleep (Buchholz, 1988).

Sedative-hypnotic medication can help stabilize sleep. However, that medication is potentially addictive and should probably be viewed as a treatment of last resort. If medication is used to treat sleep disorders, it should be viewed as an adjunct to psychotherapy (Kales, Soldatos, & Kales, 1982). Some nonprescription substances might facilitate stable sleep patterns. L-tryptophan, an amino acid available at health food stores, for example, has been found to reduce insomnia. However, the effectiveness of this and other over-the-counter preparations has not been well established.

Unlike insomnia, hypersomnia usually has a physical rather than a psychological basis (Buchholz, 1988). Consequently, treatment of hypersomnia should always include a medical evaluation. Common causes of hypersomnia include sleep apnea (particularly in middle-aged, overweight males) and narcolepsy, as well as medication. Medical treatment (for example, treatment for weight loss, stimulant medication, or surgery) is usually primary for these causes, although, regardless of the cause, clients with hypersomnia are likely to benefit from the establishment of a regular sleeping schedule and healthy eating and exercise. Psychotherapy, dealing with both underlying stressors and the stress introduced by the hypersomnia, is also indicated.

In children, the parasomnias are typically the result of a developmental lag and are usually outgrown (Kales, Soldatos, & Kales, 1982), although they may reflect a stress reaction. In adults, parasomnias are more likely to be linked to underlying emotional disorders. Kales, Solatos, and Kales recommend insight-oriented treatment for these disorders, so that clients can understand the precipitants of the disorder and acquire more effective coping mechanisms. Assertiveness training may facilitate better self-expression, and desensitization may reduce fears that are contributing to the parasomnia.

In addition to specific treatment for the sleep disorder, therapists also should attend to any underlying conflicts or sources of excessive arousal (Kales, Soldatos, & Kales, 1982). If the sleep disorder has been longstanding and chronic, it may have damaged clients' occupational and social life; and these, too, might need to be addressed in therapy.

Prognosis. The prognosis for reducing sleep disorders seems quite good. However, an accurate assessment of etiology seems critical in determining outcome. Those with an organic cause are likely to respond well to medical treatment or to alleviation of the cause; those with a psychological cause are likely to respond well to psychotherapy, as long as any underlying disorders are also addressed.

Summary of Treatment Recommendations

This chapter has focused on the diagnosis and treatment of five groups of disorders of behavior and impulse control: psychoactive substance use disorders, eating disorders, sexual disorders, other impulse control disorders, and sleep disorders. Although the symptoms of these disorders vary widely, they do have an underlying commonality, behavioral dysfunction. The following general treatment recommendations, organized according to the format of the client map, are provided for disorders of behavior and impulse control.

Diagnoses. Disorders of behavior and impulse control
Objectives. Behavioral change: reduction of dysfunctional behaviors; acquisition of new and more positive ones
Assessment. Physical examination, symptom inventory
Clinician. Professional or paraprofessional with knowledge of individual, group, and family therapy as well as extensive information on the specific disorder; able to be structured and directive yet supportive; able to manage potential negative feelings toward client behaviors; able to work effectively with client's resistance and hostility
Location. Usually outpatient, but short-term inpatient treat-

ment may be necessary for severe cases of substance use
disorder or eating disorders

Interventions. Multifaceted intervention program emphasizing behavioral therapy, including measurement of
change, education, improvement of communication and
relationship skills, attention to aspects of client's life (for
example, career, leisure activities, family) that have been
harmed by the behavioral disorder

Emphasis. High in directiveness, moderate in supportiveness, focus on present behaviors and coping mechanisms

Nature. Group therapy is particularly important when client
resistance is high; individual therapy and family therapy
also are important

Timing. Rapid pace, therapy of short to medium duration

Medication. Not the primary mode of treatment, but such
drugs as Antabuse, methadone, and antidepressant medication can accelerate progress in some cases. Medical examination typically is very important

Adjunct services. Nonprofessional support groups (such as
AA or NA)

Prognosis. Good prognosis for significant improvement if
client is (or becomes) motivated toward change, although
relapse is common

Client Map of George W.

This chapter began with a description of George W., a thirty-
six-year-old male with a twenty-two-year history of alcohol abuse.
George was also experiencing legal, interpersonal, and marital
problems, although he had been a stable and responsible employee.
Some underlying depression and social discomfort were reported.
George was seen in therapy after his arrest for driving while intoxicated. The following client map outlines the treatment provided to
George, typical of that recommended for clients with alcohol abuse
or other behavioral disorders.

Diagnosis. Axis I: 303.90—Alcohol dependence, severe.
         Axis II: 799.90—Diagnosis deferred on Axis II.

Rule out avoidant personality disorder or avoidant personality traits.

Axis III: High blood pressure, intestinal discomfort.

Axis IV: Psychosocial stressors: incarceration, conviction for third DWI, family stress. Severity: 4—severe, primarily acute.

Axis V: Current Global Assessment of Functioning: 55; highest GAF past year: 55.

Objectives. (1) Establish and maintain abstinence from alcohol.

(2) Improve marital relationship.

(3) Improve social skills.

(4) Obtain diagnosis and treatment for medical complaints.

Assessments. A thorough medical evaluation was conducted to determine the impact George's drinking has had on his physical condition and to obtain treatment for his physical complaints. The Minnesota Alcoholism Screening Test was used to clarify the extent of his alcohol use and nature of his symptoms.

Clinician. Clinician should have knowledge of the development and symptoms of alcohol dependence; should be structured and directive and skilled at limit setting.

Location. George had already been alcohol-free for several weeks as a result of his incarceration. Under other circumstances, his treatment would probably have begun with a twenty-eight-day inpatient program to evaluate his medical condition and provide medical supervision while he was adjusting to being without alcohol. However, because he was alcohol-free when therapy was begun, efforts would be made to treat George in an outpatient setting.

Interventions. A multifaceted treatment plan was established for George's longstanding disorder. The primary approach was behavior therapy, conducted in a group setting, with others who had abused alcohol. The therapy emphasized abstinence, established behavioral goals and consequences, provided peer support and feedback, taught more effective ways to manage stress and solve problems, and provided education on the impact of alcohol and patterns of abuse.

George and his wife also were seen for marital therapy. They needed help in communicating more clearly and effectively, in establishing a more rewarding marriage, and in changing patterns that facilitated George's alcohol abuse. They needed to establish an alcohol-free home and to build leisure and social activities that did not focus on drinking. Individual therapy also was a component of treatment at the outset.

Emphasis. Therapy would be directive, focused on present behavior, and include both supportive and exploratory elements.

Nature. Individual, group, and couples therapy.

Timing. Rapidly paced medium-term treatment with extended follow-up and participation in AA.

Medication. Antabuse was considered in light of George's longstanding alcohol problem, but he stated that he wanted to try remaining alcohol free without the help of medication. If an early relapse occurs, Antabuse will be considered again.

Adjunct services. George returned to work and, as a condition of his work-release program, met with his therapist and employer to discuss his difficulties and enlist the employer's help in monitoring and maintaining George's sobriety. George was referred to Alcoholics Anonymous and made a commitment to attend at least three meetings a week. In time, he would also be referred to an Adult Children of Alcoholics (ACOA) group. His wife was referred to an Al-Anon group.

Prognosis. George has both internal and external motivation. He acknowledged a need to reduce or eliminate his drinking, although he was reluctant to make a commitment to long-term abstinence. He knows that his job and his marriage are in jeopardy if he continues to abuse alcohol. He also knows that another conviction may lead to a lengthy incarceration. These factors all improve the prognosis. However, relapses are common for clients who abuse drugs and alcohol. Therefore, although the intensive phase of George's treatment will probably end when he leaves prison in six months, long-term follow-up and participation in Alcoholics Anonymous are indicated.

Recommended Readings

Agras, W. S. (1987). *Eating disorders.* Elmsford, NY: Pergamon Press.

Berger, P. A., & Dunn, M. J. (1982). Substance induced and substance use disorders. In J. H. Greist, J. W. Jefferson, & R. L. Spitzer (Eds.), *Treatment of mental disorders* (pp. 78–142). New York: Oxford University Press.

Borkovec, T. D. (1982). Insomnia. *Journal of Consulting and Clinical Psychology, 50,* 880–895.

Boskind-White, M., & White, W. C., Jr. (1983). *Bulimarexia: The binge-purge cycle.* New York: Norton.

Brandsma, J. M., Maultsby, M. C., & Welsh, R. J. (1980). *Outpatient treatment of alcoholism: A review and comparative study.* Baltimore: University Park Press.

Bratter, T. E., & Forrest, G. G. (Eds.). (1985). *Alcoholism and substance abuse.* New York: Free Press.

Kaplan, H. S. (1979). *Disorders of sexual desire.* New York: Brunner/Mazel.

Chapter Eight

Disorders Combining Physical and Psychological Factors

Case Study: Melvin B.

Melvin B., a sixty-two-year-old black male, was referred for therapy by his physician. He had been diagnosed as having gastric ulcers and was being treated by his physician for that disorder. However, the physician believed that his patient's medical complaints were exacerbated by his emotional condition, and therefore referred him for therapy.

Dr. B. had been a dentist with his own practice for almost thirty-five years. The neighborhood where he was practicing was deteriorating, as was the number of patients who sought out his services. He was losing many of his affluent patients to younger, more technologically sophisticated dentists; and the people from lower socioeconomic groups in his area seemed to have less inclination to consult dentists. In addition, Dr. B. was experiencing stress at home. He had been divorced ten years ago and had remarried five years ago. His second wife is twenty years younger than he. He felt that she was disappointed in him because of his current decline in income, and he was afraid that his marriage would end. He worked long hours in an effort to improve his practice and took a great deal of often self-prescribed medication for his gastric symptoms. He was rarely at home, had few friends and leisure activities, and had considerable difficulty verbalizing his feelings.

Overview of Disorders Combining Physical and Psychological Factors

Description of Disorder. Dr. B. is experiencing a disorder called "psychological factors affecting physical condition," one of three groups of disorders in which physical complaints, typically of greatest concern to the clients, are intertwined with emotional difficulties, so that treatment is required for both physical and emotional problems.

Disorders to be considered in this chapter include somatoform disorders, psychological factors affecting physical condition, and factitious disorders. Clients with these disorders generally present for treatment with concern about a physical complaint. Often, they come to therapy because of a referral from a physician who could not find an organic cause for their complaints or who believed that the clients' emotional difficulties were contributing to their physical problems. The clients may or may not be aware of the dynamics of their disorders. In either case, their focus is typically on their physical concerns, and they may be resistant to and surprised by the suggestion that they would benefit from psychotherapy.

Relevant Client Characteristics. People with disorders in which physical and psychological factors combine typically have difficulty expressing emotions directly and so channel concerns into the physiological realm. Many were sickly as children or had close contact with people who suffered long illnesses, and they learned that being sick is a way to get attention. They often are having trouble managing environmental stress and tend not to be very insightful or psychologically minded. Sometimes they have strong dependency needs and want others to take care of them.

Relevant Therapist Variables. Therapists treating clients with these disorders benefit from having some information on medical complaints and should be comfortable working collaboratively with physicians. The therapists need to be skilled at developing rapport and communicating support and interest, so that a helpful therapeutic relationship is established fairly rapidly. Clients will often be resistant and will dispute the importance of psychological variables. If the therapist is harshly confrontational or unsympathetic, the client may well terminate treatment. On the other hand, if the therapist overemphasizes the physical complaints, little progress will be made. The therapist, then, must walk a fine line in treating these clients. In treatment, the therapist should be concrete and structured and should be comfortable using styles of intervention that are flexible and involve little in-depth analysis.

Intervention Strategies. There is a dearth of controlled studies on the treatment of the disorders in this section. However, case studies and theoretical articles provide a good indication of the sort of treatment that is most likely to be effective.

The first step in treating clients who present with interrelated physical and psychological complaints is to obtain a medical consultation (or to confer with physicians whom the client has already consulted). The therapist then can determine whether a physical disorder is really present, become familiar with its impact on the client, and ensure that appropriate medical treatment is provided if needed. Clients should be kept informed about their medical condition and should be involved in decisions about their medical treatment. If they believe that their medical symptoms are being ignored, they may try to obtain medical attention by manifesting an increase in somatization.

Therapy with these clients generally deemphasizes interpretation and analysis, because of the resistance those approaches might provoke in clients who are primarily seeking relief of physical complaints. Therapy is typically eclectic, focusing on affective, cognitive, and behavioral areas to build up the clients' coping mechanisms, reduce depression and anxiety, modify cognitions promoting hopelessness and dependency, and help clients meet their needs more effectively, so that they do not need to somatize or use illness to gain attention. Leisure and career counseling can facilitate that process; and family counseling can prevent reinforcement of secondary gains, such as the extra attention the clients receive when they feel ill. Such models as Gestalt counseling, stress management, and hypnotherapy can be particularly useful in helping clients integrate physical and emotional aspects of themselves.

Prognosis. The prognosis for treating disorders in which physical and psychological factors combine varies greatly, depending on the dynamics of the clients' concerns and their receptivity to therapy. If they can acknowledge that they do have emotional concerns that might benefit from therapy and are able to shift their focus from their physical concerns to their emotional difficulties, they may well derive considerable benefit from therapy, not only in reducing their perceived physical complaints but also in increasing their self-confidence and self-esteem and improving the quality of their lives.

8.1 Somatoform Disorders

Description of Disorder. Somatoform disorders are characterized by physical complaints that have no known physiological or organic cause and are, therefore, believed to be caused by psychological factors. However, people with these disorders genuinely believe that they are afflicted with the symptoms and physical illnesses they are presenting and are typically very distressed about both their physiological complaints and the failure of the medical community to find and resolve an organic cause for their symptoms.

The *DSM-III-R* (1987) lists five types of somatoform disorders. *Body dysmorphic disorder* involves a "preoccupation with some imagined defect in physical appearance" (p. 255). People with this disorder are not experiencing a delusion and can acknowledge that they might be exaggerating, but they do not have a realistic image of themselves. *Conversion disorder* was well known in Freud's time but is relatively rare today. It involves a loss or change in physical functioning (for example, blindness or paralysis of a limb) with no organic cause. *Hypochondriasis,* probably the best known of these disorders, is typically characterized by an assumption that minor physical complaints, such as a cough or a headache, are symptoms of serious disease, such as lung cancer or a brain tumor. People with *somatization disorder* have multiple chronic physical complaints for which they seek medical treatment and modify their lifestyle. Finally, *somatoform pain disorder* entails either an excessive reaction to an existing physical pain or a preoccupation with a pain that is not shown to have a medical origin.

Relevant Client Characteristics. Somatoform disorders tend to begin in people before they are thirty years old, and these disorders follow a chronic but often inconsistent course (Gutsch, 1988). They seem to be more common in women (Viederman, 1986). People with these disorders tend to become preoccupied with their illness and medical history and deemphasize other areas of their lives, often experiencing social or occupational impairment as a result. Use of both prescription and nonprescription medication to relieve symptoms is common, and clients' lives may revolve around medication schedules and medical appointments and tests. Some become dependent on analgesics.

Clients with somatoform disorders also restrict their activities, movement, and level of stimulation, in the belief that they might thereby prevent a worsening of the pain or other symptoms (Philips, 1987). Their focus on and amplification of their bodily symptoms often leads to social isolation and depression, which, in turn, intensify their experience of and focus on symptoms. These clients often manifest attitudes of learned helplessness, reinforced by early family and social experiences, and tend to be discouraged, worried, angry, and low in self-esteem. They often have a sense of emptiness and a poverty of affect, feeling that they cannot build rewarding lives until their physical complaints have been alleviated. Underlying depression may be reflected in sleeping and eating patterns, and it may be difficult for therapists as well as clients to separate out physical concerns related to depression, somatoform disorders, and organically based physical problems.

Clients often report a family history of illness, and the clients' symptoms may mirror those experienced by family members while the clients were children. The clients themselves may have been sickly when younger and may have learned that physical illness gained more attention than verbal expressions of emotional discomfort.

In addition to the above research on the relationship between somatoform disorders and personality patterns, some research also has been conducted on the personality patterns of people with specific types of somatoform disorders. Gutsch (1988) notes that people with somatoform pain disorder often had close friends or family members who experienced chronic pain; tend to be in strenuous, routinized, difficult jobs where experiencing pain is common; and reject the idea that their pain has a psychological origin. Their experience of pain is often connected to a threatened loss or an unresolved conflict, which has given rise to negative feelings that they are expressing through somatization (Kaufman & Aronoff, 1983). Viederman (1986) found that somatoform pain disorder often reflects masked depression and that the families of people with this disorder have a high incidence of chronic pain, alcoholism, and depression.

Disability associated with conversion disorder is often localized in body parts that have been affected previously by injury or illness or that have some special significance. Clients with this disorder tend to describe their symptoms in rich detail but seem almost indifferent to the potential for impairment inherent in their symptoms (Viederman, 1986). Some are alexithymic and have little capacity for experiencing and expressing feelings (Kaplan & Sadock, 1985). These clients tend to feel dependent and helpless, and they use their physical complaints as a way to relate to others and to gain attention. Conversion disorder seems particularly common among those from lower socioeconomic groups and among blacks (Maxmen, 1986) and is often associated with dependent or histrionic personality disorders (sections 9.9 and 9.5) (Meyer, 1983).

Viederman (1986) reports that 4–14 percent of the people in the United States have experienced hypochondriasis. Men and women seem to be equally represented among those with this disorder. Hypochondriasis tends to begin in childhood or adolescence, but not infrequently it first appears in mid-life and is often related to the mid-life transition (Meyer, 1983). Hypochondriasis is often associated with an early bereavement, a history of illness in the family, and overprotective parents; like conversion disorder, it is particularly common in those from lower socioeconomic backgrounds. Other disturbances—such as anxiety, depression, mistrust, underlying anger and hostility, obsessive compulsive traits, fear of disease, a low pain threshold, personality disorders, and disturbed early relationships—often accompany hypochondriasis; and the disorder may be situational or chronic, typically worsening during times of stress or emotional arousal (Kellner, 1985).

Somatization disorder, also known as Briquet's syndrome, is more common in females than in males and may be found in as many as 1–2 percent of women (Viederman, 1986). The disorder also is prevalent among blacks and those who are not well educated or affluent (Maxmen, 1986). Somatization disorder tends to appear in young adulthood and, without treatment, is typically persistent and exacerbated by stress. Some of the physical symptoms presented refer to prior or current medical conditions that can be treated; others do not seem to have a physiological cause.

Somatization disorder seems to have a familial component. The female relatives of people with this disorder often have the same disorder, while their male relatives, particularly their husbands or fathers, often manifest alcohol abuse or antisocial behavior. The families of origin of people with somatization disorder tend to be disorganized, and the clients themselves often had problems of adjustment as children and may have been abused.

These clients are often manipulative, suicidal, dependent, overemotional, exhibitionistic, and narcissistic (Kaplan & Sadock, 1985). Lilienfeld, VanValkenburg, Larntz, and Akiskal (1986) suggest that somatization disorder and histrionic and antisocial personality disorders (sections 9.5 and 9.4) are different stages of the same disorder and share an underlying structure. The three often overlap, coexist, and are found in the same families. Histrionic personality disorder frequently accompanies somatization disorder in females, and those females have an unusual number of male relatives with antisocial personality disorders.

Relevant Therapist Variables. It seems important for the therapist to assume a warm, positive, optimistic stance with these clients. They need a stable relationship that provides acceptance, approval, and empathy. Viederman (1986) suggests that the therapist should communicate admiration for the suffering these clients have endured. At the same time, the therapist needs to be careful not to reinforce clients' assumption of a sick role but, rather, to gradually shift the focus off the physical illness and encourage stress management, increased activities and socialization, and positive verbalization. The therapist needs to take a structured and relatively directive approach, to prevent the sessions from becoming just a place where clients can complain about how awful they feel (Getto & Ochitill, 1982), and also needs to promote a sense of self-efficacy on the part of clients, giving them a feeling of control over their medical and psychological treatments.

Some therapists may experience annoyance and even anger with these clients if they refuse to let go of their belief that they have a serious physical disorder, or if they view therapists and physicians as adversaries because they have not found a physical cause for the clients' complaints. Therapists need to be aware of their reactions to these client behaviors and attitudes in order to prevent countertransference reactions from harming the therapeutic relationship.

Intervention Strategies. As with all the disorders in this chapter, a team approach to treatment is indicated, with physician and therapist working together. This approach reassures clients that their physical symptoms are not being ignored and also gives needed attention to their emotional difficulties. Education can help clients realize that their symptoms are benign and that they are receiving appropriate treatment. Presenting both physiological and psychological components to treatment as an integrated treatment package can promote treatment compliance.

Allergies and other difficult-to-diagnose medical disorders may be responsible for the clients' physiological symptoms. Therapists should monitor medical treatment of these clients, to make sure that an agitated client with a long medical history is not being dismissed prematurely by a busy physician but, rather, is receiving appropriate medical tests and treatment. At the same time, therapists should encourage these clients to avoid excessive and unnecessary medical tests and treatments.

Overall treatment goals should focus on improving functioning rather than on reducing physical symptoms; in most cases, symptoms will spontaneously decrease if functioning is improved. In general, insight-oriented therapy is not effective in treating these disorders. Therapy should focus on the present rather than on the past (Viederman, 1986) and should emphasize techniques designed to increase stress management and coping skills, facilitate verbal expression of feelings, promote clients' sense of self-control, and reinforce healthy cognitions as well as increased activity and socialization.

Thought stopping, flooding, and exercise have been found to contribute to treatment (Kellner, 1985). Techniques designed to reduce the fear of death as well as the anxiety and depression associated with somatoform disorders should also facilitate progress. In addition, clients with these disorders often benefit from relaxation, particularly when counterpoised with pain symptoms, to give them control over their symptoms (Gutsch, 1988). Biofeedback is another technique that can promote a sense of control and reduce physical symptoms. The clients' tendency toward selective perception, exaggerating physiological symptoms, can be reduced through cognitive-behavioral therapy.

Group therapy is often an important component of treatment for these disorders. It can promote socialization, provide support, and facilitate direct expression of emotions. Hendler (1981) recommends eclectic group therapy as the primary form of treatment because it can change clients' expression of symptoms, reduce depression, modify avoidance behaviors, help clients assume responsibility for their symptoms, enhance their ability to enjoy life, provide information and support as well as reinforcement, and teach relaxation and other positive behaviors.

Kellner (1982b) suggests an approach to treating hypochondriasis that has application to the other somatoform disorders. Beginning with a physical examination and information gathering, therapy next focuses on helping clients understand how distress can aggravate symptoms. Clients then are helped to reduce the stressors in their lives. Once that has been accomplished, therapy typically encompasses the following five steps: (1) exploration of attitudes toward illness, (2) information provided on the client's medical condition, (3) perceptual retraining to help client focus more on external information and less on internal cues, (4) suggestion that symptoms will be reduced, and (5) encouragement of self-talk and internal dialogue to reduce anxiety.

Rogers (1983) recommends a Gestalt approach to treating psychogenic pain. The approach also seems to have application to other somatoform disorders because of the Gestalt emphasis on the mind-body relationship. Rogers uses fantasy, physical expression of anger, and other techniques to promote awareness and more appropriate expression of feelings.

Some hospitals have pain treatment units that can facilitate treatment of clients with somatoform pain disorder. These programs typically involve four to twelve weeks of inpatient treatment, aimed at decreasing clients' experience of pain as well as their reliance on medication while increasing their activity level, their cognitive control over the pain, and their effective use of coping mechanisms (Getto & Ochitill, 1982). Also, these programs usually offer a multidisciplinary approach to treatment, including detoxification from medication (if needed); physical, occupational, and recreational therapy; group, individual, and family therapy; and various forms of relaxation (such as biofeedback or progressive relaxation).

Whatever approach to treatment of somatoform disorders is used, healthy, independent, responsible behavior should be encouraged. Family members should be involved in the treatment, so that they can learn to reinforce positive behavior and, when appropriate, ignore or deemphasize clients' physical complaints. Clients need to learn to get attention and affection by means other than physical illness; and these alternative means can best be practiced and reinforced, for most clients, in the family environment. Moreover, Getto and Ochitill (1982) found that clients are more receptive to therapy if it is endorsed by a family member, friend, or professional whose opinion they value. If the client has a history of conflicted and dysfunctional family relationships or is still troubled by the illness or death of a family member, therapy may need to pay some attention to those issues in an effort to reduce their present impact on the client.

Because many people with somatoform disorders have neglected social and occupational areas of their lives, those areas should receive attention through therapy. Clients often will need to build support systems, to develop leisure activities that they have been avoiding because these activities might exacerbate the physical problems, and to establish and work toward realistic and rewarding career goals. Environmental modifications, such as walking to work with a neighbor, may encourage some of these lifestyle changes by reducing secondary gains and altering patterns of activity.

In general, medication is not integral to the treatment of somatoform disorders. It usually does not eliminate the physical symptoms, and clients may continue to rely on medication to resolve their complaints. Medication prescribed for use on an as-needed basis seems particularly risky. However, if clients have severe anxiety or depression related to their physical complaints, a short course of medication may help to reduce the affective symptoms, so that clients are more accessible to therapy.

Prognosis. Somatoform disorders tend to be persistent and resistant to treatment. Kaplan and Sadock (1985) report that a good prognosis is associated with the ability to form stable relationships, to feel and express emotions directly, to form a therapeutic alliance, and to be introspective. A good prognosis also is associated with symptoms that are circumscribed and stress related.

Prognosis varies, depending on the specific disorder and the individual client. Somatization disorder, for example, seems to have a particularly poor prognosis (Viederman, 1986). The prognosis for hypochondriasis has also been regarded as poor, but Getto and Ochitill (1982) and others have reported relatively positive treatment outcomes. Kellner (1985), for example, reports a positive prognosis for treatment of hypochondriasis in which clients were from a high socioeconomic background, were young, did not have coexisting personality disorders or organicity, had few previous medical problems, and had a disorder that was of sudden onset and relatively brief duration. Pain treatment centers report a 60–80 percent rate of significant improvement among clients with somatoform pain disorder, and the improvement has been well maintained after discharge. Symptoms of conversion disorder often spontaneously disappear within a few weeks or months but tend to be difficult to treat once they become entrenched (Maxmen, 1986).

8.2 Psychological Factors Affecting Physical Condition

Description of Disorder. According to the *DSM-III-R* (1987), a condition diagnosed as "psychological factors affecting physical condition" differs from somatoform disorder in that, in the former, there is a medically verifiable physical disorder or condition that is related to (initiated, worsened, or maintained by) the client's emotional condition. (In somatoform disorder, the client's reported physical complaint is not medically verified.) The physical disorder that has been diagnosed would be listed on Axis III of a multiaxial diagnosis and might include such physical conditions as obesity, migraine headaches, acne, asthma, rheumatoid arthritis, ulcers, and nausea and vomiting. Psychological factors affecting physical condition are often reflected in a negative cycle, in which stress and related emotional difficulties worsen the client's physical ailment while concern about and discomfort from the physical ailment increase the client's stress.

Pomerleau and Rodin (1986) have noted the frequent relationship between physical illness and stress: "The magnitude of critical life changes in a given period is related to the likelihood of subsequent bodily illness" (p. 486). Severe or chronic stress has been linked to a broad range of physical disorders and is often a factor in the development of psychological factors affecting physical condition.

In mild forms, these are common disorders, occurring in up to 50 percent of the population (Blanchard, 1981). In most cases, the manifestations of psychological factors affecting physical condition are brief, transient reactions that do not receive psychotherapy and may not even receive medical treatment. For example, a recent college graduate recently employed as a business executive experienced a great deal of stress because of the many changes in her life. For several months, she felt fatigued and had painful headaches. However, her busy schedule prevented her from seeking medical attention; and, as she became comfortable in her new role, the headaches and fatigue gradually dissipated. However, in other cases, the severity of the physical disorder and its lack of response to traditional medical treatment will prompt a referral for psychotherapy.

Relevant Client Characteristics. People with this disorder are often experiencing considerable life stress and have coping mechanisms that are inadequate to help them handle the stress effectively. These people tend to have difficulty dealing with emotions, particularly aggression, and so channel feelings into physical disorders (Ramsey, Wittkower, & Warnes, 1976). People with this disorder typically have a physical weakness or predisposition that evolves into a medical disorder under conditions of stress and excessive arousal. Underlying depression is a common accompaniment of psychological factors affecting physical condition. Interpersonal conflicts, associated with deficits in assertiveness skills, often precede the onset of symptoms (Blanchard, 1981). This disorder, like somatoform disorders, tends to run in families and is often associated with a history of family dysfunction, particularly disruption in the mother/child relationship (Kaplan & Sadock, 1985).

Relevant Therapist Variables. Therapists treating this disorder need to be comfortable with and skilled at collaborating with both physicians and clients. Clients should be viewed as partners in treatment, to increase their sense of responsibility and reduce their need to somatize in order to gain attention. Therapists seem most likely to be successful if they communicate interest, empathy, and optimism and promote a sense of hopefulness in their clients (Ramsey, Wittkower, & Warnes, 1976). Support and acceptance will help the client accept the need for therapy. Therapists should familiarize themselves with the client's medical condition, so that they can help the client become properly informed about the condition.

Intervention Strategies. Psychological factors affecting physical condition is another disorder for which little data-based research on treatment is available. Suggestions for treatment, then, must be made tentatively, based on available case studies and theories. Everly (1986) recommends what he calls a biopsychosocial approach to treating this disorder. In this holistic model, attention is paid to clients' social, physical, and economic environments; their psychological coping and defense mechanisms and cognitive-affective style; and such biological factors as heredity, trauma, and predisposing organ vulnerability. The medical treatment recommended by a physician and any exercise and dietary program suggested by the physician or therapist would be the focus of the biological aspect of treatment.

Treatment of this disorder must involve collaboration between therapist and physician. The two should be consistent in the messages they are giving clients about the nature of their disorders, and both therapist and physician should try to ensure that clients are complying with the treatment recommended by the other.

Behavioral treatment of psychological factors affecting physical condition would be similar to that for the somatoform disorders; a present-oriented approach—facilitating expression of feelings, stress management, improved self-esteem, increased socialization and activity, and development of coping mechanisms—is indicated. Pomerleau and Rodin (1986) divided relevant behavioral treatment approaches into two groups: rest therapies (relaxation, biofeedback, systematic desensitization) and coping therapies (assertiveness training, social skills training, behavioral rehearsal, self-efficacy statements, and imaginal techniques) and found that a combination of these approaches could promote stress management and appropriate self-expression in clients. Cognitive-behavioral therapies, designed to relieve discouragement and preoccupation with the illness, also seem likely to contribute to the effective treatment of psychological factors affecting physical condition. A package of these approaches, planned in consultation with the physician and the client, seems likely to reduce symptoms.

The specific ingredients of the treatment would be determined primarily by (1) the stressors in the client's life and the client's ability to manage them and (2) the specific physical condition. For example, if the physical condition were obesity, the treatment plan would probably include such elements as self-monitoring of food intake, nutritional and health counseling, an exercise program, and self-presented consequences (Gutsch, 1988). According to Lambert's (1982) findings, relaxation training, biofeedback, hypnosis, assertiveness training, and cognitive self-control procedures contribute to the effective treatment of tension headaches; and hypnosis, systematic desensitization, and assertiveness training are useful in treating respiratory disorders. Biofeedback on heart rate, muscle tension, and blood pressure seems particularly useful when the medical illness is related to those processes.

For any illness with a psychological component, having clients chart the incidence and severity of their symptoms as well as recording their simultaneous emotional changes can clarify the relationship between emotional and physiological disorders. This process can facilitate treatment as well as the client's awareness of the mind-body connection and possibly also the client's increased acceptance of psychotherapy. Other homework assignments, such as practicing relaxation or using biofeedback techniques, also seem likely to accelerate progress.

Interpretation or analysis of the underlying dynamics of the physical condition generally does not seem advisable. That process can discourage clients and give them the message that they are being blamed for their illness (Maxmen, 1986).

Therapists should be sure to gather adequate information on clients' environment, so that specific interventions designed to reduce the stressors in the environment may be included in the treatment plan. The environmental component of treatment would focus on family, social and economic support systems, living situation, and career. The family might be taught to reduce the client's secondary gains, to encourage treatment compliance, and to understand the client's capabilities and limitations. Group therapy also can be useful in offering support, promoting coping mechanisms and socialization, and reinforcing improvement.

Prognosis. The overall prognosis for treatment of psychological factors affecting physical condition seems better than for treatment of somatoform disorders but also varies greatly, depending on the individual client and the nature of the medical concern. Improvement in the medical condition can begin a cycle that, with psychotherapy, will lead to improvement in both the physical and the emotional disorders. However, some clients leave treatment prematurely, primarily because they have difficulty accepting the need for therapy (Kaplan & Sadock, 1985).

Blanchard (1981) reports an effectiveness of 30–80 percent in studies of the behavioral treatment of psychological factors affecting physical condition. The prognosis seems particularly good for clients who take an active role in their own treatment and seek out information and therapy in an effort to understand and improve their physical conditions (Felton & Revenson, 1984).

8.3 Factitious Disorders

Description of Disorder. Factitious disorders are "character-ized by physical or psychological symptoms that are intentionally produced or feigned" (*DSM-III-R*, 1987, p. 315). Unlike people with somatoform disorders and psychological factors affecting physical condition, who really experience and believe in their physical com-plaints, people with factitious disorders simulate having symptoms in order to be treated as though they are ill. They are not feigning the symptoms in order to escape work or other obligations; rather, their primary goal is to assume the role of a patient. In a variation of this disorder, parents will attribute nonexistent medical symptoms to their children and coach the children to confirm the symptoms. Factitious disorders are among the most difficult disorders to diag-nose because of the client's untruthfulness and hidden agendas (Meyer, 1983).

The onset of this disorder usually occurs in early adulthood, often following a medically verified physical illness that places these clients in the patient role, a role they find rewarding and seek to repeat. Sometimes people with factitious disorders have worked in medical settings or are otherwise familiar with medical personnel and illnesses, thereby facilitating their simulation of the symptoms of illness. This disorder seems more common in males (*DSM-III-R*, 1987) and is severe in that it typically prevents clients' involvement in normal social and occupational activities.

Relevant Client Characteristics. Clients with factitious dis-orders tend to be immature, dramatic, grandiose, and demanding, insisting on attention but often refusing to comply with prescribed treatment. Maxmen (1986) reports that 50 percent engage in drug abuse, primarily of medication. The disorder is often accompanied by a personality disorder, particularly histrionic (section 9.5) or borderline (section 9.7) disorders, involving instability, self-destruc-tive and acting-out behavior, dependency, and manipulation. The ability of these clients to fool medical personnel is often gratifying and gives them a sense of power (Maxmen, 1986).

Males with this disorder tend to be unstable and egocentric, while the females tend to be younger, more stable, and more likely to be in the medical field (Viederman, 1986). As children, many were abused or neglected, with illness possibly being the only way for them to get attention. Relatives often have a history of mental disorders (Pope, Jones, & Jones, 1982). These clients may have undergone many surgical procedures and other medical treatments, which may have produced genuine physical complaints that require attention and complicate the picture.

Relevant Therapist Variables. Establishing a therapeutic alliance with these clients will almost always be extremely difficult. Therapists should be supportive and empathic but should gently confront the deception. They should avoid power struggles, open conflict, and humiliation of these clients and must manage their own feelings of anger and frustration in dealing with the clients' deception and manipulation.

Intervention Strategies. Clients with factitious disorders are rarely seen for psychotherapy, since they are typically not motivated to address their disorder. However, they may appear in treatment as a result of pressure from a family member or after discovery of their dissembling. Some may remain in treatment if attention is also paid to their feigned complaints and if the treatment meets some of their dependency needs, but most will leave treatment once they realize they have been found out. While in treatment, these clients are likely to be hostile and resistant, fighting the formation of a therapeutic relationship.

Information on treatment of this disorder is nearly all anecdotal or theoretical. Obtaining a sample size large enough for controlled research is extremely difficult. At present, there are no interventions known to be consistently effective in treatment of factitious disorders (Maxmen, 1986). Treatment recommendations, then, must be hypothetical and based on theory rather than data.

Only a few authors provide suggestions for treating factitious disorders. Meyer (1983) suggests that Reality Therapy can help these clients see that their current behavior is not really meeting their needs and can also help them find more rewarding ways of operating. Jefferson and Ochitill (1982) suggest focusing on any stressor that may have precipitated the disorder, providing support, and encouraging the development of more effective stress management and coping mechanisms. Kaplan and Sadock (1985) recommend initiating treatment with the clients on a closed ward, to prevent their disappearing or otherwise avoiding treatment.

Prognosis. In some cases, a factitious disorder is a response to environmental stress, and the disorder remits spontaneously when the stressor has passed. However, once the disorder becomes chronic and reflects a deeply entrenched lifestyle, the prognosis for treatment is poor (Jefferson & Ochitill, 1982).

Summary of Treatment Recommendations

This chapter has focused on three groups of disorders in which physical and psychological factors combine. Treatment recommendations for these disorders are summarized below according to the client map format.

Diagnoses. Disorders in which physical and psychological factors combine (somatoform disorders, psychological factors affecting physical condition, factitious disorder).

Objectives. Reduce somatization, promote more constructive expression of feelings and stress management, improve socialization and use of leisure time.

Assessments. Physical examination.

Clinician. Should have knowledge of physical disorders; also should be willing to collaborate with physicians, skilled at handling resistance, structured, concrete, warm, optimistic, and high in frustration tolerance.

Location. Usually outpatient.

Interventions. Team approach to treatment, holistic (cognitive, behavioral, and affective), increase stress management and coping skills, teach relaxation techniques, improve socialization.

Emphasis. Supportive; some attention to history but primarily present oriented; moderately directive; integrated focus on cognitive, behavioral, and affective areas.

Nature. Primarily individual therapy, with family therapy to reduce secondary gains and group therapy as indicated to promote socialization.

Timing. Pace geared to readiness of client; may need to be gradual.

Medication. As indicated by the physical disorder.

Adjunct services. Leisure and career counseling.

Prognosis. Fair.

Client Map of Melvin B.

This chapter opened with a description of Dr. B., a dentist who had been diagnosed as having gastric ulcers. He was referred for therapy by his physician, who believed that emotional factors were exacerbating the medical condition. Dr. B. was experiencing considerable stress related to his declining business, conflict in his second marriage, and his limited number of friends and leisure activities. Although resistant to psychotherapy, he agreed to try it in the hope that it would relieve his discomfort from his ulcer condition. Information on treatment of his disorder is presented below.

Diagnosis. Axis I: 316.00—Psychological factors affecting physical condition.

Axis II: V71.09—No diagnosis on Axis II.

Axis III: Gastric ulcers.

Axis IV: Psychosocial stressors: occupational and financial dissatisfaction, marital conflict. Severity: 3—moderate (primarily enduring events).

Axis V: Current Global Assessment of Functioning: 65; highest GAF past year: 70.

Objectives. (1) Improve stress management and coping mechanisms.

(2) Improve marital relationship.

(3) Facilitate development of realistic occupational and financial goals.

(4) Improve medical condition.

Assessments. Physical evaluation.

Clinician. Warm, optimistic, yet skilled at handling resistance; knowledgeable about medical concern; mature and experienced. Throughout the therapy, the therapist would be supportive and accepting, yet directive and structured.

Location. Outpatient.

Interventions. Although the therapist was the primary engineer of Dr. B.'s treatment, both Dr. B. and his physician were involved in developing the treatment—in order to be sure that physical and psychological treatments were compatible and to give Dr. B. a sense of control, which he was lacking in other areas of his life.

Treatment was multifaceted and involved the following elements: (1) Education on the impact of stress on gastric ulcers and on diet designed to reduce the discomfort of the ulcers. (2) Supportive and reflective counseling designed to promote Dr. B.'s awareness of his feelings and his ability to verbalize those feelings. (3) Stress management techniques, including progressive relaxation and development of some leisure activities. (4) Exploration of career-related attitudes, abilities, and opportunities, in order to help Dr. B. establish more realistic and rewarding career goals. Partial retirement and half-time work in area nursing homes was an avenue that held considerable appeal for him and seemed likely to reduce stress and stabilize (though perhaps not improve) his financial situation. (5) Marital therapy to improve communication between Dr. B. and his wife, help him understand her feelings, and define a lifestyle that was mutually acceptable and realistic for them.

Emphasis. Structured, relatively directive, but encouraging client to take appropriate responsibility for his own treatment.

Nature. Individual and couples.

Timing. Rapid pace, medium duration, weekly sessions.

Medication. Carefully monitored medication for ulcer.

Adjunct services. Financial and retirement planning, leisure counseling.

Prognosis. Fair to good.

Recommended Readings

Everly, G. S., Jr. (1986). A biopsychosocial analysis of psychosomatic disease. In T. Millon & G. Klerman (Eds.), *Contemporary directions in psychopathology* (pp. 535–551). New York: Guilford Press.

Getto, C. J., & Ochitill, H. (1982). Psychogenic pain disorder. In J. H. Greist, J. W. Jefferson, & R. L. Spitzer (Eds.), *Treatment of mental disorders* (pp. 277–286). New York: Oxford University Press.

Gutsch, K. U. (1988). *Psychotherapeutic approaches to specific DSM-III-R categories*. Springfield, IL: Thomas.

Kellner, R. (1982). Psychotherapeutic strategies in hypochondriasis: A clinical study. *American Journal of Psychotherapy, 36,* 146–157.

Viederman, M. (1986). Somatoform and factitious disorders. In A. M. Cooper, A. J. Frances, & M. H. Sacks (Eds.), *The personality disorders and neuroses* (pp. 363–382). Philadelphia: Lippincott.

Chapter Nine

▌▌

Personality
Disorders

Case Study: Bill M.

Bill M., a twenty-nine-year-old male, was completing a prison term
after a conviction for possession and sale of a controlled substance,
cocaine; he was referred to therapy as a condition of his participation in a prerelease program. Bill grew up in a lower socioeconomic
neighborhood, where he had little supervision. His mother left the
family when Bill's older brothers were seven and eight years old and
Bill was five. His father, an alcoholic, worked inconsistent hours,
was away from home a great deal, and paid little attention to his
children. Discipline was harsh if the boys made noise at home or
stole from the house, but otherwise the children were largely ignored. Bill's brother introduced him to marijuana and alcohol
when he was nine years old, and he had been using drugs and
alcohol since that time.

Bill rarely had attended school and spent most of his time
there in the principal's office. Bill cursed the teachers, stole money
from the younger children, and wrote his name on the walls of the
school. He was popular among those who shared his values, dated
extensively, and was married at sixteen when his girlfriend became
pregnant. They were divorced when Bill was nineteen, and he has
had little contact with his ex-wife or their child since. He had a

child with another woman two years later. That child was severely retarded and was placed in an institution. When he was twenty-four, Bill married again and had two more children. He and his wife, also a drug and alcohol abuser, were planning to separate.

Bill had good skills as a landscape gardener and was able to locate short-term employment easily, but he worked only when he could find no easier way to obtain funds. He had been selling drugs for many years, and this was his third conviction. According to Bill, his arrest was unjustified; he had been set up for arrest by a friend who was seeking a reduced sentence for his own conviction. As Bill put it, "I wasn't really doing anything wrong. It's not like I was selling drugs to children. I didn't force anybody to buy drugs."

Overview of Personality Disorders

Bill has a personality disorder. As can be seen from the case study, personality disorders are longstanding, deeply ingrained disorders that are characterized by maladaptive attitudes and behaviors. Like Bill, most people with personality disorders have difficulty accepting appropriate responsibility for their concerns and have poor coping mechanisms and relationship skills. Because their disorders are enduring and deeply entrenched, people with personality disorders are difficult to treat. This chapter will begin with an overview of personality disorders and will then review information on the diagnosis and treatment of twelve types of personality disorders.

Description of Disorder. According to the *DSM-III-R* (1987), "Personality traits are enduring patterns of perceiving, relating to, and thinking about the environment and oneself, and are exhibited in a wide range of important social and personal contexts. It is only when *personality traits* are inflexible and maladaptive and cause either significant functional impairment or subjective distress that they constitute *personality disorders*" (p. 335). Personality disorders, the focus of this chapter, are, therefore, longstanding, deeply embedded, pervasive, and dysfunctional patterns of functioning. In Millon's (1981) view, personality disorders are characterized by adaptive inflexibility in relating and coping; vicious circles in which problems are generated and perpetuated by constriction, distortion, and generalization; and instability leading to overreaction to difficulty and change. Personality disorders are usually evident by early adolescence and tend to continue throughout life, although some personality disorders commonly become less prominent in the middle or later years.

Personality disorders tend to be ego-syntonic; although people with personality disorders may be dissatisfied with their relationships or the way their lives are going, they have difficulty taking responsibility for their concerns and are resistant to change. Even for those whose personality disorders are ego-dystonic or in conflict with their self-images, change is difficult because they lack earlier healthy personality patterns.

In the *DSM-III-R*, the personality disorders are grouped into the following three clusters:

1. Cluster A (appear odd or eccentric)—paranoid, schizoid, and schizotypal personality disorders.
2. Cluster B (appear dramatic, emotional, or unpredictable)—antisocial, borderline, histrionic, and narcissistic personality disorders.
3. Cluster C (appear anxious and fearful)—avoidant, dependent, obsessive compulsive, and passive aggressive personality disorders.

In addition, the *DSM-III-R* has a category called "personality disorder not otherwise specified" (NOS), which encompasses mixed personality disorders that do not completely fit the criteria for any one personality disorder. This category also includes other personality disorders that are under consideration but have not yet been made full-fledged diagnoses (for example, self-defeating or sadistic personality disorders).

Although this framework provides some organization to the array of personality disorders, its usefulness has been controversial, and little literature is available on the clusters of personality disorders (Millman, Huber, & Diggins, 1982). Consequently, this chapter will follow the order of the clusters but will discuss the personality disorders individually rather than in groups.

According to Gunderson (1988), personality disorders are

present in approximately 15 percent of the general population and in 30–50 percent of clinical populations. In his view, the paranoid and schizotypal personality disorders are the most dysfunctional of these disorders. Millon (1981) adds the borderline personality disorder—characterized by very poor social skills, isolation, hostility, confusion, and fragility—to this group. Gunderson views the obsessive compulsive, passive aggressive, dependent, histrionic, and avoidant personality disorders as the least dysfunctional; Millon places dependent, histrionic, narcissistic, and antisocial personality disorders in this group. People with these disorders are able to seek out and deal with others in a relatively coherent fashion and can adapt to or control their environments in meaningful ways.

Relevant Client Characteristics. People with personality disorders tend to have a history of dysfunctional and inconsistent parenting (Leaff, 1974). Families typically afforded them little support or security and did not encourage development of self-esteem and an appropriate degree of independence (Kaplan & Sadock, 1985). The form taken by their personality disorder often makes sense in light of the messages received from their parents.

Several personality disorders run in families and are transmitted through genetics, modeling, or both. Personality disorders tend to be proportionally overrepresented among lower socioeconomic and disadvantaged groups (Gunderson, 1988). However, whether those circumstances predispose people to develop personality disorders or whether the dysfunction of those with personality disorders has limited their socioeconomic advancement is unclear.

Personality disorders are often accompanied by other disorders that are more transient. Common are depression (Chapter Five), anxiety (Chapter Six), and substance use disorders (section 7.1). Suicidal ideation is also frequently found in people with personality disorders.

In addition, longstanding patterns of pervasive dysfunction, affecting social and occupational areas, are usually presented. Achieving intimacy seems particularly difficult for those with personality disorders, and others often find them irritating (Kaplan & Sadock, 1985). The behavior of people with personality disorders is often socially inappropriate, since their strong sense of entitlement leads them to violate interpersonal boundaries. In addition, people with personality disorders tend to have poor self-esteem, weak ego strength, and poor impulse control (Leaff, 1974). They tend to be dependent, narcissistic, pessimistic, and passive. They have little insight into themselves or others and have little empathy or compassion (Kaplan & Sadock, 1985). Underlying fear and rage also are often present. According to Vaillant and Drake (1985), people with personality disorders are much more likely to use immature defense mechanisms (such as projection, fantasy, passive aggression, dissociation, hypochondriasis, and acting out) than are those without personality disorders.

Relevant Therapist Variables. In treating clients with personality disorders, therapists should manifest qualities integral to the development of an effective therapeutic alliance: empathy, warmth, compassion, acceptance, respect, and genuineness (Kellner, 1982a). Strong confrontation, punishment, or expressions of negative feelings can destroy the often fragile therapeutic bond established with clients with personality disorders. Therapists should not take sides or argue with these clients but should remain supportive. Patience seems to be an essential ingredient, since treatment of these disorders tends to be long term, with progress and the building of trust often very gradual.

Also, many of these clients are not motivated toward self-examination or change but really want the therapist to change their lives for them or to take care of them. Their motivation tends to be external rather than internal. Therapists working with these clients, then, must be skilled at developing client motivation and maintaining a productive focus to the sessions.

Clients with personality disorders tend to have strong transference reactions to their therapists; some become hostile and resistant, while others become needy and dependent. Therapists must monitor and manage their own countertransference reactions so that they become neither overinvolved nor rejecting toward the clients but are appropriately available to them. Judicious use of limit setting, gentle interpretation, rewards, and modeling also help elicit positive client behavior.

Intervention Strategies. Despite the prevalence of personality disorders in both the general and clinical populations, empirical studies of treatment of these disorders are scarce; and personality disorders received little attention in the research literature until the mid-1980s. Millon's (1981, 1987) writings and personality inventories—as well as the *Journal of Personality Disorders,* which he currently edits—seem to have spurred recent interest in the study of these disorders. However, most of the available literature consists of case studies and theoretical discussions of these disorders; little database research is available (Turkat & Maisto, 1985). Research is particularly sparse on the more recently defined personality disorders (obsessive compulsive, schizotypal, avoidant, self-defeating, and sadistic) (Millman, Huber, & Diggins, 1982).

Several approaches to treatment have received support for use with clients with personality disorders. Probably most has been written about the use of psychodynamic psychotherapy or psychoanalysis. The longstanding nature of these disorders, as well as their apparent origin in childhood and family dynamics, suggests an approach that will not just relieve symptoms but will also effect change in overall functioning as well as in clients' views of themselves and their world.

Behavior therapy has also been used successfully in treating personality disorders, either alone or in combination with psychodynamic psychotherapy. Behavior therapy seems particularly helpful to clients who may be resistant to long-term treatment or who have severely dysfunctional and self-destructive behavioral patterns that require rapid modification. Through behavior therapy, they can learn new social and occupational skills as well as practical approaches to coping and stress management.

Although little research is available on the efficacy of cognitive and interpersonal approaches in treating personality disorders, aspects of those techniques may also be helpful when integrated with psychodynamic or behavioral approaches. However, person-centered therapy does not seem useful, because of the limited internal motivation of people with these disorders and the severity of their dysfunction.

In general, therapy for clients with personality disorders will be multifaceted, including a psychodynamic or behavioral basis and other elements designed to mesh with the clients' defense systems and individual concerns. Adjunct services such as career counseling and Alcoholics Anonymous often will be part of the treatment package.

In severe forms or exacerbations of personality disorders, brief hospitalization may be indicated, especially for those with antisocial, borderline, or schizotypal personality disorders (Millman, Huber, & Diggins, 1982). In addition, low doses of medication (such as narcoleptics, benzodiazepines, lithium, or antiseizure drugs) may be useful (Kellner, 1982a). However, these forms of treatment do not cure the client of the personality disorder but, rather, only reduce the severity of the accompanying symptoms and perhaps facilitate the client's involvement in psychotherapy. In addition, many of these clients readily become dependent on external sources of help and tend to abuse drugs. Consequently, care must be taken in using medication or hospitalization as part of their treatment.

If the client is living in a family situation, family therapy may be a useful adjunct to individual therapy. Family members themselves often present disorders that merit attention, and they also can be helped to understand the client's personality disorder and react to it in helpful ways. The client's social and occupational dysfunction has probably already damaged family relationships, and family therapy can offer the client an opportunity to improve those relationships and develop new ways of relating to family members. However, Harbin (1981) cautions therapists against forming separate alliances with family members; that may jeopardize the tenuous level of trust the client has in the therapeutic process and may be experienced by the client as a rejection.

Group therapy also can be a useful adjunct to individual therapy, although it should generally be initiated after clients with personality disorders have made some progress in individual therapy. Otherwise, their poor social skills and their strong mistrust or dependency needs might turn group therapy into just one more disappointing interpersonal experience for them. Once clients are ready for group involvement, the feedback and support they receive from others can provide encouragement for positive change; and the group setting can serve as a safe place to experiment with new ways of relating to peers and authority figures.

Prognosis. Because of the deeply ingrained and pervasive nature of these disorders, the prognosis for effecting major change in personality disorders seems poor. However, the prognosis for reduction of symptoms and improvement in social and occupational functioning is fair to good if the client can be persuaded to remain in and cooperate with treatment. Unfortunately, clients with personality disorders often are not motivated to change and may leave treatment abruptly and prematurely. Whether prognosis is determined more by the specific disorder or by the severity and dynamics of the disorder is unclear, although at least one study found that specific diagnosis was not predictive of outcome (Millon & Klerman, 1986).

9.1 Paranoid Personality Disorder

Description of Disorder. People with paranoid personality disorder have a persistent expectation that they will be harmed or taken advantage of by others (*DSM-III-R*, 1987). They often misinterpret the behavior of others, tend to personalize experiences, and may have ideas of reference. As a result of their apprehension about being exploited or made to feel helpless, they are constantly on guard and ready to attack at the slightest provocation. They have little tenderness or sense of humor and tend to be critical, moralistic, grandiose, insecure, resentful, suspicious, defensive, and jealous. They share little of themselves with others and are typically resentful, rigid, and controlling. They tend to be interested in things rather than in people or ideas and have little empathy for or understanding of others. They have a strong sense of hierarchy and are often fiercely independent. They crave power and envy those with more power and success than they have achieved. Sometimes they achieve a semblance of power by becoming leaders of fringe religious or political groups.

There is a self-defeating element to the behavioral dynamics of these people. They believe that others dislike them and treat them badly; consequently, they protect themselves by treating others badly. Others often respond to such treatment with dislike, thereby giving people with paranoid personality disorders the responses they have feared yet invited.

This disorder is more than twice as common among men as among women (Millon, 1986). Approximately 5 percent of people with personality disorders have a paranoid personality disorder.

Relevant Client Characteristics. Little research is available on the early antecedents of paranoid personality disorder. Turkat and Maisto (1985) suggest that most people with this disorder have had at least one parent who was perfectionistic. There are at least four theories concerning the origin of this disorder; it is seen as a repression of homosexual wishes, a projection of unconscious hostility, an effort to maintain equilibrium and ward off upset, and an effort to avoid humiliation by projecting blame and one's own shortcomings onto others (Siever & Kendler, 1986).

People with paranoid personality disorder often have concurrent disorders. The most common are other personality disorders, anxiety disorders (discussed in Chapter Six), and psychotic disorders (Chapter Ten) (Millon, 1981).

People with this disorder rarely seek therapy voluntarily. They may be seen in clinical settings as a result of pressure or threats from a spouse or supervisor but have great difficulty acknowledging a need for help. Even though they often have both interpersonal and occupational difficulties, particularly conflict with family and co-workers, they externalize blame for those difficulties and insist that they do not need to make changes. Projection is a common defense (Millon & Klerman, 1986). These clients may take pride in what they perceive as their independence and objectivity and criticize those who express feelings more easily as being weak or troubled. In their family lives, they typically expect obedience and rigid organization and may experience considerable stress when children and spouses resist their control. Some establish a comfortable work and family situation for themselves as long as they are in charge and do not need to cooperate with others, but that stability may be a tenuous one.

People with this disorder do tend to be fairly consistent and predictable, unlike many of those with other personality disorders.

This consistency can help family members and therapists identify and deal with patterns of relating and reacting. At the same time, these clients have considerable difficulty handling stress; and their symptoms are likely to worsen under pressure or during experiences of humiliation or failure.

Relevant Therapist Variables. Perhaps the most fundamental goal of therapy with these clients is the establishment of trust, so that the clients become willing to engage in therapy and lower some of their defenses. To establish a trusting therapeutic alliance, the therapist will need to assume a respectful, courteous, and professional stance; be totally honest though tactful; and not intrude on the client's privacy and independence. Soloff (1985) suggests that therapists working with these clients should be emotionally visible and responsive, offering a mild, gentle, interested presence, so that they do not evoke undue suspiciousness. Because these clients are often hostile and abrasive, therapists will need to monitor their own reactions and resist being intimidated. The therapist should avoid arguing with the client, communicating excessive warmth and concern, and developing therapeutic plans that might evoke suspicion—such as meeting with the client's family when the client is not present.

Intervention Strategies. Individual therapy is usually the treatment of choice for clients with paranoid personality disorders. Therapy should not emphasize either interpretation or reflection of feelings; both are likely to be threatening. Rather, a behavioral approach that emphasizes client rather than therapist control and focuses on stress management and skill development seems most likely to engage the client in the therapeutic process and effect some positive change. These clients often respond approvingly to the logic and organization of behavior therapy and tend to be more trusting of a therapist who uses an externally directed approach than one who focuses on inner dynamics and feelings. Reinforcement, modeling, and education can help these clients develop more effective coping mechanisms and social skills.

Millon (1981) has recommended a cognitive approach, low in directiveness, for working with these clients. That model, too, offers the appeal of a logical and clear approach. Cognitive therapy might focus on issues of shame, self-esteem, blame and self-blame, and overgeneralization. Behavior therapy, integrated with cognitive therapy, might enhance outcome by helping to reduce the clients' exposure to humiliation while desensitizing them to uncomfortable situations (Colby, 1979).

Gentle reality testing can enhance any form of therapy with these clients (Kaplan & Sadock, 1985). Clients faced with legal, professional, or marital consequences of their behaviors may need help in appreciating the genuine threat their actions and attitudes present to themselves and the potential importance of modifying those behaviors and attitudes in order to avert negative consequences.

Group therapy is rarely indicated for these clients. They are acutely uncomfortable in group settings, particularly those that are intimate or confrontational, unless they are in charge; and they will tend to sabotage or flee group therapy.

Transient psychotic symptoms and severe anxiety are sometimes present in these clients. Medication may ameliorate those symptoms. However, it should be presented and used cautiously lest clients feel manipulated and controlled.

Prognosis. Therapy with clients with paranoid personality disorder usually does not have a very positive prognosis. Because of their resistance to treatment, clients often terminate prematurely or refuse to engage in the therapeutic process. Even if they do seem to cooperate with therapy and manifest some positive change, treatment is not likely to result in extensive modification of the clients' pervasive patterns of relating (Gunderson, 1988).

9.2 Schizoid Personality Disorder

Description of Disorder. According to the *DSM-III-R* (1987), the schizoid personality disorder is characterized by "a pervasive pattern of indifference to social relationships and a restricted range of emotional experience and expression" (p. 340). This pattern is evident by early adulthood and is manifested in all or nearly all contexts. People with this disorder tend to be loners, shun family and social activities, and are usually perceived as cold and detached.

In reality, people with schizoid personality disorders feel extremely shy, anxious, and self-conscious in social settings. They have great difficulty expressing their feelings and typically seem preoccupied and indecisive. They tend to be guarded, suspicious, critical, and tactless and often alienate others (Gutsch, 1988).

Schizoid personality disorder is a relatively rare disorder and is not commonly seen in clinical settings. Millon (1986) reports that schizoid personality disorder represents 4 percent of the personality disorders. This disorder seems to be three to four times more common among males than females.

Relevant Client Characteristics. People with schizoid personality disorder have typically experienced inadequate, neglectful, and unreliable parenting with impaired attachment (Siever & Kendler, 1986). The parents themselves may have modeled schizoid behavior. Since childhood, people with this disorder have had few good interpersonal experiences and have an expectation that relationships are frustrating and disappointing. Rather than exposing themselves to what they perceive as more negative experiences, they shun socialization and develop private and isolated lives.

This disorder usually is not accompanied by other prominent disorders. However, some people with schizoid personality disorder exhibit symptoms of anxiety, depersonalization, obsessional thinking, or brief manic states (Millon, 1981). Coexisting personality disorders may also be present.

Significant social impairment is, by definition, central to this disorder. Males generally do not date or marry. While the females may engage in more social and family activities, they tend to assume a passive role and allow others to make their social decisions. Both sexes have poor social skills and few if any close friends. Their capacity for empathy and introspection seems to be severely constricted. People with schizoid personality disorder also may have considerable occupational impairment, particularly if their chosen occupations involve interpersonal contact. However, some manage to find a stable and secure occupational role that is congruent with their need for solitude. They may become skilled at scientific, theoretical, creative, or mechanical pursuits and have relatively successful careers. Although they are not typically interested in becoming successful or in competing for recognition, they may attain success and recognition by accident, through their immersion in their work or hobbies and their lack of interest in social diversions.

People with this disorder tend to fantasize extensively but almost never lose contact with reality, even though they may prefer fantasy to reality (Meyer, 1983). Their affect is typically flat, and their behavior is lethargic. They tend to be relatively satisfied with their lives, although some engage in considerable intellectualization and denial to justify their lives to themselves and others (Millon & Klerman, 1986). In general, people with schizoid personality disorder have a relatively stable existence, as long as outside pressures do not intrude. One client with this disorder, for example, devoted his energy to raising pit bulldogs and collecting poisonous snakes. He had no social life and saw others only for business transactions. He was referred to therapy after his neighbors felt endangered by his activities and complained to the police. He reported being quite contented with his life; his only concern was his neighbors.

Relevant Therapist Variables. With these clients, as with those with paranoid personality disorder (section 9.1), building trust is a critical ingredient of treatment. These clients have little experience in expressing their feelings, engaging in close and collaborative relationships, or trusting others. Confrontation or scrutiny of these clients' emotions generally makes them very uncomfortable and may lead to premature termination of the therapeutic relationship.

Instead, they need what Siever and Kendler (1986) call a reconstructive relationship to decrease their withdrawal and increase their optimism about relationships. A gentle, consistent, patient, accepting, optimistic, available, and supportive therapist is needed to establish a therapeutic alliance. Therapists will need to take an active and encouraging stance, yet avoid being threatening to these clients.

These clients are rarely self-referred for therapy. Typically, they are encouraged to seek therapy by concerned parents or employers who are hoping for a change in the clients' ability to relate to others. On occasion, clients may take the initiative in seeking therapy when someone breaks through their reserve and increases their anxiety, but they rarely experience an internalized wish to change. Consequently, they are likely to manifest a passive resistance to therapy and see little need for that process. Getting past this initial resistance will be challenging. Therapists will need a high tolerance for distance, silences, and possibly even some acting out. Also, these clients probably will be more amenable to therapy if that process is clarified for them as much as possible and if they believe that the therapist will respect their privacy. Although clients with schizoid personality disorder present a challenge, under the proper conditions they may become "devoted if distant" clients (Kaplan & Sadock, 1985, p. 368).

Intervention Strategies. Almost no research exists on therapy with these clients, but some generalizations can be made with caution. Therapy would probably be similar to that suggested for clients with paranoid personality disorder. If clients with schizoid personality disorder can be engaged in therapy, it is likely to be a long, slow process. Maxmen (1986) recommends supportive individual and group therapy for these clients, combined with assertiveness training. Maxmen also suggests that intrusive interpretations and forced interactions be avoided. Group therapy can offer needed feedback and opportunities for socialization but can be threatening.

The sequencing of the components of a treatment plan for these clients seems critical. They should not be overwhelmed by a multifaceted treatment strategy, nor should they be pushed into group therapy before they are ready for that intervention. A stable therapeutic alliance should first be established through individual therapy; only when the client is ready should group or family therapy, assertiveness training, career counseling, or other more active and more threatening interventions be introduced.

Some cognitive therapy may promote increased motivation and insight. Clients' fantasies and their apprehension about dependency are other areas that might be productively explored through cognitive or other forms of therapy (Kaplan & Sadock, 1985).

Behavioral therapy is another potentially useful ingredient of treatment; it can be combined with supportive interventions to effect behavioral changes and improve socialization. Systematic desensitization, for example, may be useful in reducing social anxiety. Gutride, Goldstein, and Hunter (1973) report some success in promoting the socialization of schizoid clients through such behavioral techniques as modeling socially appropriate behavior, role playing, rehearsal, feedback, and social reinforcement.

However, clients with schizoid personality disorder generally do not respond well to reinforcement, because of their lack of reactivity and the limited importance they attach to interpersonal relationships. They may also resent the intrusive and manipulative aspects of some behavioral approaches. A more intellectual approach to behavioral change (for example, education to increase assertiveness, self-expression, and social skills) might meet with more success.

Medication is rarely needed in treatment of this disorder. However, in some cases it can help to reduce severe anxiety or depression sufficiently to facilitate therapy (Gunderson, 1988).

Family therapy and conferences with the clients' employers may be useful to those people as well as to the clients. Often, those who have contact with people with schizoid personality disorder have trouble dealing with them because of their limited social interest and skills. Some family or work-site meetings can help others accept the differentness of these clients, appreciate their strengths, and deal with them more effectively. Pressure from family or coworkers for the client to date or to socialize more at work is likely to exacerbate this condition, even though it may be well intended. At the same time, gentle encouragement and increased acceptance on the part of family and colleagues can help these clients socialize more comfortably.

Prognosis. The prognosis for treating this disorder is not promising (Millon, 1981). Clients have little insight and minimal motivation to change. Most have established a relatively stable lifestyle for themselves and are not interested in modification. Some increased socialization may be developed, especially if it is required by the client's place of employment, but fundamental change is not likely.

9.3 Schizotypal Personality Disorder

Description of Disorder. People with schizotypal personality disorder, like those with paranoid and schizoid personality disorders, have pervasive deficits in interpersonal relations and social skills. They tend to be guarded, suspicious, and hypersensitive; have few close friends other than first-degree relatives; and are uncomfortable and awkward in social situations. In addition, they manifest "pecularities of ideation, appearance, and behavior" (*DSM-III-R,* 1987, p. 341) that might involve ideas of reference, magical thinking, unusual perceptual experiences, eccentric actions or grooming, or idiosyncratic speech patterns. People with schizotypal personality disorder, then, typically are more dysfunctional and unusual in their presentation than are those with paranoid and schizoid personality disorders.

Schizotypal personality disorder is found in approximately 3 percent of the general population (*DSM-III-R,* 1987). It is slightly more common in males than in females and represents nearly 8 percent of those diagnosed as having personality disorders (Millon, 1986).

Relevant Client Characteristics. The personalities of these clients are poorly integrated and chaotic, and they are rarely free of significant social and occupational impairment. They usually do not marry or have children but tend to drift from one endeavor to another with little investment in or enthusiasm about anything (Millon, 1981). Their peculiar habits and attitudes are generally evident to those around them, who regard them as strange and troubled. They seem to experience more discomfort than do those with schizoid or paranoid personality disorder and often appear distraught, agitated, and emotionally labile. Some have a sense that they are missing something and may fear disintegration or disappearance (Millon, 1981).

There seem to be both genetic and environmental components to this disorder. People with schizotypal personality disorder have a higher percentage of first-degree biological relatives with schizophrenia than does the general population (*DSM-III-R,* 1987). In addition, the parents of people with schizotypal personality disorder were commonly inadequate, inconsistent, and overcritical (Millon, 1981).

Torgersen (1984) found that more than half of these clients have a coexisting affective disorder and that anxiety and depression, as well as psychotic symptoms, often accompany this disorder. These clients also tend to somatize and may present vague physical complaints (Siever & Kendler, 1986).

Relevant Therapist Variables. Clients with schizotypal personality disorder, like those with schizoid and paranoid personality disorders, are likely to be resistant to treatment. Building trust will be a challenging yet critical ingredient in engaging the client in the therapeutic process. An available, reliable, encouraging, positive, and nonintrusive orientation can help therapists interact effectively with these clients. Allowing the clients to establish the degree of intimacy also can increase their sense of control and comfort in therapy.

People with schizotypal personality disorder have particular difficulty expressing their feelings and dealing appropriately with interpersonal situations; therapists should therefore be prepared for unusual reactions and behaviors on the part of these clients. Therapists will need to manage their own discomfort with the strange and possibly offensive mannerisms of these clients and should communicate acceptance and support while at the same time providing some reality testing and education. On the positive side, these clients do not tend to be manipulative and will generally be sincere though guarded and cautious (Gunderson, 1984).

Intervention Strategies. Schizotypal personality disorder is one of the newer diagnoses and has been defined only in the last ten years. Consequently, research on its course and treatment is quite limited.

Like clients with the previously discussed personality disorders, those with schizotypal personality disorder are unlikely to seek out treatment on their own. Most people with this disorder seem to accept their own lifestyles. Siever and Kendler (1986) report that they are seen more often in inpatient than in outpatient settings, coming into contact with mental health services only when their symptoms become so severe that they can no longer function on their own.

Treatment for these clients in both inpatient and outpatient settings is likely to be similar to that for schizoid personality disorder (section 9.2). Therapy would typically be supportive and slowly paced, making gentle use of cognitive and behavioral strategies to promote self-awareness, reality testing, and more socially acceptable behavior. The focus of therapy with these clients is likely to be a very basic one, dealing with personal hygiene and minimal human interaction, and seeking to prevent isolation and total dysfunction. Meyer (1983) suggests that family therapy might be useful in preventing the development of psychosis in these clients. For the milder cases, group therapy also may be useful, but the group must be carefully chosen so that it does not prove too threatening to the clients.

Medication, particularly neuroleptics, is sometimes needed to treat the psychotic symptoms of these clients (Reid, 1983). Serban and Siegel (1984), for example, found that 84 percent of clients with schizotypal personality disorder were markedly improved after three months of treatment with major neuroleptic medication. Reduction was effected in cognitive disturbance, derealization, ideas of reference, anxiety, depression, social dysfunction, and negative self-image. Although medication may reduce the degree of impairment, it does not change the basic symptoms of the disorder.

Prognosis. According to Millon (1981), the schizotypal personality disorder has the worst prognosis of all the personality disorders. McGlashan's (1986b) long-term follow-up of clients with schizotypal personality disorder treated in an inpatient setting (Chestnut Lodge) indicated a relatively poor social adjustment at follow-up and an average of 2.5 additional hospitalizations in the fifteen years after initial treatment. Prognosis seemed worst for those with schizophrenia-like symptoms and best for those with some capacity for warmth and empathy. Despite the poor prognosis for significant positive change, most with this disorder do not deteriorate into schizophrenia but do manage to achieve a stable though marginal existence.

9.4 Antisocial Personality Disorder

Description of Disorder. Antisocial personality disorder, by definition, begins before the age of fifteen with a pattern of behavior consistent with a diagnosis of conduct disorder. It would be typified by such behaviors as theft, lying, truancy, cruelty to people and animals, vandalism, fighting, and running away from home. This disorder persists beyond the age of eighteen via a pattern of irresponsible and antisocial behavior.

People with antisocial personality disorder typically are unable to sustain employment or monogamous relationships; are transient, impulsive, reckless, irritable, deceptive, and aggressive; fail to abide by social and legal guidelines for behavior; are often in financial difficulty; behave irresponsibly in their parenting; and feel no guilt or remorse for their actions (*DSM-III-R*, 1987). They embrace a socially deviant lifestyle and disdain generally acceptable values and behaviors, although not all actually engage in criminal behavior. Millon (1981) reports that many find a place for themselves in business, politics, or the military. Symptoms are likely to be most evident in early adulthood and diminish spontaneously in mid-life.

Antisocial personality disorder is two to three times more common among males than it is among females and seems particularly prevalent in urban areas (Gunderson, 1988). Approximately 3 percent of men and less than 1 percent of females can be diagnosed with this disorder. Maxmen (1986) reports that 30–80 percent of clients with this disorder are in prison settings and that up to 75 percent of those in prison may have antisocial personality disorder.

Relevant Client Characteristics. Genetic and environmental influences both seem to be factors in the development of this disorder, as they are with many of the personality disorders. People with antisocial personality disorder typically lacked secure and stable parenting and grew up in inconsistent, excessively punitive, contentious, and disrupted families with others who manifested antisocial behavior (Gunderson, 1988). Fathers of these clients often are antisocial and alcoholic (Maxmen, 1986).

People with antisocial personality disorder tend to be amoral and irresponsible. They justify their behaviors and project blame for their difficulties onto others. They are easily bored, have a high need for excitement and stimulation, and typically enjoy their lifestyles, although they do not want to bear the consequences of their activities. They have difficulty with rejection and delayed gratification and want to impress others despite their professed need for independence (Soloff, 1985). They have faith only in themselves and tend to attack in anticipation of being attacked (Millon, 1981). They are often shrewd judges of others and can use insight to manipulate; at the same time, they rarely engage in introspection and have little sense of themselves.

Despite their bravado, these clients often have painful underlying disorders, typically depression and anxiety (see Chapters Five and Six) (Gunderson, 1988). They also are prone to substance use disorders (section 7.1) and somatization (see Chapter Eight) (Maxmen, 1986). Antisocial personality disorder also may be accompanied by other personality disorders—notably narcissistic (section 9.6), paranoid (section 9.1), and histrionic (section 9.5) personality disorders (Millon, 1981). Occupational and interpersonal dysfunction is almost always present. These people have considerable difficulty sustaining warm, intimate relationships and tend to change both partners and jobs frequently.

Relevant Therapist Variables. It is not surprising that these clients rarely seek therapy on their own initiative, since they attribute all their difficulties to others. However, they often are seen in therapy as a result of breaking the law. Therapy may be a condition of their parole or probation, or they may have been seen for therapy while incarcerated. They tend to be very resistant to therapy, although some are manipulative and appear superficially cooperative in order to avoid negative consequences. These clients may afford the therapist an initial honeymoon phase in treatment, but their resistance is likely to surface once therapy progresses beyond superficial interactions (Lion, 1981). These clients typically resent authority figures and may see therapists as part of that group.

The role of the therapist is very different with these clients than it is with clients with paranoid, schizoid, and schizotypal personality disorders. The therapist still needs to be genuine, accepting, clear, warm, empathic, and straightforward (Kellner, 1982a);

and the development of trust, again, is a critical ingredient. However, directive and confrontational techniques often are necessary to persuade clients with antisocial personality disorder to engage in therapy.

These clients are not likely to be threatened by the therapist; more likely the therapist will be threatened by the client, and countertransference reactions must be monitored. Setting clear limits for the therapeutic relationship can help prevent clients from becoming hostile and abusive and seeking to engage the therapist in battles.

Intervention Strategies. A structured, active, and directive approach to therapy is indicated with clients with antisocial personality disorder, although research has yet to identify an approach that has a high degree of effectiveness with them (Maxmen, 1986). The failure to find an effective form of treatment is not due to a lack of research, since antisocial personality disorder seems to be the most studied of the personality disorders (Turkat & Maisto, 1985). Rather, the discouraging results of outcome research reflect the guarded prognosis for treating this disorder.

Some approaches have achieved limited success in treating antisocial personality disorder. Therapeutic communities and other directive, authoritarian settings that involve peer pressure and clear consequences can sometimes succeed in breaking through the clients' resistance and effecting some change (Kellner, 1982a). Wilderness programs can accomplish similar ends. Many of these programs have been established specifically for offenders and focus on increasing responsibility, trust in self and others, sense of mastery, and an appreciation of the consequences of one's behavior.

Prerelease or halfway programs also can be helpful in facilitating the transition to a more socially acceptable lifestyle for those who are incarcerated. An important benefit to these residential communities is that they remove the clients from their former environments, where their antisocial behavior may have been reinforced by their peers. Developing new support systems and a sense of belonging through employment or self-help groups such as Narcotics Anonymous can accomplish a similar end. Although individual therapy is certainly an integral ingredient in treatment of these clients, some believe that individual therapy can only be effective for them in the context of a structured program (Woody, McLellan, Luborsky, & O'Brien, 1985).

Although the focus of treatment is generally on present behavior, these clients are sometimes less defensive when talking about the past, and that may provide a useful bridge to a discussion of current activities. Behavior therapy and Reality Therapy are the therapeutic approaches that seem most likely to be effective in treating antisocial personality disorder (Kellner, 1982a). Those approaches can help these clients substitute new behaviors and coping mechanisms for the old, self-destructive ones. The less confrontive cognitive approaches have also been recommended (Millon, 1981). However, person-centered and insight-oriented therapies are not indicated with these clients.

An early sign of progress is the emergence of underlying depression (Reid, 1983). This development can be upsetting to clients and may precipitate a resumption of old patterns of behavior. In order to encourage client persistence in treatment, therapists might increase support and empathy when the depression surfaces.

Medication is almost never needed for treatment of clients with antisocial personality disorder, although lithium and antiseizure medication have been successful with some in controlling anger and violent outbursts (Tupin, 1981). Whenever possible, medication should be avoided because of clients' tendency to abuse drugs and their reliance on external rather than internal solutions to problems.

Family therapy has been suggested, especially when these clients are young, in an effort to reverse patterns in the family that are being transmitted to the client. Therapy might also help the family members separate from the client and deal with their own guilt and anger toward the client.

Treatment specifically for substance use disorders (see section 7.1) can also be helpful to these clients and can reduce their motivation to engage in antisocial behavior. Reduction of the substance abuse seems to improve the prognosis for treatment (Reid, 1986).

One issue that often arises in treatment of these clients is the relationship between therapy and punishment, since many of them come into therapy as a consequence of breaking the law. According to Maxmen (1986), clients are more likely to use therapy constructively, and not manipulate or deceive the therapist, if therapy is separated from punishment. At the same time, the threat of punishment can have a powerful coercive effect and can promote an initial involvement in therapy. This issue has not yet been clearly resolved but must be considered by most therapists working with clients with antisocial personality disorder.

Prognosis. The prognosis for treating antisocial personality disorder is not good, primarily because the clients lack motivation (Gunderson, 1988). However, therapy does seem to be helpful to some people with this disorder.

9.5 Histrionic Personality Disorder

Description of Disorder. The *DSM-III-R* (1987) describes the histrionic personality disorder as characterized by "a pervasive pattern of excessive emotionality and attention-seeking, beginning by early adulthood and present in a variety of contexts" (p. 349). Prominent in this disorder are such features as constant demands for praise or reassurance; inappropriate seductiveness; a need to be the center of attention; overemphasis on physical attractiveness; exaggerated, shallow, and labile expression of emotion; self-centeredness; poor impulse control; and a vague, disjointed, and general way of speaking (*DSM-III-R*, 1987).

People with this disorder tend to be other-directed, and their moods as well as their feelings about themselves come largely from the reactions they receive from others (Millon & Klerman, 1986). They tend to avoid responsibility, feel helpless, and want others to take care of them. They usually appear affected and flighty, but their vivacity, imagination, and attractiveness can be engaging. They readily become impatient, jealous, and volatile. Suicidal threats are common but are a part of the exaggerated expression of emotion and are rarely fatal, although they should usually be taken seriously (Maxmen, 1986). Repression and denial are common defenses (Horowitz, Marmar, Krupnick, Wilner, Kaltreider, & Wallerstein, 1984).

Histrionic personality disorder is much more common in females than in males. Kernberg (1986) found that many men with this disorder are bisexual. Approximately 9 percent of those with personality disorders will be diagnosed as histrionic (Millon, 1986).

Relevant Client Characteristics. Histrionic personality disorders tend to run in families (Maxmen, 1986). These families also frequently have a history of antisocial and other personality disorders, and alcohol abuse, as well as characteristic interactional patterns. Millon (1981) reports a history of excessive stimulation, combined with inconsistent parenting and sibling rivalry, in clients with histrionic personality disorder. Reinforcement received from their families was irregular and typically focused on externals. Gunderson (1988) found that females with histrionic personality disorder often experienced insufficiency, conflict, and disapproval in their early interactions with their mothers and so seek attention primarily from their fathers. As they mature, their heterosexual relationships become overemphasized.

Histrionic personality disorder is often accompanied by other disorders. A particularly strong connection has been found between histrionic personality disorder and dissociative (section 10.5) and somatoform (section 8.1) disorders, particularly conversion disorders (section 8.1) (Kernberg, 1986). Males with histrionic personality disorder sometimes have a concurrent diagnosis of antisocial personality disorder (section 9.4). Lilienfeld, VanValkenburg, Larntz, and Akiskal (1986) suggest that histrionic and antisocial personality disorders and somatoform disorders represent different stages or manifestations of the same disorder and often coexist. Depression is also common but tends not to be pervasive or consistent. Bipolar (section 5.4) and cyclothymic (section 5.5) disorders have also been reported in clients with histrionic personality disorder (Millon, 1981).

These clients usually are sexually and socially active but typically make poor choices of partners in their quest for the ideal mate. They tend to be easily bored and typically shift partners just as they achieve the commitment they seem to be seeking. This pattern is exacerbated by their tendency to choose partners who are detached and unemotional and who cannot give them the strong responses they crave (Bergner, 1977).

Their tendency to seek out new sources of challenge and

stimulation can interfere with the occupational and social adjustment of people with histrionic personality disorder, and they may have unstable work histories. Their lack of attention to detail and their illogical thinking can also contribute to a poor occupational adjustment, although if they choose a field that can accommodate to their unstable temperaments, they may be quite successful because they can be driven and energetic in their pursuits.

Although many of the personality disorders seem to moderate with age, people with histrionic personality disorder seem to deteriorate as they get older (Kernberg, 1986)—possibly because their overemphasis on physical appearance leads them to have great difficulty accepting the changes associated with aging.

Relevant Therapist Variables. Clients with histrionic personality disorder tend to be sociable and outgoing, and therapy may begin on a positive note. These clients often seek therapy voluntarily and may temporarily appear to be charming, ingratiating, expressive, and motivated clients, eager to please the therapist. However, they often want the therapist to fix their problems, to retrieve a relationship, or to make someone else (usually a spouse or partner) change. They continue in therapy because of the secondary gains of the attention provided by the therapist and the opportunity to talk about themselves. However, as therapy progresses, their manipulative and seductive patterns will probably become more evident. Their strong need for approval and attention may lead them to seek a romantic relationship with an opposite-sex therapist and to compete with a same-sex therapist. They may resist introspection and specificity, tasks that tend to be difficult for them.

It is important that therapists quickly set limits with these clients and maintain a professional relationship at all times. Therapists should avoid reinforcing dramatic behavior with attenion. Soloff (1985) suggests focusing on process and on the facts of the clients' histories as a way of setting limits and appropriate distance. Gentle confrontation also seems to have a place here, to help clients look at the self-destructive nature of their behaviors. Keeping these clients on task will be a challenge, since they tend to be distractible and talk at length in vague, general terms. They also have often repressed much of their past (Millon, 1981).

Such therapeutic strategies as limit setting and confrontation may make the clients feel rejected and unappreciated, and they may become reproachful and demanding, engaging in acting out and regression. With these clients, too, therapists must monitor their countertransference reactions and remain warm, genuine, and accepting yet professional. Clarity and consistency can help to build and maintain the clients' trust. Therapists can also make productive therapeutic use of the clients' transference reactions to help clients examine how they relate to others and appreciate the negative impact those behaviors can have.

Persuading clients with histrionic personality disorder to engage in long-term therapy may be difficult in light of their high need for change, challenge, and stimulation. Setting a series of short-term goals can facilitate extended therapy, as can initiating therapy in an active and engaging fashion.

Intervention Strategies. As with most of the personality disorders, few systematic studies exist on the treatment of histrionic personality disorder (Turkat & Maisto, 1985). However, most of the literature points to the use of long-term individual psychodynamic or modified psychoanalytic therapy as the core of the treatment. Maxmen (1986) recommends that such an approach be used to help the clients think more systematically, reduce emotional reactivity, improve reality testing, increase self-reliance, promote appropriate expression of feeling, and increase their awareness of the impact of their behaviors on others. Cognitive reorientation, combined with the above approaches, can often help clarify the thinking of these clients (Millon, 1981). Therapy should usually be fairly systematic and goal directed, providing an external structure.

For clients whose disorders are too severe to allow them to benefit from psychodynamic therapy, Reid (1983) recommends supportive treatment as another route to helping clients with histrionic personality disorder develop more self-awareness and more positive ways of expressing their feelings and relating to others. However, most researchers seem to believe that support alone will effect little change in these clients, although it can help them maintain an equilibrium (Gutsch, 1988).

Behavior therapy usually is not recommended for treatment

of histrionic personality disorder. However, Woolson and Swanson (1972) report that a modified cognitive-behavioral approach was used successfully in the treatment of four women with this disorder. The therapists presented themselves as experts on goal clarification and attainment and provided structure and feedback. In the initial phases of the treatment, clients' goals and the dynamics of their disorders were explored. Operant conditioning and other cognitive and behavioral techniques then were used to teach empathy and improved interpersonal skills and to reduce provocativeness and manipulation.

Kass, Silvers, and Abroms (1972) were successful in using similar behavioral techniques (videotaping, role playing, assertiveness training, rehearsal, and feedback) in treating clients with histrionic personality disorder. Although the most recent literature does not support the use of a heavily behavioral approach in the treatment of this disorder, some behavioral techniques might be judiciously and effectively combined with a psychodynamic model during the middle to later stages of treatment.

Accompanying disorders should also receive attention. Unless the depression, anxiety, or somatic symptoms are relieved, the clients may not be willing or able to modify their pervasive dysfunctional patterns.

Couples and group therapy can be very useful in treating clients with histrionic personality disorder (Gunderson, 1988). Those therapeutic experiences can provide helpful feedback, enable the clients to see that their behaviors are not getting them the approval and affection they seek, and afford them the opportunity to try new ways of establishing both casual and intimate relationships.

Medication is rarely needed in treatment of these clients. If it is recommended, considerable caution should be exercised because these clients are prone to suicidal threats and gestures.

Prognosis. Kernberg (1986) reports a moderately favorable prognosis for the treatment of histrionic personality disorder via expressive or exploratory psychoanalytic psychotherapy. Unlike most clients with paranoid, schizoid, schizotypal, and antisocial personality disorders, clients with histrionic personality disorder are motivated to make some changes and have sufficiently good interpersonal skills to allow them to engage in therapy.

9.6 Narcissistic Personality Disorder

Description of Disorder. Narcissistic personality disorder is characterized by "a pervasive pattern of grandiosity (in fantasy or behavior), lack of empathy, and hypersensitivity to the evaluation of others, beginning by early adulthood and present in a variety of contexts" (*DSM-III-R*, 1987, p. 351). People with this disorder tend to have strong, negative reactions to criticism; take advantage of others to accomplish their own goals; have an exaggerated sense of self-importance; have a sense of entitlement; seek constant attention and admiration; have little appreciation for the feelings of others; are envious of others; have persistent fantasies of high achievement in both personal and professional areas; and believe that only special people can understand their special difficulties.

Narcissistic personality disorder seems to be at least twice as common among men as among women. This disorder is found in approximately 6 percent of those with personality disorders (Millon, 1986). Some researchers believe that it has increased in prevalence in recent years (Meyer, 1983).

Relevant Client Characteristics. Narcissistic personality disorder seems particularly prevalent in people from families lacking in warmth as well as from abusive and neglectful families, especially if those families idealized a particular attribute of the child (Gunderson, 1988). Masterson (1981) hypothesizes that an incomplete separation from the mother and an impaired relationship with the father are important in the development of this disorder. He also suggests that, in many instances, the mothers of people with this disorder had little empathy for their children and also had such emotional disorders as depression and narcissistic personality disorder themselves. Gutsch (1988) believes that narcissistic personality disorder represents a defensive withdrawal from parental rejection. Millon (1981) also reports the development of this disorder in those who were pampered and overindulged as children and who were given little discipline or structure by self-demeaning parents. Although the research is not consistent on the family antecedents of narcissistic personality disorder, the disorder does seem strongly related to dysfunction in the family of origin.

People with narcissistic personality disorder tend to have low self-esteem, despite their sense of entitlement and grandiosity and their appearance of self-confidence. They often feel like frauds and failures and conceal their real selves from others lest they be discovered. They are often troubled by an underlying sense of emptiness. In addition, people with narcissistic personality disorder tend to be shallow, easily bored, and emotionally unstable. Extensive use of rationalization, denial, and projection is common, and these people have difficulty seeing the part they play in their own difficulties (Millon & Klerman, 1986). They do tend to have some guilt about their actions, however (Kernberg, 1986).

Narcissistic personality disorder often is accompanied by other disorders, notably various forms of depression (see Chapter Five). Brief paranoid and other psychotic symptoms (see Chapter Ten) also may be present. Clients with narcissistic personality disorder sometimes express their symptoms through their bodies and seek medical rather than psychological treatment (see Chapter Eight).

People with this personality disorder tend to avoid intimacy and seek to control and manipulate others. They may become contentious, arrogant, and demanding if they do not receive the treatment they feel they deserve. Consequently, their interpersonal relationships typically are at least somewhat impaired and may reflect sexual conflicts. Their quest for the perfect partner to affirm their own perfection can also be extremely damaging to their relationships.

Some people with this disorder manifest occupational impairment; others, driven by their self-absorption and their fantasies of unlimited success, have an impressive occupational history (DSM-III-R, 1987). Their tendency to be self-reliant and to take control of their own lives contributes to their sense of direction.

Like those with histrionic personality disorder, people with narcissistic personality disorder tend to deteriorate with age. However, Kernberg (1986) believes that this deterioration may weaken their grandiose façade and lead them to be more receptive to therapy.

Relevant Therapist Variables. Clients with narcissistic personality disorder are typically quite resistant to treatment. They feel, at the same time, too fragile to acknowledge that they have any problems and too special for anyone else to be able to help them. Consequently, as in treatment of most of the personality disorders, it is important that therapists communicate acceptance, warmth, genuineness, and understanding. Any hint of criticism may provoke a premature termination of therapy. Although therapists should not be judgmental, indifference can be as painful as rejection to these clients, and so therapists might be wise to engage in some cautious sharing of reactions to the clients as well as extensive use of empathy. In general, these clients are more trusting than those with other personality disorders, so the therapist can take a few cautious risks.

Clients with this disorder tend to be very conscious of authority and are fearful of losing self-determination; therapists can use these qualities to their own advantage. The therapeutic relationship should be a professional one: the clients should be viewed as the experts on their own concerns, while the therapist is the expert on psychotherapy. This collaborative relationship can facilitate the clients' acceptance of help and their engagement in a working alliance. Kernberg (1985) has emphasized that these clients must receive full credit for any positive changes; otherwise, they might sabotage the therapy in order to avoid admitting that someone else has helped them.

Clients with narcissistic personality disorder tend to be concerned with and to seek perfection in themselves and in their relationships, and they frequently alternate between idealizing and devaluing others, including the therapist (Millon, 1981). The development of an idealistic transference is not unusual and will need to be dealt with, lest the client subsequently become disillusioned with the therapist's lack of perfection and leave therapy.

Intervention Strategies. Descriptions of this disorder have appeared in the literature only in the last ten years. Consequently, little conclusive information is available on treatment. As with most of the other personality disorders, however, inferences can be drawn about the types of treatment that are most likely to be successful.

Long-term treatment of the narcissistic personality disorder is difficult because of clients' resistance to treatment and their extensive rationalization. Reid (1983) suggests, therefore, that treatment should focus on symptoms and current crises rather than on the underlying disorder. Gutsch (1988), too, suggests a present-oriented therapy, one focusing on rapport building, cognitive reorienting, reality testing, development of better communication skills, rehearsal of new behaviors, and application of these behaviors outside therapy. These clients often have particular difficulty with loss and failure and may be amenable to therapy that focuses on those matters. Other goals that are relevant and that might be addressed in therapy include stabilizing and improving the self-concept, developing an internal locus of control, and promoting a capacity for empathy (Stolorow, 1976).

The use of a psychodynamic or modified psychoanalytic approach with those who have narcissistic personality disorders is controversial. Although they typically need long-term treatment to modify their disorder, extended psychotherapy often does not seem appropriate because of the clients' lack of introspection and their reluctance to engage in treatment. As Maxmen (1986) puts it, long-term psychoanalytic treatment is usually recommended for these clients but has little chance of producing significant change. However, Kernberg (1985), Kohut (1971), and others have used a modified psychoanalytic approach with some success to help these clients develop a more accurate sense of reality. Kernberg's approach is interpretive, focusing on such basic issues as anger, envy, self-sufficiency, and demands of the self and others in reality and in transference; Kohut makes use of the transference relationship to explore early development as well as the client's wish for a perfect relationship and an ideal self. Both explore defenses as well as needs and frustrations in an empathic context. A psychodynamic approach seems to have a fair chance of succeeding with clients who have mild dysfunction and who are motivated to engage in therapy but not with those who have significant disturbances of affect or impulse control (Gunderson, 1988). Those clients seem to respond better to exploratory, expressive, and supportive forms of therapy than they do to analytic approaches (Kernberg, 1986).

Behavior therapy is not recommended as the primary form of intervention in treating narcissistic personality disorder, although techniques such as modeling, role playing, and contracting can modify some dysfunctional symptoms. Medication and hospitalization, too, are rarely indicated.

It is important not to underestimate the fragility of clients with this disorder. Loss of their defenses can precipitate transient psychotic symptoms and regression. Consequently, although these clients may appear powerful, they must be handled gently.

Group therapy can be useful to these clients if they are able to tolerate the exposure and negative feedback that may accompany that mode of treatment and do not become disruptive to the group. Group therapy can help them develop a more realistic sense of themselves, deal with others in less abrasive ways, and stabilize their functioning.

These clients often come into treatment at the urging of an unhappy spouse. In such cases, marital therapy might be useful to help the couple understand the roles they have assumed in the marriage and their patterns of relating and learn ways of communicating with each other more effectively.

Prognosis. As Winberg and Sheverbush (1980) have observed, clients with this disorder are very difficult to treat. However, despite the challenges presented to therapists by these clients, Kernberg (1986) reports a favorable prognosis unless the clients have strong borderline or antisocial features. Kernberg (1985) also suggests that the prognosis for treatment is particularly good for those clients who are creative and have some capacity to work toward their desired roles.

9.7 Borderline Personality Disorder

Description of Disorder. The borderline personality disorder has been receiving increasing attention from clinicians and theorists in recent years. The very name of this disorder reflects the precariousness of people with this condition. (The name—as Millon, 1981, points out—was originally intended to indicate that they are on the border between psychosis and neurosis.) People with this disorder are characterizd primarily by a pervasive instability of mood, relationships, behavior, and self-image (*DSM-III-R*, 1987). This instability affects all or nearly all areas of their lives. The following patterns are typical: intense and fluctuating interpersonal relationships; self-destructive and impulsive behavior (for example, substance abuse, binge eating, and promiscuity); labile moods; difficulty controlling and expressing anger; self-mutilation (such as cutting or burning); suicidal threats and attempts; lack of a stable, internalized sense of self; a persistent sense of emptiness and boredom; and frantic efforts to avoid loneliness or abandonment (*DSM-III-R*, 1987). Gunderson has developed a Diagnostic Interview for Borderlines (DIB), which seems useful and reliable in diagnosing this disorder (Cornell, Silk, Ludolph, & Lohr, 1983).

According to Millon (1986), borderline personality disorder is second only to dependent personality disorder in prevalence and represents 12 percent of personality disorders. According to Gunderson (1988), borderline personality disorder is the most common diagnosis in client populations, occurring in 15–25 percent of those seen in treatment. This disorder is at least twice as common in females as it is in males and may be diagnosed in 2–4 percent of the general population (Maxmen, 1986).

Relevant Client Characteristics. Those with borderline personality disorder often have coexisting disorders. Common are dysthymia (section 5.2), cyclothymia (section 5.5), anxiety disorders (sections 6.1 to 6.5), impulse control disorders (sections 7.1 to 7.4), severe premenstrual syndrome, temporal lobe epilepsy, somatization disorders (sections 8.1 and 8.2), and other personality disorders (Maxmen, 1986; Stone, 1986). Borderline personality disorder seems to be closely linked to the affective disorders (Chapter Five) (McGlashan, 1983a). Transient psychotic symptoms (such as dissociation or paranoia—see sections 10.1 to 10.5) may also appear, particularly at times of real or imagined abandonment. Sleeping, eating, and grooming habits are often erratic (Gutsch, 1988). In addition, these clients almost always experience some occupational and social impairment, rarely achieving commensurate with their potential.

Alcoholism is prevalent in the family backgrounds of these clients. Loranger and Tulis (1985) found that one-third of the fathers of clients with borderline personality disorder abused alcohol. A history of incest, brutality, early loss, and neglect also is common (Gunderson, 1988). Some people with borderline personality disorder are amnesiac for much of their childhood, reflecting their experience of chidhood traumas (Searles, 1986). Mothers of clients with borderline personality disorder were often very troubled themselves and may have had borderline personality disorder, depression, or psychotic symptoms. These mothers typically tried to prevent the individuation of their children by threatening withdrawal, thereby producing in the children a fear of abandonment and an impaired development (Masterson, 1981).

Problems concerning separation and individuation persist from childhood into adulthood for these clients. They tend to have little sense of themselves and seek to avoid individuation by attaining a symbiotic relationship with another, typically a romantic partner or the therapist. Because they often are uncertain of what they are feeling or how they are expected to be feeling and are fearful of incurring anger and rejection if they make a mistake, they have considerable difficulty expressing feelings. They seem to have a false self, built around an effort to please others (Masterson, 1981). They are troubled by incomplete emotional experiences and limited by their own poor sense of self. Fantasy and reality often become confused.

People with borderline personality disorder seem to have a great deal of underlying anger combined with revengeful impulses, which also occasion self-doubt and interpersonal difficulties. Sometimes these feelings are denied and suppressed lest their expression precipitate abandonment; at other times, these feelings are expressed in self-destructive ways that provoke considerable anger in others.

Borderline personality disorder tends to be particularly severe in late adolescence and early adulthood (Gunderson, 1988). Like many of the personality disorders, it decreases in severity with age.

Relevant Therapist Variables. Masterson (1981) describes two ways in which clients with borderline personality disorder are likely to relate to their therapists. The higher-functioning clients with this disorder have a strong fear of abandonment and so tend to cling to their therapists, making constant demands for extra time and attention. Those who are less well functioning are more fearful of engulfment and tend to use distancing maneuvers to avoid being overwhelmed by the therapeutic relationship. Some clients seem to alternate between the two fears.

Therapists working with these clients will need to maintain a careful balance; too much attention can promote dependency or flight, while too little attention can promote suicidal threats, panic, anger, and the failure to develop a therapeutic alliance. Therapists should remain calm and nonjudgmental, actively maintaining control in the face of clients' manipulative endeavors. Although therapists must communicate availability, reliability, interest, acceptance, support, genuineness, and empathy, they must also establish and adhere to clear and consistent limits and guidelines. Extra sessions may be given and supportive telephone calls may be made when therapeutically advisable, but not because of client manipulation or suicidal threats. Therapists need to make clear that they cannot take responsibility for the lives of these clients and should not become their rescuers. At the same time, the clients need to feel secure and trusting of their therapists. Accordingly, therapists must take steps to protect the safety of these clients, perhaps by providing them with emergency resources, other sources of therapeutic support, and outside contacts to whom they can turn in time of crisis.

Splitting is a common dynamic in the self-images and relationships of these clients. They tend to perceive people in extremes, either idealized or devalued. They may view one person alternately in both ways or may idealize one helping figure while devaluing another. The devaluation sometimes has elements of projective identification as clients project unacceptable aspects of themselves onto others. These clients typically begin a therapeutic relationship by idealizing the therapist; then, when the therapist has failed to yield to their demands for special attention, this view will shift and the clients will devalue the therapist, often terminating treatment with that person and moving on to the next idealized therapist.

Therapists will need to deal with their own reactions to these often frustrating and complicated clients and should not be lulled into confidence by positive phases of therapy. Countertransference reactions can be a useful route to understanding the client and so should be examined. Inevitably, if therapy is to succeed, therapists will need to find a gentle and supportive way to deal with the resistance and transference manifested by these clients.

Intervention Strategies. Although, once again, little systematic study has been conducted, there does seem to be some agreement on the treatment of choice for borderline personality disorder. Most concur that long-term psychodynamic or modified psychoanalytic psychotherapy is most effective in treating clients with this disorder (Maxmen, 1986; Reid, 1983). However, as Dorr, Barley, Gard, and Webb (1983) put it, "A passive classical analytic approach is not recommended. Rather, the psychotherapist is advised to be more direct, real, confrontive and, in some cases, even more directive than he or she would be with a neurotic patient" (p. 403).

Many clients with borderline personality disorders need to be seen several times a week to maintain stability in their lives, avert suicide, and ensure the therapeutic alliance. The therapeutic relationship can serve as a model to help clients work through separation and individuation concerns that date back to childhood. Although some attention should be paid to working through past issues, the primary focus of therapy should be on bolstering ego defenses and on treating the present, since it mirrors the past for most of these clients. Mendelsohn (1981) emphasizes the importance of keeping these clients focused on pertinent issues and encouraging them to analyze and process current material (focusing and active attention). Reality testing, neutralizing rage, and managing the transference relationship are other important ingredients of therapy with these clients. Therapeutic use of silences and nonverbal communication is particularly important with these clients, since they have considerable difficulty with direct expression of feelings (Searles, 1986).

Gunderson (1984) recommends a supportive-expressive approach to therapy with these clients. His approach seems to integrate many of the ingredients that have been found effective in the treatment of borderline personality disorder. His long-term plan of treatment includes the following five phases:

1. Establishing boundaries by clarifying anger, demands, and manipulativeness.
2. Focusing on the therapeutic relationship and past experiences, to provide corrective emotional experiences and promote appropriate expression of feeling, shifting clients from acting out to verbalization.
3. Promoting separation and individuation.
4. Encouraging development of new feelings, interests, and social skills.
5. Planning termination carefully.

Gunderson uses inquiry more than interpretation in treating clients with borderline personality disorder and seeks to promote an observing and moderating self rather than unlimited expression of feeling. Adjuncts to treatment (for example, group and family therapy, hospitalization, medication, or art therapy) are used as needed.

Because of the self-destructive and potentially lethal behavior of many clients with borderline personality disorder, therapists—whatever approach they use—must make an effort to reduce acting out and promote more effective functioning and reality testing. In general, the self-destructive behaviors of these clients are ego-dystonic, evoking considerable shame, guilt, and anxiety as well as the wish to be forgiven and to change. For most of these clients, the acting out is a way to defend against boredom and depression and prevent abandonment; dealing with those concerns can reduce the pressure toward self-destructive behavior. Masterson (1981) recommends confrontation rather than interpretation as the most effective route to behavioral change. Although a directive approach may help these clients manage their lives more effectively, it also may undermine their efforts toward individuation. Support is needed to provide stability, strengthen the self-concept, and reinforce motivation. A careful balance must be maintained.

After some progress has been made in individual therapy,

group therapy can be a useful adjunct to treatment of borderline personality disorder, particularly for those clients who are inhibited or abrasive (Stone, 1986). Care must be taken, however, to be sure the client does not monopolize or disrupt the group and is able to share the therapist.

Antidepressant, antiseizure, and antipsychotic medication occasionally can be useful in treating the secondary symptoms of these clients, but medication does not relieve the basic personality disorder. Masterson (1981) reports that these clients generally do not respond well to antipsychotic medication, even if they are experiencing transient psychotic symptoms; however, more positive results also have been reported (Goldberg & others, 1986). Use of medication should be closely monitored because of the tendency of clients with this disorder to make suicide attempts.

Hospitalization, too, may be indicated when the client is experiencing psychotic or suicidal ideation. Typically, hospitalization will be brief but may be a frequent component in the treatment of some of these clients. For most, however, a sort of stable instability will be achieved (Soloff, 1985).

Prognosis. Pope, Jones, Hudson, Cohen, and Gunderson (1983) report a prognosis for treatment of borderline personality disorder that is somewhat better than for treatment of schizophrenia but not as good as that for treatment of schizoaffective and bipolar disorders. McGlashan (1986a) conducted a long-term follow-up of eighty-one inpatients diagnosed as having borderline personality disorder who were seen for an average of two years of intensive treatment. Although they had an average of one or two subsequent hospitalizations, most were living independently and functioning fairly well. Stone (1986) found that in treatment approximately 20 percent of clients with borderline personality disorder show considerable improvement, 40 percent show some improvement, and 40 percent stay the same or deteriorate. The prognosis seems better for those with histrionic, depressive, obsessive, or phobic features and worse for those with paranoid or narcissistic features.

According to Gunderson (1988), treatment of clients with borderline personality disorder may require as long as four to five years. He found that those who complete treatment are much improved but are still vulnerable. Improvement is signaled by reduced acting out and a more direct expression of hostility and dependency needs. Unfortunately, clients with this disorder frequently leave treatment prematurely. However, for those who complete treatment, the prognosis seems to be at least fair.

9.8 Avoidant Personality Disorder

Description of Disorder. The *DSM-III-R* (1987) describes avoidant personality disorder as characterized by "a pervasive pattern of social discomfort, fear of negative valuation, and timidity, beginning by early adulthood and present in a variety of contexts" (p. 352). Typical manifestations of this disorder include emotional fragility and hypersensitivity to criticism, no more than one close friend other than first-degree relatives, reluctance to become involved in interpersonal contact without guarantees of acceptance, fear of being embarrassed by doing something inappropriate or foolish in public, and exaggeration of the difficulties and risks involved in deviating from the usual routine (*DSM-III-R*, 1987).

Males and females are affected by this disorder in approximately equal numbers. Millon (1986) found avoidant personality disorder to be one of the more prevalent personality disorders, representing over 10 percent of those with personality disorders.

Relevant Client Characteristics. People with avoidant personality disorder often have first-degree relatives who are also acutely uncomfortable in social situations (Millon, 1986). Whether this similarity is genetic or is based on modeling and identification is unclear, but avoidant personality disorder does tend to run in families. People with this disorder often had cold, rejecting parents who exposed them to humiliation. The personality disorder seems to be an internalization of those early messages (Millon, 1986). Even as children, people with avoidant personality disorder had limited social experiences and poor peer relationships. Consequently, they had little opportunity to learn the skills needed for appropriate adult socialization.

Unlike those with schizoid personality disorder, people with avoidant personality disorder typically long for companionship and involvement in social activities, but their great anxiety and shyness prevent them from increasing their socialization. These people usually have low self-esteem, are self-effacing, and berate themselves for their refusal to take risks in social situations. They fantasize about having a different lifestyle and anguish over their inability to change. However, without assistance, they typically remain alienated, introverted, mistrustful, and guarded in social situations and avoid them whenever possible. Their need for control and self-protection outweighs their need for companionship.

By definition, then, people with avoidant personality disorder have considerable social impairment. Social impairment is typically accompanied by occupational impairment, since their fear of risk and embarrassment prevents them from seeking promotions, taking an active part in meetings, attending business-related social events, and calling attention to their accomplishments. The lives of people with avoidant personality disorder tend to be unsatisfying and disappointing, even if they manage to achieve a comfortable occupational situation. Some marry or develop another close relationship; but, typically, their friends tend to be shy and unstable, providing little help to these clients (Meyer, 1983).

Females with avoidant personality disorder often have a strongly traditional gender identification. They tend to be passive, insecure, and dependent, looking to others to direct their lives. Although they may have underlying anger at their situations, they are afraid of the consequences of change.

Other disorders and symptoms frequently accompany avoidant personality disorder. Common are disorders involving anxiety and depression (see Chapters Six and Five). Social phobia (section 6.3.3) also seems closely related to this disorder. Agoraphobia (section 6.3.1), dissociative disorders (section 10.5), somatoform disorders (section 8.1), and schizophrenia (section 10.1) have also been reported (Millon, 1981). Gunderson (1988) found that when clients with this disorder are seen in treatment, another disorder is usually the focus of treatment.

Relevant Therapist Variables. Clients with avoidant personality disorder rarely seek treatment specifically for the symptoms of their personality disorder, because that process in itself is threatening and potentially embarrassing to them. If they do enter treatment, they often have one foot out the door, testing whether the therapist can be trusted, and may leave at any hint of ridicule or embarrassment.

These clients sometimes are seen in treatment as a result of another disorder, such as agoraphobia or depression, particularly at the urging of a family member or employer. The therapist should proceed gradually in light of the apprehension these clients have about treatment and the fragile equilibrium they have established. Therapists should communicate concern, availability, empathy, acceptance, and support. Building trust may be slow but is integral to the establishment of an effective therapeutic relationship with these clients. Focusing on the clients' strengths, at least initially, can build self-confidence and contribute to the establishment of rapport. Contracting for a specific number of sessions may increase commitment to treatment and prevent the client's using therapy to avoid confronting real situations.

One advantage for the therapist in working with these clients is that they are in pain, are not happy with themselves, and want to change. In addition, they typically appreciate safe attention, have a good capacity for introspection and insight, and can even be too introspective (Millon, 1981). If they can be convinced that therapy can help them and is not likely to embarrass them, they may have the motivation needed to work successfully on their dysfunctional symptoms.

Intervention Strategies. As with most of more recently defined personality disorders, little research is available to guide treatment of avoidant personality disorder. Some clinicians view this disorder as a sort of phobia and treat it with behavior therapy, using relaxation and desensitization to help clients confront frightening situations (Gunderson, 1988). An educational component, emphasizing social skills and assertiveness training, also can help clients cope more effectively with social situations once they are willing to face them. Attention to dysfunctional cognitions that are promoting the social avoidance also should accelerate behavioral change. Although these models of treatment (behavioral, educational, and cognitive) typically involve homework assignments, Kaplan and Sadock (1985) caution against assignments that may lead to failure and humiliation for these clients.

Therapy for avoidant personality disorder might be relatively brief and directive in nature, emphasizing improvement in socialization; or, if the client is motivated, it might be lengthier and seek to modify the underlying personality disorder. Millon (1986) suggests that therapy with these clients should involve some exploration and analysis, so that clients can review past worries and disappointments and deal with underlying anxiety and depression. This suggestion makes sense, since avoidant personality disorder is a pervasive disorder and not just a behavioral deficit. However, interpretations should be made with caution, since these clients sometimes receive them as criticisms.

As clients improve, group therapy can be an important addition to treatment. It can help clients learn and practice new social skills, receive feedback and encouragement, and increase their comfort with others. However, these clients should not be put into a therapy group prematurely. That can be very threatening and can lead them to leave treatment abruptly.

Family therapy, too, can be useful if the client is actively involved with family. Family therapy can help clients relate more successfully to their families, and it can help the families understand the clients and stop pressuring them to change.

Medication is almost never needed in treatment of avoidant personality disorder. In addition, clients with that disorder seem uncomfortable with the idea of taking medication, probably because of the loss of control it may suggest. They benefit from being able to take credit for positive changes rather than attributing them to medication.

Prognosis. Millon (1981) found that the prognosis for treating avoidant personality disorder tends to be poor because of the clients' reluctance to engage in treatment. However, prognosis seems likely to improve significantly if a commitment to therapy can be obtained from the client.

9.9 Dependent Personality Disorder

Description of Disorder. The dependent personality disorder is characterized by "a pervasive pattern of dependent and submissive behavior" (*DSM-III-R*, 1987, p. 354). People with this disorder typically have great difficulty making decisions independently and without reassurance; look to others to make major decisions for them; avoid disagreeing with others lest they be rejected; feel uncomfortable and helpless when alone or when required to take initiative; go out of their way to be helpful in order to be liked; are hypersensitive to criticism or disapproval; fear being abandoned; and are devastated if close relationships end (*DSM-III-R*, 1987).

According to Millon (1986), dependent personality disorder is the most commonly diagnosed personality disorder, found in approximately 14 percent of those with personality disorders. This disorder seems more common among females than among males, and some have questioned whether women who embrace traditional roles are being inappropriately diagnosed as having dependent personality disorder.

Relevant Client Characteristics. Often, dependent personality disorder stems from an early separation anxiety disorder or chronic illness. Youngest children in families are more likely to have this disorder, perhaps because their upbringing encouraged them to depend on older family members and did not lead to sufficient independence (Maxmen, 1986). Not surprisingly, many clients with dependent personality disorder report a history of being overprotected (Esman, 1986). They were typically pampered children who were expected to behave perfectly. As Millon (1981) puts it, their home lives were often too good.

People with dependent personality disorder have very low self-esteem and are frequently self-critical. They feel that they have little to offer and therefore must assume a secondary, even subservient, relationship to others in order to be accepted; and they tend to be inordinately tolerant of destructive relationships. They typically are other-directed, and their gratifications and disappointments hinge on the reactions they receive from others. At the same time, they are egocentric in that they are pleasing others to gain appreciation. Other disorders—such as depression (Chapter Five), anxiety

(Chapter Six), agoraphobia (section 6.3.1), somatoform disorders (section 8.1), and other personality disorders—may be diagnosed along with dependent personality disorder (Esman, 1986).

People with this disorder tend to have a small number of relatives or friends on whom they are dependent and who seem to accept their passive and submissive attitudes. They bind those significant others to them through guilt and service and rarely seek to broaden their social circle. They may function satisfactorily in an occupation that is consistent with their need to be told what to do but have difficulty with tasks that require independent action and decisions; and they may appear fragile, indecisive, placating, inept, and immature to those around them (Millon & Klerman, 1986). Even when these clients' lives seem to be going well, they experience little happiness but seem to have a pervasive underlying pessimism and depression (Millon, 1981), appearing rigid, judgmental, and moralistic, especially under stress. In crisis, despondency and rage as well as suicidal ideation may surface (Reid, 1983).

Relevant Therapist Variables. Clients with dependent personality disorder may seek therapy voluntarily following an experienced or threatened loss of a relationship, particularly via bereavement or divorce; or they may seek therapy at the suggestion of a spouse, other relative, or employer. These clients also may ask for help with secondary symptoms such as depression and substance abuse (Gunderson, 1988). They are likely to be apprehensive about therapy but want help to avert any threatened loss. However, they are not likely to have much interest in becoming more assertive and independent. They tend to view their therapist as someone else on whom to depend, a magic helper, and will probably work hard to please the therapist rather than themselves.

The challenge for therapists will be to use these dynamics constructively. The clients' wish to please may be used to develop rapport and encourage increased independence. However, changes made only to please the therapist are not likely to persist outside of the sessions and do not reflect internalized change.

In working with clients with dependent personality disorder, therapists probably should begin in a directive and structured way to give focus to the session. In order to establish rapport with these clients, therapists also will need to communicate a great deal of support, acceptance, and empathy and should guard against appearing critical. With the development of a therapeutic alliance, therapists should gradually assume less responsibility and encourage clients to take more control of the session. Therapists should continue to convey empathy, appreciation, and optimism but also should ask the clients to make a commitment to working on their concerns. The overall goal of treatment with these clients is to promote self-reliance, self-expression, and independence in a safe context and then facilitate the transfer of those experiences outside of the therapy room. Termination is likely to be particularly difficult with these clients, and therapists will need to be cautious lest clients feel abandoned.

Some have recommended that women with dependent personality disorder be seen by a woman therapist, to provide a positive role model and to make dependency less likely (Hill, 1970). This recommendation might be considered when treatment is planned.

Strong countertransference reactions to these clients are common (Esman, 1986). Therapists may find them frustrating and annoying but should be careful that these reactions do not destroy the therapeutic alliance.

Intervention Strategies. Dependent personality disorder is another disorder that made its first appearance in the *DSM-III* in 1980. Two approaches to therapy with this disorder seem prominent. Some advocate a psychodynamic or modified psychoanalytic approach (Maxmen, 1986). Such an approach can help to improve clients' self-esteem; increase their sense of autonomy and individuation; teach them to manage their own lives and ask for help and support without being manipulative; and relieve their fears of harming others or being devastated by rejection. However, a psychodynamic approach requires both commitment to therapy and introspection and may not be right for some clients with dependent personality disorder. In addition, some clients respond to long-term insight-oriented therapy with increased dependency (McDaniel, 1981).

Behavior therapy has also been used effectively to ameliorate some of the symptoms of dependent personality disorder and may eliminate some of the risks of psychodynamic treatment if carefully integrated with that model. Treatment would be fairly similar to that recommended for avoidant personality disorder (section 9.8). It would include relaxation and desensitization, to help clients handle challenging interpersonal situations, and would emphasize assertiveness training and communication skills, to help clients identify and express their feelings and wants in more functional ways. Standard behavioral techniques—such as modeling, reinforcement, and rehearsal—can contribute to the improvement of these clients. Homework assignments are likely to be completed, since these clients follow directions and want to please.

Practical matters such as housing and employment will often require attention, since many clients with dependent personality disorder seek therapy after the end of a marriage. Therapists who help these clients successfully reestablish themselves will probably also succeed in promoting and reinforcing behavioral change; in the process, the clients can apply what they have learned in therapy.

Family therapy and group therapy are often indicated for these clients. Those settings will afford them the opportunity to try out new ways of expressing themselves and relating to others while receiving support and encouragement along the way.

Clients with this disorder sometimes request medication and also may seek multiple therapists to give them extra support (Gutsch, 1988). Both are rarely needed, except in cases of severe affective symptoms, and can detract from the goals of therapy.

Prognosis. Treatment of dependent personality disorder is difficult; the patterns are deeply entrenched, and the clients really want to be saved rather than to change (Esman, 1986). Nevertheless, Millon (1981) reports a relatively good prognosis. These clients are trusting, they can form relationships and make commitments, they want to please, and they can ask for help. All these characteristics lead to a somewhat better prognosis than is found for most of the personality disorders.

9.10 Obsessive Compulsive Personality Disorder

Description of Disorder. Perfectionism and inflexibility characterize the obsessive compulsive personality disorder. Typical manifestations of this pervasive pattern include impaired performance on tasks and activities because of preoccupation with details, rules, duties, and perfection; a strong need to control others out of fear that they will not do things correctly; overinvolvement in work, accompanied by minimal attention to leisure and social activities; indecisiveness; rigid moral and ethical beliefs; restricted expression of emotion; reluctance to give to others without promise of personal gain; and difficulty discarding objects that no longer have value (*DSM-III-R*, 1987). Oldham and Frosch (1986) list the three major characteristics of obsessive compulsive personality disorder as orderliness, stinginess, and obstinacy. This disorder differs from obsessive compulsive disorder (discussed in section 6.4) in that obsessive compulsive personality disorder is pervasive and ego-syntonic and typically does not include discrete, specific obsessions or compulsions that are unwanted and intrusive.

According to Millon (1986), obsessive compulsive personality disorder is somewhat more common among males than females. This disorder also seems more common among oldest children (Maxmen, 1986). People with obsessive compulsive personality disorder represent approximately 11 percent of those with personality disorders (Millon, 1986).

Relevant Client Characteristics. According to Gunderson (1988), the early history of people with obsessive compulsive personality disorder reveals demanding, punitive, and authoritarian parents, and struggles between parents and child over questions of control, authority, and autonomy. The children typically were made to feel shame and guilt, and independent thought or action was not encouraged. Home environments of people with this disorder have usually been rigid, emphasizing a work ethic (Turkat & Maisto, 1985). Obsessive compulsive personality disorder is more common among first-degree relatives of those with the same disorder than it is in the general population (*DSM-III-R*, 1987), and parents' punitive and authoritarian behavior may be a reflection of their own obsessive compulsive personality disorder.

People with this disorder almost inevitably have interpersonal and social difficulties, although it is not uncommon for them to achieve stable marriages (Gutsch, 1988). They tend to be cold, mistrustful, demanding, and uninteresting and put little time or effort into building relationships and communicating feelings. Their lives tend to be joyless and focused on work and obligations. Their occupational development may or may not be impaired, and they seem to have the greatest occupational success of those with personality disorders because they are tireless and dedicated workers (Oldham & Frosch, 1986). However, they have difficulty delegating, collaborating, and supervising; tend to be self-righteous and domineering; and usually have poor relationships with co-workers, whom the clients tend to view negatively because the co-workers do not manifest the clients' own overconscientiousness. People with obsessive compulsive personality disorder tend to have difficulty bringing projects to closure because of their indecisiveness, poor planning, and perfectionism.

Although people with obsessive compulsive personality disorder seem indifferent to the feelings of others, they are very sensitive to slights themselves and typically overreact to real or imagined insults. Their common defenses include sublimation, intellectualization, isolation, reaction formation, and undoing (Horowitz, Marmar, Krupnick, Wilner, Kaltreider, & Wallerstein, 1984). Rules are used to insulate them from their emotions (Millon, 1981).

Anxiety and depression (Chapters Six and Five) are frequent accompaniments of this disorder. Anxiety seems to be particularly interrelated with obsessive compulsive personality disorder (Frances, 1988); depression frequently follows a perceived loss or failure (Gutsch, 1988). Paranoia (sections 10.1 to 10.4) has also been reported (Oldham & Frosch, 1986). Without treatment, obsessive compulsive personality disorder is relatively stable over time and neither improves nor deteriorates.

Relevant Therapist Variables. People with obsessive compulsive personality disorder are difficult clients because they have trouble giving up control and accepting help from others and because they have little facility for self-expression. They are not often self-referred and tend to emphasize physical rather than psychological complaints in treatment (Meyer, 1983). New situations make them anxious, and they are likely to become even more than usually obstinate and resistant in therapy (Gunderson, 1988). If they can become engaged in conversation, they tend to complain bitterly about how incompetent others are and how unappreciated they feel. Their interest is in changing others rather than in changing themselves, and they may attack a therapist who suggests that they themselves need to make changes.

Involving these clients in a productive therapeutic relationship, then, clearly presents a considerable challenge. However, people with obsessive compulsive personality disorder are persevering, respect authority, and comply with rules and direction (although they may feel inwardly defiant). Therapists may initially be able to use the authority of their educations and positions to elicit a short-term commitment to therapy from these clients. Therapists should be sure not to engage in power struggles and arguments with these clients and should treat them in a respectful and professional way; not violate their defenses and need for privacy; collaborate with them on therapeutic decisions; and be prompt, organized, and efficient. Providing support and empathy can also help convince these clients that the therapist is not the enemy.

Intervention Strategies. Little empirical research exists on the etiology and treatment of obsessive compulsive personality disorder (Turkat & Maisto, 1985). Although long-term psychodynamic or modified psychoanalytic therapy might seem ideal for these clients, it is difficult to involve them in therapy that is extended, intensive, and introspective. Consequently, more present- and action-oriented approaches—approaches consistent with the clients' limited insight and intolerance for yielding control—will often need to be used.

Gunderson (1988) suggests short-term dynamic therapy for those who are reluctant to become involved in lengthier therapy. Dynamic therapy with these clients might focus on such issues as the need for control and perfectionism and on their relationships. Gentle confrontation might be used to help clients focus realistically on their current difficulties and to promote expression of affect. According to Oldham and Frosch (1986), a fundamental goal of treatment is to make the obsessive compulsive behaviors and attitudes ego-dystonic, so that clients are motivated to change.

Behavior therapy can be useful in reducing some of the dysfunctional behaviors of these clients and in increasing their tolerance, their ability to plan and make decisions, their involvement in leisure and social activities, and their facility for communicating their feelings and reactions positively and assertively. Meyer (1983) recommends a behavioral approach to treating these clients, using such techniques as covert conditioning and sensitization, in which the image of an aversive event is paired with a dysfunctional behavior in an effort to motivate clients to make behavioral changes. He also recommends paradoxical interventions as a way to give clients choices and a sense of control. Modeling humor and spontaneity in controlled ways can teach these clients new ways of behaving. Stress management techniques also can contribute to the improvement of this disorder (Maxmen, 1986).

Cognitive approaches have generally not been found effective in treating obsessive compulsive personality disorder (Millon, 1981). Neither has a person-centered model proven effective, although support and empathy should be part of any approach used with these clients.

Clients with obsessive compulsive personality disorder typically will be resistant to participation in group and family therapy because of their reluctance to disclose their feelings to others and their fear of humiliation. However, if their commitment to individual therapy can be sustained long enough for them to make some positive changes, they may later be able to make productive use of group or family therapy. Those approaches can offer them feedback as well as the opportunity to learn and experiment with new interpersonal behaviors and improve relationships.

Medication generally is not necessary for treatment of these clients. However, some medications not yet widely used (for example, Anafranil) have demonstrated effectiveness in treating obsessive compulsive disorder and may be beneficial in the treatment of obsessive compulsive personality disorder as well. Medication is occasionally indicated for symptom relief of severe anxiety and depression accompanying obsessive compulsive personality disorder (Millon, 1981).

Prognosis. Little outcome research is available on the treatment of this disorder (Oldham & Frosch, 1986). Gutsch (1988) reports that some people with obsessive compulsive personality disorder do seek therapy voluntarily and respond well to treatment, but most of the literature presents a rather bleak picture of outcome. As with most of the personality disorders, a small number of these clients probably will make major changes as a result of therapy, a larger number will make some important behavioral and attitudinal changes, and another large number will either leave therapy prematurely or resist its impact. Overall, then, there is probably only a fair prognosis for treatment of obsessive compulsive personality disorder.

9.11 Passive Aggressive Personality Disorder

Description of Disorder. Passive aggressive personality disorder is one of the more controversial and less well defined of the personality disorders (Esman, 1986). Some insist that it is not even a true personality disorder because it tends to be relatively context dependent. The *DSM-III-R* (1987) describes this disorder as characterized by "a pervasive pattern of passive resistance to demands for adequate social and occupational performance" (p. 357). Typical ways in which clients manifest this disorder include procrastinating; becoming irritable and argumentative when asked to do something undesirable; performing tasks excessively slowly or inadequately; forgetting obligations; complaining of unfair treatment; resenting suggestions; becoming inordinately critical of those in authority; failing to take part in shared tasks; and perceiving themselves as doing better than others think they are (*DSM-III-R*, 1987).

Passive aggressive personality disorder is diagnosed with equal frequency in males and females. This disorder represents approximately 9 percent of the existing personality disorders (Millon, 1986) and is found in about 1 percent of the general population (Maxmen, 1986).

Relevant Client Characteristics. Histories of people with passive aggressive personality disorder often indicate that they were difficult children and received inconsistent parenting (Esman, 1986). The disorder seems to be associated with a childhood diagnosis of oppositional defiant disorder (*DSM-III-R*, 1987). People with passive aggressive personality disorder sometimes resented having been replaced by a younger child (Millon, 1981). Kaplan and Sadock (1985) describe a common history in which parents blocked the child's developing assertiveness and only partially met dependency needs. Small, Small, and Alig (1970) report a high incidence of alcholism in the families of origin of these clients. As they mature, people with passive aggressive personality disorder internalize contradictory parental messages and fail to develop clear and realistic pictures of themselves and their interactions.

People with passive aggressive personality disorder avoid both responsibility and blame. They externalize and project blame onto others and view themselves as helpless victims of fate (Millon, 1981). They tend to be pessimistic, manipulative, excitable, obstinate, discontented, and envious of others and are troubled by low self-esteem (Soloff, 1985). Their personal relationships tend to be negative and dysfunctional; their behavior evokes hostility and rejection from others, which the clients greet with a sense of outrage and injustice. Dysfunction is evident in their careers, too, and they are often chronically ineffective, unambitious, and dissatisfied (Meyer, 1983).

Anxiety and depression (Chapters Six and Five) are common accompaniments of this disorder (Reid, 1983). Alcohol abuse (section 7.1.1) has also been reported as common (Esman, 1986). Suicidal gestures, too, are part of this disorder and seem to be both an expression of hostility and a way to evoke sympathy and attention (Maxmen, 1986).

Relevant Therapist Variables. Clients with passive aggressive personality disorder tend to undermine the work of the therapist, just as they undermine other endeavors, and are resistant to change. In an effort to prevent this tendency to undermine their work, therapists should set clear limits and guidelines for the therapeutic relationship (Reid, 1983). Therapists will also need to deal with the oppositional and critical attitudes common in these clients and their tendency to project blame onto others. Therapists themselves will often be blamed for misunderstanding the clients and for being unduly demanding.

If a rapport can be developed with these clients, dependency needs may surface, and therapists will have another set of transference issues to cope with (Esman, 1986). It is difficult to deal with these clients openly and directly on concerns, and efforts to do so will usually result in frustration. Strong confrontation of both sabotaging and dependency behaviors should be avoided, but they do need to be pointed out to clients and limits set to ensure a healthy therapeutic relationship and to promote self-observation. A firm, professional stance can provide some stability to the therapeutic relationship (Gutsch, 1988).

Intervention Strategies. Long-term treatment will usually be needed for this disorder, although Gunderson (1988) found that short-term dynamic therapy is sometimes sufficient to help clients identify and understand their concerns and effect some improvement. Initially, only a brief course of treatment should be anticipated, since these clients typically are resistant to therapy and tend to terminate treatment when distressing symptoms have abated (Millon, 1981). Emphasizing consequences rather than interpretation may facilitate initial progress.

Once they are engaged in treatment, these clients' defenses tend to weaken, and depression and anxiety emerge (Esman, 1986). The goal of therapy at that time is to reduce the distress and help the clients learn more effective ways of orienting themselves toward others and toward their work. An eclectic model—combining supportive, psychodynamic, and behavioral elements—seems most likely to be effective in accomplishing those goals. Behavior therapy can promote such desirable changes as increasing direct and assertive communication and the ability to deal with anger. Techniques such as imagery, relaxation, modeling, feedback, rehearsal, and role playing have been useful (Gutsch, 1988). Cognitive techniques, combined with the behavioral ones, can promote reality testing and accelerate development of alternate behaviors. Encouraging environmental changes to reduce stress can also be helpful.

Meyer (1983) recommends group and family therapy as a source of consensual feedback and a vehicle for teaching and facilitating development of new ways of relating to others. Consensual feedback is likely to have a more powerful impact on clients with passive aggressive personality disorder than is feedback from the therapist alone. Group therapy can also help diffuse dependency needs, promote control and consistency, and encourage acceptance of responsibility. However, without some prior individual therapy, the vulnerability and defensiveness of these clients will probably prevent them from working productively in a group context.

As with most of the personality disorders, medication usually is not indicated to treat this disorder. However, severe symptoms of anxiety and depression may be relieved through a short-term, carefully monitored course of medication.

Prognosis. Little clear information is available on the outcome of treatment for passive aggressive personality disorder. In a possibly outdated study, Small, Small, and Alig (1970) report that only nine out of one hundred clients studied in a long-term followup had recovered from this disorder. although those who had participated in therapy had benefited. As with most of the personality disorders, there seems to be a good chance of ameliorating the symptoms of the disorder if clients can be engaged in treatment; but it seems unlikely that the underlying personality disorder can be eliminated or that a consistent pattern of stable and positive interpersonal interactions can be established.

9.12 Personality Disorder Not Otherwise Specified

An additional diagnostic category, personality disorder not otherwise specified, is used for mixed personality disorders in which features of several personality disorders are present but the criteria for any single personality disorder are not met. "Personality disorder not otherwise specified" is also used for personality disorders that have not yet been fully accepted as diagnoses: sadistic personality disorder, self-defeating personality disorder, impulsive personality disorder, and immature personality disorder. These four personality disorders have been proposed as diagnostic categories and have begun to receive some attention in the literature, but little is known, as yet, about their etiology and treatment. These mixed or additional personality disorders comprise approximately 6 percent of the existing personality disorders (Millon, 1986). Impulsive personality disorder and immature personality disorder will not be discussed here because of the lack of clear information on these disorders. By the time the *DSM-IV* is published (currently planned for 1993), enough information probably will have been gathered on these personality disorders, as well as the other disorders cited in this section, to determine whether each should be made a diagnosis in its own right and to provide guidelines for treatment.

9.12.1 Sadistic Personality Disorder

Sadistic personality disorder is defined as "a pervasive pattern of cruel, demeaning, and aggressive behavior" (*DSM-III-R*, 1987, p. 371). People with this disorder use cruelty, lying, intimidation, and humiliation to gain power over others; are amused by the suffering of others; and are intrigued by violence and its instruments. Sadistic personality disorder is far more prevalent in males than in females.

Clients with sadistic personality disorder frequently have associated personality disorders and substance use disorders (section 7.1) as well as interpersonal, occupational, and legal difficulties. A history of growing up in an abusive family is common.

These clients rarely present voluntarily for treatment but may be seen in legal settings dealing with spouse or child abuse. The clients are likely to be angry and defensive and to blame others for their difficulties.

9.12.2 Self-Defeating Personality Disorder

People with self-defeating personality disorder have "a pervasive pattern of self-defeating behavior . . . present in a variety of contexts. The person often may avoid or undermine pleasurable experiences, be drawn to situations or relationships in which he or she will suffer, and prevent others from helping him or her" (*DSM-III-R*, 1987, p. 373). People with this disorder seem to seek out disappointment and failure, respond negatively to positive experiences, invite criticism and rejection, fail to accomplish needed tasks, and are excessively self-sacrificing. These behaviors do not occur solely out of fear for their own safety or as a symptom of depression. Early indications are that this is one of the more common personality disorders and is particularly prevalent among females (*DSM-III-R*, 1987).

People with self-defeating personality disorder complain of being victims and feel debased, helpless, and miserable (Gunderson, 1988). At the same time, their behavior makes them feel needed and gives them a sense of power over those they perceive as abusing them. They seem to believe that if they make others feel guilty for mistreating them, then the guilt will somehow lead to love and commitment (Asch, 1986).

Depression (Chapter Five), substance abuse (section 7.1), and suicidal ideation often accompany self-defeating personality disorder. A history of growing up in an abusive family seems to predispose people to develop this disorder, as does having first-degree relatives with the same disorder. The aggressive impulses of these clients were not tolerated when they were growing up, and they were often taught to be subservient (Gunderson, 1988). This personality disorder is one of the few that seems to worsen with age (Asch, 1986).

Both transference and countertransference reactions will need attention in therapy with these clients. They tend to turn themselves into victims in therapy, are mistrustful and suspicious of the therapist, and perceive the therapist as critical and harmful. These attitudes can evoke anger in therapists, which will probably be gratifying to the clients (Gunderson, 1988). In addition, these clients blame the outside world for their problems and have difficulty accepting the need to change (Asch, 1986). It is probably advisable for therapists to communicate considerable understanding, warmth, and acceptance and to guard against interventions that may be interpreted as critical. Role modeling by the therapist can be a useful adjunct to treatment.

On the positive side, these clients tend to be dependable, hard working, and reasonably sociable. Those traits should enable them to work productively in therapy if a positive therapeutic relationship can be established. However, forming that alliance probably will be extremely difficult.

Little is available on the treatment of this newly defined disorder. However, Gunderson (1988) recommends dynamic psychotherapy, focusing on the clients' self-esteem, interpersonal needs, relationships, and inhibited aggression. These clients need help in becoming more conscious of their self-destructive patterns and in becoming less accepting and comfortable with those patterns. Long-term treatment may well be necessary to ameliorate this deeply ingrained disorder.

Neither medication nor group therapy seems indicated in treating clients with self-defeating personality disorder. They are likely to manipulate the group, so that it feeds into their wish to be criticized, and can create a negative experience for all involved.

Asch (1986) found self-defeating personality disorder to be one of the most difficult personality disorders to treat. Clients have little motivation to change and little insight into their self-destructive patterns. In addition, failure of the therapy is consistent with their self-defeating patterns and is rewarding to them.

Summary of Treatment Recommendations

Recommendations on treating personality disorders are summarized below according to the framework of the client map:

Diagnosis. Personality disorders (paranoid, schizoid, schizotypal, antisocial, histrionic, narcissistic, borderline, avoidant, dependent, obsessive compulsive, passive aggressive, and personality disorder not otherwise specified).

Objectives. Short to medium term: improve social and occupational functioning, communication skills, self-esteem, and coping mechanisms and develop appropriate sense of responsibility. Long term: modify underlying dysfunctional personality patterns.

Assessment. Broad-based personality inventory (such as the Millon Clinical Multiaxial Inventory) is often useful, as well as measures of specific symptoms (such as substance use, depression, or anxiety) to clarify dynamics.

Clinician. Needs to be consistent and able to set limits; capable of communicating acceptance and empathy in the face of resistance or dependency; able to manage countertransference reactions; patient and comfortable with slow progress.

Location. Usually outpatient, but with emergency and inpatient services available to respond to suicidal ideation and to deterioration.

Interventions. Usually psychodynamic interventions to modify dysfunctional personality; behavioral and some cognitive interventions to effect change in coping skills and relationships.

Emphasis. Strong emphasis on establishing a therapeutic relationship; fairly structured and directive while simultaneously fostering client responsibility; balance of supportive and exploratory elements.

Nature. Individual therapy is usually primary, with accompanying family or couples therapy; group therapy may be useful once functioning has improved.

Timing. Long-term therapy usually indicated, although short-term goals should be developed, since many clients with personality disorders terminate treatment prematurely; gradual but steady pace; may require more than one session per week when in crisis.

Medication. Rarely needed, though occasionally may help to alleviate depression, anxiety, or psychotic symptoms; should be used with caution in light of clients' tendency to abuse substances and make suicide attempts.

Adjunct services. Multifaceted treatment plan important in modifying clients' pervasive dysfunction; adjunct services might include AA, NA, social groups, career counseling, assertiveness training.

Prognosis. Varies, usually fair; can be good for short-term behavioral changes but is fair for underlying personality changes and is poor if client is unwilling to engage in long-term treatment.

Client Map of Bill M.

This chapter opened with the case of Bill M., a twenty-nine-year-old male who was seen for therapy as part of his participation in a prerelease program. Bill's background included neglect and emotional abuse. He presented a twenty-year history of substance abuse, instability in relationships and employment, and a broad range of illegal activities. He tended to blame others for his problems and was resistant to treatment. The client map below presents recommendations for treating Bill's personality disorder.

Diagnosis. Axis I: 303.90—Alcohol dependence; 304.20—Cocaine abuse.

Axis II: 301.70—Antisocial personality disorder.

Axis III: Persistent gastric complaints.

Axis IV: Psychosocial stressors: incarceration, financial difficulty due to delinquent child support payments. Severity: 4—severe (predominantly acute events).

Axis V: Current Global Assessment of Functioning: 50; highest GAF past year: 50.

Objectives. (1) Elimination of substance abuse.

(2) Improved coping mechanisms (for example, stress management and verbal self-expression).

(3) Establishment of rewarding and realistic goals and direction.

(4) Increased stability and sense of responsibility.

(5) Improved relationships (for example, development of non-substance-abusing friendships, establishment of contact with his children).

Assessment. Millon Clinical Multiaxial Inventory, Michigan Alcoholism Screening Test, physical examination.

Clinician. Bill was a resistant client who entered treatment only because it was a required condition of his participation in a prerelease program. He was defensive and tended to project blame onto others. His therapist needed to be stable, genuine, accepting, structured, and directive; knowledgeable about patterns of personality disorders and substance abuse; and able to deal with client resistance and hostility and set appropriate limits and consequences.

Location. Initially, in a residential prerelease setting; later, in an outpatient program.

Interventions. Bill's capacity for insight was limited, and he had little facility for expressing his feelings. In light of these limitations, as well as his history and diagnosis, Reality Therapy with a strong behavioral emphasis and a psychodynamic component was made the core of Bill's treatment. That model was used in an effort to help Bill see the self-destructive nature of his behavior and to develop new and more effective ways of managing his life and relating to others. As progress was made, the psychodynamic focus of treatment would increase.

Emphasis. Balance of supportive and exploratory elements; initially directive but promoting client responsibility; emphasis at outset on behavior, later on underlying dysfunction and dynamics.

Nature. Initially, individual would be primary; marital therapy also would be used to help Bill and his wife make a decision on their marriage and, if appropriate, attempt a reconciliation. Group therapy was also included in the treatment plan, in the hope that the peer pressure and support provided by the group would increase Bill's openness to change and might improve his socialization once behavioral patterns had improved.

Timing. Long-term therapy, if client is willing, but treatment plan must recognize that premature termination of therapy is very possible; steady pace, communicating clear expectations.

Medication. None, except what might be needed for Bill's gastric complaints.

Adjunct services. Participation in Alcoholics Anonymous and Narcotics Anonymous on a regular, predetermined schedule was made part of Bill's treatment. In addition, education was provided Bill on such topics as the physiology of drug and alcohol abuse, adult children of alcoholics, stress management, assertiveness, and job seeking. He was helped to develop a budget that would enable him to gradually pay off his child support debts.

Prognosis. Had treatment not been required of Bill, the prognosis for his benefiting from treatment, or even beginning treatment, probably would be poor. However, Bill was aware that he must cooperate with treatment or be sent back to prison. In addition, if he violated his parole after release, he would be returned to jail for an additional five-year prison term. Consequently, there was considerable incentive for Bill to make positive use of his therapy. Even so, the rate of recidivism is high for clients with antisocial personality disorders and substance use disorders, and the prognosis probably can be viewed as no better than fair.

Recommended Readings

Cooper, A. M., Frances, A. J., & Sacks, M. H. (Eds.). (1986). *The personality disorders and neuroses*. Philadelphia: Lippincott.

Gunderson, J. G. (1988). Personality disorders. In A. M. Nicholi, Jr. (Ed.), *The new Harvard guide to psychiatry* (pp. 337-357). Cambridge, MA: Harvard University Press.

Kernberg, O. F. (1985). *Borderline conditions and pathological narcissism*. New York: Jason Aronson.

Kohut, H. (1971). *The analysis of self*. New York: International Universities Press.

Lion, J. R. (Ed.). (1981). *Personality disorders: Diagnosis and management* (2nd ed.). Baltimore: Williams & Wilkins.

McGlashan, T. H. (1983). The borderline syndrome. *Archives of General Psychiatry, 40,* 1319-1323.

McGlashan, T. H. (1986). Schizotypal personality disorder. *Archives of General Psychiatry, 43,* 329-334.

Millon, T. (1981). *Disorders of personality: DSM-III: Axis II*. New York: Wiley.

Millon, T., & Klerman, G. (1986). *Contemporary directions in psychopathology*. New York: Guilford Press.

Searles, H. F. (1986). *My work with borderline patients*. New York: Jason Aronson.

Turkat, I. D., & Maisto, S. A. (1985). Personality disorders: Application of the experimental method to the formulation and modification of personality disorders. In D. H. Barlow (Ed.), *Clinical handbook of psychological disorders* (pp. 502-570). New York: Guilford Press.

▪▮

Chapter Ten

Disorders Involving Loss of Contact with Reality

Case Study: Thomas F.

Thomas F. was brought to therapy by his wife, who reported that he was having "crazy ideas about her." Tom maintained that his ideas were not crazy and insisted that his wife was having affairs with at least two men, both family friends.

Tom, forty-seven, and Carmen, forty-two, had married three years ago after a courtship of five years' duration. This was the second marriage for both. Tom had three children from his first marriage; these children lived out of the country with their mother. Carmen's only child from her first marriage had been killed in an accident when he was ten years old. Since they had lost the children from their first marriages, Tom and Carmen hoped that they would be able to have children together and reported being extremely happy when Tom, Jr., was born almost a year ago. However, their son brought considerable stress into their lives.

Tom and Carmen had met at the computer firm where both worked, Tom as programmer and Carmen as administrative assistant. They were together almost constantly, both at work and at home. However, when their son was born, Carmen took a position at a local hospital, working nights in the admissions room, so that someone would always be available to care for their son. Tom was home with him during the evenings and nights, and Carmen was with the child during the day. They saw very little of each other, and nearly all their energy was focused on parenting. Both had few friends or outside interests to give them support. They had bought a new house, and added debts prevented them from going out frequently, as they had when they were dating. In addition, Tom's mother had cancer, and Tom and Carmen were trying to spend as much time as possible helping her.

About two months ago, Tom began to express suspicions about how Carmen was spending her daytime at home. She assured him that she was too exhausted to do much more than care for Tommy, maintain the house, and try to get some sleep. However, Tom's accusations grew worse, and he insisted that Carmen was having sexual relationships with at least two men in his absence. During this time, he continued his job as a programmer; and, except for several days in which he had left work precipitously in an effort to catch Carmen with her purported lovers, his performance at work had been unaffected. There was no prior history of mental disorder in either Tom or any of his first-degree relatives.

Overview of Disorders Involving Loss of Contact with Reality

Description of Disorder. Interviews with Tom and Carmen indicated that Tom was experiencing a mental disorder that involved loss of contact with reality. This chapter will consider a diverse array of disorders that are characterized by a loss of contact with reality: schizophrenic disorders, delusional disorders, dissociative disorders, and organic disorders. These disorders are different in origin, treatment, and prognosis. What does connect them is a similarity in their symptoms: a distortion or loss of contact with reality. These are the most severe of the mental disorders in their impact on clients' lives, usually producing significant dysfunction in at least one area.

As a result of their similar symptoms, these disorders often present a challenge to the diagnostician and, unfortunately, are sometimes misdiagnosed. A misdiagnosis can, of course, lead to incorrect treatment and a failure to ameliorate the disorder. Symptoms characterizing each group of disorders will be reviewed in the sections on each disorder.

Relevant Client Characteristics. The adjustment of clients with these disorders prior to their development of the disorder covers the spectrum. Some will have poor previous adjustment, while others will have developed positive social skills and coping mechanisms. The development of the disorders in this chapter also differs. Some people will experience gradual deterioration, while others will suffer a rapid alteration in consciousness in response to an immediate stressor or physiological change. People with these disorders typically are aware that something is wrong but may not understand what is happening, may conceal their symptoms out of fear that they will be rejected or institutionalized, and may not be receptive to help that is offered. While the disorder is present, their social and occupational adjustment almost invariably will be affected, although the degree of disturbance ranges from mild and circumscribed to pervasive, depending on the particular disorder and its severity.

Relevant Therapist Variables. Treatment of these disorders, with the exception of multiple personality disorder, generally requires medical as well as psychological intervention. Clients with schizophrenic disorders and severe organic disorders typically will require a period of hospitalization as well as medication. Although nonmedical mental health professionals may be involved in treating these disorders as part of a treatment team, medical expertise will almost always be needed to make a definitive diagnosis of most of these disorders. The psychiatrist also will often be the primary treatment provider.

Intervention Strategies. As disorders involving a loss of contact with reality differ greatly, so does the nature of the treatment that is indicated, varying with respect to the duration and approaches to treatment. Specifics will be provided in the sections on the individual disorders.

Prognosis. Prognosis for these disorders is uncertain but bears some relationship to the duration of the disorder. Those disorders that are of shorter duration (such as brief reactive psychosis or psychogenic amnesia) typically respond well to relatively brief treatment; on the other hand, those of longer duration, especially those of insidious onset (such as schizophrenia, primary degenerative dementia, or multiple personality disorder), have a less favorable prognosis and usually require long-term treatment.

10.1 Schizophrenia

Description of Disorder. Schizophrenia is, by definition, a relatively longstanding and pervasive disorder. According to the *DSM-III-R* (1987), symptoms characteristic of the disorder include bizarre delusions, hallucinations (usually auditory), flat or very inappropriate affect, and markedly impaired functioning. Other common symptoms include a confused sense of self, limited insight, dependency conflicts, loose associations, concrete thinking, psychomotor disturbances (for example, catatonic symptoms), and a dysphoric mood. Impairment in memory is not characteristic of this disorder, although it frequently accompanies other disorders considered in this chapter.

Schizophrenia typically involves a prodromal or initial phase, when functioning declines and symptoms begin; an active phase, when prominent delusions, hallucinations, and incoherence are present; and a residual phase, in which the most severe symptoms have abated but signs of the disorder are still clearly present. To warrant a diagnosis of schizophrenia, the course of the disorder must be at least six months in duration.

The *DSM-III-R* (1987) specifies three major types of schizophrenia. The paranoid type seems to be the most common; it is characterized by systematized delusions and hallucinations related to a single theme of grandiosity and persecution. Anger and suspiciousness are usually present (Meyer, 1983). Incoherence, disorganization, and inappropriate affect are less prominent. Paranoid schizophrenia tends to have a later onset and a better prognosis than the other types of schizophrenia. The disorganized type, formerly known as the hebephrenic type, tends to appear early and is associated with poor previous functioning, an insidious onset, extreme impairment, confusion and disorganization, and flat or inappropriate affect. The third type, catatonic schizophrenia, is presently very rare; it is characterized by some form of catatonia (stupor, rigidity, excitement, or posturing).

Schizophrenia most commonly begins in adolescence or early adulthood and generally starts earlier in males than in females, who tend to have less severe forms of the disorder (*DSM-III-R*, 1987; Loranger, 1984). It is very unusual for an initial episode of this disorder to occur after the age of forty-five.

Schizophrenia has a lifetime prevalence of approximately 1 percent (Tsuang, Farone, & Day, 1988). It is found in one to ten people per thousand and is slightly more common in females than in males (Helzer, 1986).

Relevant Client Characteristics. Clients with schizophrenia are more likely to come from lower socioeconomic classes and urban environments and to be born during the winter, possibly because of the increased risk of infectious diseases during that time (Tsuang, Farone, & Day, 1988). Nonwhites have a higher incidence of schizophrenia (Atwood & Chester, 1987); so do recent immigrants, probably because of the stress and confusion associated with their situation (Helzer, 1986). In general, people with schizophrenia seem unusually likely to experience stressful events in the three weeks prior to onset of the disorder (Bebbington, 1986). This pattern has been interpreted to suggest that stress activates a biological predisposition toward the disorder, rather than that stress causes the disorder.

Conflict tends to be more prevalent in families of those with schizophrenia. In addition, the parenting received by people with schizophrenia is likely to be distant, critical, and egocentric, failing to promote adequate separation or reality testing in the children (Atwood & Chester, 1987). Roy (1981) found the combination of depression and chronic schizophrenia to be associated with a parental loss before the age of seventeen.

Schizophrenia tends to run in families, and most research suggests that those with this disorder are unusually likely to have first-degree relatives who are also schizophrenic (Kendell, 1986). Chances of developing schizophrenia are two in five for those with two schizophrenic parents and one in two for a monozygotic twin when the other twin develops schizophrenia. At the same time, factors other than genetics are clearly relevant; only about 10 percent of those with schizophrenia have a schizophrenic parent.

To date, no clear explanation for the cause of schizophrenia has been found, although many explanations have been advanced. The most accepted explanation seems to be the vulnerability model, which considers genetic, biological, and psychological sources of vulnerability (Atwood & Chester, 1987).

Prior adjustment often reflects precursors of the disorder. People with schizophrenia tend to have been socially awkward and isolated, passive, mildly eccentric, impulsive, uncomfortable with competition, and absorbed with fantasy (Kendell, 1986). An unstable employment history is common (Kaplan & Sadock, 1985). Personality disorders—especially paranoid (section 9.1), schizoid (section 9.2), schizotypal (section 9.3), or borderline (section 9.7) personality disorders—may also be present (*DSM-III-R*, 1987).

Relevant Therapist Variables. McGlashan (1983b) found that a comfortable therapist-client relationship and client identification with the therapist are important ingredients in promoting change in people with schizophrenia. A therapeutic alliance that reduces anxiety and enhances treatment compliance can be integral to the recovery of these clients (Retterstøl, 1986). Warmth, reassurance, optimism, empathy, genuineness, stability, support, and acceptance on the part of the therapist are all important to forming a positive and trusting working relationship with these clients, many of whom are suspicious, guarded, and withdrawn. Managing their strong dependency needs is also important (Atwood & Chester, 1987).

Retterstøl (1986) suggests that therapists working with schizophrenic clients should help them regain contact with reality. At the same time, arguing with or interrogating these clients about their delusions or hallucinations is likely to be nonproductive and harmful to the therapeutic relationship. Perry, Frances, and Clarkin (1985) present a case in which the therapist labels hallucinations tricks of the mind; this strategy avoids the need to debate a client's veracity and can increase understanding and appropriate discussion of the phenomena.

Therapists must find a balance between overwhelming and undersupporting these vulnerable clients. Too much closeness can lead to regression, while too much distance can result in alienation (Kaplan & Sadock, 1985). Therapists should respect the clients' privacy and need for distance and should individualize treatment, reducing interpretation and being flexible as needed. Taking a walk with a suspicious, agitated client may be more effective than discussing symptoms.

Intervention Strategies. According to Tsuang, Farone, and Day (1988), "no known cure exists for schizophrenia" (p. 272), although treatment can reduce the impact of the disorder. Treatment usually entails a combination of interventions.

Psychotherapy, without accompanying medication, usually has little impact on schizophrenia (Klerman, 1986). However, the combination of psychosocial interventions and pharmacotherapy seems better than either alone (Simpson & May, 1982). Consequently, pharmacotherapy is almost always a component of treatment and is beneficial to most but not all who are diagnosed as schizophrenic. Neuroleptic drugs (phenothiazines) can effectively alleviate the positive symptoms of thought disorder (delusions and hallucinations). Medication is less effective in treating the negative symptoms (flat affect, depression, withdrawal) (Hughes, Preskorn, Adams, & Kent, 1986).

May, Tuma, and Dixon (1981) compared five approaches to treating schizophrenic clients in their first hospitalization. The combination of psychotherapy, medication, and milieu therapy was most effective, while psychotherapy alone and milieu therapy alone were least effective; medication alone and ECT and milieu therapy achieved intermediate results.

Medication is also important in reducing the risk of relapse. Sixty percent of people treated for schizophrenia seem to need continued medication after symptoms have been alleviated (Kaplan & Sadock, 1985). Without medication, 50-75 percent relapse within four years, while only 20 percent relapse when maintained on medication (Tsuang, Farone, & Day, 1988). Medication groups, held regularly during the maintenance phase of treatment, can promote treatment compliance and socialization as well as providing support and practical help (Simpson & May, 1982).

Hospitalization is often required for people with schizophrenia, particularly during the active phase of the disorder. Approximately 62 percent of those diagnosed as schizophrenic will be hospitalized (Szymanski & Keill, 1985). The average hospital stay for these clients has declined in length and is now less than two weeks; hospitalizations of over sixty days are rarely indicated (Klerman, 1986). Symptoms most strongly correlated with hospitalization include self-neglect; disorganized thought processes; delusions or hallucinations; impulsivity; suspiciousness; and suicidal, dangerous, or violent behavior (Mezzich, Evanczuk, Mathias, & Coffman, 1984). As many as 20 percent of people with schizophrenia commit suicide, sometimes in response to hallucinated directions (Murphy, 1986). The higher the number of symptoms, the greater the likelihood of hospitalization.

Day treatment centers, partial hospitalization, and halfway houses often are helpful once recovery has begun and acute symptoms have subsided (Atwood & Chester, 1987). Use of these resources is increasing as length of hospitalization is decreasing. The population of hospitalized psychiatric patients declined from 560,000 in 1955 to 160,000 in 1977, as a result of the development of antipsychotic medication, the growth of alternative forms of treatment, and the emphasis on deinstitutionalization (Atwood & Chester, 1987). Transitional settings can promote socialization, ease clients' return to independent living, and, if necessary, provide long-term maintenance.

Behavior therapy, often taking the form of milieu therapy during hospitalization, is another common component to treatment that has achieved some success with schizophrenic clients (Kaplan & Sadock, 1985). Most people with schizophrenia benefit from clear rules and guidelines, a reward system such as a token economy, and social reinforcement designed to reduce bizarre and destructive behavior. Some psychotic clients have a measure of control over their symptoms, and behavior therapy can teach self-monitoring and self-control procedures to increase this control (Breier & Strauss, 1983). Behavioral education, such as social skills training and development of practical life skills, can also be beneficial in facilitating clients' resocialization and their adjustment to living with families or on their own after a period of hospitalization. Training in useful occupational skills and increased involvement in recreational activities also can facilitate adjustment and improve prognosis (Perry, Frances, & Clarkin, 1985).

Psychodynamic psychotherapy has not received much support in the treatment of schizophrenia. According to Richelson (1986), "Well-controlled studies are generally lacking to show that a good doctor-patient relationship, . . . psychotherapy in the traditional sense, or sociotherapy can influence the course of schizophrenia" (p. 64). However, the establishment of a strong therapeutic alliance, in the context of a supportive or behaviorally oriented treatment program, may well increase treatment compliance and accelerate progress. Individual therapy should generally be present oriented, focusing on life issues and family and other relationships, exploring feelings, clarifying ego boundaries, and promoting readjustment (Atwood & Chester, 1987; Simpson & May, 1982). Short, frequent therapeutic contacts are often particularly helpful (Maxmen, 1986).

Education and counseling for the family are other important components of treatment for schizophrenia. Family members are often confused and angered by the clients' delusions and may benefit from understanding the nature of this disorder. What has been called high expressed emotion (EE) in the families of people with schizophrenia seems to be a significant factor, as is stress, in provoking a reemergence of acute symptoms (Bebbington, 1986). High EE is the tendency of the family to be critical, emotionally overinvolved, and hostile toward the schizophrenic person. According to Vaughn and Leff (1976), the best single predictor of relapse during the nine months following discharge is the number of critical comments made about a client by family members at the time of admission to the hospital.

Hogarty and colleagues (1986) concluded that only a combination of treatments—including social skills training, family treatment, and medication—could "sustain a remission in households that remain high in EE" (p. 633). None of the clients in their study who received that treatment combination relapsed in a two-year period, while 41 percent who received only support and medication did relapse. Support groups such as the National Alliance for the Mentally Ill can also be useful to families with schizophrenic members (Johnson, 1988).

Such experimental treatments as electroconvulsive therapy, megavitamins, psychosurgery, and hemodialysis have not been shown to be generally effective in treating schizophrenia (Richelson, 1986). They rarely are included in current treatment plans.

Prognosis. According to the *DSM-III-R* (1987), "A return to full premorbid functioning in this disorder is not common" (p. 191). Tsuang, Farone, and Day (1988) report that 20 percent of people with schizophrenia seem to recover completely, 33 percent remain only mildly impaired after treatment, and 47 percent stay severely impaired. Approximately 50 percent are hospitalized again within two years of an initial episode of schizophrenia (Meyer, 1983). The risk of personality deterioration seems to increase greatly after the second relapse and seems to worsen with each successive episode, as does the risk of another relapse (Kaplan & Sadock, 1985). The prognosis is particularly poor if the disorder begins with a gradual deterioration extending over many years or if the client has extensive exposure to a high-EE family (Kendell, 1986; Maxmen, 1986). Although the acute symptoms of this disorder may be controlled with medication or may remit spontaneously, clients are frequently left feeling apathetic, socially uncomfortable, depressed, and uneasy in handling emotions.

A more positive prognosis for the treatment of schizophrenia is associated with abrupt onset, particularly when there is an identifiable precipitant; positive premorbid functioning, especially in social areas; a positive work history; mid-life onset; symptoms of confusion; depression; a family history of depression and mania; a positive living situation to return to; an absence of both psychotic assaultiveness and schizoid personality disorders; intelligence that is average or higher; being married; and no family history of schizophrenia (*DSM-III-R*, 1987; Maxmen, 1986). A positive prognosis is also associated with compliance with recommended medication and aftercare, an adequate financial and living situation, and involvement in social and recreational activities (Maxmen, 1986).

In addition to relapses and residual symptoms, people with

schizophrenia often must cope with severe and sometimes permanent side effects to their neuroleptic antipsychotic medication. Of those with chronic schizophrenia, 10–70 percent have tardive dyskinesia, a side effect primarily characterized by involuntary smacking and sucking movements of the lips and tongue (Kendell, 1986). This condition gives the clients a peculiar appearance and can interfere with their social and occupational adjustment.

10.2 Brief Reactive Psychosis and Schizophreniform Disorder

Description of Disorder. Brief reactive psychosis and schizophreniform disorder are characterized by symptoms of schizophrenia: impaired reality testing, extremely inappropriate behavior, bizarre delusions and hallucinations, incoherence, and catatonic symptoms. However, despite the limited amount of research available on brief reactive psychosis and schizophreniform disorder, it seems clear that their development, causes, treatments, and prognosis differ in important respects from those of schizophrenia.

According to the *DSM-III-R* (1987), the essential feature of brief reactive psychosis is the "sudden onset of psychotic symptoms of at least a few hours', but no more than one month's, duration, with eventual full return to premorbid level of functioning" (p. 205). The onset of symptoms is preceded by an identifiable stressor or stressors (such as the loss of a loved one, rape, or combat experience) and is accompanied by extreme and rapid emotional shifts and a strong feeling of confusion. Multiple concurrent stressors seem particularly likely to precede this disorder. Unlike people with schizophrenia, people with brief reactive psychosis usually do not have prodromal symptoms.

Schizophreniform disorder is more like schizophrenia than is brief reactive psychosis, since it may include a prodromal phase, does not necessarily have an identifiable precipitant, and includes passive as well as active features of schizophrenia. Agitation and high anxiety are common in this disorder while flat affect is unusual (Tsuang & Loyd, 1986). Schizophreniform disorder is distinguished from schizophrenia primarily because of its brief duration; schizophreniform disorder, by definition, has a duration of less than six months, including prodromal, active, and residual phases.

Although some believe that schizophreniform disorder is closely related to schizophrenia, schizophreniform disorder is currently categorized as a separate disorder, partly because it seems to have a superior prognosis to schizophrenia.

Schizophreniform disorder, then, may be viewed as a sort of bridge between brief reactive psychosis and schizophrenia, with brief reactive psychosis having the best prognosis and schizophrenia, the worst. Schizophreniform disorder would be diagnosed when symptoms originally thought to be brief reactive psychosis persist for more than one month but less than six months or when symptoms do not have a clear precipitant or rapid onset but, once again, remit in less than six months.

If diagnosis of either brief reactive psychosis or schizophreniform disorder is made before recovery, the diagnosis is viewed as provisional and would be changed if the duration of the disorder were longer than anticipated. Both disorders, then, are sometimes actually the early stages of schizophrenia.

Relevant Client Characteristics. Like schizophrenia, both brief reactive psychosis and schizophreniform disorder usually appear in adolescence or early adulthood. Both disorders are more common in people who had preexisting emotional disorders, particularly personality disorders typified by emotional instability, suspiciousness, and impaired socialization. Schizophreniform disorder seems to run in families as does schizophrenia, although first-degree relatives of those with schizophreniform disorder seem to be less likely than relatives of those with schizophrenia to develop a psychotic disorder. Relatives of those with brief reactive psychosis seem to be at an increased risk for affective disorders as well as for brief reactive psychoses, but not for schizophrenia (Tsuang & Loyd, 1986).

Relevant Therapist Variables. Clients with brief reactive psychosis or schizophreniform disorder typically benefit from supportive, safe, and structured therapeutic relationships that avoid casting them in a sick role. Acceptance, respect, genuineness, and empathy often are instrumental in helping these clients come to terms with events that triggered their disorders and in restoring their awareness of reality. Modeling by therapists can promote clients' effective coping mechanisms and efforts to take control of their lives, as can identification with the therapist.

Intervention Strategies. Initial treatment of brief reactive psychosis and schizophreniform disorder has many similarities to treatment of schizophrenia. Clients may be suicidal, aggressive, or so disoriented and out of touch with reality that hospitalization and antipsychotic medication are required to protect them and to alleviate acute symptoms. However, long-term medication or extended inpatient treatment is unusual; after the psychotic symptoms have subsided, the focus of treatment usually will shift quickly, with psychotherapy rather than medication being the primary ingredient of treatment.

Attention should be paid, in this second phase of treatment, to the nature of the precipitant, and interventions should be used to help clients deal with the events that seemed to trigger their symptoms. These clients are often in crisis, and a crisis intervention approach to therapy can provide a useful direction. According to that model, clients would be assisted to take a realistic look at their situations, to become aware of and express their feelings and reactions, to identify and mobilize coping mechanisms they have used effectively in the past, and to apply those mechanisms to the present situation. Specific additional interventions would be determined by the nature of the precipitant, but those interventions would generally be short term and symptom focused, emphasizing cognitive, behavioral, and supportive rather than long-term exploratory techniques. Brief dynamic psychotherapy may also be helpful to these clients (Perry, Frances, & Clarkin, 1985; Tsuang & Loyd, 1986). However, if underlying personality disorders are also present, long-term treatment may be needed for those disorders after the clients' recovery from the schizophreniform disorder or the brief reactive psychosis.

Group and family treatment can help clients and their families deal with the aftermath of the disorder. It also can promote effective resolution of the crisis that precipitated the disorder and restore positive social and occupational functioning. Encouraging clients to draw on support systems can facilitate recovery as well as crisis resolution and abatement of residual symptoms.

Prognosis. Some clinicians distinguish between process and reactive psychotic disorders; reactive disorders have a rapid onset and a clear precipitant, and process disorders are more likely to have an insidious onset, a genetic component, and no identifiable precipitant. In general, the prognosis is better for those disorders that follow a reactive pattern. Over 90 percent of clients recover from reactive psychoses, and only 50 percent recover from the process conditions (Atwood & Chester, 1987).

The prognosis for brief reactive psychosis is, by definition, excellent. Symptoms typically remit in a few days, although the active phase of this disorder may be followed by temporary symptoms of depression, confusion, and anxiety as people deal with the stressors that precipitated the disorder and with the experience of having had their functioning severely impaired. They often feel embarrassed at having had psychotic symptoms and fear a recurrence and its accompanying loss of control.

The prognosis for schizophreniform disorder is not as good as that for brief reactive psychosis but is better than that for schizophrenia (Coryell & Tsuang, 1986). According to the *DSM-III-R* (1987), the following features are associated with a positive prognosis for recovery from schizophreniform disorder: a brief prodromal period (four weeks or less), confusion and disorientation during the active phase of the disorder, good previous functioning, and an affect that is depressed rather than flat or blunted.

10.3 Delusional Disorder

Description of Disorder. Delusional disorder tends to be less pervasive and disabling than brief reactive psychosis, schizophreniform disorder, or schizophrenia but may have some similar symptoms. A delusional disorder is characterized by the presence of a "persistent, nonbizarre delusion" of at least one month's duration (*DSM-III-R*, 1987, p. 199). The delusion typically is circumscribed; and the clients' overall behavior, apart from the delusion, usually does not seem odd or severely impaired. The following six types of delusional disorder have been identified: erotomanic, grandiose, jealous, persecutory, somatic, and unspecified. The jealous and persecutory types seem to be the most prevalent (Day & Manschreck, 1988). The type of delusional disorder experienced by a client should be indicated when this diagnosis is made.

The onset of delusional disorder typically occurs between the ages of forty and fifty-five (*DSM-III-R*, 1987) and may be acute or, more commonly, insidious (Kaplan & Sadock, 1985). Delusional disorder is fairly rare, occurring in less than 0.1 percent of the population, and is slightly more common in females than in males.

Relevant Client Characteristics. People with this disorder typically demonstrate satisfactory premorbid functioning, although preexisting personality disorders are not uncommon. As with schizophrenia, people who are recent immigrants and who come from lower socioeconomic backgrounds are more prone to develop delusional disorder. Isolated elderly people and people who are incarcerated also are overrepresented among those with this disorder (Kaplan & Sadock, 1985; Maxmen, 1986). Delusional disorder often is preceded by a period of stress and by an experience that evokes strong feelings of insecurity and self-doubt (Retterstøl, 1986). Genetic transmission of this disorder has not been well established, although there is some evidence that first-degree relatives of people with this disorder are more likely to have avoidant or paranoid personality disorder or delusional disorder (Day and Manschreck, 1988; *DSM-III-R*, 1987).

According to Retterstøl (1986), people with delusional disorder commonly had difficult and unstable childhoods. They may have had conflicted home environments or may have lost a parent when they were young. Kaplan and Sadock (1985) describe a typical family pattern of an "overcontrolling, seductive, rejecting mother" and a "distant, rigid, sadistic or weak and ineffectual father" (p. 227) who expect perfection from their children.

People with delusional disorder tend to be low in self-esteem, shy and isolated, easily frustrated, mistrustful, and fearful of intimacy. They view the world as a hostile and unfriendly place. They are very concerned with how they are perceived by others, often feel taken advantage of, and tend to overreact to criticism. They typically project blame onto others for their own failures and shortcomings and may be perceived as hostile, suspicious, and overcritical of themselves and others. Their social and sexual adjustment often is flawed. Sometimes they have physical problems (such as hearing or visual loss) that contribute to their feeling different and isolated. Their delusion may be a way of protecting themselves from overwhelming feelings of rejection and inadequacy.

Relevant Therapist Variables. Clients with delusional disorder tend to be defensive and argumentative, particularly with authority figures (Meyer, 1983). They are reluctant to acknowledge a need for treatment and tend to deny affective symptoms. They resist acceptance of the idea that stress may have precipitated their symptoms, have little empathy and insight, and often block attempts to reassure them and modify their typically ego-syntonic delusions (Retterstøl, 1986).

Therapists should deal gently with these clients, respecting their need for privacy and not arguing with them about their delusional beliefs. Instead, therapists should be stable and structured, warm, reassuring, genuine, supportive, accepting, and empathic, serving as positive role models, in an effort to engage these clients in treatment and encourage more effective coping methods. Therapists should discuss the delusions but should not participate in the clients' delusional belief systems. Confrontation should be avoided. These conditions of the therapeutic relationship are particularly important in treating delusional disorder; unless a positive relationship is established, therapy is not likely to take place; but with it, much can be accomplished.

Intervention Strategies. People with delusional disorder rarely seek treatment on their own volition and typically function well enough to avoid involuntary treatment; as a result, they are rarely seen in treatment, and little research is available on the effective treatment of this disorder. However, some inferences can be drawn from the literature.

Medication and hospitalization are less likely to be needed in treating this disorder than they are in the treatment of schizophrenia. Most clients with this disorder can be treated on an outpatient basis, although a day treatment center may provide a helpful change in environment. Medication sometimes is helpful in reducing anxiety and, because of the close connection between anxiety and delusion in this disorder, often is effective in achieving a concurrent reduction in delusions. However, the suspiciousness that is typical of these clients may lead them to refuse medication or fail to comply with prescribed treatments. Antipsychotic medication generally has not been shown to be effective in treatment of this disorder (Day & Manschreck, 1988), although it is more likely to be effective in cases where there are an apparent precipitant and an early diagnosis (Simpson & May, 1982).

Amelioration of environmental stressors and encouragement of improved coping mechanisms typically are more essential to effective treatment of this disorder than medication (Reid, 1983). Treatment should focus on improving adjustment and helping clients deal with loss and frustration (Day & Manschreck, 1988). Independence and expression of feelings also should be encouraged (Kaplan & Sadock, 1985). Clients' motivation toward treatment may be increased if the therapy initially focuses on secondary symptoms (such as insomnia or occupational concerns), rather than on the delusions and their precipitants and consequences (Kaplan & Sadock, 1985). However, some attention also should be paid to the delusion itself, because it typically has a symbolic function that, if understood, could facilitate the client's treatment (Retterstøl, 1986). A supportive therapeutic relationship is essential and is sometimes sufficient to give these clients the courage they need to deal more effectively with their lives.

Depression and anxiety that had been masked by the delusional symptoms may emerge as clients begin to improve. Both therapists and clients should be prepared for this pattern and should view it as a sign of progress, shifting the focus of treatment in order to ameliorate the affective symptoms.

Family therapy often is an important ingredient of treatment. Because these clients continue to function relatively well, family members may not understand that the clients are experiencing a mental disorder. Especially if the family members have been cast in undesirable roles in the delusional belief system, they may feel angry and unsympathetic and might benefit from help in understanding the nature of this disorder. Reducing any family stress and conflict that may be contributing to the delusional disorder also can help alleviate symptoms.

Although people with this disorder often need to improve their social skills and relationships, they typically do not derive much benefit from group therapy (Retterstøl, 1986). They tend to use their delusions to protect themselves from the group and wind up alienating the group.

Prognosis. Although this disorder seems to have a somewhat better prognosis than schizophrenia and does not have the same pervasive impact on functioning as that disorder, the prognosis for treatment of delusional disorder is uncertain. Some clients recover from the disorder rapidly, particularly those for whom the disorder had a rapid onset and an apparent precipitant. For others, however, the disorder has a chronic course, and clients may experience alternating periods of remission and relapse over many years. Some develop schizophrenia. Retterstøl (1986) found that the shorter the duration of the delusion, the better the prognosis. In 55–75 percent of clients with this disorder, particularly those whose delusions are not strongly systematized, the delusions seem to vanish. The prognosis also seems better for females, those under thirty, and those who are married (Kaplan & Sadock, 1985).

10.4 Schizoaffective Disorder

Description of Disorder. Schizoaffective disorder is one of the most controversial diagnoses in the *DSM-III-R*. By definition, it includes symptoms of a significant mood disorder—either a major depression (section 5.1) or a bipolar disorder (section 5.4)—that coexist with symptoms of schizophrenia (section 10.1), including at least two weeks of delusions or hallucinations that are *not* accompanied by symptoms of the mood disorder (*DSM-III-R*, 1987). The early and late phases of schizoaffective disorder usually feature the affective symptoms; the psychotic symptoms typically begin abruptly following the onset of the mood disorder (Kaplan & Sadock, 1985). Some view schizoaffective disorder as two discrete disorders, schizophrenia and an affective disorder, or as an atypical form of mania or depression; others believe that it is a separate diagnostic entity, a sort of hybrid with its own distinguishing features (Kaplan & Sadock, 1985). This disorder is diagnosed in less than 1 percent of the population. Little research is available on this confusing disorder and on its relationship to either schizophrenia or mood disorders, although some tentative information has appeared in the literature.

Relevant Client Characteristics. Like schizophrenia, schizoaffective disorder most commonly appears in early adulthood and is more prevalent among those with first-degree relatives who have been diagnosed as having schizophrenia, schizoaffective disorder, or a major affective disorder (Rice & McGuffin, 1986). Williams and McGlashan (1987) found that the demographic backgrounds and premorbid patterns of adjustment for those with this disorder were more like those with major depression (section 5.1) than those with schizophrenia (section 10.1) or bipolar disorders (section 5.4), although their functioning at follow-up was more like clients with schizophrenia.

Schizoaffective disorder often appears in relatively healthy people following a stressful precipitant. A sudden onset, accompanied by marked turmoil and confusion, occurs in some cases, although this disorder seems more likely to follow a chronic and insidious pattern (Tsuang & Loyd, 1986). Little clear information is available about the cause of schizoaffective disorder. It seems equally prevalent among males and females (Kaplan & Sadock, 1985), and a high suicide risk is present for both men and women with this disorder.

Relevant Therapist Variables. Almost no information is available on therapist variables that are conducive to treatment of schizoaffective disorder. Guidelines offered in the section on treating schizophrenic clients (section 10.1) are probably applicable, with therapists providing support, structure, reality testing, empathy, acceptance, and reassurance to allay the resistance and suspiciousness that often accompany psychotic symptoms. The relatively positive motivation toward treatment and previous functioning often found in people with mood disorders may make it easier to form a therapeutic alliance with clients with schizoaffective disorder than with those with schizophrenia.

Intervention Strategies. Little clear information is available about the treatment of schizoaffective disorder. According to Reid (1983), treatment should focus on both affective and schizophrenic symptoms and must be individualized to meet the needs of each client, since the symptom picture associated with this disorder varies widely. Tsuang and Loyd (1986) suggested basing the treatment on the most prominent symptoms.

Medication is often useful in reducing both psychotic and affective symptoms, and a referral for a medical evaluation of clients with schizoaffective disorder should almost always be made. However, determining the appropriate drugs can be challenging, since multiple medications may be needed and since the side effects of a medication designed to ameliorate one facet of this disorder may exacerbate the symptoms of another facet. Consequently, a trial-and-error approach often is necessary in determining the best medication for this disorder. Drugs such as lithium, antidepressants, and neuroleptics, which have been found effective with related disorders, also have been found useful in treating some cases of schizoaffective disorder (Tsuang & Loyd, 1986). Lithium has seemed particularly beneficial for maintenance of clients with this disorder. Most people diagnosed as having a schizoaffective disorder require some period of hospitalization in addition to medication (Kaplan & Sadock, 1985). Extensive treatment, following hospitalization, is often needed for clients with severe forms of this disorder (Williams & McGlashan, 1987).

No definitive information was located on the use of psychotherapy with these clients. Research on the components of the disorder suggests an interpersonal, cognitive, or cognitive-behavioral approach for the affective symptoms and a supportive and behavioral approach for the psychotic symptoms. Some mix of these, with the balance determined by the nature of a particular client's symptoms, seems a reasonable choice, but caution should be exercised in planning psychotherapy with these clients because of the dearth of research.

Prognosis. The prognosis for this disorder, not surprisingly, seems to be better than that for schizophrenia but not as good as that for a mood disorder (*DSM-III-R*, 1987). Details of outcome studies are contradictory. Tsuang and Loyd (1986) report that 70–80 percent of people with schizoaffective disorder follow a chronic course, although other studies found that only a small percentage follow a course reminiscent of chronic schizophrenia (Coryell, Lavori, Endicott, Keller, & Van Eerdewegh, 1984).

10.5 Dissociative Disorders

Description of Disorder. The dissociative disorders present a very different picture from the psychotic disorders, although they, too, involve reduced contact or changes in contact with reality. Nemiah (1988) describes the dissociative disorders as involving a "sudden alteration in mental functioning leading either to an altered state of consciousness or to a change in identity, or both" (p. 246). These disorders seem to serve the purpose of "removing painful mental events from consciousness" (p. 249). Dissociative disorders are believed to be uncommon and, with the exception of multiple personality disorder, seem to be diminishing in prevalence (Kaplan & Sadock, 1985). They tend to make their initial appearance in childhood or adolescence.

The *DSM-III-R* (1987) defines four types of dissociative disorders, in addition to dissociative disorder not otherwise specified. The dissociative disorder that has received most attention is multiple personality disorder. According to the *DSM-III-R*, "the essential feature of this disorder is the existence within the person of two or more distinct personalities or personality states" capable of assuming full control of the person's behavior (p. 269). Typically, personalities shift in ascendency under stress. Cases ranging from two to several hundred personalities have been reported, with an average of thirteen personalities (Kluft, 1987). Personalities often vary widely. Some clients have full or partial awareness of their various personalities; others have periods of amnesia for times when the primary personality is not the one in control. There is usually a primary personality, who tends to be rigid and moralistic, and a principal secondary personality, who is less inhibited and has greater awareness of the changing personalities (Nemiah, 1988).

The onset of multiple personality disorder is almost always in childhood, typically following a severe trauma or accompanying negative and abusive childhood experiences. Because of the longstanding and deeply ingrained nature of this disorder, the limited awareness that people with multiple personality disorder have of their condition, and their tendency to conceal their symptoms, multiple personality is difficult to diagnose and may be mistaken for other dissociative disorders, personality disorders, or psychotic disorders. Only approximately 5 percent of clients with multiple personalities present the disorder openly; in 40 percent, the disorder is heavily disguised (Kluft, 1987). Multiple personality disorder was once thought to be very rare but is being diagnosed with increasing frequency as clinicians become more familiar with its symptoms (Kluft, 1987).

Psychogenic fugue and psychogenic amnesia, also dissociative disorders, involve temporary forgetting of important components of the person's life. Both disorders, by definition, do not have an organic cause. People with psychogenic fugue typically have an inability to recall their past; they travel to a new place and assume a new identity, often developing a more energetic and adventurous personality. They are confused by what is happening to them and cannot recall the details of the fugue state upon recovery, the most common time for them to seek treatment (Gilmore & Kaufman, 1986). Psychogenic amnesia, the most common dissociative disorder (Nemiah, 1988), involves partial amnesia, forgetting important personal information (such as significant family members or one's place of employment). Both psychogenic fugue and psychogenic amnesia tend to occur suddenly at times of unusual stress, typically are of brief duration, and tend to remit without recurrence. Both disorders are rare but increase under circumstances of natural disaster, accidents, or warfare (DSM-III-R, 1987).

The DSM-III-R (1987) describes depersonalization disorder, the fourth in the group of dissociative disorders, as "a feeling of detachment from and being an outside observer of one's mental processes or body, or of feeling like an automaton or as if in a dream" (p. 275). Delusions and hallucinations are not present, and reality testing is intact. Nevertheless, the condition is sufficiently persistent to cause considerable distress. Symptoms of depression, anxiety, and somatic distress among others often accompany this disorder. The onset of depersonalization disorder tends to be rapid; the first episode is most likely to occur during adolescence or early adulthood, at a time when unusual stress is present. In fact, most young adults are reported to have experienced brief, single episodes of this disorder. This disorder is more common among females than males (Kaplan & Sadock, 1985). Recovery from depersonalization disorder is likely to be gradual, and recurrences are common.

Relevant Client Characteristics. Discussion of preexisting personality patterns and accompanying disorders has little relevance for clients with multiple personality disorder. The onset of the disorder usually is so early that the client, in effect, never really had one intact, mature personality. Accompanying disorders may include almost any mental disorder; in a given person with this disorder, some personalities may be relatively well adjusted while others may manifest severe emotional disorders in addition to the multiple personality disorder. Overall, the degree of impairment varies from mild to severe, and 60 percent of those with this disorder have periods in which symptoms are in remission (Kluft, 1987). Therapy commonly is sought by a so-called presenting personality who experiences significant symptoms of depression (found in over 90 percent with this disorder), guilt, anxiety, and suicidal ideation (Kluft, 1987). Other symptoms that frequently accompany this disorder include substance abuse, time lapses, disorientation, phobias, hallucination-like experiences, feelings of being influenced or changed, and mood swings (Kluft, 1987). The presenting personality often is the host personality, the one who is in control of the personality the largest percentage of the time. There is some indication that this disorder runs in families, and it seems to be four to nine times more common in females than in males (Kluft, 1987).

Research on the characteristics of people who experience psychogenic fugue or amnesia is limited. However, psychogenic amnesia seems to be more prevalent among adolescents and females, while psychogenic fugue is more common among those with a history of substance abuse (*DSM-III-R*, 1987). Amnesia is particularly common among people who are immature, suggestible, and rigid and who look to authority figures for direction (Meyer, 1983).

Depersonalization disorder is very common among adolescents. It also seems more prevalent among those with patterns of substance abuse and somatization (Meyer, 1983).

Relevant Therapist Variables. People with dissociative disorders typically are coping with considerable stress and anxiety. They may be confused and frightened by their disorders and fear that they are going insane. They need a supportive therapist who will give them clear information on the nature, course, and treatment of their disorders and reassure them that deterioration is unlikely and that the prognosis for improvement is good. For many clients with psychogenic fugue or amnesia or depersonalization disorder, a helpful therapeutic relationship is sufficient to promote spontaneous remission of the disorder. For multiple personality disorder or more severe versions of the other disorders, a strong therapeutic relationship must be combined with other interventions to promote improvement.

Intervention Strategies. Dissociative disorders resemble some organic disorders that involve memory loss. The first step in treatment, then, often will be a neurological examination to make certain there is no organic cause. Clouded consciousness and disorientation, particularly in a client past middle age, suggest that organicity rather than a dissociative disorder is present.

Hypnosis is an important component in treatment of many cases of dissociative disorders. In psychogenic fugue and amnesia, hypnosis and sodium amytal interviews typically form the core of the initial phase of treatment, facilitating the goal of uncovering memories as rapidly and completely as possible (Nemiah, 1988). Therapy—encouraging exploration, coping, and confidence building—also can aid in the uncovering of memories and, once memory has been regained, can help clients deal with the stressor that precipitated the amnesia. Family therapy, free association, environmental change, cognitive therapy, and behavior therapy seem particularly likely to ameliorate psychogenic fugue and amnesia and to help clients cope with their stress-related precipitants (Combs & Ludwig, 1982).

Little is known about the treatment of depersonalization disorder. One reason for the lack of research on this disorder is that clinicians have not yet agreed that it is a separate disorder; some view the symptoms as manifestations of seizures, depression, anxiety, schizophrenia, or other disorders (Gilmore & Kaufman, 1986). The overall goal of treatment of depersonalization disorder is to help clients regain their sense of reality and develop a feeling of personality integration. Nemiah (1988) suggests that sodium amytal and other medications along with hypnotherapy may relieve symptoms, but these approaches to treatment have received mixed reactions in the literature. Gilmore and Kaufman (1986) advocate the use of a psychodynamic approach to therapy, Meyer (1983) suggests Gestalt therapy because of its emphasis on integration of mind and body, while Kaplan and Sadock (1985) recommend supportive therapy. Promoting clients' contact with reality by encouraging increased involvement with other people and activities can also facilitate recovery.

Treatment of multiple personality disorder typically is a long, slow, challenging process, requiring years of therapy, although clients usually respond favorably to treatment when the disorder is properly recognized and addressed (Kluft, 1987). Hypnosis and sodium amytal interviews can be useful with this disorder, too, to facilitate diagnosis as well as to contribute to treatment. These approaches can be used to uncover personalities and to suggest to clients that they will recall the uncovered personalities (Gilmore & Kaufman, 1986). However, psychodynamic psychotherapy generally is viewed as the primary ingredient in treatment. Gilmore and Kaufman (1986) suggest a therapeutic approach that helps clients understand and accept their disorder, avoid dissociation under stress, and eventually establish one fused, integrated, and well-functioning personality (Maxmen, 1986).

Prognosis. The prognosis is excellent for a rapid and complete recovery from initial episodes of psychogenic fugue, psychogenic amnesia, and depersonalization disorder. Often, the recovery is spontaneous, although it can be facilitated by treatment. However, recurrences are common, particularly for psychogenic amnesia (Gilmore & Kaufman, 1986).

The prognosis for treatment of multiple personality disorder is not so positive. This disorder has not been known to remit without treatment. With long-term, intensive treatment, most clients will improve, but many will not achieve integration into a well-adjusted personality. Instead, they will gain better control over their personalities and will learn to live with their disorder more effectively.

10.6 Organic Mental Syndromes and Disorders

Description of Disorder. According to the *DSM-III-R* (1987), "The essential feature of all these disorders [organic mental syndromes and disorders] is a psychological or behavioral abnormality associated with transient or permanent dysfunction of the brain" (p. 98). Organic mental syndromes and disorders are a heterogeneous group with diverse origins and symptoms. Common causes include a disease of the brain (for example, Alzheimer's disease), a systemic illness, a head injury, or exposure to a psychoactive or toxic substance (such as alcohol or insecticide). Symptoms of these disorders encompass many of the symptoms associated with nonorganic mental disorders, such as depression, anxiety, personality change, paranoia, and confusion. Kaplan and Sadock (1985) report that the most common symptoms of organic mental disorders are impairments in memory (especially of recent memory), abstract thinking, ability to concentrate and perform new tasks, overall intellectual performance, judgment, attention, spatiotemporal orientation, calculating ability, and ability to grasp meaning, as well as misperceptions of body and environment. They view "impairment of abstraction, memory, and efficiency in intellectual and cognitive performance" (p. 272) as particularly characteristic of organic mental syndromes and disorders. Despite this information, it is difficult to diagnose an organic mental disorder by symptoms without information on possible causes, because the symptoms often mimic other mental disorders (Szymanski & Keill, 1985).

Diagnosis of organic mental syndromes and disorders has two parts: identification of the psychological impairment and the "cerebral impairment" (McHugh & Folstein, 1986, p. 334). A combination of a careful history taking and medical and neurological examinations typically is necessary to establish a conclusive diagnosis. Just as nonorganic mental disorders may be mistaken for the organic disorders that they resemble, organic disorders also can be mistaken for nonorganic disorders. For example, 10–20 percent of those diagnosed as having Alzheimer's disease actually seem to have a form of depression that has similar symptoms and that has been referred to as pseudodementia (Maxmen, 1986). This error is particularly unfortunate since there are effective treatments for depression whereas an effective treatment for Alzheimer's disease has yet to be found. In light of the diagnostic challenge presented by organic mental syndromes and disorders, clinicians should obtain a psychiatric or neurological evaluation when organicity is suspected. EEGs, CAT scans, and other medical tests as well as psychological tests such as the Wechsler Adult Intelligence Scales and the Halstead-Reitan can determine whether an organic mental disorder is likely to be present.

The *DSM-III-R* (1987) describes the following organic mental syndromes: delirium (typified by abrupt onset, clouded consciousness), dementia (insidious onset, progressive and pervasive course), amnestic syndrome, organic hallucinosis, organic delusional syndrome, organic mood syndrome, organic anxiety syndrome, organic personality syndrome, intoxication, withdrawal, and organic mental syndrome not otherwise specified. The *DSM-III-R* also defines the following organic mental disorders: dementias arising in the senium and presenium (primary degenerative dementia of the Alzheimer type and multi-infarct dementia), psychoactive substance–induced organic mental disorders, and organic mental disorders associated with Axis III physical disorders or conditions (for example, brain tumor) or whose etiology is unknown. Discussion of individual disorders is beyond the scope of this book, but those treating these disorders will want to consult the *DSM* for the detailed descriptions and diagnostic criteria provided there.

Relevant Client Characteristics. Organic mental disorders may occur at any age, with dementia most likely to occur in the later years. Alzheimer's disease affects 2–5 percent of people over age sixty-five and 11-15 percent of those over eighty-five (McHugh & Folstein, 1986). That disorder has a genetic component and is particularly likely to occur in first-degree relatives of those with the disorder (Shamoian & Teusink, 1987). Multi-infarct dementia, resulting from cerebrovascular disease, is more common among people with a history of diabetes and hypertension. Most of the other mental disorders have an external cause (such as excessive use of drugs or alcohol, a blow to the head, or exposure to a toxic environment). They may occur in any person, but will often be associated with habits or lifestyle. For example, psychoactive substance-induced organic mental disorder frequently will be accompanied by a concurrent diagnosis of substance abuse or dependence (section 7.1).

Relevant Therapist Variables. Therapists treating organic mental disorders should either have training in the physiological and neurological aspects of these disorders or should work collaboratively with someone who does have that training. The therapeutic relationship that is established will depend, to a large extent, on the level of functioning of the clients. In general, therapists working with clients with organic mental disorders will have to be directive, supportive, and reassuring. They will have to take charge of the therapy and determine what psychological and medical interventions are necessary to help the clients. Therapists will promote clients' awareness of reality and orientation to their environment. They also will provide information to clients, meet with clients' families, and help clients obtain adjunct services (such as residential treatment facilities or financial assistance through government programs).

Intervention Strategies. Treatment of organic mental disorders usually involves a multifaceted approach. Medical/neurological treatment, including medication or surgery, may be needed to assess and arrest or reduce the organic impairment. Environmental manipulation may be indicated to help clients cope more effectively with their living situations despite their impairment and maintain some form of employment as long as possible. People in advanced stages of one of these disorders may need to be placed in a supervised living situation.

Family members of those with longstanding and progressive organic mental disorders are often overwhelmed with worry, guilt, and the responsibility of caring for their affected relatives. If these family members can receive counseling; information, support, and help with decision making; and encouragement to express feelings and set goals, they will be able to cope more effectively with the difficulties of dealing with someone with an organic disorder. Family members may also benefit from help in identifying and making use of community resources, such as respite care and in-home help, that are available to them.

Although psychotherapy typically plays a secondary role in direct treatment of most organic disorders, it can serve as an important complement to medical treatment. Therapy seems particularly helpful to clients in early or mild stages of primary degenerative dementia of the Alzheimer type and of multi-infarct dementia. Therapy probably will be most useful if it emphasizes behavioral intervention, encouraging clients to remain as active and independent as possible and helping them compensate for changes in their capacities by building on coping mechanisms that are still accessible to them (Reid, 1983). Behaviorally oriented therapy also can help these clients control destructive impulses and emotional lability. Attention should be paid to keeping these clients appropriately informed about the nature of their disorders and helping them express their feelings about the changes they are experiencing. These therapeutic interventions can help clients reduce the secondary symptoms (depression, denial, fear, confusion, and negative feelings about themselves) that are common in the early stages of organic mental disorders (Shamoian & Teusink, 1987).

As mentioned, people with organic mental disorders caused by psychoactive substances often will have a coexisting diagnosis of substance abuse (section 7.1) or dependence. Psychotherapy will play an important role in treatment of those clients, with the goal of eliminating the self-destructive use of drugs or alcohol. Eliminating the substance use disorder is likely to ameliorate the accompanying organic disorder and greatly reduce chances of a recurrence.

Prognosis. The prognosis for recovery from organic mental syndromes and disorders is as variable as the disorders themselves and is usually determined by the cause of the disorder. Disorders stemming from psychoactive substances, metabolic disorders, and systemic illnesses tend to be time limited and usually are followed by full recovery or significant improvement; those caused by disease or damage to the brain have a less favorable prognosis. Presenile and senile dementia, for example, currently has no known cure and is the fourth or fifth leading cause of death (Shamoian & Teusink, 1987).

Summary of Treatment Recommendations

Treatment recommendations for disorders involving loss of contact with reality are summarized below, according to the client map format. Because disorders in this section do vary widely, readers are encouraged to review sections on specific disorders in addition to this summary.

> *Diagnosis.* Disorders involving loss of contact with reality (schizophrenia, brief reactive psychosis, schizophreniform disorder, delusional disorder, schizoaffective disorder, dissociative disorders, organic mental syndromes and disorders).
>
> *Objectives.* Reduce or eliminate prominent symptoms, if possible, and restore contact with reality; maximize clients' emotional and behavioral adjustment to the disorder as well as their coping mechanisms; prevent relapse, if appropriate; enable family members to develop understanding of the disorder, deal with their own related needs and feelings, learn how to help the affected family member, and make care-related decisions.
>
> *Assessment.* Medical, neurological, and/or psychological evaluations are usually necessary; inventories of intelligence and specific symptoms (for example, substance use, stress, depression) can clarify the diagnostic picture as well as provide useful information on level of functioning and secondary symptoms.
>
> *Clinician.* A treatment team approach is common, including medical personnel (such as psychiatrists, neurologists, and

nurses), family and individual psychotherapists, and rehabilitation therapists; all should have understanding of the
usual nature and course of the disorder and should be able
to provide support and, if needed, long-term treatment to
client and family. In some cases, clinicians will need to
deal with their own reactions to a very poor prognosis.

Location. With some exceptions (for example, multiple personality disorder and depersonalization disorder), treatment will often be inpatient initially, followed by outpatient treatment if symptoms are alleviated; residential
treatment is sometimes needed.

Interventions. Treatment will typically involve a multifaceted approach (for example, medication, hospitalization,
and psychotherapy) to reduce and, if possible, eliminate
the symptoms of the disorder. Behavioral therapy can help
clients develop coping mechanisms and stress management skills; family therapy can promote understanding
and adjustment; and other interventions (such as hypnotherapy for amnesia, psychodynamic psychotherapy for
multiple personality disorder) can be used as indicated by
the specific disorder.

Emphasis. Varies, depending on the nature of the disorder
(for example, focus on behavior and affect for the organic
mental syndromes, on exploration of dynamics for multiple personality disorder); typically will be supportive and
structured.

Nature. Primarily individual treatment, with family therapy
also important; group therapy is not usually indicated
except in specialized forms (for example, milieu therapy).

Timing. With some exceptions (for example, brief reactive
psychosis or psychogenic amnesia), long-term treatment is
indicated, sometimes with several sessions scheduled per
week.

Medication. Often indicated, but should be monitored carefully, to minimize side effects and prevent abuse or suicide.

Adjunct services. Often important in treatment; might include such services as rehabilitation counseling, occupational therapy, socialization, respite care.

Prognosis. Varies, depending on disorder: excellent for brief reactive psychosis; good for psychogenic amnesia; fair for multiple personality disorder and schizophrenia; poor for some organic mental disorders.

Client Map of Thomas F.

This chapter began with the case of Thomas F., who believed that his apparently faithful wife, Carmen, was having extramarital relationships with several men. Tom was coping with many stressful life changes: recent marriage, new baby, limited contact with wife. His poor coping mechanisms (dependent and avoidant personality traits) and fear of another failed marriage, coupled with those stressors, led to the development of a delusional disorder. This disorder is characterized by circumscribed delusions focusing on a stressful area (Tom's marriage), with relatively unimpaired functioning in other areas. The following client map outlines treatment for Tom.

Diagnosis. Axis I: 297.10—Delusional disorder, paranoid type.

Axis II: Dependent and avoidant personality traits.

Axis III: No medical problems.

Axis IV: Psychosocial stressors: birth of child, change in marital relationship, mother's illness. Severity: 4—severe (primarily acute events).

Axis V: Current Global Assessment of Functioning: 40; highest GAF past year: 70.

Objectives. (1) Eliminate delusional symptoms.

(2) Improve marital relationship and communication.

(3) Review and possibly modify child care and employment arrangements.

(4) Improve socialization, leisure activities, coping mechanisms, support systems, self-confidence, and self-reliance.

Assessment. Because of the circumscribed nature of Tom's symptoms and their sudden onset, a combination of stressful life circumstances and weak underlying coping mechanisms was assumed to be the cause of the disorder. However, Tom was evaluated to determine whether medication or hospitalization was necessary.

Clinician. Supportive and empathic, skilled at reducing resistance and restoring contact with reality, preferably a good male role model for Tom, knowledgeable about family dynamics.

Location. Tom was functioning relatively well in most areas of his life and did not seem to present a danger to himself or others. Consequently, treatment was begun on an outpatient basis.

Interventions. Marital and individual therapy were the primary components of Tom's treatment. Individual therapy combined supportive and behavioral elements. The therapist recognized Tom's need for acceptance and encouragement and emphasized the development of a strong therapeutic alliance. In addition, behavior therapy was used to build up Tom's coping mechanisms. He was taught to appraise problems more clearly, to communicate his concerns to others, to develop alternatives, to make decisions more effectively, and to gain control over his challenging life circumstances. Techniques such as time management and stress management were also included in the treatment package. Weekly marital therapy with Carmen and Tom focused on strengthening their communication skills as well as their commitment to and understanding of each other. Constructive ways to reassure and support each other were taught and practiced, and they gradually began to feel like a team that was starting to win.

Emphasis. Structured, relatively directive, present oriented, and supportive; taking a holistic approach, with focus on behavioral and affective elements.

Nature. Individual and couples therapy.

Timing. Pacing was gentle yet steady, seeking to help Tom

quickly develop a commitment to treatment and reduce symptoms. One individual and one couples session was scheduled each week. Treatment of moderate duration was anticipated.

Medication. Medication was prescribed to reduce the thought disorder and anxiety, but it was viewed as a short-term component of the treatment plan, facilitating Tom's involvement in therapy.

Adjunct services. Both Tom and Carmen felt that they were operating in isolation and had little time to enjoy each other or their new baby. They were helped to make use of community and family resources, to give them some respite and to focus attention on the couple relationship.

Prognosis. The combination of medication and psychotherapy had a rapid effect on Tom's delusional symptoms. His delusional beliefs began to fade in intensity and quickly ceased to become a dominant theme in the relationship. He was able to invest energy into improving his marriage and could accept the reassurance that Carmen provided. In approximately six months, medication was stopped, and many positive changes had been made in Tom and Carmen's marriage. They were also becoming happier and more effective parents. Although they continued to be rather dependent on each other and to focus most of their energy on their family, they became more able to use outside supports and to resume some of the activities they had enjoyed as a couple before the birth of their child. Tom seemed to be healthier at the end of treatment than he had been before treatment. In all likelihood, he will recover completely from the delusional disorder and seems unlikely to have a recurrence.

Recommended Readings

Day, M., & Manschreck, T. C. (1988). Delusional (paranoic) disorders. In A. M. Nicholi, Jr. (Ed.), *The new Harvard guide to psychiatry.* Cambridge, MA: Harvard University Press.

Helzer, J. E., & Guze, S. B. (Eds.). (1986). *Psychoses, affective disorders, and dementia.* New York: Basic Books.

Kluft, R. P. (1987). Making the diagnosis of multiple personality disorder. In F. Flach (Ed.), *Diagnostics and psychopathology* (pp. 207-225). New York: Norton.

May, P.R.A., Tuma, A. H., & Dixon, W. J. (1981). Schizophrenia. *Archives of General Psychiatry, 38,* 776-784.

McGlashan, T. H. (1983). Intensive individual psychotherapy of schizophrenia. *Archives of General Psychiatry, 40,* 909-920.

Simpson, G. M., & May, P.R.A. (1982). Schizophrenic disorders. In J. H. Greist, J. W. Jefferson, & R. L. Spitzer (Eds.), *Treatment of mental disorders* (pp. 143-183). New York: Oxford University Press.

Tsuang, M. T., Farone, S.V., & Day, M. (1988). Schizophrenic disorders. In A. M. Nicholi, Jr. (Ed.), *The new Harvard guide to psychiatry* (pp. 259-295). Cambridge, MA: Harvard University Press.

Chapter Eleven

▋▋▋▊▋▊▊▋▊▋▊▋▊▋▊▋▊▋▊▋▊▊▋▊▋▊▋▊▋▊▋▊▋▊▋▊▊▋▊▋▊▋▊▊▋▊▋▊▋

The Future
of Diagnosis
and Treatment
Planning

In this book, I have tried to provide readers with a greater understanding of the major mental disorders affecting adults and the techniques that have shown evidence of effectiveness in treating those disorders. I have also presented a systematic and comprehensive approach to developing a treatment plan, DO A CLIENT MAP. This map is designed to lead clinicians through a series of decisions that will culminate in a complete treatment plan. Although I hope that the information contained in this book will enhance clinicians' ability to diagnose and treat their clients' mental disorders, the book can only shape and refine skills that clinicians already possess. The therapist's personality, style, knowledge, and experience are the essential ingredients of treatment, and no book can turn a weak therapist into a strong one unless the basic ingredients of a good therapist were already present. This book, then, is to be used to help therapists refine their existing knowledge of diagnosis and treatment, not to provide a definitive recipe for treatment.

The Art and Science of Psychotherapy

Psychotherapy is both an art and a science. Scientific research can be used to assess the impact of various treatment approaches on

336

a particular disorder and can provide invaluable guidelines for treatment planning. Current research being conducted at the National Institute of Mental Health on the treatment of depression and of obsessive compulsive disorder, discussed elsewhere in the book (in sections 5.1 and 6.4), is a striking example of the contribution that data-based research can make to the process of psychotherapy. At the same time, because psychotherapy involves at least two people, each of whom brings unique qualities to the relationship, and an interaction different from any other interaction, it is an art.

This mixture of art and science brings both strengths and pitfalls to psychotherapy. At its best, psychotherapy is a rich process of recovery and growth, with both client and therapist benefiting from their interaction. There is ample room for creativity and individuality; and reasoned innovation is often just what is needed to change a deeply entrenched and dysfunctional personality pattern. However, because psychotherapy is not an exact science, because there is no exact recipe or formula to remedy each disorder, there is room for error and failure. Many disorders are difficult to diagnose and may be mistaken for similar disorders. The challenges presented by the process of diagnosing such disorders as multiple personality disorder, organic mental syndromes and disorders, schizoaffective disorder, and bipolar disorder have been discussed elsewhere in this book. Misdiagnosis is only one possible reason for a treatment failure. Others include lack of therapist expertise, inappropriate choice of treatment, or a disorder that is highly resistant to treatment. Although occasional treatment failures or setbacks seem inevitable, there are steps that therapists can take to maximize the likelihood of treatment success. Consulting with other mental health practitioners is one important step. Therapists should not hesitate to refer clients for an evaluation by someone from a related discipline, perhaps a neurologist or psychiatrist, to clarify a diagnosis. Discussion of a case with colleagues also can be useful in providing ideas on diagnosis and treatment. Frequent evaluation of progress made on the goals established in a client map is imperative in monitoring progress. As indicated in Chapter Two, clients typically manifest evidence of progress fairly early in therapy; if progress is not being made, something needs to change—either the goals themselves, the treatment plan, or the therapist-client interaction.

Progress often is slow and slight, especially with clients who have personality disorders. However, treatment that produces no evidence of progress over several months or more needs reevaluation and possibly modification.

Sources of Influence on Diagnosis and Treatment Planning

Perhaps the major source of error in diagnosis and treatment is the lack of adequate information. Knowledge of mental disorders and treatment is constantly changing and evolving. No sooner was the *DSM-III-R* published in 1987 than work was begun on the *DSM-IV*, with publication expected for 1993. Changes in our understanding of diagnosis and treatment come from many sources— scientific, clinical, social, political, legal, and financial.

Scientific research, such as that being conducted at the National Institute of Mental Health, has greatly modified treatment of several disorders in recent years. For example, studies have led to a reduced emphasis on medication in the treatment of major depression and an increasing emphasis on medication in the treatment of obsessive compulsive disorder.

Clinical experience commonly provides the basis for scientific research and often influences diagnoses and treatment even before being scientifically validated. For example, the *DSM-III-R* contains several diagnoses that have been proposed but that need further study—for example, late luteal phase dysphoric disorder (emotional and physiological concomitants of premenstrual syndrome), sadistic personality disorder, and self-defeating personality disorder. Data are being gathered on these disorders, to determine whether they should be included in the *DSM-IV*. Other diagnoses have also been viewed as possible additions or modifications to the *DSM*. For example, some clinicians believe that dysthymia is really a personality disorder—involving longstanding, deeply ingrained, mild to moderate depression—rather than a mood disorder. Questions have also been raised about the absence, in the *DSM-III-R*, of any diagnosis that addresses the impact of substance abuse on the family. People who can be described as Adult Children of Alcoholics, codependent, or enabling must be diagnosed according to the nature of their symptoms rather than according to a combination of symptoms and dynamics. For example, many people who might be perceived as codependent or enabling would be diagnosed as having a dependent personality disorder. That diagnosis does not reflect the familial/genetic component to their disorders, which might be better captured by a new diagnosis that encompasses both the dependency needs and the family origins of those needs. The need for a diagnosis to describe the emotional symptoms associated with AIDS has also been discussed, and certainly clinicians increasingly will be dealing with clients who are apprehensive about or affected by AIDS. Clinical work seems likely to provide a limitless source of information that will modify and alter diagnostic categories and criteria as well as treatments for mental and emotional disorders.

Social changes also have an impact on diagnosis and treatment. For example, homosexuality was viewed as a mental disorder in the 1950s, when the *DSM-II* was developed and published. That diagnosis was controversial in 1980, when the *DSM-III* was published, and was eliminated from the *DSM-III-R*. Homosexuality has not changed; however, social understanding and acceptance of homosexuality have changed greatly over the past thirty years, and those changes were reflected in the diagnostic manuals. Growing awareness of gender bias and discrimination has led several diagnoses to be viewed as sex biased because they tend to be applied to one sex far more than to the other. Dependent personality disorder, diagnosed in women more than in men, is one of these. Social changes also have had an impact on treatment. In the late 1960s and early 1970s, the antiwar movement, with its associated emphasis on individuality and freedom of expression, led to the growth of such therapies as encounter groups, rebirthing, and Gestalt therapy. These approaches seemed to receive far less attention during the late 1970s and the 1980s, but growing interest in so-called New Age approaches seems to have spawned a renewed interest in the therapies of the Vietnam era and some of their modern relatives. It is difficult to predict what impact social changes will have on diagnosis and treatment planning in the future, but certainly they will have a considerable impact.

Political changes, affecting funding of programs as well as attitudes toward mental illness, probably are equally difficult to predict but just as inevitable. For example, during the Kennedy-

Johnson era, considerable funds were made available to develop a nationwide network of community mental health centers. Decreases in funding, over the years, for these and other mental health programs seem to have contributed to a growing emphasis on brief treatment as well as on group treatment. A long-considered national health insurance plan is still on the drawing boards but seems more likely than ever to be passed. That legislation would certainly have a great impact on funding for treatment programs for mental and emotional disorders.

Present health insurance programs have been very concerned with cost containment in recent years, and their financial difficulties have had an effect on treatment. Efforts to curtail costs for medical care have led to rapid growth in health maintenance organizations, preferred provider organizations, and employee assistance programs, all typically emphasizing brief treatment of mental disorders. Some of these programs offer clients little choice of treatment provider and pay little attention to the need for extended treatment for amelioration and prevention of some mental disorders. Many clients are therefore faced with paying their own psychotherapy bills or failing to receive the treatment they need.

Finally, legislation has had an impact on the field of psychotherapy in many ways. A shortage of psychiatrists has been predicted for this country. At the same time, the number of mental health practitioners at the master's level, either counselors or social workers, has substantially increased. Legislation has reflected this increase. Virginia was the first state to pass legislation licensing counselors. Less than fifteen years later, in 1989, thirty-two states have laws requiring licensure or certification for counselors practicing independently. In addition, several states have passed freedom-of-choice legislation, mandating that insurance companies provide third-party payments to any mental health treatment providers licensed in that state. These pieces of legislation make psychotherapy increasingly available. On the other hand, the legal system has also posed a threat to nonmedical mental health treatment providers. In 1988, the Florida Psychiatric Society and other psychiatric and medical associations in Florida filed a petition against the Florida Board of Clinical Social Work, Marriage and Family Therapy and Mental Health Counseling, alleging that diagnosis and treatment of persons with mental and emotional illnesses should no longer be practiced by social workers, counselors, and related nonmedical mental health therapists. At this writing, the case is still in the courts. However, it promises to have a considerable impact on the role of psychotherapists and on clients' access to appropriate treatment for their mental and emotional disorders.

The future of diagnosis and treatment clearly will be affected by many factors and will continue to evolve through research, practice, and social, legal, political, and financial change. It is hoped that most of that change will be influenced by increased knowledge of diagnosis and treatment. Certainly, although we have already learned a great deal, the field is, at best, in its adolescence; and this book alone probably has more options for treatment than could be explored in all the doctoral dissertations and research projects that will be conducted in the next ten years. The rapid and often unpredictable changes in the field are both exciting and disconcerting. The challenge to mental health therapists is to keep aware of those changes, to incorporate them wisely and selectively in their own practices, and to promote positive changes in the field. In that way, we can maximize the rewards we receive from our profession as well as the benefits psychotherapy can bring to our clients.

References

Agras, W. S. (1987). *Eating disorders*. Elmsford, NY: Pergamon Press.

Andersen, A. E. (1987a). Anorexia nervosa, bulimia, and depression: Multiple interactions. In F. Flach (Ed.), *Diagnostics and psychopathology* (pp. 131–139). New York: Norton.

Andersen, A. E. (1987b). Psychiatric aspects of bulimia. In F. Flach (Ed.), *Diagnostics and psychopathology* (pp. 121–130). New York: Norton.

Anderson, D. J., Noyes, R. J., & Crowe, R. R. (1984). A comparison of panic disorder and generalized anxiety disorder. *American Journal of Psychiatry, 141*, 572–575.

Andreasen, N. C., & Hoenk, P. R. (1983). The predictive value of adjustment disorders: A follow-up study. *American Journal of Psychiatry, 139*, 584–590.

Andrews, G., & Harvey, R. (1981). Does psychotherapy benefit neurotic patients? *Archives of General Psychiatry, 38*, 1203–1208.

Aneshensal, C. S., & Stone, J. D. (1982). Stress and depression. *Archives of General Psychiatry, 39*, 1392–1396.

Arieti, S. (1982). Individual psychotherapy. In E. S. Paykel (Ed.), *Handbook of affective disorders* (pp. 297–306). New York: Guilford Press.

343

Asch, S. S. (1986). The masochistic personality. In A. M. Cooper, A. J. Frances, & M. H. Sacks (Eds.), *The personality disorders and neuroses* (pp. 291–299). Philadelphia: Lippincott.

Ascher, L. M. (1981). Employing paradoxical intention in the treatment of agoraphobia. *Behaviour Research and Therapy, 19,* 533–542.

Atwood, J. D., & Chester, R. (1987). *Treatment techniques for common mental disorders.* New York: Jason Aronson.

Baker, A. L., and Wilson, P. H. (1985). Cognitive-behavior therapy for depression: The effects of booster sessions on relapse. *Behavior Therapy, 16,* 335–344.

Bale, R. N., Zarcone, V. P., Van Stone, W. W., Kuldau, J. M., Engelsing, T.M.J., & Elashoff, R. M. (1984). Three therapeutic communities. *Archives of General Psychiatry, 41,* 185–191.

Barbaree, H. E., & Marshall, W. L. (1985). Anxiety-based disorders. In M. Hersen & S. M. Turner (Eds.), *Diagnostic interviewing* (pp. 55–77). New York: Plenum Press.

Barlow, D. H., Cohen, A. S., Waddell, M. T., Vermilyea, B. B., Klosko, J. S., Blanchard, E. B., & DiNardo, P. A. (1984). Panic and generalized anxiety disorders: Nature and treatment. *Behavior Therapy, 15,* 431–449.

Barlow, D. H., & Waddell, M. T. (1985). Agoraphobia. In D. H. Barlow (Ed.), *Clinical handbook of psychological disorders* (pp. 1–68). New York: Guilford Press.

Barrow, J. (1979). Cognitive self-control strategies with the anxious student. *Psychotherapy: Theory, Research and Practice, 16,* 152–157.

Bebbington, P. E. (1986). Psychosocial etiology of schizophrenia and affective disorders. In J. E. Helzer & S. B. Guze (Eds.), *Psychoses, affective disorders, and dementia* (pp. 171–192). New York: Basic Books.

Beck, A. T., & Emery, G. (1985). *Anxiety disorders and phobias.* New York: Basic Books.

Beck, A. T., Rush, A. J., Shaw, B. F., & Emery, G. (1979). *Cognitive therapy of depression.* New York: Guilford Press.

Beech, H. R., & Vaughn, M. (1978). *Behavioral treatment of obsessional states.* New York: Wiley.

Beiman, I., Israel, E., & Johnson, S. A. (1978). During training and posttraining effects of live and taped extended progressive relaxation, self-relaxation, and electromyogram biofeedback. *Journal of Consulting and Clinical Psychology, 46,* 314–321.

Bellack, A. S., Hersen, M., & Himmelhoch, J. M. (1983). A comparison of social-skills training, pharmacotherapy and psychotherapy for depression. *Behaviour Research and Therapy, 21,* 101–107.

Berger, P. A., & Dunn, M. J. (1982). Substance induced and substance use disorders. In J. H. Greist, J. W. Jefferson, & R. L. Spitzer (Eds.), *Treatment of mental disorders* (pp. 78–142). New York: Oxford University Press.

Bergin, A. E. (1971). The evaluation of therapeutic outcomes. In A. E. Bergin & S. L. Garfield (Eds.), *Handbook of psychotherapy and behavior change.* New York: Wiley.

Bergin, A. E., & Lambert, M. J. (1978). The evaluation of psychotherapeutic outcomes. In S. L. Garfield & A. E. Bergin (Eds.), *Handbook of psychotherapy and behavior change* (2nd ed., pp. 139–189). New York: Wiley.

Bergner, R. M. (1977). The marital system of the hysterical individual. *Family Process, 16,* 85–95.

Berman, J. S., Miller, R. C., & Massman, P. J. (1985). Cognitive therapy versus systematic desensitization: Is one treatment superior? *Psychological Bulletin, 97,* 451–461.

Berman, J. S., & Norton, N. C. (1985). Does professional training make a therapist more effective? *Psychological Bulletin, 98,* 401–407.

Beutler, L. E., Crago, M., & Arizmendi, T. G. (1986). Therapist variables in psychotherapy process. In S. L. Garfield & A. E. Bergin (Eds.), *Handbook of psychotherapy and behavior change* (3rd ed., pp. 257–310). New York: Wiley.

Bibring, E. (1954). Psychoanalysis and the dynamic psychotherapies. *Journal of American Psychoanalytic Association, 2,* 754–770.

Billings, A. G., & Moos, R. H. (1985). Life stressors and social resources affect posttreatment outcomes among depressed patients. *Journal of Abnormal Psychology, 94,* 140–153.

Biran, M., & Wilson, G. T. (1981). Treatment of phobic disorders using cognitive and exposure methods: A self-efficacy analysis. *Journal of Consulting and Clinical Psychology, 49,* 886–899.

Blanchard, E. B. (1981). Behavioral assessment of psychophysiologic disorders. In D. H. Barlow (Ed.), *Behavioral assessment of adult disorders* (pp. 239–269). New York: Guilford Press.

Blazer, D., Hughes, D., & George, L. K. (1987). Stressful life events and the onset of a generalized anxiety syndrome. *American Journal of Psychiatry, 144,* 1178–1183.

Bloch, S., Crouch, E., & Reibstein, J. (1981). Therapeutic factors in group psychotherapy. *Archives of General Psychiatry, 38,* 519–526.

Bloom, B. L. (1981). Focused single-session therapy: Initial development and evaluation. In S. H. Budman (Ed.), *Forms of brief therapy* (pp. 167–216). New York: Guilford Press.

Bolles, R. (1988). *What color is your parachute?* Berkeley, CA: Ten Speed Press.

Borkovec, T. D. (1982). Insomnia. *Journal of Consulting and Clinical Psychology, 50,* 880–895.

Boskind-White, M., & White, W. C., Jr. (1983). *Bulimarexia: The binge-purge cycle.* New York: Norton.

Bourque, P., & Ladouceur, R. (1980). An investigation of various performance-based treatments with acrophobics. *Behaviour Research and Therapy, 18,* 161–170.

Boyd, J. H., & Weissman, M. M. (1982). Epidemiology. In E. S. Paykel (Ed.), *Handbook of affective disorders* (pp. 109–125). New York: Guilford Press.

Brandsma, J. M., Maultsby, M. C., & Welsh, R. J. (1980). *Outpatient treatment of alcoholism: A review and comparative study.* Baltimore: University Park Press.

Bratter, T. E. (1985). Special clinical psychotherapeutic concerns for alcoholic and drug-addicted individuals. In T. E. Bratter & G. G. Forrest (Eds.), *Alcoholism and substance abuse* (pp. 523–574). New York: Free Press.

Bratter, T. E., Collabolletta, E. A., Fossbender, A. J., Pennacchia, M. C., & Rubel, J. R. (1985). The American self-help residential therapeutic community. In T. E. Bratter & G. G. Forrest (Eds.), *Alcoholism and substance abuse* (pp. 461–507). New York: Free Press.

Breier, A., Charney, D. S., & Heninger, G. R. (1985). The diagnostic validity of anxiety disorders and their relationship to depressive illness. *American Journal of Psychiatry, 142,* 787–797.

Breier, A., & Strauss, J. S. (1983). Self-control in psychotic disorders. *Archives of General Psychiatry, 40,* 1141–1145.

Brown, R. A., & Lewinsohn, P. M. (1984). A psychoeducational approach to the treatment of depression: Comparison of group, individual, and minimal contact procedures. *Journal of Consulting and Clinical Psychology, 52,* 774–783.

Bruch, H. (1982). Anorexia nervosa: Therapy and theory. *American Journal of Psychiatry, 139,* 1531–1538.

Buchholz, D. (1988, April). Sleep disorders. *Treatment Trends, 3,* 1–9.

Buckley, P., Conte, H. R., Plutchik, R., Wild, K. V., & Karasu, T. B. (1984). Psychodynamic variables as predictors of psychotherapy outcome. *American Journal of Psychiatry, 141,* 742–748.

Budman, S. H. (Ed.). (1981). *Forms of brief therapy.* New York: Guilford Press.

Butler, G., Cullington, A., Munby, M., Amies, P., & Gelder, M. (1984). Exposure and anxiety management in the treatment of social phobia. *Journal of Consulting and Clinical Psychology, 52,* 642–650.

Cadoret, R. J., Troughton, E., O'Gorman, T. W., & Heywood, E. (1986). An adoption study of genetic and environmental factors in drug abuse. *Archives of General Psychiatry, 43,* 1131–1136.

Caine, L. (1974). *Widow.* New York: Bantam Books.

Carroll, E. M., Rueger, D. B., Foy, D. W., & Donahoe, C. P., Jr. (1985). Vietnam combat veterans with posttraumatic stress disorder: Analysis of marital and cohabiting adjustment. *Journal of Abnormal Psychology, 94,* 329–337.

Carter, E. A., & McGoldrick, M. (1988). *The family life cycle.* New York: Gardner Press.

Christensen, H., Hadzi-Pavlovic, D., Andrews, G., & Mattick, R. (1987). Behavior therapy and tricyclic medication in the treatment of obsessive-compulsive disorder: A quantitative review. *Journal of Consulting and Clinical Psychology, 55,* 701–711.

Cofer, D., & Wittenborn, J. (1980). Personality characteristics of formerly depressed women. *Journal of Abnormal Psychology, 89,* 309–315.

Colby, K. M. (1979). Cognitive therapy of paranoid conditions: Heuristic suggestions based on a computer simulation model. *Cognitive Therapy and Research, 3,* 55–60.

Combs, G., Jr., & Ludwig, A. M. (1982). Dissociative disorders. In J. H. Greist, J. W. Jefferson, & R. L. Spitzer (Eds.), *Treatment of mental disorders* (pp. 309–319). New York: Oxford University Press.

Connors, M. E., Johnson, C. L., & Stuckey, M. K. (1984). Treatment of bulimia with brief psychoeducational group therapy. *American Journal of Psychiatry, 141,* 1512–1516.

Conte, H. R., Plutchik, R., Wild, K. V., & Karasu, T. B. (1986). Combined psychotherapy and pharmacotherapy for depression. *Archives of General Psychiatry, 43,* 471–479.

Cornell, D. G., Silk, K. R., Ludolph, P. S., & Lohr, N. E. (1983). Test-retest reliability of the diagnostic interview for borderlines. *Archives of General Psychiatry, 40,* 1307–1310.

Coryell, W., Lavori, P., Endicott, J., Keller, M., & Van Eerdewegh, M. (1984). Outcome in schizoaffective, psychotic, and nonpsychotic depression. *Archives of General Psychiatry, 41,* 787–791.

Coryell, W., & Tsuang, M. T. (1986). Outcome after 40 years in *DSM-III* schizophreniform disorder. *Archives of General Psychiatry, 43,* 324–328.

Coryell, W., & Winokur, G. (1982). Course and outcome. In E. S. Paykel (Ed.), *Handbook of affective disorders* (pp. 93–106). New York: Guilford Press.

Craighead, W. E., Kennedy, R. E., Raczynski, J. M., & Dow, M. G. (1984). Affective disorders—unipolar. In S. M. Turner & M. Hersen (Eds.), *Adult psychopathology and diagnosis* (pp. 184–244). New York: Wiley.

Custer, R. L. (1984). Profile of the pathological gambler. *Journal of Clinical Psychiatry, 45,* 35–38.

Day, M., & Manschreck, T. C. (1988). Delusional (paranoic) disorders. In A. M. Nicholi, Jr. (Ed.), *The new Harvard guide to psychiatry* (pp. 296–308). Cambridge, MA: Harvard University Press.

Deitch, J. T. (1981). Diagnosis of organic anxiety disorders. *Psychosomatics, 22,* 661–669.

Diagnostic and statistical manual of mental disorders (DSM-III-R) (3rd ed. rev.) (1987). Washington, DC: American Psychiatric Association.

Donovan, J. M., Bennett, M. J., & McElroy, C. M. (1981). The crisis group: Its rationale, format, and outcome. In S. H. Budman (Ed.), *Forms of brief therapy* (pp. 283–303). New York: Guilford Press.

Dorr, D., Barley, W. D., Gard, B., & Webb, C. (1983). Understanding and treating borderline personality organization. *Psychotherapy: Theory, Research and Practice, 20,* 397–407.

DSM-III-R. See *Diagnostic and statistical manual . . .*

Durham, R. C., & Turvey, A. A. (1987). Cognitive therapy vs. behavior therapy in the treatment of chronic general anxiety. *Behaviour Research and Therapy, 25,* 229–234.

Emmelkamp, P.M.G. (1986). Behavior therapy with adults. In S. L. Garfield & A. E. Bergin (Eds.), *Handbook of psychotherapy and behavior change* (3rd ed., pp. 385–442). New York: Wiley.

Endicott, J., Cohen, J., Nee, J., Fleiss, J., & Sarantakos, S. (1981). Hamilton Depression Rating Scale. *Archives of General Psychiatry, 38,* 98–103.

Esman, A. H. (1986). Dependent and passive-aggressive personality disorders. In A. M. Cooper, A. J. Frances, & M. H. Sacks (Eds.), *The personality disorders and neuroses* (pp. 283–289). Philadelphia: Lippincott.

Everaerd, W., & Dekker, J. (1985). Treatment of male sexual dysfunction: Sex therapy compared with systematic desensitization and rational emotive therapy. *Behaviour Research and Therapy, 23,* 13–25.

Everly, G. S., Jr. (1986). A biopsychosocial analysis of psychosomatic disease. In T. Millon & G. Klerman (Eds.), *Contemporary directions in psychopathology* (pp. 535–551). New York: Guilford Press.

Eysenck, H. J. (1952). The effects of psychotherapy: An evaluation. *Journal of Consulting Psychology, 16,* 319–324.

Eysenck, H. J. (1966). *The effects of psychotherapy.* New York: International Science Press.

Feinberg, M., & Carroll, B. J. (1984). Biological "markers" for endogenous depression. *Archives of General Psychiatry, 41*, 1080–1085.

Felton, B. J., & Revenson, T. A. (1984). Coping with chronic illness: A study of illness controllability and the influence of coping strategies on psychological adjustment. *Journal of Clinical and Consulting Psychology, 52*, 343–353.

Fishbein, D. (1985). Biofeedback applications to psychiatric disorders. *Psychological Record, 35*, 3–21.

Flach, F. (Ed.). (1987). *Diagnostics and psychopathology*. New York: Norton.

Foa, E. B., Grayson, J. B., Steketee, G. S., Doppelt, H. G., Turner, R. M., & Latimer, P. R. (1983). Success and failure in the behavioral treatment of obsessive-compulsives. *Journal of Consulting and Clinical Psychology, 51*, 287–297.

Foa, E. B., & Steketee, G. S. (1979). Obsessive-compulsives: Conceptual issues and treatment interventions. *Progress in Behavior Modification, 8*, 1–53.

Foa, E. B., Steketee, G. S., Grayson, J. B., & Doppelt, H. G. (1982). Treatment of obsessive-compulsives: When do we fail? In E. B. Foa & P.M.G. Emmelkamp (Eds.), *Failures in behavior therapy*. New York: Wiley, 1982.

Foreyt, J. P., & Kondo, A. T. (1985). Eating disorders. In M. Hersen & S. M. Turner (Eds.), *Diagnostic interviewing* (pp. 243–259). New York: Plenum Press.

Forrest, G. G. (1985). Psychodynamically oriented treatment of alcoholism and substance abuse. In T. E. Bratter & G. G. Forrest (Eds.), *Alcoholism and substance abuse* (pp. 307–336). New York: Free Press.

Fowler, R. C., Rich, C. L., & Young, D. (1986). Substance abuse in young cases. *Archives of General Psychiatry, 43*, 962–965.

Frances, A., Clarkin, J., & Perry, S. (1984). *Differential therapeutics in psychiatry*. NY: Brunner/Mazel.

Frances, A. J. (1988). Introduction to personality disorders. In A. M. Nicholi, Jr. (Ed.), *The new Harvard guide to psychiatry* (pp. 171–176). Cambridge, MA: Harvard University Press.

Frances, R. J., & Allen, M. J. (1986). The interaction of substance-use disorders with nonpsychotic psychiatric disorders. In A. M.

Cooper, A. J. Frances, & M. H. Sacks (Eds.), *The personality disorders and neuroses* (pp. 425–437). Philadelphia: Lippincott.

Friedman, J. M., & Hogan, D. R. (1985). Sexual dysfunction: Low sexual desire. In D. H. Barlow (Ed.), *Clinical handbook of psychological disorders* (pp. 417–461). New York: Guilford Press.

Frosch, W. A., Frosch, J. P., & Frosch, J. (1986). The impulse disorders. In A. M. Cooper, A. J. Frances, & M. H. Sacks (Eds.), *The personality disorders and neuroses* (pp. 275–282). Philadelphia: Lippincott.

Frye, J. S., & Stockton, R. A. (1982). Discriminant analysis of posttraumatic stress disorder among a group of Viet Nam veterans. *American Journal of Psychiatry, 139,* 52–61.

Fyer, A. J., & Klein, D. F. (1986). Agoraphobia, social phobia, and simple phobia. In A. M. Cooper, A. J. Frances, & M. H. Sacks (Eds.), *The personality disorders and neuroses* (pp. 339–352). Philadelphia: Lippincott.

Garakani, H., Zitrin, C. M., & Klein, D. (1984). Treatment of panic disorder with imipramine alone. *American Journal of Psychiatry, 141,* 445–448.

Garfield, S. L. (1986). Research on client variables in psychotherapy. In S. L. Garfield & A. E. Bergin (Eds.), *Handbook of psychotherapy and behavior change* (3rd ed., pp. 213–256). New York: Wiley.

Gawin, F. H., & Kleber, H. D. (1984). Cocaine abuse treatment. *Archives of General Psychiatry, 41,* 903–909.

Getto, C. J., & Ochitill, H. (1982). Psychogenic pain disorder. In J. H. Greist, J. W. Jefferson, & R. L. Spitzer (Eds.), *Treatment of mental disorders* (pp. 277–286). New York: Oxford University Press.

Gilmore, M. M., & Kaufman, C. (1986). Dissociative disorders. In A. M. Cooper, A. J. Frances, & M. H. Sacks (Eds.), *The personality disorders and neuroses* (pp. 383–394). Philadelphia: Lippincott.

Glassner, B., & Haldipur, C. V. (1983). Life events and early and late onset of bipolar disorder. *American Journal of Psychiatry, 140,* 215–217.

Goldberg, S. C., Schultz, S. C., Schultz, P. M., Resnick, R. J., Havner, R. M., & Friedel, R. O. (1986). Borderline and schizotypal personality disorders treated with low-dose thiothixene vs. placebo. *Archives of General Psychiatry, 43,* 680–686.

Goodwin, D. W. (1984). Studies of familial alcoholism: A review. *Journal of Clinical Psychiatry, 45,* 14–17.

Goplerud, E., & Depue, R. A. (1985). Behavioral response to naturally occurring stress in cyclothymia and dysthymia. *Journal of Abnormal Psychology, 94,* 128–139.

Gorman, J. M., & Liebowitz, M. R. (1986). Panic and anxiety disorders. In A. M. Cooper, A. J. Frances, & M. H. Sacks (Eds.), *The personality disorders and neuroses* (pp. 325–337). Philadelphia: Lippincott.

Gotlib, I. H., & Colby, C. A. (1987). *Treatment of depression.* Elmsford, NY: Pergamon Press.

Greenblatt, D. J., & Shader, R. I. (1974). *Benzodiazepines in clinical practice.* New York: Raven Press.

Greenspan, M., & Kulish, N. M. (1985). Factors in premature termination in long-term psychotherapy. *Psychotherapy: Theory, Research and Practice, 22,* 75–82.

Gunderson, J. G. (1984). *Borderline personality disorder.* Washington, DC: American Psychiatric Association.

Gunderson, J. G. (1988). Personality disorders. In A. M. Nicholi, Jr. (Ed.), *The new Harvard guide to psychiatry* (pp. 337–357). Cambridge, MA: Harvard University Press.

Gurman, A. S. (1981). Integrative marital therapy: Toward the development of an interpersonal approach. In S. H. Budman (Ed.), *Forms of brief therapy* (pp. 415–457). New York: Guilford Press.

Gurman, A. S., Kniskern, D. P., & Pinsof, W. M. (1986). Research on the process and outcome of marital and family therapy. In S. L. Garfield & A. E. Bergin (Eds.), *Handbook of psychotherapy and behavior change* (3rd ed., pp. 565–624). New York: Wiley.

Gutride, M. E., Goldstein, A. P., & Hunter, G. F. (1973). The use of modeling and role playing to increase social interaction among asocial psychiatric patients. *Journal of Consulting and Clinical Psychology, 40,* 408–415.

Gutsch, K. U. (1988). *Psychotherapeutic approaches to specific DSM-III-R categories.* Springfield, IL: Thomas.

Hafner, R. J. (1984). Predicting the effects on husbands of behaviour therapy for wives' agoraphobia. *Behaviour Research and Therapy, 22,* 217-226.

Harbin, H. T. (1981). Family therapy with personality disorders. In J. R. Lion (Ed.), *Personality disorders: Diagnosis and management* (2nd ed.). Baltimore: Williams & Wilkins.

Harmon, T., Nelson, R., & Hayes, S. (1980). Self-monitoring of mood versus activity by depressed clients. *Journal of Consulting and Clinical Psychology, 48,* 30-38.

Harris, E. L., Noyes, R., Jr., Crowe, R. R., & Chaudhry, D. R. (1983). Family study of agoraphobia. *Archives of General Psychiatry, 40,* 1061-1064.

Helzer, J. E. (1986). Schizophrenia: Epidemiology. In J. E. Helzer & S. B. Guze (Eds.), *Psychoses, affective disorders, and dementia* (pp. 45-61). New York: Basic Books.

Hendler, N. (1981). Group therapy with chronic pain patients. *Psychosomatics, 22,* 333-340.

Herzog, D. B. (1984). Are anorexic and bulimic patients depressed? *American Journal of Psychiatry, 141,* 1594-1597.

Herzog, D. B., Norman, D. K., Gordon, C., & Pepose, M. (1984). Sexual conflict and eating disorders in 27 males. *American Journal of Psychiatry, 141,* 989-990.

Hesselbrock, M. N., Meyer, R. E., & Keener, J. J. (1985). Psychopathology in hospitalized alcoholics. *Archives of General Psychiatry, 42,* 1050-1055.

Hesselbrock, V., Stabenau, J., Hesselbrock, M., Mirkin, P., & Meyer, R. (1982). A comparison of two interview schedules. *Archives of General Psychiatry, 39,* 674-677.

Hill, D. (1970). Outpatient management of passive-dependent women. *Hospital and Community Psychiatry, 21,* 402-405.

Hirschfeld, M. A., & Cross, C. K. (1982). Epidemiology of affective disorders. *Archives of General Psychiatry, 39,* 35-46.

Hirschfeld, R.M.A., Klerman, G. L., Clayton, P. J., & Keller, M. B. (1983). Personality and depression. *Archives of General Psychiatry, 40,* 993-998.

Hoffman, J. J. (1985). Client factors related to premature termination of psychotherapy. *Psychotherapy: Theory, Research and Practice, 22,* 83-85.

Hogarty, G. E., Anderson, C. M., Reiss, D. J., Kornblith, S. J.,

Greenwald, D. P., & Javna, C. D. (1986). Family psychoeducation, social skills training, and maintenance chemotherapy in the aftercare treatment of schizophrenia. *Archives of General Psychiatry, 43*, 633–642.

Hollon, S. D., & Beck, A. T. (1986). Cognitive and cognitive-behavioral therapies. In S. L. Garfield & A. E. Bergin (Eds.), *Handbook of psychotherapy and behavior change* (3rd ed., pp. 443–482). New York: Wiley.

Horowitz, M., Marmar, C., Krupnick, J., Wilner, N., Kaltreider, N., & Wallerstein, R. (1984). *Personality styles and brief psychotherapy*. New York: Basic Books.

Horowitz, M. J., Marmar, C., Weiss, D. S., DeWitt, K. N., & Rosenbaum, R. (1984). Brief psychotherapy of bereavement reactions. *Archives of General Psychiatry, 41*, 438–448.

Horvath, P. (1984). Demand characteristics and inferential processes in psychotherapeutic change. *Journal of Consulting and Clinical Psychology, 52*, 616–624.

Howard, G. S., Nance, D. W., & Myers, P. (1987). *Adaptive counseling and therapy: A systematic approach to selecting effective treatments*. San Francisco: Jossey-Bass.

Howard, K. I., Kopta, S. M., Krause, M. S., & Orlinsky, D. E. (1986). The dose-effect relationship in psychotherapy. *American Psychologist, 41*, 159–164.

Hudson, J. I., Pope, H. G., Yurgelun-Todd, D., & Jonas, J. M. (1987). A controlled study of lifetime prevalence of affective and other psychiatric disorders in bulimic outpatients. *American Journal of Psychiatry, 144*, 1283–1287.

Hughes, C. W., Preskorn, S. H., Adams, R. N., & Kent, T. A. (1986). Neurobiological etiology of schizophrenia and affective disorders. In J. E. Helzer & S. B. Guze (Eds.), *Psychoses, affective disorders, and dementia* (pp. 193–208). New York: Basic Books.

Hughes, P. L., Wells, L. A., Cunningham, C. J., & Ilstrup, D. M. (1986). Treating bulimia with Desipramine. *Archives of General Psychiatry, 43*, 182–186.

Hurt, S. W., Holzman, P. S., & David, J. M. (1983). Thought disorder. *Archives of General Psychiatry, 40*, 1281–1285.

Hutchings, D. F., Denney, D. R., Basgall, J., & Houston, B. K.

(1980). Anxiety management and applied relaxation in reducing general anxiety. *Behaviour Research and Therapy, 18,* 181–190.

Jacobson, A., & McKinney, W. T. (1982). Affective disorders. In J. H. Greist, J. W. Jefferson, & R. L. Spitzer (Eds.), *Treatment of mental disorders* (pp. 184–233). New York: Oxford University Press.

Jarrett, R. B., & Rush, A. J. (1986). Psychotherapeutic approaches for depression. In J. E. Helzer & S. B. Guze (Eds.), *Psychoses, affective disorders, and dementia* (pp. 209–243). New York: Basic Books.

Jefferson, J. W., & Ochitill, H. (1982). Factitious disorders. In J. H. Greist, J. W. Jefferson, & R. L. Spitzer (Eds.), *Treatment of mental disorders* (pp. 387–397). New York: Oxford University Press.

Jellinek, E. M. (1971). Phases of alcohol addiction. In G. D. Shean (Ed.), *Studies in abnormal behavior.* Skokie, IL: Rand McNally.

Johnson, C., & Flach, A. (1985). Family characteristics of 105 patients with bulimia. *American Journal of Psychiatry, 142,* 1321–1324.

Johnson, D. L. (1988, March). A father: The search for help leads to NAMI. *APA Monitor,* p. 9.

Kahn, R. J., McNair, D. M., Lipman, R. S., Covi, L., Rickels, K., Downing, R., Fisher, S., & Frankenthaler, L. M. (1986). Imipramine and chlordiazepoxide in depressive and anxiety disorders. *Archives of General Psychiatry, 43,* 79–85.

Kales, J. D., Soldatos, C. R., & Kales, A. (1982). Diagnosis and treatment of sleep disorders. In J. H. Greist, J. W. Jefferson, & R. L. Spitzer (Eds.), *Treatment of mental disorders* (pp. 473–500). New York: Oxford University Press.

Kanfer, F. H. (1972). Self-regulation and its clinical application: Some additional conceptualizations. In R. C. Johnson, P. R. Dokecki, & O. H. Mowrer (Eds.), *Socialization: Development of character and conscience.* New York: Holt, Rinehart & Winston.

Kanter, N. J., & Goldfried, M. R. (1979). Relative effectiveness of rational restructuring and self-control densensitization in the reduction of interpersonal anxiety. *Behavior Therapy, 10,* 472–490.

Kaplan, H. I., & Sadock, B. J. (1985). *Modern synopsis of comprehensive textbook of psychiatry.* Baltimore: Williams & Wilkins.

Kaplan, H. S. (1979). *Disorders of sexual desire.* New York: Brunner/Mazel.

Kaplan, H. S. (1986). Psychosexual dysfunctions. In A. M. Cooper, A. J. Frances, & M. H. Sacks (Eds.), *The personality disorders and neuroses* (pp. 467–479). Philadelphia: Lippincott.

Karasu, T. (1982). Psychotherapy and pharmacotherapy: Toward an integrative model. *American Journal of Psychiatry, 139,* 1102–1113.

Karasu, T. (1986). The specificity versus nonspecificity dilemma: Toward identifying therapeutic change agents. *American Journal of Psychiatry, 143,* 687–695.

Kass, D. J., Silvers, F. M., & Abroms, G. M. (1972). Behavioral group treatment of hysteria. *Archives of General Psychiatry, 26,* 42–50.

Kaufman, G. B., Jr., & Aronoff, G. M. (1983). The use of psychomotor therapy in the treatment of chronic pain. *Psychotherapy: Theory, Research and Practice, 20,* 449–456.

Kazdin, A. E. (1986). The evaluation of psychotherapy: Research design and methodology. In S. L. Garfield & A. E. Bergin (Eds.), *Handbook of psychotherapy and behavior change* (3rd ed., pp. 23–68). New York: Wiley.

Kazdin, A. E., & Wilson, G. T. (1978). *Evaluation of behavior therapy: Issues, evidence and research strategies.* Cambridge, MA: Ballinger.

Keller, M. B., Lavori, P. W., Endicott, J., Coryell, W., & Klerman, G. L. (1983). "Double depression": Two-year follow-up. *American Journal of Psychiatry, 140,* 689–694.

Kellner, R. (1982a). Personality disorders. In J. H. Greist, J. W. Jefferson, & R. L. Spitzer (Eds.), *Treatment of mental disorders* (pp. 429–454). New York: Oxford University Press.

Kellner, R. (1982b). Psychotherapeutic strategies in hypochondriasis: A clinical study. *American Journal of Psychotherapy, 36,* 146–157.

Kellner, R. (1985). Functional somatic symptoms and hypochondriasis. *Archives of General Psychiatry, 42,* 821–833.

Kendell, R. E. (1986). Schizophrenia: Clinical features. In J. E. Helzer & S. B. Guze (Eds.), *Psychoses, affective disorders, and dementia* (pp. 25–44). New York: Basic Books.

Kernberg, O. F. (1985). *Borderline conditions and pathological narcissism.* New York: Jason Aronson.

Kernberg, O. F. (1986). Hysterical and histrionic personality disorders. In A. M. Cooper, A. J. Frances, & M. H. Sacks (Eds.), *The personality disorders and neuroses* (pp. 231–241). Philadelphia: Lippincott.

Kleber, H. D., & Gawin, F. H. (1984). The spectrum of cocaine abuse and its treatment. *Journal of Clinical Psychiatry, 45,* 18–23.

Klein, D. F., Zitrin, C. M., Woerner, M. G., & Ross, D. C. (1983). Treatment of phobias: II. Behavior therapy and supportive psychotherapy: Are there any specific ingredients? *Archives of General Psychiatry, 40,* 139–145.

Klerman, G. L. (1986). Drugs and psychotherapy. In S. L. Garfield & A. E. Bergin (Eds.), *Handbook of psychotherapy and behavior change* (3rd ed., pp. 777–818). New York: Wiley.

Klerman, G. L., Dimascio, A., & Weissman, M. (1974). Treatment of depresson by drugs and psychotherapy. *American Journal of Psychiatry, 131,* 186–191.

Klerman, G. L., Lavori, P. W., Rice, J., Reich, T., Endicott, J., Andreasen, N. C., Keller, M. B., & Hirschfield, R.M.A. (1985). Birth-cohort trends in rates of major depressive disorder among relatives of patients with affective disorders. *Archives of General Psychiatry, 42,* 689–693.

Klerman, G. L., Weissman, M. M., Rounsaville, B. J., & Chevron, E. S. (1984). *Interpersonal psychotherapy of depression.* New York: Basic Books.

Kluft, R. P. (1987). Making the diagnosis of multiple personality disorder. In F. Flach (Ed.), *Diagnostics and psychopathology* (pp. 207–225). New York: Norton.

Kocsis, J. H., & Mann, J. J. (1986). Drug treatment of personality disorders and neuroses. In A. M. Cooper, A. J. Frances, & M. H. Sacks (Eds.), *The personality disorders and neuroses* (pp. 129–137). Philadelphia: Lippincott.

Kohut, H. (1971). *The analysis of self.* New York: International Universities Press.

Kornblith, S. H., Rehm, L. P., O'Hara, M. W., & Lamparski, D. M. (1983). The contribution of self-reinforcement training and behavioral assignments to the efficacy of self-control therapy for depression. *Cognitive Therapy and Research, 7,* 499-528.

Koss, M. P., & Butcher, J. N. (1986). Research on brief psychotherapy. In S. L. Garfield & A. E. Bergin (Eds.), *Handbook of psychotherapy and behavior change* (3rd ed., pp. 627-670). New York: Wiley.

Kosten, T. R., Rounsaville, B. J., & Kleber, H. D. (1986). A 2.5-year follow-up of depression, life crises, and treatment effects on abstinence among opioid addicts. *Archives of General Psychiatry, 43,* 733-738.

Kovacs, M., Rush, A. J., Beck, A. T., & Hollon, S. D. (1981). Depressed outpatients treated with cognitive therapy or pharmacotherapy. *Archives of General Psychiatry, 38,* 33-39.

Lambert, M. J. (1982). *The effects of psychotherapy.* New York: Human Sciences Press.

Lambert, M. J., Shapiro, D. A., & Bergin, A. E. (1986). The effectiveness of psychotherapy. In S. L. Garfield & A. E. Bergin (Eds.), *Handbook of psychotherapy and behavior change* (3rd ed., pp. 157-211). New York: Wiley.

Lars-Göran, O. (1987). Age of onset in different phobias. *Journal of Abnormal Psychology, 96,* 223-229.

Layne, C. (1984). Painful truths about depressives' cognitions. *Journal of Clinical Psychology, 39,* 848-853.

Leaff, L. A. (1974). Psychodynamic aspects of personality disturbances. In J. R. Lion (Ed.), *Personality disorders* (pp. 1-15). Baltimore: Williams & Wilkins.

Leckman, J. F., Weissman, M. M., Merikangas, K. R., Pauls, D. L., & Prusoff, B. A. (1983). Panic disorder and major depression. *Archives of General Psychiatry, 40,* 1055-1066.

Leigh, G. (1985). Psychosocial factors in the etiology of substance abuse. In T. E. Bratter & G. G. Forrest (Eds.), *Alcoholism and substance abuse* (pp. 3-48). New York: Free Press.

Lewinsohn, P. M., & Hoberman, H. M. (1982). Behavioural and cognitive approaches. In E. S. Paykel (Ed.), *Handbook of affective disorders* (pp. 338-345). New York: Guilford Press.

Lewinsohn, P. M., Sullivan, M., & Grosscup, S. (1980). Changing reinforcing events: An approach to the treatment of depression. *Psychotherapy: Theory, Research and Practice, 17,* 322-334.

Liberman, R. P., & Eckman, T. (1981). Behavior therapy vs. insight-oriented therapy for repeated suicide attempters. *Archives of General Psychiatry, 38,* 1126–1130.

Liebowitz, M. R., Gorman, J. M., Fyer, A. J., & Klein, D. F. (1985). Social phobia. *Archives of General Psychiatry, 42,* 729–736.

Lief, H. I. (1981). *Sexual problems in medical practice.* Chicago: American Medical Association.

Lilienfeld, S. O., VanValkenburg, C., Larntz, K., & Akiskal, H. S. (1986). The relation of histrionic personality disorder to antisocial personality and somatization disorders. *American Journal of Psychiatry, 143,* 718–722.

Linden, W. (1981). Exposure treatments for focal phobias. *Archives of General Psychiatry, 38,* 769–775.

Linehan, M. M., Goldfried, M. R., & Goldfried, A. P. (1979). Group versus individual assertion training. *Journal of Consulting and Clinical Psychology, 47,* 1000–1002.

Lion, J. R. (1981). Countertransference and other psychotherapy issues. In W. H. Reid (Ed.), *The treatment of antisocial syndromes.* New York: Van Nostrand Reinhold.

Longabough, R., Fowler, D. R., Stout, R., & Kriebel, G., Jr. (1983). Validation of a problem-focused nomenclature. *Archives of General Psychiatry, 40,* 453–461.

Loranger, A. W. (1984). Sex difference in age at onset of schizophrenia. *Archives of General Psychiatry, 41,* 157–161.

Loranger, A. W., & Tulis, E. H. (1985). Family history of alcoholism in borderline personality disorder. *Archives of General Psychiatry, 42,* 153–157.

Luborsky, L. (1972, June). *Comparative studies of psychotherapies—Is it true that everybody has won and all must have prizes?* Paper presented at 3rd annual meeting of the Society for Psychotherapy Research, Nashville, TN.

Luborsky, L., McLellan, A. T., Woody, G. E., O'Brien, C. P., & Auerbach, A. (1985). Therapist success and its determinants. *Archives of General Psychiatry, 42,* 602–611.

Luborsky, L., Singer, B., & Luborsky, L. (1975). Comparative studies of psychotherapies. *Archives of General Psychiatry, 32,* 995–1008.

Maddux, J. F., & Desmond, D. P. (1982). Residence relocation inhibits opioid dependence. *Archives of General Psychiatry, 39,* 1313–1317.

Marks, I. (1982). Anxiety disorders. In J. H. Greist, J. W. Jefferson, & R. L. Spitzer (Eds.), *Treatment of mental disorders* (pp. 234–264). New York: Oxford University Press.

Marshall, W. L. (1985). The effects of variable exposure in flooding therapy. *Behavior Therapy, 16,* 117–135.

Marshall, W. L., & Barbaree, H. E. (1984). Disorders of personality, impulse, and adjustment. In S. M. Turner & M. Hersen (Eds.), *Adult psychopathology and diagnosis* (pp. 406–452). New York: Wiley.

Marziali, E. A. (1984). Prediction of outcome of brief psychotherapy from therapist interpretive interventions. *Archives of General Psychiatry, 41,* 301–304.

Masters, W. H., & Johnson, V. E. (1970). *Human sexual inadequacy.* Boston: Little, Brown.

Masterson, J. F. (1981). *The narcissistic and borderline disorders.* New York: Brunner/Mazel.

Matthews, A., Gelder, M., & Johnson, D. (1981). *Agoraphobia: Nature and treatment.* New York: Guilford Press.

Mavissakalian, M. R., & Barlow, D. H. (1981). Assessment of obsessive-compulsive disorders. In D. H. Barlow (Ed.), *Behavioral assessment of adult disorders* (pp. 209–238). New York: Guilford Press.

Mavissakalian, M., Michelson, L., Greenwald, D., Kornblith, S., & Greenwald, M. (1983). Cognitive-behavioral treatment of agoraphobia: Paradoxical intention vs. self-statement training. *Behaviour Research and Therapy, 21,* 75–86.

Mavissakalian, M., Turner, S. M., Michelson, L., & Jacob, R. (1985). Tricyclic antidepressants in obsessive-compulsive disorder: Antiobsessional or antidepressant agents? *American Journal of Psychiatry, 142,* 572–576.

Maxmen, J. S. (1986). *Essential psychopathology.* New York: Norton.

May, P.R.A., Tuma, A. H., & Dixon, W. J. (1976). Schizophrenia: A follow-up study of results of treatment. *Archives of General Psychiatry, 33,* 474–478.

May, P.R.A., Tuma, A. H., & Dixon, W. J. (1981). Schizophrenia. *Archives of General Psychiatry, 38,* 776–784.

McConaghy, N. (1984). Psychosexual disorders. In S. M. Turner & M. Hersen (Eds.), *Adult psychopathology and diagnosis* (pp. 370–405). New York: Wiley.

McCormick, R. A., Russo, A. M., Ramirez, L. F., & Taber, J. I. (1984). Affective disorders among pathological gamblers seeking treatment. *American Journal of Psychiatry, 141,* 215–218.

McCrady, B. S. (1985). Alcoholism. In D. H. Barlow (Ed.), *Clinical handbook of psychological disorders.* New York: Guilford Press.

McDaniel, E. (1981). Personality disorders in private practice. In J. R. Lion (Ed.), *Personality disorders: Diagnosis and management* (2nd ed.). Baltimore: Williams & Wilkins.

McGlashan, T. H. (1983a). The borderline syndrome. *Archives of General Psychiatry, 40,* 1319–1323.

McGlashan, T. H. (1983b). Intensive individual psychotherapy of schizophrenia. *Archives of General Psychiatry, 40,* 909–920.

McGlashan, T. H. (1986a). Long-term outcome of borderline personalities. *Archives of General Psychiatry, 43,* 20–30.

McGlashan, T. H. (1986b). Schizotypal personality disorder. *Archives of General Psychiatry, 43,* 329–334.

McHugh, P. R., & Folstein, M. F. (1986). Organic mental disorders. In J. E. Helzer & S. B. Guze (Eds.), *Psychoses, affective disorders, and dementia* (pp. 333–353). New York: Basic Books.

McLean, P. D., & Hakstian, A. R. (1979). Clinical depression: Comparative efficacy of out-patient treatment. *Journal of Consulting and Clinical Psychology, 47,* 818–836.

McLellan, A. T., Luborsky, L., Woody, G. E., O'Brien, C. P., & Druley, K. A. (1983). Predicting response to alcohol and drug abuse treatments. *Archives of General Psychiatry, 40,* 620–625.

Meichenbaum, D. H., & Deffenbacher, J. L. (1988). Stress inoculation training. *The Counseling Psychologist, 16,* 69–90.

Mellinger, G. D., Balter, M. B., & Uhlenhuth, E. H. (1985). Insomnia and its treatment. *Archives of General Psychiatry, 42,* 225–232.

Meltzoll, J., & Kornreich, M. (1970). *Research in psychotherapy.* Hawthorne, NY: Aldine.

Mendelsohn, R. (1981). "Active attention" and "focusing" on the transference/countertransference in the psychotherapy of the borderline patient. *Psychotherapy: Theory, Research and Practice, 18,* 386–393.

Merikangas, K. R. (1984). Divorce and assortive mating among depressed patients. *American Journal of Psychiatry, 141,* 74–76.

Meyer, R. (1983). *The clinician's handbook.* Boston: Allyn & Bacon.

Mezzich, J. E., Evanczuk, K. J., Mathias, R. J., & Coffman, G. A. (1984). Symptoms and hospitalization decisions. *American Journal of Psychiatry, 141,* 764–769.

Miller, P. M. (1981). Assessment of alcohol abuse. In D. H. Barlow (Ed.), *Behavioral assessment of adult disorders* (pp. 271–299). New York: Guilford Press.

Miller, W. R., & Hester, R. K. (1986). Inpatient alcoholism treatment: Who benefits? *American Psychologist, 41,* 794–805.

Millman, H. L., Huber, J. T., & Diggins, D. R. (1982). *Therapies for adults: Depressive, anxiety, and personality disorders.* San Francisco: Jossey-Bass.

Millon, T. (1981). *Disorders of personality: DSM-III: Axis II.* New York: Wiley.

Millon, T. (1986). The avoidant personality. In A. M. Cooper, A. J. Frances, & M. H. Sacks (Eds.), *The personality disorders and neuroses* (pp. 263–273). Philadelphia: Lippincott.

Millon, T. (1987). *Manual for the MCMI-II.* Minneapolis: National Computer Systems.

Millon, T., & Klerman, G. (1986). *Contemporary directions in psychopathology.* New York: Guilford Press.

Mindham, R.H.S. (1982). Tricyclic antidepressants and amine precursors. In E. S. Paykel (Ed.), *Handbook of affective disorders* (pp. 231–245). New York: Guilford Press.

Minuchin, S., Rosman, B. L., & Baker, L. (1978). *Psychosomatic families: Anorexia nervosa in context.* Cambridge, MA: Harvard University Press.

Mitchell, J. E., Hatsukami, D., Eckert, E. D., & Pyle, R. D. (1985). Characteristics of 275 patients with bulimia. *American Journal of Psychiatry, 142,* 482–487.

Mogul, K. M. (1982). Overview: The sex of the therapist. *American Journal of Psychiatry, 139,* 1–11.

Monroe, S. M., Bellack, A. S., Hersen, M., & Himmelhoch, J. M.

(1983). Life events, symptom course, and treatment outcome in unipolar depressed women. *Journal of Consulting and Clinical Psychology, 51,* 604–615.

Moras, K., & Strupp, H. H. (1982). Pretherapy interpersonal relations, patients' alliance, and outcome in brief therapy. *Archives of General Psychiatry, 39,* 405–409.

Morgan, R., Luborsky, L., Crits-Cristoph, P., Curtis, H., & Solomon, J. (1982). Predicting the outcomes of psychotherapy by the Penn Helping Alliance Rating Method. *Archives of General Psychiatry, 39,* 397–402.

Morgan, W. P. (1979). Anxiety reduction following acute physical activity. *Psychiatric Annals, 9,* 24–45.

Murphy, G. A. (1986). Suicide and attempted suicide. In J. E. Helzer & S. B. Guze (Eds.), *Psychoses, affective disorders, and dementia* (pp. 299–315). New York: Basic Books.

Murphy, G. E., Simons, A. D., Wetzel, R. D., & Lustman, P. J. (1984). Cognitive therapy and pharmacotherapy. *Archives of General Psychiatry, 41,* 33–41.

Myers, I. B., & McCauley, M. H. (1985). *A guide to the development and use of the Myers-Briggs Type Indicator.* Palo Alto, CA: Consulting Psychologists Press.

Myers, J. K., Weissman, M. M., Tischler, G. L., Holer, C. E., III, Leaf, P. J., Orvaschel, H., Anthony, J. C., Boyd, J. H., Burke, J. D., Jr., Kramer, M., & Stoltzman, R. (1984). Six-month prevalence of psychiatric disorders in three communities. *Archives of General Psychiatry, 41,* 959–967.

Myers, R. A. (1986). Research on educational and vocational counseling. In S. L. Garfield & A. E. Bergin (Eds.), *Handbook of psychotherapy and behavior change* (3rd ed., pp. 715–738). New York: Wiley.

National Institutes of Health (n.d.). *Mood disorders: Pharmacologic prevention of recurrences. Consensus Statement* (Vol. 4). Bethesda, MD: National Institutes of Health.

Nemiah, J. C. (1988). Psychoneurotic disorders. In A. M. Nicholi, Jr. (Ed.), *The new Harvard guide to psychiatry* (pp. 234–258). Cambridge, MA: Harvard University Press.

Nichols, M. (1984). *Family therapy.* New York: Gardner Press.

Nicholson, R. A., & Berman, J. S. (1983). Is follow-up necessary in evaluating psychotherapy? *Psychological Bulletin, 93,* 261–278.

Nies, A., & Robinson, D. S. (1982). Monoamine oxidase inhibitors. In E. S. Paykel (Ed.), *Handbook of affective disorders* (pp. 246–261). New York: Guilford Press.

Nietzel, M. T., Russell, R. L., Hemmings, K. A., & Gretter, M. L. (1987). Clinical significance of psychotherapy for unipolar depression: A meta-analytic approach to social comparison. *Journal of Consulting and Clinical Psychology, 55,* 156–161.

O'Brien, C. P., Woody, G. E., & McLellan, A. T. (1984). Psychiatric disorders in opioid-dependent patients. *Journal of Clinical Psychiatry, 45,* 9–13.

O'Connor, J. (1984). Strategic individual psychotherapy with bulimic women. *Psychotherapy: Theory, Research and Practice, 21,* 491–499.

Oldham, J. M., & Frosch, W. A. (1986). The compulsive personality disorder. In A. M. Cooper, A. J. Frances, & M. H. Sacks (Eds.), *The personality disorders and neuroses* (pp. 243–250). Philadelphia: Lippincott.

Orlinsky, D. E., & Howard, K. I. (1978). The relation of process to outcome in psychotherapy. In S. L. Garfield & A. E. Bergin (Eds.), *Handbook of psychotherapy and behavior change* (2nd ed., pp. 283–329). New York: Wiley.

Orlinsky, D. E., & Howard, K. I. (1986). Process and outcome in psychotherapy. In S. L. Garfield & A. E. Bergin (Eds.), *Handbook of psychotherapy and behavior change* (3rd ed., pp. 311–381). New York: Wiley.

Ost, L., Jerremalm, A., & Jansson, L. (1984). Individual response patterns and the effects of different behavioral methods in the treatment of agoraphobia. *Behavioural Research and Therapy, 24,* 697–707.

Paquin, M. J. (1979). The treatment of obsessive compulsions by information feedback: A new application of a standard behavioral procedure. *Psychotherapy: Theory, Research and Practice, 16,* 292–296.

Parloff, M. B. (1986). Psychotherapy outcome research. In A. M. Cooper, A. J. Frances, & M. H. Sacks (Eds.), *The personality disorders and neuroses.* Philadelphia: Lippincott.

Perris, C. (1982). The distinction between bipolar and unipolar affective disorders. In E. S. Paykel (Ed.), *Handbook of affective disorders* (pp. 45–58). New York: Guilford Press.

Perry, S., Frances, A., & Clarkin, J. (1985). *A DSM-III casebook of differential therapeutics.* New York: Brunner/Mazel.

Person, E. S. (1986). Paraphilias and gender identity disorders. In A. M. Cooper, A. J. Frances, & M. H. Sacks (Eds.), *The personality disorders and neuroses* (pp. 447–465). Philadelphia: Lippincott.

Peselow, E. D., Dunner, D. L., Fieve, R. R., & Lautin, A. (1982). Lithium prophylaxis of depression in unipolar, bipolar II, and cyclothymic patients. *American Journal of Psychiatry, 139,* 747–757.

Philips, H. C. (1987). Avoidance behaviour and its role in sustaining chronic pain. *Behaviour Research and Therapy, 25,* 273–279.

Pilkonis, P. A., Imber, S. D., Lewis, P., & Rubinsky, P. (1984). A comparative outcome study of individual, group, and conjoint psychotherapy. *Archives of General Psychiatry, 41,* 431–437.

Polich, J. M., Armor, D. J., & Braiker, H. B. (1980). *The course of alcoholism: Four years after treatment.* Santa Monica, CA: Rand Corporation.

Pomerleau, O. F., & Rodin, J. (1986). Behavioral medicine and health psychology. In S. L. Garfield & A. E. Bergin (Eds.), *Handbook of psychotherapy and behavior change* (3rd ed., pp. 483–522). New York: Wiley.

Pope, H. G., Jr. (1987). Differential diagnosis of acute psychotic disorders. In F. Flach (Ed.), *Diagnostics and psychopathology* (pp. 39–48). New York: Norton.

Pope, H. G., Jr., Jones, J. M., Hudson, J. I., Cohen, B. M., & Gunderson, J. G. (1983). The validity of *DSM-III* borderline personality disorder. *Archives of General Psychiatry, 40,* 23–30.

Pope, H. G., Jr., Jones, J. M., & Jones, B. (1982). Factitious psychosis: Phenomenology, family history, and long-term outcome of nine patients. *American Journal of Psychiatry, 139,* 1480–1483.

Queiraz, L. O., Motta, M. A., Madi, M. B., Sossai, D. L., & Boren, J. J. (1981). A functional analysis of obsessive-compulsive problems with related therapeutic procedures. *Behaviour Research and Therapy, 19,* 377–388.

Rabin, A. S., Kaslow, N. J., & Rehm, L. P. (1985). Factors influencing continuation in a behavioral therapy. *Behaviour Research and Therapy, 23,* 695–698.

Rachman, A. W., & Raubolt, R. R. (1985). The clinical practice of group psychotherapy with adolescent substance abusers. In T. E. Bratter & G. G. Forrest (Eds.), *Alcoholism and substance abuse* (pp. 349–375). New York: Free Press.

Ramsey, R. A., Wittkower, E. D., & Warnes, H. (1976). Treatment of psychosomatic disorders. In B. B. Wolman (Ed.), *The therapist's handbook* (pp. 451–519). New York: Van Nostrand Reinhold.

Rapoport, J. L. (1989). *The boy who couldn't stop washing.* New York: Dutton.

Raskin, M., Peeke, H.V.S., Dickman, W., & Pinsker, H. (1982). Panic and generalized anxiety disorders. *Archives of General Psychiatry, 39,* 687–689.

Rehm, L. P. (1984). Self-management therapy for depression. *Advances in Behaviour Research and Therapy, 6,* 83–98.

Reid, W. H. (1983). *Treatment of the DSM-III psychiatric disorders.* New York: Brunner/Mazel.

Reid, W. H. (1986). Antisocial personality. In A. M. Cooper, A. J. Frances, & M. H. Sacks (Eds.), *The personality disorders and neuroses* (pp. 251–261). Philadelphia: Lippincott.

Retterstøl, N. (1986). Paranoid disorders. In J. E. Helzer & S. B. Guze (Eds.), *Psychoses, affective disorders, and dementia* (pp. 245–263). New York: Basic Books.

Rice, J. P., & McGuffin, P. (1986). Genetic etiology of schizophrenia and affective disorders. In J. E. Helzer & S. B. Guze (Eds.), *Psychoses, affective disorders, and dementia* (pp. 147–170). New York: Basic Books.

Richelson, E. (1986). Schizophrenia: Treatment. In J. E. Helzer & S. B. Guze (Eds.), *Psychoses, affective disorders, and dementia* (pp. 63–90). New York: Basic Books.

Rickels, K., & Case, G. W. (1982). Trazodone in depressed outpatients. *American Journal of Psychiatry, 139,* 803–806.

Robins, L. N., Helzer, J. E., Croughan, J., & Ratcliff, K. S. (1981). National Institute of Mental Health Diagnostic Interview Schedule. *Archives of General Psychiatry, 38,* 381–389.

Rogers, R. (1983). Role of retroflection in psychogenic pain: A treatment perspective. *Psychotherapy: Theory, Research and Practice, 20,* 435–444.

Roose, S. P., Glassman, A. H., Walsh, B. T., Woodring, S., & Vital-Herne, J. (1983). Depression, delusions, and suicide. *American Journal of Psychiatry, 140,* 1159–1162.

Rosenthal, T. L., & Rosenthal, R. H. (1985). Clinical stress management. In D. H. Barlow (Ed.), *Clinical handbook of psychological disorders* (pp. 145–205). New York: Guilford Press.

Rounsaville, B. J., Dolinsky, Z. S., Babor, T. F., & Meyer, R. E. (1987). Psychopathology as a predictor of treatment outcome in alcoholics. *Archives of General Psychiatry, 44,* 505–513.

Rounsaville, B. J., Weissman, M. M., Kleber, H., & Wilber, E. (1982). Heterogeneity of psychiatry diagnosis in treated opiate addicts. *Archives of General Psychiatry, 39,* 161–166.

Roy, A. (1981). Depression in the course of chronic undifferentiated schizophrenia. *Archives of General Psychiatry, 38,* 296–297.

Roy, A. (1983). Family history of suicide. *Archives of General Psychiatry, 40,* 971–974.

Roy-Byrne, P. P., Unde, T. W., & Post, R. M. (1986). Effects of one night's sleep deprivation on mood and behavior in panic disorder. *Archives of General Psychiatry, 43,* 895–899.

Rush, A. J., Beck, A. T., Kovacs, M., & Hollon, S. (1977). Comparative efficacy of cognitive therapy and pharmacotherapy in the treatment of depressed out-patients. *Cognitive Therapy and Research, 1,* 17–37.

Sachs, J. S. (1983). Negative factors in brief psychotherapy: An empirical assessment. *Journal of Consulting and Clinical Psychology, 51,* 557–564.

Sacks, M. H. (1986). Depressive neurosis. In A. M. Cooper, A. J. Frances, & M. H. Sacks (Eds.), *The personality disorders and neuroses* (pp. 395–408). Philadelphia: Lippincott.

Sanchez-Craig, M., Annis, H. M., Bornet, A. R., & MacDonald, K. R. (1984). Random assignment to abstinence and controlled drinking: Evaluation of a cognitive-behavioral program for problem drinkers. *Journal of Consulting and Clinical Psychology, 52,* 390–403.

Satir, V. (1983). *Conjoint family therapy*. Palo Alto, CA: Science and Behavior Books.

Scarf, M. (1987). *Intimate partners*. New York: Ballantine.

Schmitt, J. P. (1983). Focus of attention in the treatment of depression. *Psychotherapy: Theory, Research and Practice, 20*, 457-463.

Schramski, T. G., Beutler, L. E., Lauver, P. J., Arizmendi, T. A., & Shanfield, S. B. (1984). Factors that contribute to posttherapy persistence of therapeutic change. *Journal of Clinical Psychology, 40*, 78-85.

Schwartz, A. H., & Schwartzburg, M. (1976). Hospital care. In B. B. Wolman (Ed.), *The therapist's handbook* (pp. 199-226). New York: Van Nostrand Reinhold.

Searles, H. F. (1986). *My work with borderline patients*. New York: Jason Aronson.

Searles, J. S. (1985). A methodological and empirical critique of psychotherapy meta-analysis. *Behaviour Research and Therapy, 23*, 453-463.

Seligman, L. (1980). *Assessment in developmental career counseling*. Cranston, RI: Carroll Press.

Seligman, L. (1986). *Diagnosis and treatment planning in counseling*. New York: Human Sciences Press.

Seligman, M. (1975). *Helplessness: On depression, development, and death*. New York: Freeman.

Serban, G., & Siegel, S. (1984). Response of borderline and schizotypal patients to small doses of thiothixene and haloperidol. *American Journal of Psychiatry, 141*, 1455-1458.

Shamoian, C. A., & Teusink, J. P. (1987). Presenile and senile dementia. In F. Flach (Ed.), *Diagnostics and psychopathology* (pp. 171-185). New York: Norton.

Shapiro, D. A., & Shapiro, D. (1982). Meta-analysis of comparative therapy outcome research: A critical appraisal. *Behavioral Psychotherapy, 10*, 4-25.

Shear, M. K., & Frosch, W. A. (1986). Obsessive-compulsive disorder. In A. M. Cooper, A. J. Frances, & M. H. Sacks (Eds.), *The personality disorders and neuroses* (pp. 353-362). Philadelphia: Lippincott.

Siever, L. J., & Kendler, K. S. (1986). Schizoid/schizotypal/paranoid personality disorders. In A. M. Cooper, A. J. Frances, & M. H.

Sacks (Eds.), *The personality disorders and neuroses* (pp. 191–201). Philadelphia: Lippincott.

Silverman, J. S., Silverman, J. A., & Eardley, D. A. (1984). Do maladaptive attitudes cause depression? *Archives of General Psychiatry, 41*, 28–30.

Simons, A. D., Garfield, S. L., & Murphy, G. E. (1984). The process of change in cognitive therapy and pharmacotherapy for depression. *Archives of General Psychiatry, 41*, 45–51.

Simpson, D. D. (1981). Treatment for drug abuse. *Archives of General Psychiatry, 38*, 875–880.

Simpson, D. D., Joe, G. W., & Bracy, S. A. (1982). Six-year follow-up of opioid addicts after admission to treatment. *Archives of General Psychiatry, 39*, 1318–1323.

Simpson, G. M., & May, P.R.A. (1982). Schizophrenic disorders. In J. H. Greist, J. W. Jefferson, & R. L. Spitzer (Eds.), *Treatment of mental disorders* (pp. 143–183). New York: Oxford University Press.

Skinner, L. J., & Becker, J. V. (1985). Sexual dysfunctions and deviations. In M. Hersen & S. M. Turner (Eds.), *Diagnostic interviewing* (pp. 205–242). New York: Plenum Press.

Sloane, R. B., Staples, F. R., Cristol, A. H., Yorkston, N. J., & Whipple, K. (1975). *Psychotherapy versus behavior therapy.* Cambridge, MA: Harvard University Press.

Small, I., Small, J., & Alig, V. (1970). Passive-aggressive personality disorder: A search for a syndrome. *American Journal of Psychiatry, 126*, 973–981.

Smith, M. L., Glass, G. V., & Miller, T. I. (1980). *The benefits of psychotherapy.* Baltimore: Johns Hopkins University Press.

Smith, R. E., & Winokur, G. (1984). Affective disorders. In S. M. Turner & M. Hersen (Eds.), *Adult psychopathology and diagnosis* (pp. 245–262). New York: Wiley.

Sobell, M. B., & Sobell, L. C. (1978). *Behavioral treatment of alcohol problems.* New York: Plenum Press.

Soloff, P. H. (1985). Personality disorders. In M. Hersen & S. M. Turner (Eds.), *Diagnostic interviewing* (pp. 131–159). New York: Plenum Press.

Speilberger, C. D., Pollans, C. H., & Worden, T. J. (1984). Anxiety disorders. In S. M. Turner & M. Hersen (Eds.), *Adult psychopathology and diagnosis* (pp. 263-303). New York: Wiley.

Stanton, M. D. (1985). The family and drug abuse. In T. E. Bratter & G. G. Forrest (Eds.), *Alcoholism and substance abuse* (pp. 398-430). New York: Free Press.

Stearns, A. K. (1984). *Living through personal crisis*. New York: Ballantine.

Steinbrueck, S. M., Maxwell, S. E., & Howard, G. S. (1983). A meta-analysis of psychotherapy and drug therapy in the treatment of unipolar depression with adults. *Journal of Consulting and Clinical Psychology, 51,* 856-863.

Steinmetz, J. L., Lewinsohn, P. M., & Antonuccio, D. O. (1983). Prediction of individual outcome in a group intervention for depression. *Journal of Clinical and Consulting Psychology, 51,* 331-337.

Steketee, G., & Foa, E. B. (1985). Obsessive compulsive disorder. In D. H. Barlow (Ed.), *Clinical handbook of psychological disorders* (pp. 69-144). New York: Guilford Press.

Steketee, G., Foa, E. B., & Grayson, J. B. (1982). Recent advances in the behavioral treatment of obsessive-compulsives. *Archives of General Psychiatry, 39,* 1365-1371.

Stern, R. S., & Cobb, J. P. (1978). Phenomenology of obsessive compulsive neurosis. *British Journal of Psychiatry, 132,* 233-239.

Stewart, J. W., McGrath, P. J., Liebowitz, M. R., Harrison, W., Quitkin, F., & Rabkin, J. G. (1985). Treatment outcome validation of *DSM-III* subtypes. *Archives of General Psychiatry, 42,* 1148-1153.

Stewart, J. W., Quitkin, F. M., Liebowitz, M. R., McGrath, P. J., Harrison, W. M., & Klein, D. F. (1983). Efficacy of desipramine in depressed outpatients. *Archives of General Psychiatry, 40,* 202-207.

Stiles, W. B., Shapiro, D. A., & Elliott, R. (1986). Are all psychotherapies equivalent? *American Psychologist, 41,* 165-180.

Stolorow, R. D. (1976). Psychoanalytic reflections on client-centered therapy in the light of modern conceptions of narcissism. *Psychotherapy: Therapy, Research and Practice, 13,* 26-29.

Stone, M. H. (1986). Borderline personality disorder. In A. M.

Cooper, A. J. Frances, & M. H. Sacks (Eds.), *The personality disorders and neuroses* (pp. 203-217). Philadelphia: Lippincott.

Strupp, H. H. (1981). Toward the refinement of time-limited dynamic psychotherapy. In S. H. Budman (Ed.), *Forms of brief therapy* (pp. 219-242). New York: Guilford Press.

Suinn, R. M., & Deffenbacher, J. L. (1988). Anxiety management training. *The Counseling Psychologist, 16*, 31-49.

Szymanski, H. V., & Keill, S. I. (1985). Schizophrenia. In M. Hersen & S. M. Turner (Eds.), *Diagnostic interviewing* (pp. 111-130). New York: Plenum Press.

Telch, M. J. , Agras, W. S., Taylor, C. B., Roth, W. T., & Gallen, C. C. (1985). Combined pharmacological and behavioral treatment for agoraphobia. *Behaviour Research and Therapy, 23*, 325-335.

Terr, L. C. (1983). Chowchilla revisited: The effects of a psychic trauma four years after a school-bus kidnapping. *American Journal of Psychiatry, 140*, 1543 1550.

Thiers, N. (1988, June 16). Therapy as powerful as drugs, study shows. *Guidepost*, pp. 1, 17.

Thyer, B. A. (1987). *Treating anxiety disorders*. Newbury Park, CA: Sage.

Torgersen, S. (1984). Genetic and nosological aspects of schizotypal and borderline personality disorders. *Archives of General Psychiatry, 41*, 546-554.

Tsuang, M. T., Farone, S. V., & Day, M. (1988). Schizophrenic disorders. In A. M. Nicholi, Jr. (Ed.), *The new Harvard guide to psychiatry* (pp. 259-295). Cambridge, MA: Harvard University Press.

Tsuang, M. T., & Loyd, D. W. (1986). Other psychotic disorders. In J. E. Helzer & S. B. Guze (Eds.), *Psychoses, affective disorders, and dementia* (pp. 20-39). New York: Basic Books.

Tupin, J. P. (1981). Treatment of impulsive aggression. In W. H. Reid (Ed.), *The treatment of antisocial syndromes*. New York: Van Nostrand Reinhold.

Turkat, I. D., & Maisto, S. A. (1985). Personality disorders: Application of the experimental method to the formulation and modification of personality disorders. In D. H. Barlow (Ed.), *Clinical handbook of psychological disorders* (pp. 502–570). New York: Guilford Press.

Turner, S. M., & Hersen, M. (Eds.), (1984). *Adult psychopathology and diagnosis.* New York: Wiley.

Tyrer, S., & Shopsin, B. (1982). Symptoms and assessment of mania. In E. S. Paykel (Ed.), *Handbook of affective disorders* (pp. 12–23). New York: Guilford Press.

Uhlenhuth, E. H., Balter, M. B., Mellinger, G. D., Cisin, I. H., & Clinthorne, J. (1983). Symptom checklist syndromes in the general population. *Archives of General Psychiatry, 40,* 1167–1173.

Vaillant, G. E., & Drake, R. E. (1985). Maturity of ego defenses in relation to *DSM-III* Axis II personality disorders. *Archives of General Psychiatry, 42,* 597–601.

Vaillant, G. E., & Milofsky, E. S. (1982). Natural history of male alcoholism: Paths to recovery. *Archives of General Psychiatry, 39,* 127–133.

VandenBos, G. R. (1986). Psychotherapy research: A special issue. *American Psychologist, 41,* 111–112.

VanValkenburg, C., & Akiskal, H. S. (1985). Affective disorders. In M. Hersen & S. M. Turner (Eds.), *Diagnostic interviewing* (pp. 79–110). New York: Plenum Press.

Vaughn, C. E., & Leff, J. P. (1976). The influence of family and social factors on the course of psychiatric illness. *British Journal of Psychiatry, 129,* 125–137.

Viederman, M. (1986). Somatoform and factitious disorders. In A. M. Cooper, A. J. Frances, & M. H. Sacks (Eds.), *The personality disorders and neuroses* (pp. 363–382). Philadelphia: Lippincott.

Viorst, J. (1986). *Necessary losses.* New York: Fawcett.

Wallerstein, R. S. (1986). *Forty-two lives in treatment.* New York: Guilford Press.

Waterhouse, G. J., & Strupp, H. H. (1984). The patient-therapist relationship: Research from the psychodynamic perspective. *Clinical Psychology Review, 4,* 77–92.

Weinrach, W., Dawley, H., & General, D. (1976). *Self-directed systematic desensitization.* Kalamazoo, MI: Behaviordelia.

Weissman, M. M., Klerman, G. L., Prusoff, B. A., Sholomskas, D.,

& Padian, N. (1981). Depressed outpatients. *Archives of General Psychiatry, 38*, 51–55.

Wierzbicki, M., & Bartlett, T. S. (1987). The efficacy of group and individual cognitive therapy for mild depression. *Cognitive Therapy and Research, 11*, 337–342.

Williams, P. V., & McGlashan, T. H. (1987). Schizoaffective psychosis: Comparative long-term outcome. *Archives of General Psychiatry, 44*, 130–137.

Wilson, G. T. (1981). Behavior therapy as a short-term therapeutic approach. In S. H. Budman (Ed.), *Forms of brief therapy* (pp. 131–166). New York: Guilford Press.

Winberg, J. S., & Sheverbush, R. L. (1980). Cooperative treatment of narcissistic personality disorder by two therapists. *Psychotherapy: Theory, Research and Practice, 17*, 105–109.

Wogan, M., & Norcross, J. C. (1983). Dimensions of psychotherapists' activity: A replication and extension of earlier findings. *Psychotherapy: Theory, Research and Practice, 20*, 67–74.

Wolman, B. B. (Ed.). (1976). *The therapist's handbook*. New York: Van Nostrand Reinhold.

Woodward, R., & Jones, R. B. (1980). Cognitive restructuring treatment: A controlled trial with anxious patients. *Behaviour Research and Therapy, 18*, 401–407.

Woody, G. E., McLellan, A. T., Luborsky, L., & O'Brien, C. P. (1985). Sociopathy and psychotherapy outcome. *Archives of General Psychiatry, 42*, 1081–1086.

Woolfolk, R. L., & McNulty, T. F. (1983). Relaxation treatment for insomnia: A component analysis. *Journal of Consulting and Clinical Psychology, 51*, 495–503.

Woolson, A. M., & Swanson, M. G. (1972). The second time around: Psychotherapy with the "hysterical woman." *Psychotherapy: Theory, Research and Practice, 9*, 168–175.

Yost, J. K., & Mines, R. A. (1985). Stress and alcoholism. In T. E. Bratter & G. G. Forrest (Eds.), *Alcoholism and substance abuse* (pp. 74–103). New York: Free Press.

Zitrin, C. M., Klein, D. F., Woerner, M. S., & Ross, D. C. (1983). Treatment of phobias: I. Comparison of imipramine hydrochloride and placebo. *Archives of General Psychiatry, 40*, 125–138.

Name Index

Subject Index